THE Notre Dame
FOOTBALL
ENCYCLOPEDIA

THE
Notre Dame
FOOTBALL
ENCYCLOPEDIA

THE ULTIMATE GUIDE TO AMERICA'S FAVORITE COLLEGE TEAM

KEITH MARDER, MARK SPELLEN,
AND JIM DONOVAN

CITADEL PRESS
KENSINGTON PUBLISHING CORP.
www.kensingtonbooks.com

This book is for my father, Donald Marder, who was a great man and a better father. He taught me the value of honesty, integrity, hard work and a love of football. I hope this book shows I was listening.

KM

CITADEL PRESS books are published by

Kensington Publishing Corp.
850 Third Avenue
New York, NY 10022

All Kensington titles, imprints, and distributed lines are available at special quantity discounts for bulk purchases for sales promotions, premiums, fund raising, educational, or institutional use. Special book excerpts or customized printings can also be created to fit specific needs. For details, write or phone the office of the Kensington special sales manager: Kensington Publishing Corp., 850 Third Avenue, New York, NY 10022, attn: Special Sales Department, phone 1-800-221-2647.

Citadel Press and the Citadel logo are trademarks of Kensington Publishing Corp.

Photos courtesy of the University of Notre Dame Sports Information Department and Bill Panzica.

First printing: November 2001

10 9 8 7 6 5 4 3 2 1

Printed in the United States of America

Library of Congress Control Number: 2001092623

ISBN 0-8065-2108-2

CONTENTS

ACKNOWLEDGMENTS

The authors wish to acknowledge the contributions of Bill Panzica, who is a lifelong resident of South Bend and a sports photographer who specializes in Notre Dame sports, especially football. Also thanks to the staff at the Notre Dame Sports Information Department for their help in researching this book. Doug Jacobs, Matt McHale and Vinny Bonsignere (a true Notre Dame fan) at the *Los Angeles Daily News* as well as Tim Wilkin and Matt "TMA" Graves at the *Albany Times Union*, and Paul McGuire at the WB must be recognized for their guidance and support.

NOTRE DAME
A-Z

ADAMS, JOHN
Tackle (1942–44), 6′7″, 218 lbs.

Adams was an all-state high school football and basketball player at Subiaco Academy, thirty-five miles down the road from his hometown of Charleston, Arkansas. He was urged to go to Notre Dame by Reverend George Strassner, a Notre Dame alumnus who taught at Subiaco. Adams was a huge man in his time, even for a football player. At 6-foot-7, he towered over most teammates and opponents. His official measurements may have actually understated the case: newspaper accounts from the 1940s had him more in the neighborhood of 6-foot-8 and 250 pounds. His head was so big that they had to sew two helmets together to fit him.

Adams, one of ten children, was a normal-sized kid until the age of ten, but then he had a growth spurt in which he "shot up like a tree," and that lasted until he was fifteen. "Tree" was awkward and slow when he first arrived at South Bend in 1942, but he saw some action as a reserve. The next year he filled in behind Ziggy Czarobski on the 1943 national championship team, and finally became a starter at right tackle in 1944. (His size kept him out of the service.) After graduation he was selected in the second round of the 1945 draft by the Washington Redskins and played for them for six years.

ADAMSON, KEN
Guard (1957–59), 6′2″, 205 lbs.

After bouncing around the world as an army brat, Adamson settled down long enough to become a prep All-American at Marist High School in Atlanta. At Notre Dame he earned letters in his sophomore and junior years playing behind All-American guard Al Ecuyer. His reserve status didn't prevent him from contributing—he led all sophomores in tackles, with 11 in 1957. The following year his playing time increased; he was second among guards in minutes played and made the most of his time, with 53 tackles, second on the team. After his junior year, Adamson was elected team captain. He finished his college career on a high note, with 84 tackles in 1959, again second on the team, and went on to play three seasons with the Denver Broncos.

ALM, JEFF
Defensive tackle (1986–89), 6′7″, 270 lbs.

Alm, of Orland Park, Illinois, had the physical stature to pose match-up problems for almost every opponent. His height made it possible for him to deflect and intercept passes, and his heft enabled him to clog the middle of the line while defending against the run. He earned four letters and became a starter in 1988, his junior season. His team-high 3 interceptions that year made him the first lineman to lead the team in that category since Bernie Crimmins did it forty-seven years earlier. During his senior campaign Alm was fourth on the squad, with 74 tackles. He also intercepted 1 pass, and earned second-team All-American honors. The Oilers drafted him in the second round in 1990, and he spent his entire four-year career in Houston.

ANDERSON, EDDIE
End (1918–21), 5'10", 166 lbs.

How's this for well-rounded: not only was Anderson an All-American who went on to become a great coach, he was also a practicing physician. A graduate of Oskaloosa High School in Mason City, Iowa, Anderson arrived at Notre Dame in 1918 weighing a whopping 150 pounds. Because of his less-than-imposing physique, the split end was nearly overlooked by rookie coach Knute Rockne, who quickly found out that Anderson not only had football smarts, but was also stronger than much larger men.

As a four-year starter he did nothing but get bigger and better. His junior year was outstanding (a team-leading 17 catches for 293 yards and 3 touchdowns), but that was nothing compared with his senior year. As a captain, the kid who was once thought too skinny to contribute again led the team by catching 26 passes for 394 yards and 2 touchdowns, and he was named a first-team All-American.

In 1922, he began his professional career with the Rochester Jeffersons; he went on to play for the Chicago Cardinals and Chicago Bears before retiring in 1925. While playing professionally the seemingly tireless Anderson also coached at Columbia College in Dubuque, Iowa, and from 1922–24 his team was 16–6–2. He moved on to DePaul University, where he compiled a record of 21–22–4 over seven seasons. For much of that time he also studied for a medical degree at Rush Medical College, graduating in 1929. Then he became a football-coaching doctor, somehow balancing the two careers as diverse as they were time-consuming. In 1933, his coaching took him to Holy Cross College in Worcester, Massachusetts, and in six seasons the team was an outstanding 47–7–4 (including undefeated seasons in 1935 and 1937), and quickly rose to become a national powerhouse.

Anderson wasn't done moving around. His next stop was back home, as he became head coach at the University of Iowa in 1939. Coming off a one-win campaign and only twenty-two victories in the previous nine seasons, the Hawkeyes instantly turned around under Anderson's direction. Led by Heisman Trophy winner Nile Kinnick, Iowa went 6–1–1 (including a win over Notre Dame) in 1939. In seven more seasons with Anderson running the show, the Hawkeyes were 29–32–1; during World War II, his tenure was interrupted by a three-year hitch in the U.S. Army Medical Corps. In 1950, he returned to Holy Cross and stayed there until he retired, fourteen years later. In two decades of coaching at Holy Cross, he had just three losing seasons.

As a coach, Anderson was 201–128–15 (.606). Only five coaches had reached the two-hundred-win milestone before him. His success led to his induction into the College Football Hall of Fame in 1971. He passed away five years later.

ANDERSON, HEARTLEY
Guard (1918–21); Head coach (1931–33), 5'11", 170 lbs.

Anderson was a good coach at Notre Dame, compiling a three-year record of 16–9–4, but he was an even greater player. A high school pal of Notre Dame's George Gipp, the man nicknamed "Hunk," from Hancock, Michigan, weighed only 168 pounds when he arrived on campus. He was still tough enough to impress rookie coach Knute Rockne, earning the starting left guard position as a freshman, and would not relinquish it during his four years in South Bend. Named a first-team All-American after his senior season, Anderson played for the Chicago Bears from 1922 to 1925. Professional football then was far from the full-time vocation it is today, so from 1922 to 1926, Anderson moonlighted as Rockne's assistant. He also served as the head coach at St. Louis University for two years, but returned to Notre Dame as an assistant in 1930. He replaced Rockne the following year after the coach was killed in a plane crash. Like Rockne, Anderson was a fanatic about fundamentals and preparation. In that first year as a coach he was undefeated through seven games, but the team dropped games to the University of Southern California (USC) and Army to complete his first season at 6–2–1. The following year Notre Dame was 7–2, and in his third and final year as coach the Fighting Irish were 3–5–1.

That was not the end of Anderson's coaching career. He moved on to the University of North Carolina and remained there until 1937. He held jobs as assistant coach at the University of Michigan in 1937 and Cincinnati University the following season. Anderson's next move was into the professional ranks. He became the head coach of the Detroit Lions in 1939, a position he held for a year before becoming the line coach of the Chicago Bears, his job for the next eleven years, until he retired from coaching in 1951.

ANGSMAN, ELMER
Halfback/Fullback (1943–45), 6'0", 185 lbs.

Chicago native Angsman tasted success his first year on the Notre Dame varsity football team, logging time as a reserve on the 1943 national championship squad. The following season he was promoted to starter and ranked third on the team in rushing, with 273 yards and 3 touchdowns on 58 carries. In 1945, Angsman really flourished. He was the squad's top offensive player, rushing for 616 yards on 87 carries and averaging 7.1 yards a run. He also scored 42 points.

Angsman's biggest postseason honor was a spot in the College Football All-Star Game, but he was inexplicably left off every All-America team. The professional ranks did not overlook his talent, however, and he was drafted by the Chicago Cardinals in 1946, with whom he played until 1952.

ARRINGTON, DICK
Tackle/Guard (1963–65), 5'11", 232 lbs.

Arrington, who had been captain of his Erie, Pennsylvania, high school football and wrestling teams and a member of the varsity track team, was a tremendous all-around athlete. At Notre Dame he also captained the wrestling team, and became one of the school's last outstanding two-way players on the gridiron.

Like all other first-year players, Arrington started out on the freshman team in 1962. As a sophomore in 1963, the year before two-platoon football began, he played 310 minutes of a possible 540 (over 57 percent of the time) and made 40 tackles from his left tackle position. In 1964, he played only offense, at guard, but still logged 300 minutes of a possible 600. He capped off his career as a senior starting at right offensive guard and defensive tackle, where he made 36 tackles. His play on offense was good enough to make him a consensus first-team All-American in 1965. Arrington was virtually overlooked by the pros—he wasn't selected until the eighteenth round in the 1965 draft—and he did not play in the National Football League (NFL).

BACHMAN, CHARLIE
Guard/Fullback (1914–16), 5'11", 187 lbs.

Bachman, who alternated between fullback and offensive lineman during his college career, was elected to the College Football Hall of Fame in 1978, but his induction had far more to do with what he did after he left Notre Dame, as a coach and master strategist, than his fine play as a collegian.

Bachman came to South Bend from Chicago's Englewood High School. He began his undergraduate career as an offensive lineman and became the starting right guard on the 1914 team that featured stars such as Knute Rockne and Ray Eichenlaub. He moved to fullback the following year, but was back on the line for his senior season, which turned out to be his best. His play in his final campaign earned him second-team All-American honors.

Upon graduation, Bachman went directly into coaching as an assistant at DePauw University in 1917. The next year he enlisted in the navy and played for the Great Lakes Service Team, which won the U.S. championship. Discharged in 1919, Bachman became known as the Boy Coach of the Western Conference when, at twenty-four, he became the head coach at Northwestern University. In his first and only season, Northwestern was a poor 4–7–1. The following eight seasons he coached at Kansas State University, where he compiled a far better 33–23–8 record. He then moved to the University of Florida, where his career started taking off and his prowess as an offensive whiz became apparent. Their first year under Bachman, the Gators were the highest-scoring team in the country and beat arch-enemies Georgia and Georgia Tech, both for the first time in school history. By the time he left Florida, in 1933, he had racked up an outstanding twenty-seven wins against eighteen losses and three ties.

Then it was on to Michigan State University, where he replaced another Notre Dame alum, Jim Crowley. Over the next thirteen seasons his teams were good enough to compile a 70–34–10 record. After the 1946 season, Bachman retired to enter the corporate world, but couldn't get football out of his system. In 1953, he returned to the gridiron to coach a small school, Michigan's Hillsdale College. He also wrote several football texts and became a designer of athletic equipment and clothing.

BAGARUS, STEVE
Halfback (1939–40), 5'11", 160 lbs.

You could almost say that Steve Bagarus was born to play at Notre Dame. A hometown boy, he was a three-sport standout at Washington High School in South Bend, and an all-city selection in 1937. He was the only prep star in the city to make the all-state team that season, as he led Washington High to the state championship. Eventually he would be inducted into the Indiana Football Hall of Fame.

Bagarus first attended Notre Dame on a basketball scholarship and played two seasons of hoops at the same time he was playing football as a walk-on. In 1939, under Coach Elmer Layden, he lettered as a third-string halfback; he got enough playing time to rush for 147 yards on 47 carries and catch 4 passes for 69 yards. In his spare time he worked at defensive back and made 3 interceptions. The following season, Bagarus moved up the depth chart and split time at right halfback with Steve Juzwik. The opening sequence on his highlight reel would likely be the interception he ran back for a touchdown in a 7–0 victory over Army in front of 75,000 fans at Yankee Stadium.

Bagarus was forced to leave school in 1941, when he was drafted into the army. Stationed at Camp Callan in San Diego, he became the outstanding athlete on the base as part of the championship football, basketball, and baseball teams. It was during a service all-star game that he caught the attention of Washington Redskins owner George Preston Marshall; in no time the former Notre Dame walk-on was a professional football player. He was anxious to start, so he played two games while on furlough.

In 1944, Bagarus was discharged from the service and became a full-time Redskin. The next year he was an All-Pro, as he led Washington to a 28–21 victory over the Chicago Bears in the NFL Championship Game. Bagarus then left Washington and signed with the Los Angeles Rams. In the second game of the season he was injured, and his career was over shortly after.

BANKS, ROBERT
Defensive tackle/Linebacker (1983–86), 6′5″, 246 lbs.

Banks, a versatile defender, was feared from both the defensive tackle and linebacker positions. By the time he was a sophomore, the tall athlete from Hampton, Virginia, was a starter at outside linebacker and made 68 tackles. He followed that up with 50 tackles as a junior. In his final season, Banks was shifted into the spot vacated by standout defensive tackle Eric Dorsey. Any doubts that he could handle life in the trenches was erased quickly, as he had 13 tackles against Michigan in the season opener. Despite missing two games with a knee injury, Banks had 57 tackles as a senior. He played in the NFL for the Houston Oil-

ers in 1988 and 1991, and for the Cleveland Browns from 1989 to 1990.

BARNETT, REGGIE
Defensive back (1972–74), 5′11″, 181 lbs.

Reggie Barnett was an outstanding high school athlete, and as a senior in 1970 led Michigan's Flint High School to a state championship. That year he was an All-American and also all-state in both football and track, thanks to his 9.8-second speed in the 100-yard dash.

Barnett was a key member of the defense that helped Notre Dame win the 1973 national championship, the final one under coach Ara Parseghian. In his junior season, Barnett was the starter at left cornerback, where he broke up 6 passes and had 29 tackles as well as 2 interceptions, including one in the 24–23 Sugar Bowl victory over the University of Alabama, which sealed the title. As a senior he had 37 tackles and 1 interception, and was also named a first-team Academic All-American.

BARRY, NORMAN
Halfback (1917–20), 5′10″, 170 lbs.

Barry experienced every facet of football—amateur and professional, player and coach—before becoming a prominent attorney and politician, rising to the ranks of the Illinois state senate.

At Notre Dame, the Chicago native shared the backfield with one of the all-time greats. As the other halfback on a team that starred George Gipp, Barry did his part to help the Irish go 9–0 in 1920, his senior season. After graduation he played for the Green Bay Packers and Chicago Cardinals, and in 1925 he coached the Cardinals to the NFL championship and was named Coach of the Year.

When his football days were behind him, Barry turned to law and politics. He was an Illinois state senator for ten years and then became a Cook County circuit judge. In 1978 he retired to private practice, but his life after football was not overlooked. In 1988 he received the Distinguished American Award from the National Football Foundation and his alma mater also dedicated a building to him: the Norman Barry Courtroom at the Notre Dame School of Law. A couple more honors were bestowed on him when he was elected to the Chicago Sports Hall of Fame and the Chicago Catholic League Hall of Fame.

BAUJAN, HARRY
End (1913–16), 5'8", 167 lbs.

A part of the Notre Dame family before he ever entered college, Baujan had to wait until a left end named Knute Rockne moved on to coaching before shedding his reserve status. After Rockne moved up, Baujan, from Beardstown, Illinois, started his final three years. He attended Notre Dame Prep from 1910 to 1913 before going on to the university, where he played behind Rockne as a freshman. When he became a starter, Baujan played both right and left end and was honored as All-Western and All-Indiana three times each.

After graduation, Baujan joined the army during World War I, and then, from 1920 to 1921, he played professional football for the Cleveland Indians. In 1922, he took a job as an assistant football coach at the University of Dayton; the next year he was promoted to head coach, and five years later he became athletic director, a post he occupied for thirty-five years. Baujan died in 1976 at the age of eighty-six, and fourteen years later was inducted into the College Football Hall of Fame.

BAVARO, MARK
Tight end (1981–84), 6'4", 242 lbs.

Not that he didn't have a wonderful career at Notre Dame, but the rugged, sure-handed Bavaro is probably best remembered for being an All-Pro with the 1986 Super Bowl–winning New York Giants. Bavaro was also a key component for the Giants in 1991, when they won another Super Bowl. He came from a football-playing family—his father Tony played for the San Francisco 49ers in 1960.

Bavaro had been a prep All-American at Danvers High School, in Massachusetts, but injuries made the transition to college slow. As a member of the Fighting Irish he played just three and a half minutes in his first two seasons. A healthy Bavaro caught on—and caught passes—in 1993, when he succeeded Tony Hunter as the starting tight end. He responded by finishing third on the team in catches, with 23, and he led the Irish with 3 touchdowns. At the end of his junior campaign, during the 19–18 victory over Boston College in the Liberty Bowl, he foreshadowed his spectacular senior season when he led all receivers with 5 grabs for 52 yards. As a senior in 1984, Bavaro built on his junior success. He was tops on the team in receptions with 32 for 395 yards and a touchdown, and he was named an All-American.

Bavaro was selected in the fourth round by the Giants and quickly became one of quarterback Phil Simms's favorite targets. He played for the Giants from 1985 through the Super Bowl XXV season of 1991. He then played a year for the Cleveland Browns, and after two seasons, he finished his career with the Philadelphia Eagles in 1994.

BEACOM, PAT
Guard/Tackle (1903–06), 6'2", 220 lbs.

Beacom learned the finer points of the game of football while he was at Notre Dame, and his skill level increased dramatically during his four college seasons. Beacom, who came to South Bend from Sheldon, Iowa, started at left guard for Notre Dame's undefeated team of 1903. The following season he again started at left guard and scored 2 touchdowns against Ohio Medical and was a key offensive weapon running the ball against DePauw and Purdue Universities. He came back to start again at left guard in 1905 and scored 3 touchdowns and ran for more than 60 yards against North Division High School. He also scored twice against American Medical College and DePauw, and kicked an extra point in a win over Bennett Medical College. For his final season, Beacom was moved to left tackle. He scored twice and kicked a conversion against Franklin, blocked a punt, scored a touchdown and a kick against Hillsdale, and scored three times in a shutout win over Chicago Physicians and Surgeons.

BECKER, DOUG
Linebacker (1974–77), 6'0", 223 lbs.

Becker, from Hamilton, Ohio, was a three-year starter at outside linebacker at Notre Dame, where he used his athleticism to make himself an integral member of the school's 1977 national championship squad. That year he was fifth on the team in tackles, with 91, and forced a fumble that led to a touchdown as the Fighting Irish stomped previously unbeaten Texas in the Cotton Bowl. He lettered as a freshman, and in 1975 became a starter as a sophomore, compiling 72 tackles. He continued to improve, with 89 tackles as a junior and the aforementioned 91 as a senior. That year he also received the Hering Award, given to the team's best linebacker.

Although drafted by the Pittsburgh Steelers in the tenth round in 1978, Becker played for the Chicago Bears and Buffalo Bills during his one-year NFL career.

BECTON, LEE
Tailback (1991–94), 6'0", 191 lbs.

Some players have problems moving up from high school to major college ball, and even Becton did, if only briefly. He won four varsity letters in track and basketball, and another three in football, besides possessing the leadership qualities to be senior class president. So big things were expected from the swift back from Ernul, North Carolina. Take into account that in his senior year at West Craven High School he ran for 2,011 yards

and had 32 touchdowns, and that in his high school career he totaled more than 5,000 yards and had 87 touchdowns, and you can see why.

After a period of adjustment to bigger defenders, more intricate offenses, and more difficult textbooks, Becton delivered, finishing as one of the top running backs in Notre Dame history. In his freshman season he played in only 5 games, rushing for 62 yards on 15 carries. The next year he was a valuable reserve tailback, not behind just anybody, but All-American Reggie Brooks. Still, Becton got into eleven games and was a key member of the "Killer Bee" backfield along with Brooks, Jerome Bettis, and Jeff Burris. As a sophomore he amassed 373 yards and 3 touchdowns on 68 carries.

Brooks left for the NFL the following season, and Becton earned the starting tailback spot. In his first game as starter he really went to work, rushing for 72 yards on 16 carries. He missed the following week's game against Purdue and rushed only 6 times against next-opponent Stanford, but for the rest of the season he was a juggernaut. He rushed for 142 yards against Pittsburgh, 177 versus USC, and finished the season with 1,044 yards on 164 carries. Becton became just the fourth back in school history to rush for 1,000 yards and the first to rush for more than 100 yards in six consecutive games. To cap off his successful junior campaign, he punished Texas A&M with 138 yards on 26 carries in Notre Dame's 24–21 Cotton Bowl victory, taking the game's Outstanding Offensive Player honors. Notre Dame finished 11–1 and was ranked second in the final Associated Press poll.

Brooks was a finalist for the Doak Walker Award, which goes to the nation's top running back, and he earned honorable mention All-American status, so there was much anticipation for Becton and the Irish in 1994. According to *Street and Smith's,* he was a preseason All-American, but injuries did what defenders couldn't: they stopped Becton. In the third game he pulled a groin muscle and missed nearly five entire games.

When he made it back into the lineup, he led Notre Dame to a 42–30 victory over Air Force and logged 156 yards against USC.

Becton finished his college career ninth on Notre Dame's all-time rushing list, with 2,029 yards, and somehow slipped past the watchful eyes of NFL scouts. He went undrafted, but was signed by the Green Bay Packers as a free agent. He didn't make the team.

CAREER STATS

Year	Att.	Yards	Avg.	TDs
1991	15	62	4.1	0
1992	68	373	5.5	3
1993	164	1,044	6.4	6
1994	100	550	5.5	3
Total	347	2,029	5.8	12

BEINOR, JOSEPH EDWARD
Tackle (1936–38), 6'2", 207 lbs.

Joseph Edward "Beefy" Beinor was more than a great football player at Notre Dame. He is also the answer to a trivia question: Which Notre Dame football player also competed for the Lithuanian-American team in the 1938 Lithuanian Olympics? Answer: Ed Beinor, who finished first in the shotput event.

One of the most honored linemen to wear the Fighting Irish uniform in the 1930s, Beinor, from Harvey, Illinois, was a two-time All-American. He was a large player (for those days) and was as impassioned as he was big. He won his first letter in 1936, backing up Bill Steinkemper. The following year he was the team's starting left tackle and a first-team All-American. That was a perfect prelude to his senior campaign. Beinor won more awards than nearly every other college football player, he was a key component of Notre Dame's 8–1 team, and was rewarded by a first-team selection on every All-America team. He wound up his senior season with an appearance in the College Football All-Star Game in 1939.

A 1939 draft pick of the Brooklyn (football) Dodgers, Beinor began his career the following season as a member of the Chicago Cardinals. The All-American was then plucked off waivers by the Washington Redskins near the end of the 1941 season, but he retired the following year and entered the Marine Corps during World War II.

BELL, GREG
Running back (1980–83), 6'0", 210 lbs.

It wasn't until after Bell left Notre Dame that fans of the Fighting Irish found out what they'd missed. Bell played just one full season in college, but lasted eight in the NFL. Injuries all but destroyed the college career of the former South High School basketball, football, and track star from Columbus, Ohio. As a freshman he played tailback, but carried the ball 5 times for 66 yards (an average of 13.2). He was switched to wingback as a sophomore and had his best season in South Bend by far, rushing 92 times

Running back Greg Bell rushed for only 870 yards at Notre Dame but ran for more than 5,000 yards in the pros.

for 512 yards and scoring 4 touchdowns. As a junior, and again a tailback, he got off to a phenomenal start, with a 95-yard performance in the opener against Michigan, but the next week he fractured his leg and gained just 28 yards the rest of the season. He then missed seven games as a senior, gaining 169 yards on 37 carries.

With one year of eligibility remaining, Bell opted to enter the NFL draft. In 1984, he was a first-round pick of the Buffalo Bills, and played for them through 1987. He also played for the Los Angeles Rams and Los Angeles Raiders before he retired in 1991. As a Ram, Bell led the NFL in touchdowns in 1988, with 16, and in 1989, with 15. He finished with more than 5,000 yards rushing. Not bad for a guy who had only 10 touchdowns and 870 yards during his entire college career.

CAREER STATS

Year	Att.	Yards	Avg.	TDs
1980	5	66	13.2	1
1981	92	512	5.6	4
1982	24	123	5.1	1
1983	37	169	4.6	4
Total	158	870	5.5	10

BERCICH, PETE
Linebacker (1990–93), 6'2", 237 lbs.

Bercich set a high school record in tackles at Providence High School in New Lenox, Illinois, with a whopping 170 his junior year, and he finished high school with 392 stops. At Notre Dame, Bercich earned his first letter in 1991, when he started seven games and was also second on the team in tackles, with 69. His play earned him honorable mention All-American honors, despite being bothered by an ankle injury in the season's final two games. Bercich was responsible for calling defensive signals in 1993, when he started at inside linebacker. The fiery competitor also led by example: he was second on the squad in tackles, with 71, compiling 11 of them in a victory over Michigan State. He

was a seventh-round selection of the Minnesota Vikings in 1994.

BEREZNEY, PETE
Tackle (1943–45), 6'2", 215 lbs.

Due to depth at his position, Berezney, a member of Notre Dame's national championship team in 1943, did not earn a letter. He had the personal misfortune of arriving in South Bend from Northvale, New Jersey, during the same era as All-American Jim White, John "Tree" Adams, and Ziggy Czarobski, all ahead of him at the tackle spot. That year he was a backup, but his playing time increased in 1944, and by 1945 he was a starter. Selected by the Detroit Lions in the fifth round of the 1946 draft, Berezney played for the Los Angeles Dons of the All-American Football Conference (AAFC) in 1947 and for the Baltimore Colts in 1948.

BERGMAN, ALFRED
Halfback/Quarterback (1910–14), 5'9", 160 lbs.

"Dutch" Bergman was Notre Dame's starting halfback in 1911 and 1912, and its starting quarterback in 1914. He's probably best remembered, however, for one very special play.

On October 28, 1911, in a game against Loyola University of Chicago, Bergman returned a kickoff for a record 105 yards—and he didn't score! The record will definitely stand through the ages because since he set it, college fields have been shortened from 110 to 100 yards long. He received the kick on his own goal line, and ran it back to Loyola's 5. Ironically, it was probably one of the few plays the Fighting Irish didn't score on that day, as the final was Notre Dame 80, Loyola 0.

Bergman, from Peru, Indiana, also bears another distinction among the nearly 2,500 players who have worn the blue and gold. From 1911 until 1915, he was a member of the school's football, baseball, basketball, and track and field teams, and became the first four-sport athlete in school history to letter in every one.

BERRY, BERTRAND D.
Linebacker (1993–96), 6'3", 245 lbs.

Berry was the best sacker on Notre Dame's best sacking team ever. He led the 1996 Fighting Irish defense with 10 sacks, as they set a school record by tackling the opposing quarterback in the backfield 41 times.

Berry arrived in Notre Dame after winning letters in football, baseball, and track at Humble High School, in Texas. As a senior, he was the captain of the football team and earned all-district honors in football three times and in basketball twice. In his senior year, was named one of the top five high school athletes in Texas. Berry went on to start for four years for Notre Dame. As a senior, during his stellar sack season of 1996, he made 60 tackles, including 5 for -28 yards. He was also named an honorable mention All-American. Despite the fact that he had but .5 sacks, Berry had his best statistical season as a junior, making 76 tackles, good for third on the team. As a sophomore he had 6 sacks for -44 yards. The Indianapolis Colts selected him in the third round of the 1997 NFL draft.

BERTELLI, ANGELO
Quarterback/Running back (1941–43), 6'1", 173 lbs.

A funny thing happened when Bertelli was voted winner of the Heisman Trophy. He wasn't anywhere near a college campus. With four games to play in 1943, his final collegiate season, Bertelli was called into service by the Marine Corps. It was no surprise that he was in contention for the Heisman, let alone a runaway winner; runner-up Bob O'Dell of Pennsylvania had 177 votes compared with 648 for Bertelli, who had been close to the coveted trophy twice before. As a sophomore, he had finished second in the voting behind Minnesota's Bruce Smith, and sixth, as a junior, behind winner Frank Sinkwich.

Bertelli's senior season proved to be magical. He attempted just 36 passes and completed 25, but made the most of his throws, amassing 512 yards through the air. His astounding .694 completion percentage, 10 touchdowns, and 20.5-yards-per-pass average make him one of the most efficient quarterbacks in history. The minimal pass attempt numbers are, however, directly due to his abbreviated season. Still the Fighting Irish were undefeated with him running the

Quarterback Angelo Bertelli won the Heisman Trophy in 1943.

offense. The only blemish on the otherwise perfect season was a season-ending loss to the Great Lakes Service Team. The Irish, who scored an average of 43.5 points in games Bertelli played in 1943, still finished the season 9–1 and won the national title.

Bertelli's outstanding football career, which was good for 2,578 yards in three seasons, almost never happened. Prestigious Eastern universities tried to woo "the Springfield Rifle" to play hockey for them. Schools such as Dartmouth and Boston College wanted the strapping athlete from Cathedral High School, but playing football at Notre Dame was an offer the Springfield, Massachusetts, native couldn't refuse. As a sophomore single-wing *tailback,* Bertelli displayed his arm, completing 70 of 123 passes for a nation-leading .569 percentage, and 1,027 yards and 8 touchdowns. The following season, coach Frank Leahy switched his offense to the T formation, enabling the Rifle to play quarterback. As a junior, Bertelli heaved 159 passes, completing 72 for 1,039 yards and 10 touchdowns. In a 27–10 win over Stanford, he had a season-high 4 touchdown throws and a record 10 consecutive completions.

After his discharge from the marines, Bertelli played professionally for the Los Angeles Dons and Chicago Hornets of the All-American Football Conference. Unfortunately, he blew out his knee, and his pro career lasted the same length as his college career—three seasons. He was a 1972 inductee into the College Football Hall of Fame.

CAREER STATS

Year	Att.	Comp.	Yards	TDs	Pct.
1941	123	70	1,027	8	.569
1942	159	72	1,039	10	.453
1943	36	25	512	10	.694
Total	318	167	2,578	28	.525

BETTIS, JEROME
Fullback (1990–92), 6'0", 247 lbs.

It's interesting to note that Bettis left Notre Dame numbering fourteenth on the school's all-time rushing list, a good but not overly impressive statistic. It *is* impressive, however, when you take into account that he declared himself eligible for the NFL draft after his junior year, and wasn't moved into the starting lineup until his sophomore season, to say nothing of having to share time with the other Killer Bees in the backfield (Becton, Brooks, and Burris). Bettis, who combined the speed of a halfback with the body of a fullback, was also sixth on the career rushing touchdown list, with 27. Had he stayed his final season, his name would probably be at the top of the list in most rushing categories of the Notre Dame record book.

As a freshman out of Mackenzie High School, in Detroit, Bettis played behind fullback Rodney Culver and only managed 15 carries, but he made the most of every one. With a total of 115 yards and an average of 7.7 yards per carry, he forced the coaching staff to make a move the next season. In a controversial decision, coach Lou Holtz decided to move Culver to tailback to make room for Bettis at fullback. Early in the year, second-guessing was rampant, as Bettis got off to a slow start, but he kicked it up a notch and finished the season with 972 yards on 168 carries for 16 touchdowns. He also caught 17 passes for 190 yards and another 4 touchdowns. His record 120 points in a single season remains unbroken. He was the Most Valuable Player in a 39–28 victory over Florida in the Sugar Bowl, with 150 yards and 3 touchdowns on 16 carries. He and quarterback Rick Mirer shared team MVP honors for the season, and Bettis was named a second-team All-American.

In his junior season an ankle injury hindered his production, but the rugged back still played in eleven of the team's twelve games. He rushed for 825 yards and scored 10 touchdowns, earning honorable mention All-American status. That was it for Bettis's college career, as he announced his intention to enter the NFL draft that spring. There is no debating whether Bettis was ready to make the jump, as he proved to be as tough in the professional ranks as he was in high school

A member of the "Killer Bee" backfield, fullback Jerome Bettis bulls his way past Texas defenders.

and college. The Los Angeles Rams grabbed him in the first round of the 1993 draft, and he came out of the gate full speed. He amassed 1,429 yards and scored 7 touchdowns in his first season and was named NFC Rookie of the Year. In his first three seasons in the NFL, he rushed for 3,981 yards on 363 carries and had 16 touchdowns. He was traded to the Pittsburgh Steelers in 1996 and continued his success. A four-time Pro Bowler, Bettis has rushed for 7,373 yards and 34 touchdowns (including 11 in 1996) and has compiled 965 yards receiving.

CAREER STATS

RUSHING

Year	Att.	Yards	Avg.	TDs
1990	15	115	7.7	1
1991	168	972	5.8	16
1992	154	825	5.4	10
Total	337	1,912	5.7	27

RECEIVING

Year	Rec.	Yards	Avg.	TDs
1990	0	0	0	0
1991	17	190	11.2	4
1992	15	239	15.9	2
Total	32	429	13.4	6

BEUERLEIN, STEVE
Quarterback (1983–86), 6'3", 201 lbs.

In a program that can proudly exhibit a quarterback lineage that includes Angelo Bertelli, Joe Theismann, and Joe Montana, the fact that Beuerlein graduated as Notre Dame's all-time top passer is a good reason for him to boast. Beuerlein, from Fullerton, California, was a semifinalist in the national Punt, Pass and Kick competition, but didn't even start at quarterback for his high school team until his senior year. When he won the job in 1982, he showed off his stellar arm. He led Anaheim's Servite High School to the top ranking in the state of California and was a schoolboy All-American, passing for 2,244 yards and 12 touchdowns.

Ironically, his rise at Notre Dame was much quicker. In the fourth game of his freshman season he replaced Blair Kiel as starting quarterback and completed 75 of his 145 attempts for 1,061 yards and 4 touchdowns. As the years went by, the play of the poised and gifted drop-back passer improved. As a sophomore he passed for 1,920 yards and 7 touchdowns and had a record .602 completion percentage. As a junior he passed for 1,335 yards and 3 touchdowns. All of that, however, was just prelude. As a senior he completed 151 of 259 passes for 2,211 yards and 13 touchdowns, and was named an honorable mention All-American and the Outstanding Offensive Player by his teammates. Beuerlein, who had the fortune of sharing an offense with superstar flanker Tim Brown for three years, left school as the career record holder, with 850 attempts, 473 completions, 6,527 passing yards, and 6,459 yards in total offense. Ron Powlus, a 1997 graduate, has since eclipsed most of Beuerlein's records. The only career mark he still holds is for interceptions (44), one he probably wishes would be washed off the books.

Beuerlein was a fourth-round draft pick of the Los Angeles Raiders. He remained with the Raiders until 1990, and then became a journeyman hired gun. He played for the Dallas Cowboys (1991–92), Arizona Cardinals (1993–94), Jacksonville Jaguars (1995), and is currently the starter for the Carolina Panthers, after backing up Kerry Collins for a little more than two years.

BISCEGLIA, PAT
Guard (1953–55), 5′10″, 190 lbs.

Bisceglia didn't take the most direct route to college, which is why he was the age of most graduates by the time he enrolled at Notre Dame. After starring in football, baseball, and hockey in high school in Worcester, Massachusetts, Bisceglia enlisted in the U.S. Navy. In 1952, at age twenty-two, the man among boys came to campus, and during his first two years on the football team played backup to Ray Lemek. Then Lemek was moved to tackle to make room for Bisceglia in the starting lineup. The move paid dividends. Along with halfback Paul Hornung and fullback Don Schaefer, Bisceglia was a prime contributor to Notre Dame's 8–2 season.

Bisceglia was a first-team, second-team, and third-team All-American, as voted by different news sources. The NFL, however, thought differently. He was a twenty-ninth-round selection by the Washington Redskins and did not play professionally.

BLEIER, ROBERT
Halfback (1965–67), 5′11″, 195 lbs.

It's safe to say that while playing in South Bend "Rocky" Bleier learned, or at least perfected, many of the moves he used in helping the Pittsburgh Steelers win four Super Bowls. Robert "Rocky" Bleier, the son of an Appleton, Wisconsin, tavern owner, was a two-time all-state running back and captain of the football, basketball, and track teams at Xavier High School, where all of his teams went undefeated in his senior year. He was the starting halfback on Notre Dame's 1966 national championship team and was elected captain for the following season.

During his first season on the Notre Dame varsity football team, Bleier played behind Bill Wolski at left halfback and gained 145 yards on 26 carries. The next year he moved up to the first team and was the smallest member of the starting backfield, but at the end of the championship season he had the numbers to prove his worth. He finished with 282 yards on 63 carries (third on the team) and was second on the team, with 17 receptions for 209 yards. In his spare time he punted and also led the team in that category.

During the next season, Notre Dame was Bleier's team. He was elected captain in the spring of 1967, and his hard work and skill set a great example on the field. In his senior campaign, Bleier rushed for 357 yards on 77 carries and grabbed 16 passes for 171 yards. His 42 points were third best on the team, but he made very few All-America teams, and his statistics (which were not as impressive as his play) and size made many NFL teams shy away on draft day in 1968. Taken in the sixteenth round, 417th overall, Bleier was the steal of the draft for the Pittsburgh Steelers.

Bleier's outstanding professional career almost came to a halt after one year. After his rookie season in Pittsburgh he was drafted into the army and was seriously wounded in combat duty during the Vietnam War. Medical experts said he would be lucky to ever walk normally again, let alone carry the ball in an NFL game. But mere words could not stop the Rock, who fought his way back onto the Pittsburgh roster in 1971. He continued to improve and earned more playing time; by 1974 he was starting at halfback, and he was a key member of a Steelers offense that won Super Bowls in 1975, 1976, 1979, and 1980.

Bleier retired from the NFL in 1980, with 3,864 yards rushing on 928 carries and 136 receptions for 675 yards. He also scored 23 touchdowns. His autobiography, *Fighting Back,* was adapted into a television movie.

CAREER STATS

RUSHING

Year	Att.	Yards	Avg.	TDs
1965	26	145	5.6	2
1966	63	282	4.5	4
1967	77	357	4.4	5
Total	166	784	4.7	11

RECEIVING

Year	Rec.	Yards	Avg.	TDs
1965	3	42	14.0	0
1966	17	209	12.3	1
1967	16	171	10.7	2
Total	36	422	11.7	3

BOERINGER, ART
Center (1925–26), 6'1", 186 lbs.

In 1926, "Bud" Boeringer, from St. Paul, Minnesota, had a phenomenal season anchoring the offensive line for Notre Dame. As a starter on a 9–1 team, he was showered with honors. One year after playing second string, Boeringer was named a first-team All-American. After he left South Bend he still kept his ties with Notre Dame. He was an assistant under former Notre Dame star Gus Dorais at the University of Detroit for sixteen years, and the line coach at the University of Iowa under another former Fighting Irish player, Clem Crowe. Then it was time for him to run his own program, and Boeringer served as the head coach at Cornell University from 1946 to 1950.

BOLAND, JOE
Tackle (1924–26), 6'0", 221 lbs.

Boland did it all for the Notre Dame football program—literally. After he finished his playing career, the Philadelphia, Pennsylvania, native was an assistant under his former teammate Elmer Layden from 1936 through 1940, and was the longtime "Voice of the Irish" on the radio.

As a player he was a large but quick lineman who was perfect for head coach Knute Rockne's shift offense. He was around to help block for "the Four Horsemen" in their final run and started at left tackle in 1925 and 1926. He blocked two punts against Minnesota in 1925, and blocked another one against the Golden Gophers the following season, but it proved to be his undoing. With more than eight games to play, he was kicked in the leg and lost for the season.

BOLCAR, NED
Linebacker (1986–89), 6'2", 229 lbs.

Bolcar's odd-numbered years were a lot better than his even-numbered ones. He arrived on campus from Phillipsburg, New

Jersey, in 1986 and played just 27 minutes as a freshman. The following year, 1987, he displayed the talent that made him one of the better linebackers the Fighting Irish fielded in that decade. Bolcar, a starting inside linebacker, played more time than any other defensive player, led the team with 106 tackles, and was a second-team All-American. In 1988, when Bolcar was named tri-captain, he lost his starting job to Michael Stonebreaker and logged about half the time of the previous season; he was fourth on the team in tackles, with 57. In 1989, again a captain, Bolcar was back in the starting lineup and back on top of the tacklers list, with 109. He was also named a second-team All-American. In the sixth round of the NFL draft, Bolcar was selected by the Seattle Seahawks. He played with that franchise in 1990, and for the Miami Dolphins the following two seasons.

BOWL GAMES

Notre Dame played only one bowl game prior to 1970, a 27–10 Irish victory over Stanford in the Rose Bowl on January 1, 1925. The Fighting Irish would have been invited to numerous bowl games between 1925 and 1970 if not for a decision by university officials to prevent the football team from engaging in postseason games. At the time it was thought that preparation for them would interfere with academics. In 1969, the university changed its policy in order to raise money for minority scholarships and programs. Had there not been a forty-five year hiatus from bowl games, Notre Dame most likely would hold the record for most appearances, which is held by the Crimson Tide of the University of Alabama.

BRADLEY, LUTHER
Strong safety (1973, 1975–77),
6'2", 200 lbs.

Bradley, of Muncie, Indiana, holds the Notre Dame career record for interceptions (17), and book-ended his college run by

Safety Luther Bradley holds the Notre Dame career record for interceptions (17), and played on two national championship teams.

playing on two national championship teams (1973 and 1977). The ferocious hitter made many All-America teams during his time in South Bend, and also holds the record for the most yardage on interception returns in a game (2 for 103 yards against Purdue in 1975, including a 99-yard return for a touchdown that is the second-longest return in school history). After making 153 career tackles in college, Bradley played in the Japan Bowl and was selected in the first round of the 1978 NFL draft by the Detroit Lions. He played for them for four seasons before retiring.

BRENNAN, MIKE
Offensive tackle/Guard (1986–89),
6'5", 260 lbs.

Brennan is a Notre Dame success story. The big but nimble athlete from Easton, Maryland, was not offered a scholarship to play sports at the university, but still made both the football and lacrosse teams as a walk-on. He was an excellent lacrosse player who had the talent to make teams at such powerhouses as Johns Hopkins University and the University of North Carolina, but he turned down those offers to attend Notre Dame. By his sophomore year in South Bend, Brennan decided to play only football and was rewarded with a scholarship in his junior year, when he started two games at guard. He was moved to tackle in his senior season and was fourth on the team in minutes played (287:42). A fourth-round draft pick of the Cincinnati Bengals, Brennan had a three-year NFL career.

BRENNAN, TERRY
Halfback (1945–48); Head coach (1954–58)
6'0", 170 lbs.

During his ten-year association with the Notre Dame football program, Brennan helped the Fighting Irish win an awful lot of games as both a player and coach. Playing at Notre Dame was always a goal for Brennan, an Irish Catholic who grew up in Milwaukee. His boyhood idol was Creighton Miller, a Fighting Irish halfback from 1941 to 1943. Brennan even wore Miller's number, 37, throughout high school, where he was an All-Catholic Conference halfback at Marquette High School, and in college, where he was a four-year letter winner.

While Brennan wore number 37, the Fighting Irish were a combined 33–2–3, had three undefeated seasons, won two national titles, and finished second in the final poll after another season. When Brennan returned a decade later, first as an assistant to his former coach Frank Leahy, and then when he was promoted to head coach, Notre Dame was 32–18, including a 9–1 season and an 8–2 season. Twice during his tenure, the team ranked in the Top Ten of the final Associated Press poll.

In 1946, Brennan was the team's starting left halfback, and he tied for the team's

scoring lead of 36 points with Jim Mello. He also led the 8–0–1 national championship squad in receptions, with 10 for 154 yards. In 1947, Notre Dame went 9–0 and won another national crown, and Brennan was again a key contributor. For the second consecutive season the junior led the team in receiving, with 16 catches for 181 yards and 4 touchdowns, and he scored 66 points and had 87 rushing attempts. His longest run didn't even count in that total: it was a 97-yard kick-off return for a touchdown in a 27–7 victory over Army. As a senior, Brennan rushed for 284 yards on 48 carries and caught 5 passes for 102 yards. His career rushing total was 1,249.

CAREER STATS

RUSHING

Year	Att.	Yards	Avg.	TDs
1945	57	232	4.4	2
1946	74	329	4.4	6
1947	87	404	4.6	11
1948	48	284	5.9	2
Total	266	1,249	4.7	21

CAREER COACHING RECORD

Year	Won	Lost
1954	9	1
1955	8	2
1956	2	8
1957	7	3
1958	6	4
Total	32	18

Brennan started his coaching career at Mount Carmel High School, where he helped the team win three consecutive Chicago City Championships. In 1953 he was back at Notre Dame as an assistant to Leahy, and he became the head coach the following season. During his first two seasons, Notre Dame went 9–1 and 8–2 and was ranked fourth and ninth in the final Associated Press polls, but he had a rough year in 1956, when the team went 2–8. Remove that from his record, and

Notre Dame went 30–10 with Brennan patrolling the sidelines. After the 1958 season he resigned from Notre Dame to take the job of conditioning coach for baseball's Cincinnati Reds.

BRILL, MARTY
Halfback (1929–30), 5'11", 190 lbs.

After high school Brill stayed at home, in Philadelphia, and attended the University of Pennsylvania. After two wasted seasons of riding the bench at the Ivy League school, he transferred to Notre Dame in 1929, and his talent was immediately appreciated. Brill knew how to get revenge. During his senior season, he was able to show Penn what it was missing when the two teams met. Head coach Knute Rockne must have sensed that retribution was in order, as he gave Brill an unusually large amount of runs from scrimmage, and Penn paid. In the first-ever meeting between the two schools, Notre Dame won 60–20, and Brill scored on runs of 62, 52, and 45 yards.

Brill, the son of a millionaire, played like anything but a spoiled prima donna. He was a tough football player who focused on making others look better, and he was far better known for his blocking than his running. He was the lead blocker for two-time All-American running back Marchy Schwartz and is still considered one of the best blockers in school history. He was also a topnotch defensive back who led the team in interceptions. After his final season, Brill made several All-America teams.

After graduation, he returned to the Ivy League as an assistant coach at Columbia. From 1933 to 1939 he was back in Philadelphia as the head coach of LaSalle College, and two years later he moved out to Los Angeles to coach at Loyola University before returning to Notre Dame as an assistant coach.

BROOKS, RAYMOND ANTHONY
Tailback (1987–88, 1990–91), 6'2", 223 lbs.

The first of the Brooks brothers from Tulsa, Oklahoma, to attend Notre Dame, Tony was far more consistent than his brother. He didn't have the lows, and, unfortunately, he didn't have the highs. This Brooks, who was named Gatorade High School Player of the Year while leading Booker T. Washington High School to the 1986 Oklahoma state championship, was part of a recruiting class that also included Ricky Watters. He stepped right in and contributed at Notre Dame—Watters being the only freshman to log more time on offense than him. Brooks's first season resulted in 262 yards on 54 carries (an average of 4.9 yards) and a touchdown. In 1988, he was the team's second-leading rusher, with 667 yards on 117 carries, and he caught 2 passes for 121 yards and 2 touchdowns. The following season, which coincidentally was his younger brother's freshman season, he took a break from Notre Dame and

Tailback Tony Brooks rushed for more than 2,000 yards at Notre Dame. (Bill Panzica)

transferred to nearby Holy Cross Junior College. He did not play football there and was back at Notre Dame the following fall, adding 451 yards on 105 carries to his totals.

His senior season was his best. Sharing the tailback position with Rodney Culver, Brooks played in twelve games, including four starts, and rushed for 894 yards on 147 carries. His average was a hefty 6.1 yards per rush, and he scored 5 times. Brooks was invited to play in the 1992 Senior Bowl and was an honorable mention All-American. He finished his career at Notre Dame sixth on the all-time rushing list, with 2,274 yards. He was selected in the fourth round of the NFL draft by the Philadelphia Eagles and played two years as a pro.

CAREER STATS

Year	Att.	Yards	Avg.	TDs
1987	54	262	4.9	1
1988	117	667	5.7	2
1990	105	451	4.3	4
1991	147	894	6.1	5
Total	423	2,274	5.4	12

BROOKS, REGGIE
Tailback/Defensive back (1989–92),
5′8″, 200 lbs.

In his first two years as a running back, it didn't seem as if Reggie Brooks was worth the hype and blue-chip status that he'd earned as a prep superstar. After playing a season at defensive back, it didn't even seem like he'd get another chance to prove himself on the offensive side of the ball. Brooks followed his brother Tony (a running back who graduated in 1992) to South Bend from Booker T. Washington High School in Tulsa, Oklahoma. In high school he was an all-state running back and defensive back, and rushed for more than 1,400 yards in his final two seasons while being limited to eleven games because of injuries. When he was a freshman he saw action primarily as a special-teams player, though he did rush the ball 13 times from scrimmage. As a sophomore, he moved to defense and started

three games at cornerback. He played so well that it looked like he would be a defender the rest of his college career, but in 1991 he was back on offense and ran the ball a grand total of 18 times for 122 yards, with an outstanding average of 6.8 yards per carry. He also returned 9 kickoffs for 198 yards.

In Brooks's senior year, head coach Lou Holtz finally had the wisdom to put him in the starting backfield, where he blossomed into one of the stars of college football. In that one season, Brooks ran for 89 percent of the yards he gained in college and scored 13 touchdowns. He was the best of the Killer Bee backfield, which also included Jerome Bettis, Lee Becton, and Jeff Burris. Brooks rushed for 1,343 yards on 167 carries (an average of 8 yards, or nearly a first down every rush), and finished fifth in Heisman Trophy voting. He was one of the three finalists for the Doak Walker Award for the top junior or senior running back in the nation, and was a multiteam All-American. In 1993, Brooks was drafted by the Washington Redskins and led the team in rushing his first season. He played one more year in Washington and one for the Tampa Bay Buccaneers.

CAREER STATS

Year	Att.	Yards	Avg.	TDs
1989	13	43	3.3	0
1990	Played defense			
1991	18	122	6.8	2
1992	167	1,343	8.0	13
Total	198	1,508	7.6	15

BROWN, BOB
Halfback (1895–96), 5′10″, 162 lbs.

The small town of Sheldon, Iowa, was very, very good to Notre Dame football in its early years. It was not only the hometown of Brown, but Pat Beacom, another standout who would arrive at South Bend seven years later.

Brown was a major part of the revitalization of football at Notre Dame. (There was a three-year lapse from 1889 to 1892.) He was tough and quick and liable to break a long gainer at any time. As the team's starting right halfback in 1895, Brown scored on a 40-yard run in a shutout victory over Northwestern. He also gained 130 yards and scored twice against the Illinois Cycling Club, and rushed for 155 yards and a touchdown and recovered 3 fumbles in a victory over Chicago Physicians and Surgeons.

In 1986, Brown was back in the starting lineup—at left halfback—and gained 120 yards (mainly on touchdown runs of 50 and 65 yards) and scored 3 times against South Bend Commercial Athletic Club. He also scored in a loss to Purdue and had three 60-yard runs in an 82–0 drubbing of Highland Views.

BROWN, BOBBY
Split End (1996–99), 6'2", 193 lbs.

Brown, who combined the speed to letter twice as a 400-meter runner for the Notre Dame track team and soft hands of a possession receiver, led Notre Dame in receiving for two seasons—both as a sophomore and as a senior. After an All-American career at St. Thomas Aquinas High School in Fort Lauderdale, Florida, Brown came to South Bend and got into eight games as a freshman. He caught 2 passes—of 49 and 35 yards, showing a glimpse of the ability that would carry him throughout his college career.

As a sophomore, Brown led all Notre Dame receivers with 45 catches from the flanker position, joining Malcolm Johnson to give Notre Dame its only two 40-reception receiver tandem ever. Brown was the only receiver on the team to have a catch in all thirteen games. He finished the season with 543 yards receiving and 6 touchdowns.

As a junior, Brown's receptions may have been way down (13), but his threat to break a big play was as real as ever. From his flanker position, Brown led Notre Dame with a 22.0-yard-per-catch average, including a 66-yard touchdown pass from Jarious Jackson against Baylor, the longest Notre Dame pass play in five seasons.

The National Football League's Green Bay Packers signed Brown, who was not drafted, as a free agent. He later played for the Cleveland Browns.

CAREER STATS

Year	Rec.	Yards	Avg.	TDs
1996	2	84	42.0	0
1997	45	543	12.1	6
1998	13	286	22.0	1
1999	36	608	16.9	5
Total	96	1,521	15.8	12

BROWN, CHRIS
Defensive back (1980–83), 6'1", 196 lbs.

For a former quarterback, Chris Brown sure could hit. Head coach Gerry Faust took the former signal caller from Owensboro, Kentucky, and turned this excellent athlete into a defensive back in college. During his first two seasons, Brown played backup to strongside cornerback John Krimmand, and in 1982 took over the starting spot on the weak side. In that, his junior season, Brown had 37 tackles and 2 interceptions. As a senior he upped his tackle total to 46 and added another 2 interceptions. He was drafted in the sixth round by the Pittsburgh Steelers and spent two seasons with the franchise.

BROWN, DEAN
Offensive tackle/Guard (1986–89), 6'3", 291 lbs.

Canton, Ohio, is not only the home of the Pro Football Hall of Fame, it's also the home to two outstanding linemen who played at Notre Dame. The better known is Alan Page, a Hall of Fame defensive end. The other is Brown, who started his Notre Dame career as a guard but only worked his way onto the first team when he moved outside to tackle.

An extremely strong player, Brown was Notre Dame's weight-room champion—he bench pressed 455 pounds as a senior, the most of anyone on the team. After his senior

Offensive lineman Dean Brown was a workout warrior who bench-pressed 455 pounds. (Bill Panzica)

season he was named an honorable mention All-American and was invited to play in the Hula Bowl. He played one season in the NFL, for the San Diego Chargers.

BROWN, DEREK
Tight end (1988–91), 6'6", 252 lbs.

Brown, one of the top recruits in the nation out of high school, did exactly what he was supposed to at Notre Dame and went on to be a first-round NFL draft pick when his Fighting Irish days were over. Brown, a sturdy and sure-handed receiver who was *Parade* magazine's Prep Player of the Year out of Florida's Merritt Island High School, began contributing right away and steadily improved throughout his college career. During his freshman campaign, he played in eleven games and started five. He caught 12 balls, including 3 for touchdowns, and amassed 150 yards, stats good enough to make him an honorable mention All-American.

As a sophomore, Brown logged more time than any other Notre Dame receiver and caught 13 receptions for 204 yards. As a junior, he started in all eleven games and finished second on the team, with 15 catches for 220 yards. Again he was named an honorable mention All-American. He capped his college career with an outstanding senior season. Equally adept at blocking and catching, he finished with career highs for receptions, with 22, and yards, with 325. He also scored 4 touchdowns on the way to earning first-team All-American honors.

The New York Giants, who had recently had great success with Mark Bavaro, another Fighting Irish tight end, used the fourteenth overall selection to tab Brown. He played for the New York Giants until 1994, then moved to Jacksonville to play for the Jaguars until 1996, and in 1998 joined the Oakland Raiders, along with Tim Brown, another former Notre Dame star. He is currently a member of the Arizona Cardinals.

CAREER STATS

Year	Rec.	Yards	Avg.	TDs
1988	12	150	12.5	3
1989	13	204	15.7	0
1990	15	220	14.7	1
1991	22	325	14.8	4
Total	62	899	14.5	8

BROWN, EARL
End (1936–38), 6'0", 178 lbs.

As if being a football star on some good Notre Dame football teams weren't enough, Earl Brown also played basketball in college. As a matter of fact, he is considered one of the best two-sport athletes in school history. Brown had always performed well in the two sports: he was all-state in both football and basketball at Benton Harbor High School, in Michigan.

There are plenty of tales that prove his versatility once he got to college. Look at his senior year if you want evidence. In football, Brown led the 8–1 fifth-ranked Fighting Irish with 6 receptions for 192 yards and 4 touchdowns. His 24-point scoring total tied Benny Sheridan for the school title, and was good enough to earn him All-American honors. A few months later, Brown was tearing up the gymnasiums; he was named an All-American guard on the basketball team for the second consecutive year. In the middle of the season he took a break to—what else—play football, participating in a 1939 game between the College Football All-Stars and the New York Giants.

Brown passed up playing professionally to teach others the games he excelled at, and he proved to be as diversely talented as a coach as he was a player. His first coaching post was at Brown University, where he was the head football coach and assistant basket-

ball coach. In 1941, he moved to Harvard University and switched positions. Brown was the football team's end coach under Dick Harlow, and the school's head basketball coach. Two years later he continued his Ivy League swing, finally becoming the head coach of both basketball and football at Dartmouth University. His 1943 football team went 9–1 and was ranked sixteenth, and the basketball team won the Eastern Intercollegiate Basketball Championship. In 1944, he joined the U.S. Maritime Service and later became the head football coach at the U.S. Merchant Marine Academy.

BROWN, HARVEY
Guard (1921–23), 5'9", 165 lbs.

At 165 pounds, Brown weighed half of what many of today's offensive linemen tip the scale at, but that didn't stop him from earning All-American honors. In 1922, the normal-sized guy from Youngstown, Ohio, was a reserve behind a guy named Heartley "Hunk" Anderson, an All-American and future coach of the Fighting Irish. The next year, Brown made his way onto the first string, and in his senior season there was only one Notre Dame starter smaller than him—the man the offensive lineman set out to protect: diminutive quarterback Harry Stuhldreher (5-foot-7, 151 pounds). Of Brown's 165 pounds, at least half had to be heart. Despite his size he was a starter for two years, and in his senior year he was a team captain and a second-team All-American.

After he graduated from Notre Dame, Brown stopped picking on bigger guys and went to medical school at St. Louis University. He began a private medical practice in Detroit but couldn't get football totally out of his blood. He was also a volunteer assistant for the University of Detroit football team.

BROWN, TIM
Flanker/Split end (1984–87), 6'0", 195 lbs.

Tim Brown was one of the finest players ever to don a Fighting Irish uniform. A

Heisman Trophy-winner Tim Brown was one of the best receivers in Notre Dame history and went on to an equally glorious career in the NFL. (Bill Panzica)

phenomenal athlete, he was one of the fastest quarter milers in the country at Dallas's Woodrow Wilson High School, and on the football team he gained more than 4,000 all-purpose yards and was a high school All-American. Still, in his three years of varsity play, his team won only four games.

Brown then moved on to Notre Dame—where four victories usually come in four weeks. He played for both Gerry Faust and Lou Holtz, and by the time he left to play in the pros he was regarded as one of the most explosive all-around talents in Notre Dame history. His 4.38-second, 40-yard-dash speed and Heisman Trophy may have had something to do with that. In his four years at Notre Dame, the school won twenty-five games. Although this was not close to one of the school's best eras (the team also racked up twenty losses), it was quite an improvement for Brown.

He exhibited his lightning speed as a freshman split end, when he was second on the team in receiving, with 28 receptions for 340 yards. (While at Notre Dame, Brown also lettered as a sprinter on the track team.) The following season, Faust shifted him to flanker, where he came into his own. He led the team with 25 catches for 397 yards and 3 touchdowns and also got a chance to show off his ability as a kick returner, which would become his trademark. He returned 14 kick-offs for 338 yards (an average of 24.1 yards per kick), including a 93-yard touchdown return against Michigan.

In 1986, playing for Holtz, Brown became one of the most feared players in college football. He did it all: 45 receptions for 910 yards and 5 touchdowns; 59 rushes for 254 yards and 2 touchdowns; 25 kickoff returns for 698 yards (an average of 27.9 yards per return); and 2 touchdowns and 2 punt returns for 75 yards. His 176.1 all-purpose yards per game were not only good for third in the nation, it was also a school record, and made Brown, who still had a year to play in college, a first-team All-American.

Brown, however, was even better as a senior. He had 39 receptions for 846 yards and 3 touchdowns; 34 carries for 144 yards and a touchdown; 23 kickoff returns for 456 yards; and 34 punt returns for 401 yards and 3 touchdowns, including two in one game, a 31–8 victory over Michigan State. He finished the season with 1,847 all-purpose yards. In Notre Dame's 35–10 Cotton Bowl loss to Texas A&M, Brown caught 6 passes for 105 yards. He was a unanimous first-team All-American, and was also named the college football Player of the Year by the Walter Camp Foundation, the *Sporting News, Football News,* and United Press International, as well as the national media and former winners, who honored him with the Heisman Trophy. Syracuse University quarterback Don McPherson finished a distant second in the Heisman voting. Brown also played in the Aloha Bowl, Japan Bowl, and Hula Bowl.

When he graduated the Notre Dame record book read like a Brown biography. His name was at the top of the list for receiving yardage (2,493), kickoff return yardage (1,613), combined kickoff and punt return yardage (2,089), and kickoffs and punts returned for touchdowns (6), and he was third in pass receptions, with 137.

Brown was the sixth player picked in the first round of the 1988 NFL draft. He was selected by the Los Angeles Raiders and got right to work. He led the league in kickoff returns (41 for 1,098 yards), snagged 43 passes for 755 yards and 5 touchdowns, returned 49 punts for 444 yards, and set a rookie record for all-purpose yards (2,317). In 1989 a knee injury did something to Brown that defenses couldn't do–stop him. He was limited to one game, but was back in the starting lineup the following season. He started in the Pro Bowl three consecutive seasons, from 1993 to 1995, and also made the team in 1988 and 1991. Brown, who has led the NFL in receiving on several occasions, ranks as number one in Raiders history for receptions, having grabbed 770 passes. He is also the Raiders all-time leader in total yards from scrimmage, punt returns and punt return yardage. He has caught a pass in every game dating back to October 3, 1993. Entering the 2001 season, he ranked number eight on the NFL's all-time receiving list.

Brown is the only Raider to have scored touchdowns four different ways: on a pass reception, a run from scrimmage, a kickoff return, and a punt return. He was still going strong in 2000, leading Oakland with 76 receptions, 1,128 yards receiving, and 11 touchdowns.

CAREER STATS

RECEIVING

Year	Rec.	Yards	Avg.	TDs
1984	28	340	12.1	1
1985	25	397	15.9	3
1986	45	910	20.2	5
1987	39	846	21.7	3
Total	137	2,493	18.2	12

RUSHING

Year	Att.	Yards	Avg.	TDs
1984	1	14	14.0	0
1985	4	30	7.5	1
1986	59	254	4.3	2
1987	34	144	4.2	1
Total	98	442	4.5	4

KICKOFF RETURNS

Year	No.	Yards	Avg.	TDs
1984	7	121	17.3	0
1985	14	338	24.1	1
1986	25	698	27.9	2
1987	23	456	19.7	0
Total	69	1,613	23.4	3

PUNT RETURNS

Year	No.	Yards	Avg.	TDs
1984	No punt returns			
1985	No punt returns			
1986	2	75	37.5	0
1987	34	401	11.8	3
Total	36	476	13.2	3

ALL-PURPOSE YARDS

Year	Yards
1984	475
1985	765
1986	1,937
1987	1,847
Total	5,024

BROWNER, JIM
Safety/Fullback (1975–78), 6'3", 204 lbs.

Browner had a fine career at Notre Dame. As a strong safety on the 1977 national championship team, he was the glue that held the team together. He was, however, far from the best Browner to attend Notre Dame. His older brother Ross, also a member of the 1977 team, was not only 43 pounds heavier, he was one of the best defensive linemen ever to play in South Bend.

Jim Browner, a high school All-American from Warren, Ohio, was a three-year starter who began his college career as a fullback. In his first game, against Boston College, he rushed for 95 yards. He played in nine of eleven games and finished third on the team in rushing with 394 yards on 104 carries. Despite these flashes of brilliance, Browner was moved to the defensive side of the ball. He played strong safety for the rest of his career, making 80 tackles as a sopho-more, 73 as a junior, and 75 during his se-nior season. He was drafted in the twelfth round by the Cincinnati Bengals, and joined his brother there for two seasons.

BROWNER, ROSS
Defensive end (1973, 1975–77), 6'3", 248 lbs.

Ross Browner came to Notre Dame from Warren, Ohio, with outstanding cre-dentials. He left with even better ones.

A high school All-American at War-ren Western Reserve, which he led to an Ohio state championship, Browner was a two-time college All-American (1976–77) and winner of the Outland Trophy (1976) and the Lombardi Trophy (1977). The defen-sive lineman was also fifth in the voting for the Heisman Trophy (1977), which tradi-tionally is awarded to an offensive standout.

Defensive tackle Ross Browner was the winner of the Outland Trophy and the Lombardi Trophy and had a ten-year career in pro football.

A starter from his freshman year, Browner made his presence felt from the be-ginning. In his first-ever college game he blocked a punt for a safety as Notre Dame drubbed Northwestern 44–0 in the 1973 sea-son opener. His first college team was unde-feated and won a national championship. Browner was a big contributor, especially for a first-year player. He had 68 tackles, third on the team.

Browner missed the following season with an injury, but came back in 1975 with a vengeance. He made 71 tackles and recovered 4 fumbles. Then, as a junior, he had 97 tack-les, including a school record 28 for negative yardage, and also recovered 4 fumbles. His junior season might have been a tough act to follow, but with 104 tackles in his senior year, Browner made it look easy. The team won an-other national championship, and his brother Jim was also on the same defense.

Browner holds the Notre Dame career record for tackles by a front-four lineman (post-1956), with 340. He also recovered 12 fumbles, forced 2 safeties, and scored a touch-down. He was selected eighth overall in the 1978 NFL draft by the Cincinnati Bengals, taken one pick after his Notre Dame team-mate, tight end Ken MacAfee. Browner played for the Bengals until he was suspended for three months in 1985 for failing a drug test. He then moved over to the United States Football League for a brief stint with the Hous-ton Gamblers, and returned to the Bengals later that season. He capped his decade-long career as a member of the Green Bay Packers.

Browner was inducted into the College Football Hall of Fame in 1999.

BUDKA, FRANK
Quarterback/Defensive back (1961–63), 6'0", 190 lbs.

Players who worked both sides of the ball were rare in college football in the 1960s, and Budka did it in an interesting way: he played quarterback and defensive back. Sometimes he threw passes, at other times he tried to intercept them.

Budka, from Pompano Beach, Florida, showed promise as a sophomore signal caller in 1961, splitting time with Daryle Lamonica and leading the team with 40 completions on 95 attempts for 636 yards and 3 touchdowns. He also made 21 tackles as a defensive back. In 1962, however, Lamonica won the quarterback position, and Budka threw only 9 passes. He concentrated more on defense, making 51 tackles and adding an interception. Lamonica was gone the following year, and Budka was again in a quarterback battle. He shared the position with John Huarte and Sandy Bonvechio, and led the team with 22 completions in 41 attempts for 251 yards and 4 touchdowns. He also rushed for 4 touchdowns for a total of 24 points, which led the team.

Budka, whose Notre Dame teams were far from the best in school history (the Fighting Irish were 12–17 during his career) was drafted in the fourth round by the Los Angeles Rams. He played one season for them as a defensive back.

BULLOCK, WAYNE
Fullback (1972–74), 6'1", 221 lbs.

By the end of his sophomore season, Bullock didn't give much indication that he was going to be one of the best running backs in Notre Dame history. Luckily for the Irish, though, he didn't let past performance stop him.

Bullock came to South Bend from Newport News, Virginia, where he was a two-time all-state running back and the state heavyweight wrestling champion for Washington Carver High School. His sophomore season at Notre Dame was less than sensational, as he had 27 carries for 123 yards. But the following year he had one game which was better than his entire sophomore season. He carried the ball 27 times (as he did as a sophomore), gaining 167 yards and scoring 4 touchdowns in a 31–10 victory over twentieth-ranked Pittsburgh. He finished his junior season as the team's leading rusher, with 752 yards on 162 carries as Notre Dame

went 11–0 and won the national championship. Bullock was second on the team in scoring, with 66 points, behind only kicker Bob Thomas, who scored 70 points. He also scored a touchdown in a 24–23 victory over Alabama in the Sugar Bowl.

Bullock's senior year was even better. He rushed for a team-leading 855 yards on 203 carries and was also tops on the roster with 72 points scored. In basically two seasons, he finished eighth on Notre Dame's all-time rushing list, though he has since dropped off the school's Top Twenty list. His senior season now stands as the twentieth-best season for a running back in Fighting Irish history.

Bullock, however, was passed over by most All-America teams after his two standout seasons, and the pros didn't get too excited either. In 1975, he was drafted in the fifth round by the San Francisco 49ers, but never played in the NFL.

BUONICONTI, NICK
Guard (1959–61), 5'11", 210 lbs.

Buoniconti may have enjoyed individual success at Notre Dame, but he had to wait until he made it to the professional ranks to enjoy team success. In his three seasons on the Notre Dame varsity, Buoniconti and his teammates won twelve games and lost eighteen, but he tasted victory when he moved from the Boston Patriots to the Miami Dolphins, where he was a key member of the 1973 and 1974 Super Bowl champion teams, the first of which finished 17–0, for the NFL's only undefeated season.

Buoniconti hailed from Springfield, Massachusetts, where he played at the same high school (Cathedral) as Heisman Trophy–winning quarterback Angelo Bertelli. At Notre Dame he got a chance to play during his sophomore season after left guard Myron Pottios injured his knee. With the newfound playing time, Buoniconti quickly proved his worth, finishing third on the team in tackles, with 67. The next year, Pottios was back and was elected team captain. That didn't slow down the progress of Buoniconti, however. The two men shared the position, and Buoniconti actually played more. Pottios led the team with 74 tackles, and Buoniconti was next with 71.

As a senior, Buoniconti took over. He was the starting left guard and a team cocaptain. He led by example with 74 tackles, tops on the team, and 2 blocked kicks. He was named to several All-America teams. Still, it was not until the twelfth round of the 1962 draft that the Boston Patriots called Buoniconti's name. He played with the American Football League (AFL) team until 1968, and then moved on to the Miami Dolphins in 1969. After the two Super Bowl seasons, Buoniconti missed the 1975 campaign with a broken finger, but came back in 1976 for his final season of football.

His son, Marc, broke his neck while playing for the Citadel. Since then, Marc and Nick have dedicated their lives to the awareness of and fund-raising for spinal cord injuries.

BURGMEIER, TED
Defensive back/Split end (1974–77), 5'11", 186 lbs.

Burgmeier both played receiver and guarded them during his four years at Notre Dame, but he made more of a mark in the defensive backfield than as a wide receiver. In his freshman season, Burgmeier, from East Dubuque, Illinois, backed up free safety Randy Harrison. In 1975, rookie head coach Dan Devine wanted to cash in on Burgmeier's quick feet and athletic ability and moved him to split end. Burgmeier, who was all-state in baseball and track and all-state and All-American in football at Wahlert High School, also proved to have soft hands. He caught 10 balls for 185 yards, despite missing the season's final two games with an injury.

As a junior, Devine moved Burgmeier back to defense, where he started at cornerback, making 54 tackles and intercepting 2 passes. He also led the team in punt returns, with 20 for 138 yards. During his senior sea-

son the Fighting Irish won a national championship, and Burgmeier's 54 tackles and 4 interceptions were good enough to earn him second-team All-American status. He also returned a team-leading 18 punts for 82 yards. Burgmeier lasted one season in the NFL as a member of the Kansas City Chiefs.

BURRIS, JEFF
Cornerback/Safety/Running back (1990–93), 6'0", 204 lbs.

Burris was certainly an all-around athlete. As a freshman he played in ten games. If he wasn't playing cornerback he was playing safety or tailback or returning kicks. He didn't start a game and didn't have a position, but somehow it seemed certain that he was going to have an outstanding career in South Bend.

It wasn't long before Burris, a four-year letter winner at Northwestern High School in Rock Hill, South Carolina, who led his team to a state title and was twice named South Carolina Player of the Year, gained national attention in college. As a sopho-

Jeff Burris was extremely versatile, playing on offense, defense, and special teams. He went on to a pro career as a cornerback.

more he became a starter and a known entity in college football. He split time between cornerback (eight starts) and free safety (five starts), finishing fourth on the squad in tackles. He also led his team in punt returns. Burris's heroics earned him honorable mention All-American honors.

After leading his team in interceptions and placing third in tackles, he again made honorable mention All-American as a junior. Head coach Lou Holtz even found another way to squeeze some wins out of Burris's talent: he started using him in the red zone to jam the ball into the end zone. Burris rushed just seven times during the season for an average of 2.0 yards, but made the most of it, with 3 touchdowns. The following season Notre Dame went 11–1 and finished second in the final rankings.

Unsurprisingly, Burris didn't get much rest. He was a rarity in college football, playing a major role for his team on offense, defense, and special teams. On defense, he was good for 53 tackles and 3 interceptions, and was the team leader in minutes played. He also led the Fighting Irish with 204 special-teams appearances. Burris was also called on to score as a tailback, particularly during offensive goal-line situations: he rushed for 6 touchdowns, second on the team.

Burris capped his magnificent career with 9 tackles as Notre Dame beat Texas A&M in the 1994 Cotton Bowl. The National Monogram Club, made up of Notre Dame letter winners, named him the Most

Valuable Player of the 1993 season. He also gained national acclaim and was named a first-team All-American.

The Buffalo Bills picked Burris in the first round of a bumper draft for Notre Dame. In 1994, he was selected twenty-seventh overall; teammate defensive tackle Bryant Young was picked seventh by the San Francisco 49ers, and offensive guard Aaron Taylor was taken sixteenth by the Green Bay Packers. That made seven first-round draft picks in two seasons for the Fighting Irish, as four of its players were selected in the opening round of the 1993 NFL draft. Burris played for the Bills until 1997 and then moved to the Indianapolis Colts.

CAREER STATS
DEFENSE

Year	Tackles	Int.	Yards
1991	63	2	0
1992	73	5	6
1993	53	3	61
Total	189	10	67

RUSHING

Year	Att.	Yards	Avg.	TDs
1990	6	30	5.0	1
1991	No rushing attempts			
1992	7	14	2.0	3
1993	16	92	5.8	6
Total	29	136	4.7	10

CALHOUN, MIKE
Defensive tackle (1976–78), 6′5″, 237 lbs.

Only one underclassman started on Notre Dame's defensive line during the 1977 season, when the team went 11–1 and took the national title. That man was Calhoun, who came to South Bend from Austintown High School in Ohio, where he was an all-state and All-American football player. He picked up right where he left off when he got to Notre Dame.

During his first varsity season, Calhoun had 92 tackles. As a junior, he was only seventh on the team with 72 tackles, but he had a penchant for big plays: he was second on the squad in tackles for minus yardage (13 for -63). He had his most productive year as a senior, ending the season 1 tackle shy of 100. The Dallas Cowboys selected Calhoun in the tenth round of the 1979 NFL draft; he played the following season for the San Francisco 49ers and Tampa Bay Buccaneers.

CANNON, JACK
Guard (1927–29), 5′11″, 193 lbs.

You could call Jack Cannon a lot of things. It would be fair to characterize him as a rebel, a free spirit, or as competitive or erratic, but one thing you couldn't call him was soft. Cannon, who was inducted into the College Football Hall of Fame in 1965, was one of the most outstanding guards in Notre Dame history as well as one of the last players to play without a helmet. He was one of the standouts of the 1929 Notre Dame team, which had to play its season under unusual circumstances: the team went undefeated despite having to play all of its nine games on the road due to the construction of Notre

College Football Hall of Famer Jack Cannon was one of the most outstanding guards in Notre Dame history as well as being one of the last players to play without a helmet.

Dame Stadium. The constant train rides and games in front of enemy crowds may have bothered some players, but not Cannon. It actually charged him up; he liked upsetting the home crowd with a Notre Dame victory.

During games Cannon would go all out until the contest was no longer in doubt, then he would lose interest. This lack of consistency frustrated head coach Knute Rockne. Still, he remains one of the best to play his position in school history. One of his best games came during his senior season against Army. He kicked off 3 times and beat the coverage team downfield to make the tackle after each kick. He also made the key block that sprung Jack Elder for a 96-yard interception return in the 7–0 victory. His play was rewarded, as he was named a consensus All-American.

CARBERRY, GLEN
End (1920–22), 6'0", 180 lbs.

Mr. and Mrs. J. H. Carberry of Ames, Iowa, had twelve kids. Notre Dame was fortunate enough to have the services of the best football-playing one.

Glen had six brothers, and many of them went on to play football. John and William Carberry stayed home for college and starred at the University of Iowa. Richard Carberry also remained in Iowa and played for Columbia College in Dubuque. Glen, however, did the most with his football talent. He was the captain of the 1922 Notre Dame team, which went 8–1–1. Nicknamed Judge, he arrived in South Bend in 1919 and earned his first letter the following season. He was the starting left end as a senior.

After three seasons of professional football, Carberry went into coaching and worked as an assistant to former teammate halfback Jim Crowley at Fordham University.

CAREY, TONY
Defensive back (1964–65), 6'0", 190 lbs.

It took Carey a couple of seasons to crack the varsity football team at Notre Dame, but once he got there, he was right at home. Carey, from Chicago, did not earn a letter until his junior season in 1964, but he was an instant starter and gained national attention. He played 269 minutes that season and led not only the Fighting Irish but the entire nation, in interceptions, with 8. He was also credited with 46 tackles. His first season on the big team earned him second-team All-American honors.

Carey had his sophomore slump as a senior. His interception total was down to 3, and he had about 25 percent less tackles (34). Still, he was drafted in the sixth round by both the NFL Chicago Bears and San Diego Chargers of the AFL, although he didn't play professionally. Carey's brother, Tom, preceded him at Notre Dame. The elder Carey was a quarterback in the 1950s.

CARIDEO, FRANK
Quarterback (1928–30), 5'7", 175 lbs.

Carideo was the quarterback on two Notre Dame national championship teams, yet he never led the team in passing. He was too busy doing everything else. The tough, intelligent signal caller from Mount Vernon, New York, was an all-around athlete with outstanding leadership capabilities. In his two years as a starting quarterback, Notre Dame was 19–0 and took two national titles.

Carideo was not only one of the best quarterbacks and punters in Notre Dame history, he also played defensive back and led the Fighting Irish in interceptions, with 5 for 151 yards as a junior, which was also his first season as the team's starting quarterback. That was the year he began displaying his multidimensional game. Against Navy he completed a 10-yard touchdown pass to Jack Elder. Against Georgia Tech he made it to the end zone on a 75-yard touchdown run, and he ran back an interception for 85 yards and a touchdown in a 26–6 victory over Northwestern. Carideo also nailed an extra point that was the difference in a 13–12 win over USC, and in a season-ending 7–0 victory over Army, he scored the only points the Fighting Irish would need with a 96-yard interception return. He made every prominent All-American team as a junior.

In 1930, while leading Notre Dame to its second consecutive undefeated national championship year, Carideo proved to be one of the most versatile athletes in college football. Against Southern Methodist University (SMU) he set up a touchdown with a 70-yard punt return and a second one with a 25-yard completion to end Ed Kosky. He scored a touchdown against Pennsylvania, and then kicked a game-winning extra point in a 7–6 victory over Army in front of a crowd of 110,000 at Chicago's Soldier Field. In a late-season victory over Western Conference cochampion Northwestern, the quarterback showed off his leg, kicking 4 punts that landed inside the 1-yard line and were not returned. (He learned how to kick to the coffin corner at Dean Academy from Leroy Mills, a New York City attorney who played football at Princeton University and was a kicking and punting guru of his time.) In that game, Carideo also returned a punt to the 28-yard line to set up the winning score in the 14–0 victory. A 1954 inductee into the College Football Hall of Fame, Carideo punctuated his college career with a 27–0 victory over USC by catching a 26-yard touchdown pass from halfback Marchy Schwartz. It should, then, come as no surprise that Carideo was named a consensus All-American for the second consecutive season.

After graduating, Carideo took to coaching. In 1931, he was an assistant at Purdue University; from 1932 to 1934 he was the head coach at the University of Missouri. In 1936, he became the head basketball coach and an assistant football coach at Mississippi State. He coached at the University of Iowa from 1939–42, and later served as a lieutenant in the navy. He returned to Iowa in 1946 and retired from coaching four years later.

CARNEY, JOHN
Kicker (1983–86), 5'10", 170 lbs.

Following in the footsteps of kicker Mike Johnston, who graduated in 1982 with the record for consecutive field goals (13), may have been a daunting task, but it didn't seem to bother Carney. He was an all-state kicker at Cardinal Newman High School in West Palm Beach, Florida, in 1982, but did not receive a scholarship to play in South Bend. Instead, he made the squad as a walk-on and patiently waited while Johnston kicked extra points and field goals in 1983. He was responsible for kickoffs, however, and

reached the opponent's goal line with 43 of his 59 kicks. Only 25 were returned.

The next season he took over the position, and for three seasons was recognized as one of the most accurate kickers in the game. He was good for 70 of 75 extra points and 51 of 69 field goals for a total of 223 points, despite never nailing a field goal of more than 50 yards. His 1984 kicking percentage of .895 (17 of 19) and his career mark of .739 (51 of 69) remain school records. The kid who was not offered a scholarship to play at his college also went undrafted and did not make the NFL until 1989, when he signed as a free agent with the Tampa Bay Buccaneers.

Again he proved to the teams that passed him over that they had missed out. Carney, who was born in Hartford, Connecticut, has continued to be one of the best kickers in the league. He was traded to the San Diego Chargers in 1990 and is the team's all-time scoring leader. In 1994, he also led the NFL in scoring, with 135 points, and was named to the Pro Bowl. Off the field, Carney has made a name for himself in San Diego. He started a charitable program called KickStart for Kids, which raises funds for children in need of reconstructive surgery.

CAREER STATS

Year	PATs	FGs	Points
1983	Only used on kickoffs		
1984	25–25	17–19	76
1985	21–24	13–22	60
1986	24–26	21–28	87
Total	70–75	51–69	223

CAROLLO, JOE
Tackle (1959–61), 6'2", 235 lbs.

Carollo, from Wyandotte, Michigan, was a workhorse of a tackle. In his junior season he led all tackles in playing time with more than five hours of game action (302 minutes), and averaged a tackle every 10 minutes. In 1961, as a senior, he had his best season, with 40 tackles. His varsity debut was in 1959, when he was a second-stringer and made 22 tackles. After competing in the 1962 College Football All-Star Game, Carollo was a second-round draft pick of the NFL's Pittsburgh Steelers and the AFL's Boston Patriots. He played for the Los Angeles Rams from 1962 to 1968, and in 1971. In 1969 he was a member of the Philadelphia Eagles. He also played for the Cleveland Browns in 1972 and 1973.

CARROLL, JIM
Guard/Linebacker (1962–64), 6'1", 225 lbs.

Carroll, who was born in Jonesboro, Arkansas, and grew up in Atlanta, was a football and wrestling star at Marist High School. As the starting left guard, he had 59 tackles in each of his first two seasons on the varsity. Then, in 1964, coach Ara Parseghian platooned Carroll to defense only, and he answered with more tackles than he'd made in the previous two seasons combined. He set a school record with 140 tackles, 52 more than his second-place teammate. Playing for third-ranked Notre Dame, Carroll was a first-team All-American.

After he was done in South Bend, Carroll was a twelfth-round selection by the New York Giants in the 1965 NFL draft. He played for the Giants in 1965 and 1966, with the Washington Redskins from 1966 to 1968, and finished up his career back in New York as a member of the Jets in 1969.

CARTER, PHIL
Running back (1979–82), 5'10", 197 lbs.

Carter, from Tacoma, Washington, had three exceptional years of running the ball for Notre Dame, but somehow that was lost when it came time to vote for All-America teams and pick players in the NFL draft.

Carter finished up at Notre Dame with 2,409 yards on 557 carries and 14 touchdowns, good for fifth on the school's all-time rushing list. His sophomore season was his most productive. He gained 822 yards on 186 carries for an average of 4.4 yards and 6 touchdowns, placing second on the team be-

hind Jim Stone, who gained 908 yards on 192 carries. The tandem was a terrific one-two punch, but after that season he took control of the rushing reins and was Notre Dame's leading rusher in 1981 (165 carries for 727 yards, 6 touchdowns) and 1982 (179 carries for 715 yards, 2 touchdowns).

CAREER STATS

Year	Att.	Yards	Avg.	TDs
1979	27	145	5.4	0
1980	186	822	4.4	6
1981	165	727	4.4	6
1982	179	715	4.0	2
Total	557	2,409	4.3	14

CARTER, TOM
Defensive back (1990–92), 5'11", 184 lbs.

Carter possessed 4.38 40-yard-dash speed, was very aggressive, could hit like a Mack truck, and was a threat on special teams. If he hadn't decided to go professional instead of playing his senior year at Notre Dame, he could have set some school records. After playing quarterback, cornerback, and wide receiver in high school, the St. Petersburg, Florida, schoolboy stepped right into college ball. He was a starting safety for six games as a freshman. As a sophomore he was moved to cornerback, where he became a permanent starter. He had 30 tackles and a team-high 5 interceptions, and ran one back for a 79-yard score in a 35–34 loss to the University of Tennessee.

During his junior season, Carter had 40 tackles and 5 interceptions, to raise his career total to 10. He was named a third-team All-American and opted to enter the NFL draft rather than play his senior season. He left school just 3 interceptions from breaking into the top three on Notre Dame's all-time list, and 7 behind Luther Bradley's school record of 17. After he finished with college football, Carter took his fleet feet to the track and field team, winning the Midwestern Collegiate Conference 55-meter indoor sprint championship.

Then, in 1993, Carter was the third of four Notre Dame players to be chosen in the first round of the NFL draft. He went seventeenth overall to the Washington Redskins, and made another smooth transition. He led the team, and all rookies, with 6 interceptions. In 1997, he was signed by the Chicago Bears as a free agent. The Redskins could have matched the offer but decided not to, even though Carter had led the team in interceptions, with 9, in 1995 and pass breakups, with 42, in 1996. He started every game for Chicago at cornerback in 1997. He later played for the Cincinnati Bengals.

CASEY, DAN
Guard (1894–95), 6'0", 173 lbs.

Football had taken a break at Notre Dame during the two years prior to 1892; Casey, of Crawfordsville, Indiana, was part of its resurgence. Like most players of his time, he had a multifaceted game: He could run, kick, and defend. In 1894, as the starting right guard in a shutout over Wabash, he ran for more than 145 yards, including scoring romps of 50 and 25 yards. He also ran for a 35-yard score in another victory over Wabash. Casey was named team captain in 1895 and again started at right guard. He also scored a touchdown and 2 point-after scores in a shutout over Northwestern Law School. He also ran for a 15-yard score and made 3 extra points in a victory over the Illinois Cycling Club, and had the identical scoring output in a shutout of Physicians and Surgeons.

CASPER, DAVE
Tackle/Tight end (1971–73), 6'3", 252 lbs.

Casper, who came to South Bend from Chilton, Wisconsin, is best known as a standout tight end for the Oakland Raiders in the franchise's heyday. In college, he was actually an offensive lineman for three seasons before moving to his permanent position as a senior. Casper, however, was never one to be pigeonholed. In high school he lettered in basketball, golf, baseball (he was a .446 hitter), and football (he was an All-American). During his first year on the Notre Dame cam-

Dave Casper was originally an offensive lineman who later switched to tight end, where he had spectacular success both in college and in the NFL.

pus he played the line and handled the punting duties for the freshman football team. He was a second-string offensive tackle as a sophomore in 1971, his first varsity season. As a junior he became a starter and was named an honorable mention All-American tackle. He also saw time as a wide receiver, defensive tackle, and tight end.

He was obviously impressive during his time at tight end, because he set down stakes at the position the following season. In 1973, during an undefeated national championship campaign for Notre Dame, Casper was made a tri-captain and started at tight end. He was second on the team with 19 receptions for 317 yards and scored 4 touchdowns. Casper proved to be a clutch performer. He caught a 30-yard pass from quarterback Tom Clements, which set up Bob Thomas's game-winning field goal in a 24–23 championship-clinching victory over the University of Alabama. Casper was a consensus All-American after his senior season. He played in the College Football All-Star Game and in the Hula Bowl, and was a first-team Academic All-American.

In the second round of the NFL draft he was selected by the Oakland Raiders and went on to a stellar eleven-year NFL career, during which he caught 378 passes for 5,216 yards and scored 52 touchdowns. In addition to the Raiders, for whom he played in Super Bowl XI, Casper also played for the Houston Oilers, Minnesota Vikings, and Los Angeles Rams. In 1993 he was inducted into the Academic All-American Hall of Fame.

CASTNER, PAUL
Halfback/Fullback (1920–22), 6'0", 190 lbs.

The 1920s were a freewheeling time. It was a decade when a kid who never played high school football could receive a scholarship to play on a major college football team, and not only play, but excel. That's what happened to St. Paul, Minnesota, native Castner, who was recommended to Notre Dame head coach Knute Rockne by a mutual friend. Rockne took a chance and it paid off, as Castner was a two-time All-American on Rockne's stellar teams. In his three letter-winning seasons, Castner excelled in kickoff returns and averaged an astounding 36.5 yards per carry, including an average of 44.5 his senior year.

Castner, who was as strong as he was fleet, made the varsity as a second-string fullback in 1920, playing behind Chet Wynne. Castner only ran back two kickoffs that season, but gained 55 yards for a 27.5 yards-per-carry average. The next year he started at halfback, and had just 8 kickoff returns to chalk up 222 yards (for a 27.8 average). The performance earned him a place as a second-team All-American. In his senior season Castner found himself back at fullback, where he led the team in scoring, with 64 points, 27 of which came in one game, a 27–0 win over Indiana. He scored 3 touchdowns, made 3 extra points, and was successful on dropkicks of 37 and 42 yards.

Late in the season Castner injured his back, and his absence made way for the birth of the fabled Four Horsemen. Elmer Layden moved in to replace Castner and joined Jim Crowley, with whom he was splitting time at left halfback, Don Miller at right halfback, and Harry Stuhldreher at quarterback. The quartet would go on to make up one of the most famous offensive backfields in the history of the game.

Castner coauthored a biography called *We Remember Rockne*. His name often gets lost in the shuffle of bigger names in Notre Dame history. Seventy-five years later, though, he is still in the Irish record books. He holds school records for kickoff return yards in a single game (253) and career kickoff return average (36.5 yards). Castner did more than just play football and go to class. He earned three varsity letters in baseball and went on to play for the Chicago White Sox. He also was the founder of Notre Dame's ice hockey team in 1921.

CHEVIGNY, JACK
Halfback (1926–28), 5'9", 173 lbs.

Even someone who has never seen one down of Notre Dame football will probably know the phrase, "Win one for the Gipper." However, even the most diehard fan of the Fighting Irish will probably struggle when asked which player first uttered the immortal words on the field of play. It was Chevigny, from Hammond, Iowa, who scored the first touchdown after head coach Knute Rockne's fiery pregame speech to his team. "The Rock" told them of late halfback George Gipp's dying words: When the team was up against it in a game against Army, they should win one for him. As Chevigny crossed the goal line in the come-from-behind victory he shouted, "That's one for the Gipper!"

The battle cry was not Chevigny's lone highlight. He scored a touchdown in his first varsity game, a victory over Beloit. As a backup right halfback in 1926, he scored against the University of Minnesota. Chevigny again backed up at right halfback in 1927, and finally made it into the starting lineup in 1928. He scored against the University of Wisconsin and Drake University before breaking the plane for Gipp. The famous score was a 1-yard run on fourth down. His celebration didn't last long, as he had to be carried from the field later in the game after recovering a bad snap. His final college touchdown was also his longest. He scored on a 51-yard run against USC on a fake reverse play.

CHRYPLEWICZ, PETE
Tight end (1992–96), 6'5", 267 lbs.

Chryplewicz, from Sterling Heights, Michigan, was a prep All-American who went on to become one of the best tight ends to play for coach Lou Holtz at Notre Dame, earning five letters for the Fighting Irish. His career got off to a slow start, with just 4 receptions during his first three years on the team. He made 1 catch in 1992, 3 the following year, and none in 1994, when his season was ended after two games because of a broken navicular bone in his right wrist. He suited up for games late in the season but didn't play, leading to an extra year of eligibility.

As a starter in 1995, Chryplewicz made 17 catches (for 204 yards and a touchdown), which placed him third on the team in receptions. As a fifth-year senior in 1996, he made 25 catches, which was the most for a Notre Dame tight end since Mark Bavaro's 32 catches in 1984 (for 331 yards and 4 touchdowns). It was also the best statistical season for a tight end who played for Holtz. Chryplewicz's career total of 48 catches was the second highest total, behind Derek Brown, for a tight end during Holtz's era. In his final season, the soft-handed receiver who finished his college career with 585 receiving yards was named an honorable mention All-American. He played in the East-West Shrine Game and was a fifth-round selection by the Detroit Lions in 1997.

CIFELLI, GUS
Tackle (1946–49), 6'4", 222 lbs.

What Cifelli lacked in athletic skill he more than made up for in grit and toughness. The Philadelphia native was a man when he

entered Notre Dame, having already spent two years in the Marine Corps as a gun operator and boxing instructor. He was on the varsity for four seasons, won three letters, but did not often start games. In the nineteenth round of the 1950 draft, Cifelli was selected by the Detroit Lions and bounced around the NFL, from the Green Bay Packers to the Philadelphia Eagles, and finally the Pittsburgh Steelers, before retiring in 1954.

CLARK, WILLIE
Defensive back/Tailback (1990–93), 5'10", 185 lbs.

Clark spent his college career shifting from offense to defense. As the son of military personnel, moving should have been nothing for him. Born in New Haven, Connecticut, he began high school in Madrid, Spain, and graduated from Wheatland High School, in California. He was impressive enough to earn a scholarship to Notre Dame when, as a senior, he rushed for 1,121 yards and 16 touchdowns and made the All-California team.

Clark began his college career at tailback, his high school position. In the middle of his sophomore campaign he was moved to the defensive backfield, where he played cornerback and free safety. He capped the season with a great performance in a 39–28 victory over Florida in the Sugar Bowl when he intercepted a pass, deflected 3 others, and made 6 tackles. If his on-the-field performance was not enough to convince onlookers that he was fast, after the football season, he qualified for the National Collegiate Athletic Association (NCAA) indoor track and field championships in the 55-meter run.

Back on offense as a junior, Clark's year ended shortly after the season opener against Northwestern when he injured his wrist. As a senior he played on both sides of the line of scrimmage, but again his season was limited because of injuries. Despite a shortened career and lack of a true position in college, Clark was selected in the third round of the NFL draft by the San Diego Chargers. He moved to Philadelphia to play for the Eagles in 1997.

CLASBY, BOB
Defensive tackle (1979–82), 6′5″, 259 lbs.

Clasby excelled at three sports—football, lacrosse, and hockey—but it was the first of the three that was in his blood. In his day, Clasby's father Ed was the football captain at Harvard. The family remained in Milton, Massachusetts, which was in close proximity to the Ivy League school, but when it came time to pick a college Clasby selected football and Notre Dame. His college career got off to a slow start; he arrived in South Bend in 1979 and didn't earn his first letter until 1981. As a sophomore he played just seventeen minutes as a defensive tackle.

The following season he became a mainstay, earning 184 minutes of playing time and making 56 tackles. As a senior he finished fifth on the team in tackles, with 65, and his play impressed NFL and United States Football League scouts. Clasby was a sixth-round draft pick of the San Diego Chargers. He played in the USFL for the Jacksonville Bulls in 1984 and 1985 and then joined the St. Louis Cardinals of the NFL in 1986. He retired as a member of the Arizona Cardinals in 1990.

CLATT, CORWIN
Fullback (1942, 1946–47), 6′0″, 200 lbs.

A star player from East Peoria High School in Illinois, Clatt became Notre Dame's leading rusher in 1942, gaining 698 yards on 138 carries. He also shared top scoring honors (30 points) with halfback Creighton Miller. Clatt joined the military in 1943, but returned to Notre Dame after the end of World War II. He lettered in both 1946 and 1947, and went on to play for the Chicago Cardinals in the NFL in 1948 and 1949.

CLEMENTS, TOM
Quarterback (1972–74), 6′0″, 189 lbs.

As a three-year starter at quarterback for Notre Dame, the least impressive season of the McKees Rock, Pennsylvania, native was one of the best for the Fighting Irish.

After throwing for 1,163 yards as a sophomore, a year that Notre Dame went 8–3, Clements's total was down to 882 yards as a junior. But 1973 turned out to be one of those memorable seasons for Notre Dame: the Fighting Irish went 11–0 and won the national championship. Despite a subpar passing year, Clements had a lot to say about the fabulous season. In the championship-clinching 24–23 Sugar Bowl win over Alabama, Clements engineered a 79-yard scoring drive late in regulation time, and Bob Thomas's 19-yard field goal with 4:26 to play clinched the win. It was the second national championship under head coach Ara Parseghian, and Clements was named the Most Valuable Player of the bowl game.

As a senior, Clements, an extremely accurate passer who completed more than half of his passes every year as a college starter, got his range back and passed for 1,549 yards for the 10–2 Fighting Irish. An interesting statistic is that in each of his three seasons as starting quarterback at Notre Dame, Clements threw 8 touchdown passes. He even ranked eighth on Notre Dame's all-time passing list until the career of Jarious Jackson (1999) bumped him down to ninth.

Clements never played in the NFL, but played long and prospered in the Canadian Football League (CFL). In 1975, while playing for the Ottawa Rough Riders, he won the Schenley Award as the league's Most Outstanding Rookie. The next season he led Ottawa to a Grey Cup victory, again making a clutch play by throwing the game-winning pass with nineteen seconds to go. He was named an Eastern Conference All-Star in that, the 1976 season, as well as in 1977.

He was not even close to through collecting honors. Clements won the Jeff Russel Trophy (CFL Eastern Conference MVP) in 1981. In 1984, while playing for Winnipeg, he won another Grey Cup and was named the game's Most Valuable Player. His career came to an end in 1987, but not before he had thrown for 4,600 yards, 35 touchdowns, and won the CFL's Most Outstanding Player Award. He was inducted into the Canadian Football Hall of Fame in 1994.

From 1992 through 1996 Clements was an assistant coach under Lou Holtz.

CAREER STATS

Year	Att.	Comp.	Pct.	Yards	TDs
1972	162	83	.512	1,163	8
1973	113	60	.531	882	8
1974	215	122	.567	1,549	8
Total	490	265	.541	3,594	24

COADY, ED
Quarterback (1888–89)

Coady, of Pana, Illinois, was part of the second group of players to compete in football for Notre Dame. He played quarterback in four games over two seasons, including the first two victories in the program's history.

Notre Dame had lost the first three games in its history, all to Michigan. Finally, on December 6, 1888, Notre Dame played Harvard Prep (Chicago) and won, 20–0. The following season, its lone game was against Northwestern and Notre Dame won, 9–0. Coady scored a touchdown in the latter game after faking a handoff to a lineman.

COFALL, STAN
Halfback (1914–16), 5′11″, 180 lbs.

Cofall played on some talented, and successful, Notre Dame teams. The three-year starter at left halfback definitely did his part in helping head coach Jesse Harper's teams go an incredible 21–4. Cofall was a first-team All-American in 1916 and rushed for 30 touchdowns, a figure surpassed by only three other Fighting Irish alumni. The native of Cleveland, Ohio, played two seasons of professional football: with the Cleveland Browns in 1920 and the New York Giants in 1921.

COLEMAN, HERB
Center (1942–43), 6′1″, 198 lbs.

Coleman was the starting center on head coach Frank Leahy's 1943 national championship team, following his stint as a backup at the position the previous season.

The Chester, West Virginia, native was a member of the navy V-5 program and received a medical discharge from the service because of knee and back injuries he suffered while playing football. He went on to play professional ball for the Chicago Rockets in 1946 and 1947 and for the Baltimore Colts the following season.

COLLINS, GREG
Linebacker (1972–74), 6′3″, 228 lbs.

Collins, a standout defender, had a nose for the pigskin. He was an all-state linebacker at Brother Rice High School in Troy, Michigan, and won his first letter at Notre Dame as a second-string outside linebacker in 1972. The following year he began his two-year assault on opposing offenses. He led the Fighting Irish in tackles his final two seasons, including his junior year, when Notre Dame won the national championship. As the defensive leader on a team that allowed just 66 points all season, Collins had 133 tackles and 11 sacks. Eighteen of those tackles came in one game, a 45–23 victory over USC. In that game he also forced a fumble and recovered another. Collins led all defenders with 225 minutes played, and made 16 solo tackles in the team's season-clinching 24–23 Sugar Bowl victory over Alabama.

In 1974, Collins's talent was rewarded; he was named captain, and he did not disappoint. Again he led the team in tackles, this time with 144, good enough for second-team All-American honors. He was a second-round pick of the San Francisco 49ers in the 1975 NFL draft and played one season with the franchise. Collins then played a year apiece for the Seattle Seahawks and Buffalo Bills.

CONJAR, LARRY
Fullback (1965–66), 6′0″, 212 lbs.

It took Conjar a while to catch on at Notre Dame, but once he did, the rugged fullback had no problem making up for lost time. Conjar, who came to South Bend from Oxon Hill, Maryland, didn't play a full season of varsity ball until his junior season, but he made his way directly into the team's starting lineup. He turned some heads by rushing for more than 500 yards as Notre Dame's starting fullback. He was also third on the team in points with 42. In one game he carried the ball 25 times and netted 116 yards and 4 touchdowns.

As a senior, Conjar was again an integral part of the squad's offense. Notre Dame was in the hunt for the national championship with the help of the nation's third-ranked offense. Conjar was a large part of that success. He carried the ball 112 times, gained 521 yards, and scored 7 touchdowns. The only back on the team with better numbers was consensus All-American Nick Eddy, who benefited from Conjar's selfless blocking. Conjar, who also caught 4 passes for 62 yards, was named to several All-America teams.

Conjar spent four rather unproductive seasons in the NFL. In 1967, he was drafted in the second round by the Cleveland Browns, and also played with the Philadelphia Eagles and Baltimore Colts. In his entire four years he carried the ball only 30 times, for a career total of 102 yards.

CONLEY, TOM
End (1928–30), 5'11", 175 lbs.

Tom Conley, a graduate of Philadelphia's Roman Catholic High School, earned his first letter at Notre Dame as a backup during his sophomore year in 1928, and then was ready in the wings when starting right end Manny Vezie was injured the following season. The junior's performance in place of Vezie helped Notre Dame secure a national championship. He showed unusual poise for an underclassman and impressed teammates so much that he was named team captain as a senior. Following his senior season, Conley was named a second-team All-American.

CONNOR, GEORGE
Tackle (1946–47), 6'3", 225 lbs.

It was at Pearl Harbor that Connor decided to transfer from Holy Cross College

to Notre Dame, giving the Fighting Irish one of the best linemen in school history. Connor was heavily recruited after completing an outstanding career at Chicago's DeLaSalle Institute. He could have gone anyplace, but seriously considered only two choices: Notre Dame and Holy Cross, and for good reason. His high school coach, Joe Gleason, had been a Notre Dame halfback in the 1930s, but even more compelling was the fact that his uncle, George S.L. Connor, was a monsignor at the small college of Holy Cross in Worcester, Massachusetts. As it turned out, monsignor knew best, and Connor picked Holy Cross. He entered school as a seventeen-year-old freshman and was a starter from his first college game. A natural leader, Connor was named captain in just his sophomore season and took home the George Bulger Lowe Award for the best college football player in New England; he was also named an All-American.

He would, however, never again play at Holy Cross. Connor was a member of the navy's V-12 program and was called into active duty in 1944. He was stationed at Pearl

Tackle George Connor was a phenomenal two-way player whose distinguished accomplishments include the Outland Trophy, induction into both the College and Pro Football Halls of Fame, and All-American and All-Pro honors.

Harbor where, one day, Connor was called into the office of a commander, who just happened to be Notre Dame coach Frank Leahy, who had joined the navy during World War II. Leahy, who had recruited Connor out of DeLaSalle Institute, told the sailor that he still thought a lot of him as a person and as a player. Leahy assured Connor that when the war was over there was always a place for him in South Bend. Connor took him up on the deal, partly to stay close to his father, who had taken ill.

NCAA rules were lax for servicemen returning to college in 1946, and veterans transferring to new schools were immediately eligible. Connor, an all-around athlete on the football field, was quickly inserted into the starting lineup as a tackle and achieved nothing but success as a member of the Fighting Irish. The two teams he played on—in 1946 and 1947—both won national titles, and Connor was a consensus All-American both seasons. In his junior season he won the Outland Trophy as the nation's outstanding interior lineman. He was named captain of the 1947 team and played in the East-West Shrine Game.

Connor is a member of both the College Football Hall of Fame (he was inducted in 1963) and the Professional Football Hall of Fame (he was inducted in 1975). Although he was selected in the first round of the NFL draft by the New York Giants, he spent his entire eight-year professional football career with the Chicago Bears. An All-Pro two-way lineman in 1949 and 1950, he continued to play on both sides of the ball in 1951, even though the professional ranks had already adopted the two-platoon system. He was just as strong at both positions, winning All-Pro honors on both sides of the line. In 1952, Connor was moved to outside linebacker and was named All-Pro again. He retired from professional football in 1955.

COTTON, FOREST
Tackle (1920–22), 6'1", 182 lbs.

Elgin, Illinois, native Cotton gradually moved up the ladder at Notre Dame. He was a member of coach Knute Rockne's early teams. As would have happened during any time in Rockne's tenure, "Fod," as he was called, was part of a winning team. The Fighting Irish were a phenomenal 27–2–1 during his three-year varsity stint. Cotton was a backup guard in 1920, earned his first letter the next season as a second-string tackle (playing behind All-American "Hunk" Anderson), and finally joined the starting lineup for the 1922 season.

After his Notre Dame eligibility expired, Cotton was not through with football. He played professional football for the Rock Island Independents and also coached at St. Ambrose College in Davenport, Iowa, and Catholic University in Washington, D.C.

COUTRE, LARRY
Halfback (1946–49), 5'9", 170 lbs.

Chicago native Coutre had the misfortune of coming along at the same time as Emil Sitko. For three years Coutre's playing time was limited because Sitko, an All-American and one of the best running backs in the program's history, was ahead of him on the depth chart. Coutre waited for his turn and won the Hering Award, which went to the most improved back, in 1948. His statistics that season were 27 carries for 152 yards. The following year, Coutre got to build on his junior season, and show what he had. Sitko was moved from right halfback to fullback, making room for Coutre on the first team. That season Notre Dame had a phenomenal, and deep, running game. Coutre rushed for 645 yards on 102 carries. His total yardage was surpassed that year by Sitko alone, and his yards per carry average of 6.3 was tops on the team. He was fourth in scoring, with 42 points, and second in receiving, with 13 receptions for 271 yards.

Notwithstanding the fact that he was a key contributor on an undefeated national championship team, it was not enough to place Coutre on any All-America team. Coutre's only postseason honor was a spot in the College Football All-Star Game. In 1950 he was selected in the fourth round of NFL draft by the Green Bay Packers, for whom he played in 1950 and 1953. He also spent part of the 1953 season with the Baltimore Colts before he retired.

COVINGTON, JOHN
Safety/Linebacker/Defensive end
(1990–93), 6'1", 211 lbs.

Covington, of Winter Haven, Florida, was an amazing athlete who played in all three zones of Notre Dame's defense—the line, the linebacker position, and the defensive backfield. He began as a free safety in his freshman season, finding his way into all twelve games. The following season he played free safety, strong safety, and linebacker. As a junior, in 1992, Covington added defensive end to his repertoire. In his senior year he became a full-time starter and was back to strong safety; he finished the year fourth on the team in tackles, with 58.

Covington was from a startlingly large and athletic family with twenty kids (his brother played college football and his sister was a track star). He was no different. Covington was the captain of his high school football and basketball teams before he went to Notre Dame. He was drafted in the fourth round of the NFL draft by the Indianapolis Colts, for whom he played in 1994. He finished his career in 1995 as a member of the New Orleans Saints.

COWHIG, GERRY
Fullback/Halfback (1942, 1946),
6'3", 211 lbs.

World War II broke up Cowhig's college football career. During the 1942 season, the big running back from Dorchester, Massachusetts, scored 18 points as a backup to fullback Corwin Clatt. He then left school to serve in the armed forces and would not return to Notre Dame until 1946, where he found a backfield jam-packed with talent.

Terry Brennan and Emil Sitko had the halfback spot all locked up, and Jim Mello was entrenched at fullback. Cowhig still found a way to contribute to the Fighting

Irish's national championship by scoring 2 touchdowns and gaining 199 yards. He was even captain for a game—on November 9, 1946, Cowhig acted as team captain in the one game Notre Dame did not win all season. The only blemish on the 8–0–1 year was an 0–0 tie with Army in front of 74,000 spectators at Yankee Stadium. The tie was no disgrace. It ended Army's twenty-five-game winning streak and fouled the Cadets's chances at a third-straight national title.

Cowhig played fullback in the NFL for three teams—the Los Angeles Rams from 1947 to 1949, the Chicago Cardinals in 1950, and the Philadelphia Eagles in 1952.

CRABLE, BOB
Linebacker (1978–81), 6'3", 225 lbs.

Bob Crable just couldn't shake head coach Gerry Faust. After starring for the coach at Cincinnati's Moeller High School, which Crable helped lead to three consecutive state championships, Crable moved on to star at Notre Dame. Crable, regarded as the best linebacker ever to play for Notre

Linebacker Bob Crable holds the Notre Dame record for career tackles with 521.

Dame, set a school record of 521 tackles, which still stands. Before it was all through, Crable and Faust would be back together again.

Crable did not play much in his freshman season, compiling 13 tackles, considerably less than his career average for one game. The next year, however, Crable was the team's best defender. He led the team in tackles for nine of the season's eleven games and set the single-season and one-game tackle records. Crable was named a third-team All-American. In 1980, Crable again led the team, this time with 154 tackles, and first-team All-American honors came rolling in.

In 1981, when Crable was the senior captain of the squad, Faust took over the Notre Dame head-coaching reins from Dan Devine. Crable seemed to welcome his old coach back. He made 167 tackles and intercepted 2 passes during the season and was a near-unanimous first-team All-American. He was also named the Most Valuable Player by the Notre Dame Monogram Club for the second time in two years.

Crable holds virtually every record for tackles in the history of the school. He and Bob Golic are tied for tackles in a single game, with 26. Crable made his hits in a 16–10 loss against Clemson in the 1979 season. His 187 tackles that season are also a school mark. Crable's 167 tackles in 1981 are second on the list, and his 521 career tackles are also the standard for future Fighting Irish defenders to shoot for.

Crable was selected by the New York Jets in the first round (twenty-third overall) of the 1982 NFL draft. Injuries limited his career to three seasons, and he went back to Moeller High School to take over the head coaching position that made Faust famous.

CRIMMINS, BERNIE
Fullback/Guard (1939–41), 5'11", 185 lbs.

Crimmins wrapped up a fine career at Louisville's Xavier High School, starring in three sports. Kentucky wanted him, and many Big Ten schools coveted him. Crim-

mins was being wooed hard and was having a hard time selecting a winner of the sweepstakes. Enter his dad, who, when asked his opinion, said he was high on Notre Dame.

Crimmins was a backup fullback for two years under head coach Elmer Layden, who was an outstanding running back himself. Frank Leahy took over the head coaching duties in 1941, and Crimmins, a senior, was converted into a lineman. Weighing in at 185 pounds, he still found his way into the starting lineup at right guard. He did his part, as Notre Dame finished with an 8–0–1 record. He was named to several All-America teams.

He played for the Green Bay Packers for one season before going back to his alma mater to serve as an assistant coach under Leahy. He remained a member of the staff, focusing on running backs, until 1951. At that point he accepted the post of head football coach at Indiana University, which unfortunately went 13–32 under his tutelage. After a final two-year stint, Crimmins finished up his coaching career in 1957 back in South Bend as an assistant coach.

CROTTY, JIM
Running back (1957–59), 5'10", 185 lbs.

The second of three seasons on the Fighting Irish varsity team was the best for Seattle, Washington, native Crotty. As the starting halfback he showed his versatility, with 67 rushing attempts for 315 yards and 13 receptions for 137 yards. He used his speed to compile a team-high 228 yards returning kickoffs, and he also made 38 tackles. Crotty then spent his final season as a fullback, replacing two-time All-American Nick Pietrosante, who graduated in the spring of 1959. Crotty's numbers were down across the board, but he still contributed. He finished with 184 yards on 62 carries, and caught 8 passes for 104 yards and 3 touchdowns.

Picked in the 1960 draft by both the Washington Redskins of the NFL and Dallas Cowboys of the AFL, Crotty played parts of two seasons in the nation's capital. He also played for the Buffalo Bills in 1961 and 1962.

CROWLEY, JIM
Halfback (1922–24), 5′11″, 162 lbs.

Not many players could get away with throwing barbs at legendary football coach Knute Rockne, but when you're a member of the historic backfield nicknamed the Four Horsemen, score 15 touchdowns, gain 1,841 yards during your career, and are named a consensus All-American, you have a certain amount of leniency. Jim Crowley was all of those things and took advantage of his credentials. In practice one day, Crowley blew an assignment, and Rockne was not about to let the moment pass. Rockne shouted to him, "What's dumber than a dumb Irishman?" Crowley shot back, "A smart Norwegian." Rockne, of course, was Norwegian.

Crowley didn't look like the type of sharp guy who could roll off one-liners like he was working a comedy club. Rockne called him Sleepy Jim, because the running back had droopy eyelids, but he had an agile mind as well as quick feet—and it was his feet that made Crowley one of the most memorable players in the history of the program.

It was Green Bay Packers founder and coach "Curly" Lambeau, a former Fighting Irish player himself, who discovered Crowley, a Green Bay native. Lambeau contacted Rockne, his former coach, and told him about Crowley. The Crowleys were not a rich brood and there was no way that the player could afford to go to a school like Notre Dame in the days before scholarships. In those days athletes were allowed to take on a part-time job to pay for room, board, and tuition, so Lambeau made sure that Crowley was taken care of. As a varsity sophomore, Crowley split time with Elmer Layden at the left halfback position. Despite weighing in at just 162, Layden was shifted to fullback, leaving Crowley at the left halfback spot for his final two seasons of college ball. With everyone in place during Crowley's senior season, it was time for poetic sportswriter Grantland Rice to conjure up the name that would remain a part of college football lore for all time.

It was on October 18, 1924, while reporting on Notre Dame's 13–7 victory over Army for the *New York Herald-Tribune,* that Rice called Notre Dame's starting backfield of Crowley, Layden, right halfback Don Miller, and quarterback Harry Stuhldreher, the Four Horsemen. The fame of the fearsome foursome would become bigger than the game of college football itself. With the Horsemen moving the ball, Notre Dame went 10–0 in 1924, a national championship season that was capped with a 27–10 Rose Bowl victory over Stanford. Crowley was named a consensus All-American.

Crowley followed his college career by playing for the Green Bay Packers and the Providence Steam Roller, and then went back to college as an assistant coach for the University of Georgia. In 1929 he was named head coach at Michigan State, which went an outstanding 22–8–3 during his four seasons there. His next stop was the Bronx, where he coached Fordham and a player named Vince Lombardi, who would go on to be one of the greatest sideline practitioners in the history of the game.

Crowley continued his winning ways at Fordham. In 1937 the Rams were 7–0–1 and were ranked third by the Associated Press in its final poll. Four years later the team was 7–1, including a 2–0 (yes, that's the correct score) victory over Missouri in the Sugar Bowl. Crowley's final tally as a college coach was a superlative 78–21–10, but he was not done coaching just yet. After receiving a commission as a lieutenant commander in the navy reserve, Crowley was assigned to pre-flight training school in Chapel Hill, North Carolina, where he also coached the service football team.

After his service, Crowley became the charter commissioner of the All-American Football Conference, a position he held until 1947, when he left to become the owner and coach of the Chicago Rockets. His stay as coach was short-lived, as the team won just one game in his first year and he resigned (rather than firing himself). He later became station manager and sports director at radio station WTVU in Scranton, Pennsylvania, and also provided color commentary on Canadian Football League games for NBC. Crowley entered the College Football Hall of Fame in 1966.

CAREER STATS

Year	Att.	Yards	Avg.	TDs
1922	75	566	7.5	5
1923	88	536	6.1	4
1924	131	739	5.6	6
Total	294	1,841	6.3	15

CULLINAN, JOE
Tackle (1900–1903), 5'10", 177 lbs.

"Jepers" Cullinan was a key contributor as Notre Dame gained national prominence in football. The local product from South Bend teamed with offensive whiz Louis "Red" Salmon and made up for lack of size with a good head for the game. At 177 pounds he was small for his position, even at the turn of the century. During his first two college seasons he was a backup, first at right tackle and then at left tackle. In 1902 he took over the starting left tackle position and held it in 1903 as Notre Dame went 8–0–1 and outscored its opponents by a fantastic combined score of 292–10.

CULVER, RODNEY
Defensive back/Running back (1988–91), 5'10", 226 lbs.

Culver packed a lot of meat on his 5-foot-10 frame. He got that body to move quickly, covering 40 yards in 4.38 seconds, and he also had a nose for the end zone. All of that made Culver a very versatile running back, one who could always be counted on to contribute.

The graduate of St. Martin de Porres High School in Detroit was coming off a phenomenal high school senior season during which he gained in excess of 1,500 yards and scored 20 touchdowns. He began his

Running back Rodney Culver averaged 5 yards a carry and rushed for 15 touchdowns in his Notre Dame career. (Bill Panzica)

freshman season as a defensive back but eventually was moved to offense, where he rushed the ball 30 times for 195 yards and 3 touchdowns. His sophomore season was even better: 59 carries for 242 yards and 5 scores. In 1990, as a junior, Culver replaced Anthony Johnson as the starting fullback for the Fighting Irish and his numbers took off: he gained 710 yards and scored 5 touchdowns. He became the first fullback to lead the squad in rushing since 1977, when Jerome Heavens gained 994 yards, and was named an honorable mention All-American.

As a senior, Culver was moved to tailback, mainly to pave the way for freshman back and future superstar Jerome Bettis at halfback. He responded to his new digs with 550 yards and 2 touchdowns on just 101 carries, while starting eight of eleven games. He finished up his eligibility nineteenth on Notre Dame's all-time rushing list, with 1,697 yards, but has since been knocked out of the top twenty. Culver was a fourth-round draft pick of the Indianapolis Colts, for whom he played in 1992 and 1993. He finished up his NFL career as a member of the San Diego Chargers in 1994 and 1995.

CAREER STATS

Year	Att.	Yards	Avg.	TDs
1988	30	195	6.5	3
1989	59	242	4.1	5
1990	150	710	4.7	5
1991	101	550	5.4	2
Total	340	1,697	5.0	15

CZAROBSKI, ZYGMONT
Tackle (1942–43, 1946–47), 6'0", 213 lbs.

Whether he was on the field or off, it was never difficult to tell when Ziggy Czarobski was around. The jovial, bigger-than-life tackle from the South Side of Chicago was popular from the day he arrived on campus. Czarobski, all-city and all-state as a senior for Mt. Carmel High School, could always be counted on for a joke to loosen the mood in the locker room.

But there was nothing funny about his game. On the field he was able to mow over opposing players with sheer strength or outwit them with his Ph.D. in football smarts. His disjointed career at Notre Dame included three consecutive national titles. During Czarobski's final three years playing for head coach Frank Leahy, the Fighting Irish were a combined 26–1–1.

Czarobski played in 1941 on Notre Dame's freshman squad before moving up to the varsity the following season, instantly joining the starting lineup as the right tackle. In 1943, the Fighting Irish went 9–1, and Czarobski played a major role in the school's first consensus national championship under Leahy. He was busy off serving the United States in World War II and missed the 1944 and 1945 seasons. Back on campus in time to play another season (he turned down the Chicago Cardinals of the All-American Football Conference, which drafted him in 1945 hoping he would pass up his final two seasons of college eligibility), Czarobski was again a starter at right tackle. He became a major force on two of the best all-time college football teams. In 1946 and 1947, with records of 8–0–1 and 9–0, Notre Dame won back-to-back national titles.

Czarobski went on to play professional football in 1948, signing with the Chicago Rockets and playing for two seasons before retiring. After his playing days were over, he used the same charismatic personality and sense of humor that made him one of Notre Dame's all-time favorite sons to become a formidable force on the banquet speaking circuit. Despite never being named an All-American, Czarobski was a 1977 inductee into the College Football Hall of Fame.

DABIERO, ANGELO
Halfback (1959–61), 5'8", 170 lbs.

Dabiero was an outstanding athlete who, during his senior season, played an astounding 464 minutes and 34 seconds (of a possible 600 minutes), rushed for 637 yards on 92 carries, caught 10 passes for 201 yards, scored 24 points, returned 11 punts for 97 yards, ran back 8 kickoffs for 200 yards, and on defense intercepted 5 passes for 78 yards and made 47 tackles. He was first on the team in minutes played, rushing, punt returns, and interceptions; second in receiving, scoring, and kickoff returns; and third in tackles. All of that, however, wasn't enough to impress enough voters to place Dabiero on a single All-America team, and NFL scouts weren't any different—he wasn't selected in the draft. This oversight can be attributed to the fact that he played for the Fighting Irish during a down period. The team won only twelve of thirty games during his varsity career, which included a 2–8 record his junior season.

Dabiero lettered as a sophomore, and the Donora, Pennsylvania, native ran for 118 yards on 36 rushing attempts and grabbed 6 passes for 64 yards. As a junior, his first as a starter, he ran for 325 yards on 80 carries, which made him the team leader in rushing yardage that year.

Dabiero was a tough player who led the team in rushing for two consecutive years, yet his great individual accomplishments could not overcome the deficiencies of a weak team effort.

DAHL, BOB
Defensive tackle (1988–90), 6'5", 261 lbs.

Dahl's first two seasons at Notre Dame were a wash. He didn't make the varsity football team as a freshman and only made it into three games as a sophomore. The Chagrin Falls, Ohio, native made the most of an opportunity afforded to him his junior season, however, when starting defensive tackle George Williams was lost for the season because of academic problems. It was a chance Dahl turned into two seasons as a starter, one as an All-American and, eventually, a six-year NFL career.

Dahl, who was known as a hard worker by both his teammates and the coaches, played more than 209 minutes as a junior and recorded 52 tackles. Williams was back on the active roster the following season, but coach Lou Holtz did not take that opportunity to bench Dahl. He simply moved him over to right tackle and inserted Williams at left tackle. Dahl, who started all twelve games, made 35 tackles and was an honorable mention All-American. He was a third-round draft choice of the Cincinnati Bengals and played with the franchise from 1992 through 1995. He then played for the Washington Redskins in 1996 and 1997.

DAMPEER, JOHN
Tackle (1970–72), 6'3", 237 lbs.

Dampeer proved many things at Notre Dame, including the fact that he knew how to make up for lost time. He arrived in South Bend from Kermit, Texas, in 1968, and was initially eligible to play on the varsity football team in 1969. Unfortunately, he fractured an ankle and missed his entire sophomore season. Finally, in 1970, he got a chance to suit up. Actually, he did more than suit up. Dampeer started every game at right tackle and led the team in time played, with 300:19. He was again a starter in 1971 and was named a cocaptain in 1972. The hard-nosed player was named a first-team All-American, and the Cincinnati Bengals selected him in the ninth round of the 1973 NFL draft, but he did not play in the league.

DANCEWICZ, FRANK
Quarterback (1943–45), 5′10″, 180 lbs.

The same depth that was a gift to the Fighting Irish in the mid-1940s was a curse to Dancewicz. When he landed on the varsity team in 1943, there were two outstanding quarterbacks ahead of him. Actually, Angelo Bertelli and Johnny Lujack were better than outstanding—they were two of the best in the game. Heisman Trophy winner Bertelli was the starter until he left campus for active duty in the Marine Corps, and Lujack was Bertelli's backup and replacement during the national championship season of 1943.

The next year, Bertelli graduated and Lujack was off to World War II. That left the team in the hands of Dancewicz, a somewhat erratic and yet explosive signal caller. Dancewicz completed only 68 of the 163 passes he threw for a .417 percentage, but he did throw 9 touchdown passes and nearly amassed 1,000 yards. In his final campaign, he again had accuracy problems. As a team captain, he hooked up on 30 of 90 passes (.333) for 489 yards and 5 touchdowns with 3 interceptions. Despite his less than sterling statistics, he led Notre Dame to a 7–2–1 record and made many second-team All-America squads.

Dancewicz was a first-round draft pick of the Boston Yanks in 1946 and played three

years of professional football before embarking on a coaching career. His first stop in his new profession was at Salem High School, in Massachusetts. He coached many teams in the Boston area, including his old high school, Lynn Classical, from which he graduated in 1942, and Boston University and Lafayette College. Dancewicz was also the supervisor of physical education and health of the school system for his hometown of Lynn, Massachusetts, and ended his career at Lynn Classical as a physical education teacher.

DAVIE, ROBERT (BOB) EDWIN JR.
Defensive coordinator (1994–96); Head coach (1996–present)

Twenty years as a college assistant coach was obviously plenty of time for Davie to learn enough to take over the most storied program in college football history. His first season was a winning but shaky one (7–6). Once the Sewickley, Pennsylvania, native got going, however, Notre Dame was again one of the top football programs in the nation.

On November 24, 1996, Davie became the twenty-eighth coach in Fighting Irish history, replacing Lou Holtz. He came to Notre Dame from Texas A&M, where he coached the outside linebackers and was the defensive coordinator for a total of nine seasons. Prior to his stint with the Aggies, he coached for Pittsburgh, Arizona, and Tulane. Holtz brought him in as the Fighting Irish defensive coordinator in 1994, and he held that position until succeeding Holtz. One factor that gave Davie the edge over other coaches rumored to be in line for the position, such as Northwestern coach Gary Barnett, was that he had filled in admirably as head coach when Holtz underwent neck surgery in 1995. He was familiar with the program and also had a well-deserved reputation as a superb defensive strategist. So Davie was the first assistant coach at Notre Dame to be promoted to the head coaching position since Terry Brennan replaced Frank Leahy in 1954.

In twenty years as an assistant, Davie was involved in fifteen bowl games, including seven Cotton Bowls. The teams he worked for had a combined record of 166–68–10. His Aggies defense led the nation in pass-defense efficiency in 1993. The team was also tops in the Southwest Conference in total defense for three consecutive seasons. From 1991 to 1993, Texas A&M won every conference title and had a record of 32–5.

The Fighting Irish got off to a slow start under Davie, losing four of its first five games. Notre Dame turned it around and won six of its final seven games, including the final five of the regular season, which gave Davie a winning season in his rookie year (7–6) and won the team a spot in the Independence Bowl, which it lost 27–9 to Louisiana State University (LSU). Davie was the first coach ever to take Notre Dame to a bowl game in his first season, and the first since Dan Devine, in 1975, to lead the team to a winning record in his first campaign. That 1997 squad also had a record four game-winning fourth-quarter drives.

The team built on that success in Davie's second season. By mid-season he had the Fighting Irish back in the Top Ten. In the season's penultimate game, quarterback Jarious Jackson injured his knee against LSU. The Fighting Irish were ranked ninth nationally until their quarterback's absence in the last game of the season rendered Notre Dame's offense helpless in a 10–0 loss at rival USC. Jackson came back for the Gator Bowl but looked a couple of steps slow, and Notre Dame lost on New Year's Day, 35–28, to Georgia Tech. The Fighting Irish finished the 1998 season ranked a respectable twenty-second by the Associated Press. His recruiting class in 1999 was ranked in the top ten nationally. It began paying dividends with a 9–2 regular season and a trip to the Fiesta Bowl in 2000.

CAREER RECORD

Year	W	L	T	Bowl Game
1997	7	6	0	Independence, L, LSU, 9–27
1998	9	3	0	Gator, L, Georgia Tech, 28–35
1999	5	7	0	No bowl appearance
2000	9	3	0	Fiesta, L, Oregon State, 41–9
Total	30	19	0	0–3

Head coach, Bob Davie, instructing Jarvis Edison in 1996. (Bill Panzica)

DAVIS, TRAVIS
Safety/Tailback (1991–94), 6′0″, 197 lbs.

Hailing from Carson, California, Davis only got into two games as a freshman defensive back, but by the time he was a senior he had laid the groundwork for a productive career in the NFL. He earned his first letter as a sophomore, when he got into eight games. As a senior, he was Notre Dame's starting strong safety and finished sixth on the squad in tackles, with 56, had an interception, and was a terror on special teams. Davis had his best game against USC, making 9 tackles. He also had 6 solo stops in a 21–20 win over Michigan State. After graduating from Notre Dame with a degree in psychology, he was selected in the seventh round of the NFL draft by the New Orleans Saints. He played one season with the franchise and in 1996 moved to Jacksonville to play with the Jaguars before becoming a member of the Pittsburgh Steelers in 1999.

DAWSON, LAKE
Flanker/Split end (1990–93), 6′1″, 202 lbs.

Whether he was playing flanker or split end at Notre Dame, when the ball was thrown to Dawson, he caught it. He was not only one of the best receivers of his time, twice leading the Fighting Irish in receiving (1992 and 1993), he was also one of the most consistent. Dawson, from Federal Way, Washington, played split end and safety in high school and was all-state at both positions. He was also named Gatorade Circle of Champions Player of the Year in Washington.

In college he would concentrate on offense. Dawson played behind Tony Smith at split end his freshman season. The next year he earned the position of starting flanker, and rewarded head coach Lou Holtz's decision by finishing with 24 catches for 433 yards and a touchdown. In one game, a 45–21 victory over Purdue, he caught 6 passes for 81 yards. His highlight reel also contains a 40-yard touchdown hookup with quarterback Rick

Mirer, as Notre upset third-ranked Florida 39–28 in the Sugar Bowl.

Dawson would remain a starter while shifting between flanker and split end, but his statistics were remarkably similar during his final three seasons in school. He was moved back to split end his junior season and responded with nearly identical statistics. He caught 25 passes for 462 yards and a touchdown. That team-leading total earned him honorable mention All-American honors. In 1993 he was back at flanker and kept catching passes. Again he caught 25 balls, this time for 395 yards and 2 touchdowns, and again was named honorable mention All-American. The Kansas City Chiefs selected him in the third round of the 1994 NFL draft, and he played with the team until 1997. He sat out the 1998 season with an injury, and later landed on the roster of the Indianapolis Colts.

CAREER STATS

Year	Rec.	Yards	Avg.	TDs
1990	6	107	17.8	0
1991	24	433	18.0	1
1992	25	462	18.5	1
1993	25	395	15.8	2
Total	80	1,397	17.5	4

DEMMERLE, PETE
End (1972–74), 6′1″, 190 lbs.

Some players are easier to recruit than others. For instance, Notre Dame had a pretty good shot at Demmerle when he was born—going to Notre Dame was in his genes. His father, uncle, and cousin all graduated from the school in South Bend, and Demmerle followed in their footsteps.

Demmerle's genes also helped make him an excellent football player. He was a prep All-American who led New Canaan High School to a Connecticut state championship in 1969. He scored an amazing 4 touchdowns in 4:26 during the state title game. He arrived at Notre Dame in 1971 but was a late bloomer; he didn't get much significant playing time until he was a junior, but by the time he was through with college he was a consensus All-American.

In 1973, Demmerle and quarterback Tom Clements became a formidable part of a juggernaut offense that scored 358 points and went on to win the national championship. Demmerle, who was also an excellent blocker, scored 5 touchdowns and led the team in receptions, with 26 for 404 yards. Fortunately for Notre Dame, one of his best games was in a tight Sugar Bowl in which Notre Dame beat the University of Alabama, 24–23. Demmerle caught 3 passes for 59 yards, and also caught a 2-point conversion.

As good as his junior season was, Demmerle almost doubled his output as a senior. He had 43 receptions for 667 yards and scored 6 touchdowns, earning consensus All-American status to go along with being selected as a first-team Academic All-American. He was a thirteenth-round selection by the San Diego Chargers in the 1975 NFL draft but never played professional football. Instead, the recipient of a postgraduate scholarship from the NCAA and the National Football Foundation went to law school and became a lawyer.

CAREER STATS

Year	Rec.	Yards	Avg.	TDs
1972	No receptions			
1973	26	404	15.5	5
1974	43	667	15.5	6
Total	69	1,071	15.5	11

DENMAN, ANTHONY
Inside linebacker (1997–2000), 6'2", 235 lbs.

Denman's rise at Notre Dame was steady and steep. After playing behind Cory Minor for two seasons, Denman, out of Rusk High School in Texas, was ready when it was his turn to lead the defense. And, lead he did, finishing his career with two seasons atop the team leader board in solo tackles.

Denman played only 16:27 as a freshman. The following year, as a sophomore, he

began his ascent. Although playing only 74:45 behind captain Minor, Denman made the most of his time with 18 solo tackles, 10 assists, and 3 sacks. He also started two games—against Michigan State and Purdue—when Minor was injured.

As a junior, Denman led all Fighting Irish linebackers in playing time and tackles. Denman led Notre Dame in solo tackles (59) and finished with 89 total hits, only 2 behind team leader A'Jani Sanders. He also added a sack. Denman also was tied atop the school list with 3 fumble recoveries.

As a senior, Denman, a Notre Dame captain, didn't only lead the Irish in solo tackles (55), but in assists (29) and total tackles (84). He led all linebackers in sacks (5), sharing the team lead with defensive end, Ryan Roberts and was number one on the team in yards lost caused by a sack (30). Denman's play did not go unnoticed as he was Notre Dame's only All-American in 2001 and was Notre Dame's National Monogram Club Most Valuable Player. Denman was one of six Irish players to be selected in the 2001 National Football League draft. He went to the Jacksonville Jaguars in the seventh round (213 overall).

DENSON, AUTRY
Tailback (1995–98), 5'10", 200 lbs.

Denson, a strong and quick cutback runner, was not only consistent in his four college seasons, he was consistently outstanding. There is no doubt that Denson was a key reason for Notre Dame's rebirth under head coach Bob Davie. The Fighting Irish were 18–5 when Denson rushed for more than 100 yards, which included wins in the first nine such games of his career.

Denson played high school football in Davie, Florida, and set a county record with 4,738 yards and 66 touchdowns during his prep career. He was just as explosive in college, where he began his career as a special-teams player and a backup cornerback. By his second game, however, he was moved to tailback and finished the season with 695 yards, third on the team, and just 61 yards less than Vagas Ferguson's freshman record. He was second on the team in carries, with 137. As a sophomore, Denson ran for 1,179 yards and was nineteenth in the country in all-purpose running (averaging 147.91 yards), twenty-fifth in rushing (averaging 107.18 yards), and thirty-second in punt returns (10.89 yards per runback).

During his third college season, Denson rushed for a career-high 1,268 yards for the fourth-highest single-season total in school history. He led the Irish in scoring, with 78 points, and ranked nineteenth nationally in rushing, with 105.67 yards per game, and thirty-sixth in all-purpose running (133.67 yards per game).

Denson's 1,176 yards as a senior made him the only Fighting Irish player besides Allen Pinkett to crack the 1,000-yard barrier 3 times. Speaking of Pinkett, Denson finished his career at Notre Dame with 4,318 yards rushing, breaking Pinkett's record of 4,131 yards, which had stood for more than twelve seasons.

Denson finished his career ranked twenty-ninth on the NCAA's all-time rushing list, where he is tied with former Oklahoma State rusher David Thompson and ahead of players such as Syracuse's Joe Morris and Auburn's Bo Jackson. Denson also placed first in Notre Dame history in 100-yard rushing games, with twenty-two. He is second behind Pinkett in all-time rushing touchdowns (43), rushing attempts (854), total yards (5,234 to Pinkett's 5,259), 100-yard rushing games in a season (7 in 1996 and 1997), and rushing yardage per game (96.0 to Pinkett's 96.1). All Denson needed was 6 more yards in Notre Dame's season finale against USC and he would have ranked first in that category as well. He also has the fourth-, sixth-, and seventh-best rushing seasons on file and ranks sixth in touchdowns in a season (1998), with 15.

Denson was more than just a rusher. He had 30 receptions as a junior, the most by any Fighting Irish running back since Bob Gladieux had 37 in 1968. He also returned kicks for a total of 577 yards. Among his best games were five in which he gained more than 150 yards rushing, topped by a 189-yard performance against Baylor University as a senior. His longest single run from scrimmage was 58 yards against the University of Michigan in the 1998 season opener.

Denson finished his career on a high note. He rushed for 1,785 yards (119.0 yards per game) during his final fifteen games in college, and then capped it off by gaining 130 yards on 26 carries and a touchdown against Georgia Tech in Notre Dame's 35–28 Gator Bowl loss. For his senior year efforts, Denson was named a second-team All-American, and he was honored with the National Monogram Club's MVP Award for the third straight year. He was drafted in the seventh round by the Tampa Bay Buccaneers, but he has only played for the Miami Dolphins.

CAREER STATS

RUSHING

Year	Att.	Yards	Avg.	TDs
1995	137	695	5.1	8
1996	202	1,179	5.8	8
1997	264	1,268	4.8	12
1998	251	1,176	4.7	15
Total	854	4,318	5.1	43

RECEIVING

Year	Rec.	Yards	Avg.	TDs
1995	6	65	10.8	0
1996	11	111	10.1	2
1997	30	175	5.8	1
1998	6	81	13.5	0
Total	53	432	8.2	3

KICKOFF RETURNS

Year	Ret.	Yards	Avg.	TDs
1995	4	39	9.8	0
1996	7	141	20.1	0
1997	5	93	18.6	0
Total	16	273	16.1	0

PUNT RETURNS

Year	Ret.	Yards	Avg.	TDs
1996	18	196	10.9	1
1997	7	68	9.7	0
1998	4	40	10.0	0
Total	29	304	10.5	1

ALL-PURPOSE YARDS, NOTRE DAME HISTORY

Allen Pinkett	5,259
Autry Denson	5,234
Tim Brown	5,024

DEVINE, DAN
Head coach (1975–80)

Devine's first coaching post was at East Jordan High School in Michigan, where he led the team to undefeated seasons in 1948 and 1949. The next year it was off to Michigan State, where he was freshman coach and eventually an assistant coach on the varsity, in charge of the offensive backfield. In 1955, Devine became a head college coach, accepting the post at Arizona State University. In three seasons he had phenomenal success, as Arizona State was 27–3–1. Under Devine the team went undefeated for the first time in school history and finished twelfth in the final Associated Press poll. His performance at Arizona State did not go unnoticed. The University of Missouri grabbed him, and in thirteen seasons Devine's teams were 92–38–7. The Tigers played in the Orange Bowl their second season under Devine, and in 1960 were 10–1, won the Orange Bowl 24–21 over Navy, and were ranked fifth in the nation.

Missouri never lost more than three games in a season during the Devine era. He also served as the school's athletic director from 1966 to 1971. In 1972, he left college and graduated to the professional ranks as coach of the Green Bay Packers. The Packers responded to him instantly, going 10–4 in his first season and winning the division title. He was named the NFC Coach of the Year by the United Press International and the Pro Football Writers Association of America.

Three years later, Devine was on the sidelines in South Bend. On December 17, 1974, Notre Dame announced that Devine would become the twenty-fourth head coach in the history of the program. Devine, an extremely successful college coach, was then coming off a less-than-stellar stint as head coach of the Green Bay Packers, with a record of 25–28–4. His assignment at Notre Dame was not an easy one. Not only was he taking over one of the most storied programs in the game, he was also replacing Ara Parseghian, who, in eleven years, led Notre Dame to a remarkable 95–17–4 record.

Devine's teams, though, were up for the challenge. During his six-year run, and despite underutilizing quarterback Joe Montana, the Fighting Irish were a more than respectable 53–16–1 and won the national championship in 1977, his third year in South Bend. The only blemish on that otherwise perfect record was a 20–13 loss at the University of Mississippi in the second week of the season. After that, Notre Dame steamrolled, including winning its final two games over the Air Force Academy and the University of Miami by a combined score of 97–10. The Fighting Irish went on to the Cotton Bowl and clinched the national title by cruising past number five–ranked Texas A&M, 38–10. Notre Dame impressed all the voters and was ranked number one in every poll for the first time in school history. The team didn't have any down seasons under Devine, and went 9–2–1 in his final season, 1980. Devine retired from Notre Dame after a 17–10 loss in the Sugar Bowl to Georgia on January 1, 1981. (He said that he was vacating the post because his wife was in poor health.) His overall coaching record was 126–42–7 (.742).

Devine did come out of retirement to become the executive director of the Arizona State Sun Angel Foundation in Phoenix. Then, in 1992, he went back to the University of Missouri, where he had coached for thirteen very successful seasons, to become its athletic director. He was a 1985 inductee to the College Football Hall of Fame and retired for good in 1994.

CAREER RECORD

Year	W	L	T	Bowl
1975	8	3	0	No bowl appearance
1976	9	3	0	Gator, W, Penn State, 20–9
1977	11	1	0	Cotton, W, Texas, 38–10*
1978	9	3	0	Cotton, W, Houston, 35–34
1979	7	4	0	No bowl appearance
1980	9	2	1	Sugar, L, Georgia, 10–17
Total	53	16	1	3–1

*Notre Dame won the national championship.

DEVORE, HUGH
End (1931–33); Head coach (1945, 1963), 6'0", 170 lbs.

Devore twice served as interim coach for the Fighting Irish, but the two stints were eighteen years apart. In between he coached St. Bonaventure University, New York University, the Green Bay Packers, the University of Dayton, and the Philadelphia Eagles. He also coached at Fordham University, Providence College, and Holy Cross College before taking his first job at Notre Dame.

As a player, Devore came to Notre Dame via St. Benedict's Prep, where he was one of the best and most versatile players in the history of the school. In New Jersey, he was all-state in football twice, and was the captain of the football, basketball, and baseball teams. The only thing that kept him off the Notre Dame varsity as a freshman was the rules of the day. Back then freshmen were not eligible, so Devore had to wait a year to be a star. The Notre Dame coaching staff, however, knew what they were getting, as Devore was a terror in scrimmages against the varsity team. In 1931, he joined the varsity and earned his first letter. The following sea-

son he was a starter, and as a senior he added cocaptain to his resumé.

After graduating with honors, Devore took an assistant coaching position under Elmer Layden. The following season, in 1935, he moved on to Fordham, where he was the line coach under another member of the Four Horsemen, Jim Crowley. That was where Devore stayed for three seasons, before he took the head coaching post at Providence College, which became one of the top small-college teams in the country.

In 1942, he moved to Worcester, Massachusetts, and worked as an assistant coach at Holy Cross. The following year he was summoned back to Notre Dame, where he served under Frank Leahy. In 1945, while Leahy served in the military, Devore was named the school's interim coach and led the Fighting Irish to a 7–2–1 record. The next year, Leahy came back to South Bend and Devore moved on. Next stop: Olean, New York, and St. Bonaventure University. But in 1949 it was time to leave the Bonnies and take over the New York University program.

Devore became a professional coach in 1952 and worked as an assistant for the Green Bay Packers. Two years later he was back in college as head coach at the University of Dayton, and two seasons after that was named coach of the NFL Philadelphia Eagles. His journey finally took him back to Notre Dame in 1958, when Terry Brennan brought him in to be freshman coach, a position he held simultaneously with his post of assistant athletic director. In 1963, after Joe Kuharich vacated Notre Dame's head coaching position, Devore filled in and the team went 2–7. He was replaced by Ara Parseghian the following year.

DiNARDO, GERRY
Offensive guard (1972–74), 6'1", 237 lbs.

Like his brother Larry before him, DiNardo, from Howard Beach, New York, was a decorated player at Notre Dame. Gerry had the unenviable task of following in the footsteps of an older brother who was one of the

Offensive lineman Gerry DiNardo opened holes for a Notre Dame rushing attack that garnered 3,502 yards en route to a national championship in 1973.

best offensive linemen in college football, but he was up to the task: DiNardo was a three-year starter and a key member of the 1973 national championship team, which had the fourth-ranked offense in the nation. The offensive line he was featured on was outstanding. That season the Fighting Irish set a school record with 3,502 rushing yards. In 1974, DiNardo helped lead Notre Dame to a 10–2 record and was named a consensus first-team All-American. He did not play professional football but went into coaching, first at Vanderbilt University and then at Louisiana State.

DiNardo, Larry
Offensive guard (1968–70), 6'1", 235 lbs.

Larry DiNardo was as smart off the field as he was on it. The Howard Beach, New York, native logged a lot of time in 1969, leading the team in minutes played with 283:41. He also was a dean's list student, a first-team All-American, and a cocaptain as a senior, when Notre Dame set a school record averaging 510.5 yards of total offense a game. DiNardo, whose younger brother

Gerry would arrive in South Bend in 1971, was a consensus All-American and also a first-team Academic All-American.

DiNardo was picked in the seventh round of the NFL draft by the New Orleans Saints. He opted to go to law school instead and later practiced law in Chicago.

Dingens, Greg
Defensive tackle (1982–85), 6'5", 257 lbs.

Dingens, from Bloomfield Hills, Michigan, was a prototypical student-athlete. He was a four-time letter winner and even started five games as a senior in 1985. An Academic All-American as a sophomore, junior, and senior, he was a Rhodes Scholar candidate and also earned a postgraduate scholarship from the NCAA and the National Football Foundation. During his senior season, he was playing the best football of his career, with 15 tackles in more than 111 minutes, when he suffered a catastrophic knee injury in game five and missed the second half of the season. That didn't affect his future; Dingens ended up going to medical school anyway.

Dorais, Charles
Quarterback (1910–13), 5'7", 145 lbs.

"Gus" Dorais, from Chippewa Falls, Wisconsin, and Knute Rockne were more than just teammates. They were close pals who revolutionized the way football was played.

Back in the summer of 1913, the quarterback and left end worked together as lifeguards at the Cedar Point Ranch in Sandusky, Ohio. When there were no lives to save, the two chums would toss a pigskin and work on different pass patterns. When they arrived back on campus for their senior season, the two put what they learned in their special practice sessions to use. This was cutting-edge stuff in the second decade of the century. The forward pass had only been legal since 1906 and was still considered a gimmick—that is, until Notre Dame had breakout success with its forward pass strategy, which propelled the Fighting Irish into national prominence.

Early in that season the scores that Notre Dame won by were astounding. The first victim was Ohio Northern University, which was drubbed 87–0. Next was the University of South Dakota, which went down 20–7, and the next week Alma was annihilated 62–0. The total score of Notre Dame's first three games in 1913 was 169–7, and the forward pass became a viable offensive option.

In Notre Dame's fourth game of the year, a 35–13 defeat of perennial national powerhouse Army, Dorais completed his first 12 passes, including 3 for touchdowns. He finished the game with 14 completions in 17 attempts for 243 yards, including a record 40-yard completion to Rockne. Army began to overplay the pass, and Notre Dame then used its all-around offense to hurt its opponent with the run.

Up to this point, college football was a sport of brute force. Big men plowed into other big men to open holes for smaller men to run through. The win over college football's marquee program, however, changed all that. Notre Dame, with its newfangled forward pass, changed the game's strategy forever.

The 1913 season was Notre Dame's third straight undefeated year with Dorais, a 1954 inductee into the College Football Hall of Fame, at the helm. He did much more than pass and hand off. His 7 field goal attempts in one game (he made 3 in a 30–7 victory over the University of Texas in 1913) are still a school record.

An education and an unparalleled football career weren't all that Charles Dorais got out of Notre Dame. He also got his nickname, Gus, in a freshman literature course. The class was discussing Dante's *Inferno*, and the professor brought up the novel's French illustrator, an artist named Gustave Dore. Although Dore and Dorais are spelled differently, they are both pronounced "dor-RAY." Dorais's classmates began calling him Gustave, and the nickname was shortened to simply Gus.

Dorais left Notre Dame to embark on a professional career, playing for a bunch of teams, including the Massillon Tigers. After

his playing days were over, he couldn't leave the game. He started a long run as a coach at Columbus College in Iowa, where he worked from 1914 to 1917. He then was hired as an assistant at Notre Dame for a brief period after World War I, but the brunt of his career, or at least seventeen years of it, were spent at Detroit University. He worked there from 1925 to 1942 and finished his college coaching career with a quite respectable 150–70–13 record. He also compiled a record of 20–31–2 as head coach of the Detroit Lions from 1943 to 1947.

DORSEY, ERIC
Defensive tackle (1982–85), 6'5", 270 lbs.

Dorsey improved every year of his college career. He was a starter by his sophomore season, but a recurring ankle injury limited him to just 53 minutes of playing time. By the time he was a senior, Dorsey started every game, and, in fact, led the Fighting Irish linemen with 87 tackles and 261:25 played.

Dorsey, who came to Notre Dame from McLean, Virginia, along with his cousin, tailback Allen Pinkett, was named an honorable mention All-American after his senior season. The New York Giants then selected him with the nineteenth pick of the 1986 NFL draft. He played with the Giants until 1992 and was a key defensive member of Bill Parcells's teams that won Super Bowl XXI and Super Bowl XXV.

DOVE, BOB
Left end (1940–42), 6'2", 195 lbs.

After a rocky start that included a heaping helping of hazing as a freshman, Dove settled in to have an outstanding career at Notre Dame. The initiation included a practical joke played by legendary equipment manager John "Mac" McAllister. In 1939, Dove reported for his first day of practice. He asked Mac for his socks, since he had not yet been issued any. Wrong move. McAllister rode Dove for losing the apparel and would not give him another pair. Dove, who wasn't

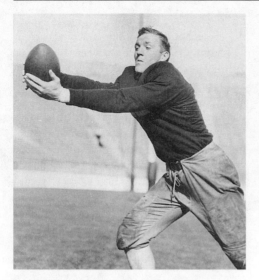

End Bob Dove was a two-time All-American and winner of the Knute Rockne Trophy.

looking for any trouble, put on his cleats without anything between them and his feet. In less than an hour, his tootsies were covered with blisters and he went off to the sidelines. This may have amused Mac and some of the other members of the team, but was not at all funny to head coach Elmer Layden.

Dove should have known better. This was not his first surprise in South Bend. One reason he picked Notre Dame, after an all-city career at South High School in Youngstown, Ohio, was what he believed would be his living accommodations. During a recruiting trip to South Bend, Dove somehow got the idea that he would live in the brand-new and somewhat swanky Breen-Phillips Hall, but when he showed up for school he was sent to his single bed and locker in Bronson Hall, a desolate place where the freshmen lived.

Despite these early setbacks, Dove turned it around and became one of the most outstanding ends in school history. After failing to win a letter as a freshman, he became a starter as a sophomore and was eventually one of the most skilled athletes to play under head coach Frank Leahy in his first two seasons, 1941 and 1942. Dove, who was inducted into the College Football Hall of Fame in

2000, was a consensus All-American in both of those years. He also won the Knute Rockne Trophy as the best lineman in college football in 1942 while playing for a 7–2–2 Notre Dame squad that was one year shy of a national championship.

Dove competed in the East-West Shrine Game, and after his Notre Dame career was over he was selected in the third round of the NFL draft by the Washington Redskins. He played his entire eight-year professional career in Chicago—for the Rockets and the Cardinals. After retiring, Dove was hired as an assistant coach by the Detroit Lions. After he left Detroit, he moved back home and became the assistant athletic director at Youngstown State University.

DRIVER, TONY
Tailback, Free safety, (1997–2000),
6'2", 220 lbs.

A versatile performer who had collegiate success at both tailback and free safety, Driver came to South Bend as a three-time all-state performer for Male High School in Louisville, Kentucky. His versatility was evident back then as Driver was the state champion in the 100-meter run as a junior and also played basketball. As a high school senior he was All-American according to *Parade*, Reebok, *USA Today*, and the Chicago *Sun-Times*, which named him the fifth best college prospect in the nation.

Driver, one of six freshmen to play for Notre Dame in 1997, predominantly worked the offensive side of the ball. As a sophomore Driver was shifted to defense and finished fourth on the team with 58 tackles. He also returned 23 kickoffs (the second highest total for a season in Notre Dame history) for 512 yards. As a junior, Driver continued his career shifting, moving back to offense and sharing tailback duties with Tony Fisher. Driver gained 187 yards in seven games. He returned to the defensive side of the ball as a senior, and became a strong contributor to the Notre Dame secondary, leading all defensive backs and finishing second on the team with 39 tackles and 26 assists. He also recovered 2 fumbles, had a sack, and 2 interceptions. Driver's 232 yards on nine kickoff returns brought his career total to 1,059 yards, placing him number 5 in school history.

Driver, whose athletic ability makes it seem as if he could play any position on the gridiron, is also a great team player, evident by him being awarded the Notre Dame Golden Helmet Award for the 2000 season. The Buffalo Bills selected Driver, who has a tremendous upside, with the 178th overall pick in the sixth round of the National Football League draft. Later in the sixth round, the Bills selected Driver's Irish teammate Dan O'Leary (195th pick).

DuBose, Demetrius
Linebacker (1989–92), 6′2″, 234 lbs.

DuBose may have been smart enough to graduate from Notre Dame a semester early with a degree in government, but it was Fighting Irish head coach Lou Holtz who knew enough to make him a starter during his sophomore season.

DuBose was an All-American football player and three-sport star at Bishop O'Dea High School in Seattle, Washington. By the time he was a college junior he led the team in tackles, and he repeated that feat in his senior season. DuBose, who started eleven games and was known for running down the opposition all over the field, made 127 tackles, was named a first-team All-American, and was one of ten semifinalists for the Butkus Award, presented each year to the best linebacker in the nation.

As a senior, despite missing two games with injuries, the savvy and agile DuBose again led Notre Dame in tackles, with 87. He was captain of the team, earned honorable mention All-American honors, and was also presented the Nick Pietrosante Award by his teammates. The award is named after the star fullback who died of cancer on February 6, 1988, and goes to the Fighting Irish player who best exemplifies courage, loyalty, team-

work, dedication, and pride. It was first given out later that year.

After his Notre Dame career was over, the Tampa Bay Buccaneers selected him in the second round of the 1993 NFL draft. He played for the team through the 1996 season.

Duerson, Dave
Defensive back (1979–82), 6′3″, 202 lbs.

As a freshman, Duerson, who hailed from Muncie, Indiana, made 24 tackles and 2 interceptions and led the team with a 17.4-yard punt return average. He also played more minutes than any other first-year player. The solidly built Duerson had outstanding foot speed and got better each season. As a sophomore he played strong safety and had 34 tackles. As a junior free safety he made 55 hits and after the season was named a third-team All-American. In his final campaign, still at free safety, Duerson upped his career best with 63 hits and added a team-high 7 interceptions. He also ran back 34 punts for 245 yards. Those numbers earned him first-team All-American honors. He is the school's all-time leader in punt returns, with 103, and second, behind Frank Carideo, in punt return yards, with 869.

The Chicago Bears selected Duerson in the third round of the NFL draft, and he set off on an eleven-year career. He played in Chicago from 1983 to 1989, including the team's Super Bowl championship game in 1986. He also played a season for the New York Giants in their Super Bowl–winning year of 1991. Duerson was also on the roster of the Arizona Cardinals before he retired in 1993.

CAREER STATS

PUNT RETURNS

Year	Ret.	Yards	Avg.
1979	12	209	17.4
1980	25	194	7.8
1981	32	221	6.9
1982	34	245	7.2
Total	103	869	8.4

DURANKO, PETE
Defensive tackle/Fullback/Linebacker
(1963–66), 6'2", 235 lbs.

Duranko suffered a broken wrist in the first game of his sophomore season, but he and the Fighting Irish made the most of his extra season of eligibility. The Fighting Irish were 9–0–1 in 1966, Duranko's fifth year on campus, and won the national championship.

In his sophomore season, his first on the varsity and the last before two-platoon football became the norm, Duranko played fullback and rushed for 93 yards on 26 carries. The next year he was moved to line-backer, but the broken wrist prematurely ended his season. He was back in 1965, and a healthy Duranko found his spot at defensive tackle. He played 267 minutes and had 95 tackles, second on the team behind line-backer Jim Lynch. During that championship season the native of Johnstown, Pennsylvania, did his part, making 73 stops, good enough for first-team All-American honors. Duranko also competed in the 1967 College Football All-Star Game. The AFL's Denver Broncos and the NFL's Cleveland Browns took him in the fourth round of the draft. He played in the Mile High City from 1967 to 1970.

EBLI, RAY
End/Tackle (1940–41), 6'2", 197 lbs.

Because he looked like the popular comic strip character, Ebli was saddled with the nickname of Lil' Abner. Ebli may have looked like Lil' Abner, but he played football like a pro. He was a two-sport standout at St. Ambrose High School in Ironwood, Minnesota, but football wasn't one of them, since St. Ambrose didn't have a gridiron team. Despite his lack of experience, he made the Notre Dame freshman football team as a walk-on in 1938, and two seasons later he was a letter-winning member of Frank Leahy's varsity squad, playing on the third team. As a senior, Ebli moved up the ladder. Leahy switched him to left tackle, where he split time with Jim Brutz.

After he was through at Notre Dame, Ebli played for the Chicago Cardinals in 1942. He then served in World War II, and was back in pro football in 1946, playing end for the Buffalo Bills. Later he was a member of the Chicago Rockets.

ECUYER, AL
Guard (1956–58), 5'10", 205 lbs.

Ecuyer was not big by guard standards, but he sure could hit. The New Orleans parochial league all-star and prep All-American made up for his size with toughness. He joined the varsity squad in 1956 and showed his grit. Despite a bunch of nagging injuries, including a broken thumb, a pinched nerve in his shoulder, and a sprained ankle, he led all guards in minutes played, with 324. As a junior the next year, Ecuyer upped his minutes-played total to

374 and, along with Jim Schaff, led the Fighting Irish in tackles, with 88. Eighteen of those stops came in one game (a 21–13 loss to Iowa). Ecuyer was also a first-team All-American.

Ecuyer again led Notre Dame in tackles as a senior, with 78 hits, and he was again named a first-team All-American. The New York Giants selected him in the eighteenth round of the 1959 draft. Ecuyer decided professional football was not in his future, however, and he went into the business world.

EDDY, NICK
Halfback (1964–66), 6'0", 195 lbs.

Eddy never rushed for 600 yards or caught passes totaling as many as 400 yards in a single season, but when you put everything together, steady Eddy from Lafayette, California, contributed a lot to the Notre Dame football program. They won a national title during his stay, and he chewed up his fair share of yards as the leading rusher during the championship season. After three seasons on the Fighting Irish varsity, his grand total of offense from scrimmage was more than 2,300 yards, and he was a unanimous All-American selection.

Eddy contributed right away in 1964, when he first made the varsity as a sophomore. He was the youngest member of one of Notre Dame's best all-time backfields. He played along with fullback Joe Farrell, halfback Bill Wolski, and that season's Heisman Trophy winner, John Huarte, who played so well that Eddy's impressive coming-out season was a bit overlooked. Eddy led the team in kickoff returns and was second in rushing (98 carries for 490 yards) and third in re-

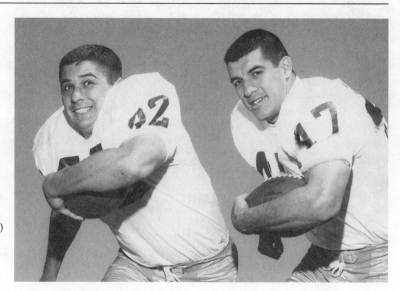

Fullback Larry Conjar
(left) and All-American
halfback Nick Eddy (right)
led Notre Dame to a
national championship
in 1966. (Laughead
Photographers)

ceiving (16 catches for 352 yards) and scoring (44 points). The following season he took over the chores of leading the backfield. He led the team in both rushing (115 for 582) and receiving (13 for 233), and was fourth in scoring (36 points). After just two seasons on varsity, Eddy was listed among the top twenty rushers in school history.

Eddy continued to build on his statistics. He got better, as did the Fighting Irish, who were 9–0–1 and national champs his senior season. He averaged more than 7 yards per carry, totaled 553 yards, and caught 15 passes. He scored 60 points, or roughly one-sixth of Notre Dame's NCAA-leading 362. If you need any more indication of Eddy's importance to Notre Dame's titanic offense you need only look at a game played in East Lansing, Michigan, on November 19. Eddy had a sore shoulder, and he slipped while disembarking the train in Michigan, further injuring the joint. He did not play, and the Fighting Irish had its only blemish of the year, a 10–10 tie with Michigan State.

Eddy finished third in Heisman Trophy voting (Florida quarterback Steve Spurrier was the winner), and he was a consensus first-team All-American after his senior season. He was invited to play in the College

Football All-Star Game and finished school with 1,625 yards, which, at the time, was eighth on Notre Dame's all-time list. (He no longer ranks among the top twenty.) The Detroit Lions of the NFL and Denver Broncos of the AFL selected Eddy in the second round of the 1966 draft. He played in the Motor City from 1967 to 1970, missed the 1971 season with a knee injury, but played in 1972 before retiring, with 523 yards on 152 carries.

CAREER STATS

RUSHING

Year	Att.	Yards	Avg.	TDs
1964	98	490	4.8	5
1965	115	582	5.1	4
1966	78	553	7.1	8
Total	291	1,625	5.6	17

RECEIVING

Year	Rec.	Yards	Avg.	TDs
1964	16	352	22.0	2
1965	13	233	18.0	2
1966	15	123	8.2	0
Total	44	708	16.1	4

EDWARDS, EUGENE
Quarterback (1924–26), 6'1", 165 lbs.

Edwards was not what you would call a conventional quarterback. For instance, in 1925, his first year as a starter, he was not even the team's leading passer. He was the Fighting Irish's leading receiver, though, with 4 catches for 28 yards. Despite not being anything close to a classic drop-back passer, he led Notre Dame to a 16–3–1 record in his two years as a starter.

During Edwards's first year on the varsity, All-American quarterback Harry Stuhldreher helmed the offense while "Red" had to patiently wait his turn. After playing backup for a season Edwards was on the first team, and he proved to be a leader of the first rank.

One year after his graduation, Edwards was hired as an assistant coach at St. Vincent College in Latrobe, Pennsylvania. After two years he returned home to Weston, West Virginia, where he took a civilian job. He couldn't keep off the gridiron, though. After one season of work he was back on the sidelines as St. Vincent's head coach.

EDWARDS, MARC
Fullback (1993–96), 6'0", 237 lbs.

Edwards's college football career was rolling right along until a knee injury in the eighth game of his senior year prematurely ended his tenure. He had been a phenomenon at Norwood High School, where he was the Ohio Back of the Year, an all-state running back as a junior and senior, and a member of the National Honor Society.

Edwards was, if nothing else, a steady rusher for Notre Dame. He was one of the school's three captains as a senior, along with quarterback Ron Powlus and linebacker Lyrone Cobbins. He gained 186 yards as a freshman and showed great promise as a sophomore, when he started four of eleven games and gained 307 yards on 48 carries (a 6.4-yards-per-carry average). His best season was his junior year, his first as a starter. He gained 717 yards on 140 carries and scored a career-high 9 touchdowns, numbers good enough for honorable mention All-American honors. He was also a finalist for the Doak Walker Award, given annually to the top running back in the country. Before suffering a knee injury in his senior year, Edwards gained 381 yards and scored 8 touchdowns, which was still good enough to share the team lead despite his shortened season. His damaged knee didn't stop him from being selected to play in the Senior Bowl, or by the San Francisco 49ers in the second round of the NFL draft. He played two seasons for the 49ers before joining the Cleveland Browns.

EGGEMAN, JOHN
Center (1897–99), 6'5", 256 lbs.

Eggeman was a giant among men in the early days of Notre Dame football. Along with being big and tall and hefty, Eggeman from Fort Wayne, Indiana, was strong enough to move back an opponent's defensive line 5 to 6 yards all by himself. When he played defense, Eggeman was known to hold off a blocker with one arm and tackle a runner with his free hand.

Eggeman started at center all three seasons and in 1898 he saved a game by blocking an Illinois field goal. In another game he recovered a Michigan State fumble, and ambled 4 yards for a score in a 53–0 shutout. Later in the season, the University of Michigan took advantage of the inexperience of Notre Dame's other linemen and tripleteamed Eggeman during a 23–0 victory.

EICHENLAUB, RAY
Fullback (1911–14), 6'0", 210 lbs.

While Gus Dorais was chucking passes and Knute Rockne was hauling them in, it was fullback Eichenlaub, from Columbus, Ohio, who kept defenses honest with a stellar running game. He was a key member of the team that upset perennial powerhouse Army, 35–13, during the fourth week of the 1913 season. What is most memorable about that game was that Dorais and Rockne changed the college game for good by making the forward pass a viable weapon. The win put Notre Dame on the map as a program to be reckoned with. When the Cadets began playing the pass, Eichenlaub's running gave Notre Dame a balanced attack, and he scored the Fighting Irish's two rushing touchdowns.

Eichenlaub was a four-year starter and compiled 176 career points. During his tenure, Notre Dame had a stunning 25–2–2 record. In the 1913 season, Eichenlaub scored 12 touchdowns in just seven games, earning him second-team All-American honors. He was a spirited gridder whose play has become part of Notre Dame's lore. Here's a great moment in Fighting Irish history. It is up to you to believe it or not.

By the fall of 1917, Rockne was an assistant coach in South Bend and was trying to talk future legend George Gipp into trying out for the football team.

During his sales pitch, Rockne said, "I've got just the pair of cleats for you."

This apparently impressed the Gipper, who said, "A special pair?"

"Yeah," answered Rockne. "They belonged to Ray Eichenlaub."

The rest is history.

EILERS, PAT
Split end/Flanker (1987–89),
5'11", 193 lbs.

Eilers started his college career at Yale. The St. Paul, Minnesota, native then made a very smart move—he transferred to Notre Dame. Eilers made the team and earned a letter as a walk-on, in 1987. In 1988, with a void left by the graduation of Heisman Trophy winner Tim Brown, Eilers was named the starting flanker and caught 6 passes for 70 yards. He moved to split end for his senior season and started every game. His performance, which was marked by intelligence

and great blocking, helped the team in ways that don't show up in statistical categories. He also had good hands and caught what was thrown to him, but that was only 5 passes for 53 yards.

Not surprisingly, he was not selected in the NFL draft, but the Los Angeles Rams brought him in as a free agent to take a look. He hung around the NFL for seven seasons, contributing to the Minnesota Vikings (1990–91), the Phoenix Cardinals (1992), the Washington Redskins (1993–94), and the Chicago Bears (1995–96).

ELDER, JACK
Halfback (1927–29), 5'8", 165 lbs.

Elder hailed from the horse country of Louisville, Kentucky, and had the speed of a thoroughbred. He had outrun Olympic 100-yard sprinters and was one of the fastest players ever to suit up for head coach Knute Rockne. He was also part of one of the greatest moments in Notre Dame's long history of great moments. In the last game of the 1929 season, in Yankee Stadium, he intercepted a pass from perpetual powerhouse Army and ran it back 95 yards for the game's only score. Notre Dame won the game 7–0 and a second consecutive national championship.

ELLIS, CLARENCE
Defensive back (1969–71), 6'0", 178 lbs.

Once Ellis became a starter at Notre Dame, he was not about to give up his spot. During his sophomore season he became a member of the varsity team and instantly won a spot on the first team. Thanks to his good play at defensive back, Ellis, from Grand Rapids, Michigan, never relinquished the position. He finished up with 13 career interceptions and a touchdown. His interception total places him in a five-way tie, along with Ralph Stepniak (1971), Joe Restic (1978), John Lattner (1963), and Mike Townsend (1973), for third place on the school's all-time list.

As a sophomore, Ellis had 31 tackles and 3 interceptions, 1 for a touchdown. He also set a school record, which still stands, by breaking up 13 passes. The following year, as the iron man of defensive backs (269:49 played), he intercepted 7 passes and made 27 tackles. He played a great game in the Cotton Bowl, in which Notre Dame beat Texas, 24–11. His 6 tackles and 3 defended passes made him the game's Most Valuable Defensive Player, and he was also named a first-team All-American.

Ellis's senior season was his best. He had 3 interceptions and 35 tackles and was again named a consensus first-team All-American. He also made the rosters of the College Football All-Star Game and the Senior Bowl. Atlanta picked Ellis in the first round of the 1972 NFL draft, and he played three seasons of professional ball for the Falcons.

CAREER STATS

Year	Int.	Yards	Avg.	TDs
1969	3	98	32.6	1
1970	7	25	3.6	0
1971	3	34	11.3	0
Total	13	157	12.1	1

EVANS, FRED
Fullback/Halfback (1940–42),
5'11", 178 lbs.

Head coach Elmer Layden didn't have to go far to find "Dippy" Evans, who was an all-state player at South Bend's Riley High School and arrived on the campus in 1939. He made the varsity and won a letter in 1940 as a sophomore halfback. The next year a new coach, Frank Leahy, took over the program and shifted Evans to starting fullback. Evans responded by leading the team in rushing, with 480 yards on 141 carries and scoring a team-high 11 touchdowns. He also was credited with an extra point to bring his team-leading total to 67 points.

Evans was obviously penciled in to start his senior year, but he got hurt in a preseason practice and played a grand total of 1 minute the entire regular season. He was a member of the Army Air Corps reserve during World War II, and after the war returned to football on the professional level. Evans played for the Cleveland Browns (1946), the Buffalo Bills (1947), and the Chicago Rockets (1947) of the All-American Football League. He also played for the Chicago Bears in 1948 before retiring.

FANNING, MIKE
Defensive end/Defensive tackle (1972–74),
6′6″, 250 lbs.

Fanning, from Tulsa, Oklahoma, was as
outstanding a wrestler as he was a football
player. At Tulsa's Edison High School he was
captain of the football and wrestling teams.
As a senior, he was on All-American and all-
state, as well as being hailed as the city's lineman of the year.

Fanning's success was good news for the
Fighting Irish. He earned his first letter as a
sophomore second-stringer at defensive end.
During his junior season, Fanning excelled at
both football and wrestling. He was a starting defensive end on Ara Parseghian's 11–0
national championship team, and finished
fourth on the team in tackles, with 61. He
also played more minutes than any other
defensive lineman on the squad. He did his
part in the team's opening week 44–0 drubbing of Northwestern, sacking the opposing
quarterback 3 times to earn the title of Midwest Lineman of the Week.

After the Sugar Bowl against Alabama,
which Notre Dame won 24–23, Fanning
competed on the wrestling team and qualified for the heavyweight championship of the
NCAA tournament after going 18–0.

As a senior on the football team, Fanning made 85 tackles, which was again good
for fourth on the squad and first-team All-
American honors.

In the 1975 NFL draft, Fanning was a
first-round pick (ninth overall) of the Los
Angeles Rams. During his nine-year professional career he played both defensive end
and defensive tackle. He played for the Rams
from 1975 to 1982, moved to Detroit for the

All-American defensive lineman Mike Fanning was
also an NCAA heavyweight wrestling champ.

1983 season, and to Seattle for the 1984 season before retiring.

FARLEY, JOHN
End/Fullback (1897–1900), 5′9″, 160 lbs.

Paterson, New Jersey, native Farley had
many attributes that couldn't be coached. He
was fast and possessed an extraordinary will
to win—and more specifically, to score.

Farley was Notre Dame's starting left
end in 1897 and had what many players
would consider a successful season in one
game. In a 62–0 victory over Chicago Dental Surgeons he ran for 184 yards, including
an 80-yard score, in the first half alone. In

the second half he came back and gained 280 more yards (and 3 more touchdowns) for a whopping total of 464 yards rushing.

Farley was a starting left end again in 1898 and gained in excess of 220 yards and 2 touchdowns against Michigan State. In 1900, after another year at left end, he started at full-back. He scored many more touchdowns on many more long runs, including a 75-yarder against Englewood High School and 2 touchdowns and a 50-yard run against South Bend Howard Park, and he preserved a win over Rush Medical College with a 25-yard run and a blocked field goal. After he graduated from college, Farley entered the priesthood and remained at Notre Dame. Unfortunately, he lost the legs that defenses couldn't stop due to complications from diabetes.

FARRAGHER, JIM
Tackle (1900–1901), 5'10", 190 lbs.

Farragher didn't let his handicap of having only one eye stop him from contributing to his college football team. The tough little tackle from Youngstown, Ohio, also had the ability to score when needed. In 1900 he did it three times in a 64–0 victory over Howard Park. The following year he scored a touchdown on a fumble recovery against the South Bend Commercial Athletic Club.

FAUST, GERARD ANTHONY
Head coach (1981–85)

Gerry Faust's selection as the twenty-fourth head football coach at Notre Dame, which was announced on November 24, 1980, was a bit of a shock. Instead of promoting from within its own program, picking a former Fighting Irish star, or going to another program to pluck either one of the best young minds in the game or a time-tested winner, Notre Dame hired a man with a great personality and a proven record as a teacher, but no college experience other than as a player.

Before coming to Notre Dame for the 1981 season, Faust had coached at Cincin-

nati's Moeller High School for almost twenty years. His record there was an unbelievable 174–17–2 (.901), and he had a well-deserved reputation as a winner. In eighteen seasons, beginning in 1963, Moeller won five state championships and twelve city championships. In four years, at season's end, the team was ranked the top prep program in the nation. Faust coached 250 players who received college football scholarships, including twenty of whom went to Notre Dame, most notably All-Americans linebacker Bob Crable and defensive lineman Steve Niehaus. He coached twenty-two prep All-Americans and was national high school Coach of the Year in 1979, two years before moving on to South Bend.

But, in the end, the critics were right. Jumping into college ball and taking over a program with the stature of Notre Dame proved to be too much for Faust, who barely escaped his five-year run there with a winning record. He lost four of his first six games and coached the team to 5–6 records his first and final seasons. During his best regular season, in 1982, the Fighting Irish only managed a 6–4–1 record. The team went 7–5 in both 1983 and 1984, qualifying for bowls, albeit small ones, in both seasons. After the 1983 season, Notre Dame beat Boston College, 19–18, in the Liberty Bowl but lost to SMU, 27–20, in the 1984 Aloha Bowl.

CAREER RECORD

Year	W	L	T	Bowl
1981	5	6	0	No bowl appearance
1982	6	4	1	No bowl appearance
1983	7	5	0	Liberty Bowl, W, Boston College, 19–18
1984	7	5	0	Aloha Bowl, L, SMU, 20–27
1985	5	6	0	No bowl appearance
Total	30	26	1	1–1

Faust resigned from Notre Dame after one more losing season. Only Joe Kuharich (17–23–0) and Hugh Devore (9–9–1 in two seasons) had worse records at Notre Dame than Faust. He was back in the game the next season, as the University of Akron scooped him up. But was even less successful there. He compiled a 45–53–3 record in nine seasons and left the post in 1994 to take a job in the institution's development office.

FEENEY, AL
Center (1910–13), 5'11", 180 lbs.

There's no arguing with the success Notre Dame had when Feeney was its starting snapper. After one season as a reserve, Feeney made the first team varsity, and during the next three seasons the Fighting Irish won twenty games, lost none, and tied two. There's also no arguing that Feeney, from Indianapolis, Indiana, was successful in life after he left South Bend. He played professionally for the Canton Bulldogs in 1920 and 1921 before entering public life. He was the head of the Indiana state police and, in 1947, was elected the mayor of Indianapolis.

FERGUSON, VAGAS
Running back (1976–79), 6'1", 194 lbs.

Ferguson was so good at Notre Dame that his phenomenal statistics have passed the test of time. He finished up his football career in 1979 as the school's all-time leading rusher, with 3,472 yards. Only Autry Denson, who played until 1998, and Allen Pinkett, who played until 1985, have since surpassed his mark.

As a senior, Ferguson's 301 rushing attempts for a season is still a school record. His 255 yards in one game against Georgia Tech in his junior season is still the Notre Dame record. (Ferguson was a real Georgia Tech killer—he also rushed for 177 yards against the Yellowjackets the following year.) His 130.6 rushing yards per game as a senior is still number one on the list, as is his 1,437-yard performance in his last year on campus.

Those aren't the only places that Ferguson's name appears in the school record book. He has some near misses as well. Ferguson's 39 carries against Georgia Tech is second behind Pinkett's 40 carries in a game. His 637 carries in a career trails only Pinkett's 889 and Autry Denson's 854. And his 13 career 100-yard games places him third in Fighting Irish history.

Ferguson, a big-play runner, did come in during a fat period for Notre Dame's offense. In 1977, as a sophomore, he gained 493 yards on 80 carries and had to pick up whatever plays were left after quarterback Joe Montana and running back Jerome Heavens (229 carries for 994 yards) were through with the ball. However, after that season, in the Cotton Bowl, Ferguson showed flashes of what was ahead. He gained 100 yards and scored 3 touchdowns, earning Outstanding

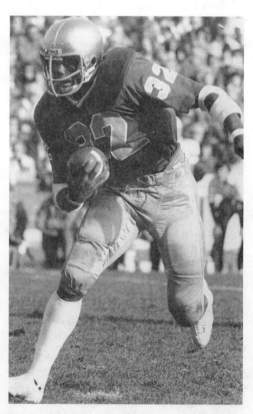

Running back Vagas Ferguson rushed for nearly 3,500 yards, a mark which ranks third all time in the Notre Dame record books.

Offensive Player of the Game honors, as Notre Dame beat Texas 38–10 and won the national title.

During Ferguson's junior season Heavens was still around, and he is a major reason that the rusher from Richmond, Indiana, became one of the top in college ball. Heavens, who had proved that he could run the year before, used his outstanding blocking skills to open holes and lead the way for his quicker teammate. Ferguson finished the season with 1,192 yards, including 255 in one game against Georgia Tech. All season Heavens was more than a blocking dummy, as his 728 yards gave the Fighting Irish one of the most fearsome one-two running combinations in the game.

By the time Ferguson was a senior Heavens and Montana were gone, and he was more than ready to shoulder the load. Over the eleven-game season he was a workhorse. He set a record for rushing attempts, 301, which works out to an average of 27.4 a game. He also set the Notre Dame single-season rushing record, despite being nearly shut out in his final game, a 35–34 come-from-behind victory over the University of Houston in the Cotton Bowl. That day Ferguson gained only 19 yards on 10 carries. His attempts were limited, as Notre Dame trailed 34–12 and had to take to the air.

Ferguson was a consensus All-American in 1979 and was subsequently selected by the New England Patriots with the twenty-fifth selection in the NFL draft. He played for the Patriots, Oilers, and Browns in a less than sensational professional career, finishing with 1,163 yards on 290 carries and 5 touchdowns. After retiring he returned home to become the athletic director at Richmond High School.

CAREER STATS

Year	Att.	Yards	Avg.	TDs
1976	81	350	4.3	2
1977	80	493	6.2	6
1978	211	1,192	5.6	7
1979	301	1,437	4.8	17
Total	673	3,472	5.2	32

FIGARO, CEDRIC
Linebacker (1984–87), 6′2″, 246 lbs.

Figaro had an extremely consistent career at Notre Dame, contributing to the team's defense in each of his four seasons. As a freshman from Lafayette, Louisiana, he logged the most minutes of any first-year defender. He made the starting lineup as a sophomore and made 62 tackles. His performance led to a second-team All-American selection. As a junior he made 59 tackles and was named a third-team All-American. In his final campaign he made 53 tackles and was again named a third-team All-American. The San Diego Chargers used their sixth-round pick in the NFL draft to select Figaro, who went on to have a seven-year career. He played in San Diego from 1988 to 1990, in Cleveland in 1991 and 1992, and in St. Louis in 1995 and 1996.

FILLEY, PATRICK JOSEPH
Guard (1941–44), 5′8″, 175 lbs.

"Peanut" Filley played alongside some of the most talented players in Notre Dame history. He was the smallest player in the starting lineup on the 1943 team, which was 9–1, and gave the Fighting Irish its first national title in thirteen years. Filley, a local product from South Bend, was as spirited as he was talented. He was the team's emotional leader, and although the team was packed with eventual College Football Hall of Famers (halfback Creighton Miller, tackle Ziggy Czarobski, and quarterbacks Angelo Bertelli and Johnny Lujack), it was Filley, a junior, who was named the team's captain. He was also the captain of the team his senior season, becoming the first player to hold the title twice. After his junior season he was selected a first-team All-American; the rich-with-talent Fighting Irish dressed five other All-Americans that year. Filley ended up his four-year college career in 1945 with another All-American campaign.

The Cleveland Browns selected Filley

in the tenth round of the draft, but he never played a down as a pro. He took a job at Cornell, working as an assistant for former Notre Dame coach Ed McKeever, but ten years later, an arthritic condition cut his coaching career short. He moved into the front office, where he worked more than thirty years in sundry positions, such as assistant director, ticket manager, director of operations, and associate director in charge of scheduling.

FISCHER, BILL
Tackle/Guard (1945–48), 6'2", 230 lbs.

"Moose" Fischer was one of the best linemen in Notre Dame history. He was even named best lineman in the land as a senior, and as a member of the College Football Hall of Fame, he is considered one of the best athletes ever to play college football.

If Fischer hadn't had a last-minute change of heart, he would have achieved his accomplishments for the University of Illinois. He was pretty much hand-delivered to the Fighting Illinois. He had led Lane Tech High School of the Chicago Public League to a city championship and was named to the all-state team as a senior. He and the other members of the team were then honored at a banquet on the Champaign campus of the University of Illinois. Illinois head coach Ray Eliot gave him the hard sell, and it apparently worked. Fischer liked the football program, its coach, and his would-be teammates. Staying home and being a local hero also had a nice ring, so Illinois won the Fischer derby. In those days, however, there were no national letters of intent. College football was run on the honor system. If a player announced his intention to attend a school, all other coaches were expected to back off.

This usually worked, but not this time, and not with Notre Dame head coach Hugh Devore. It was the summer of 1945, and pre-season practice at Illinois was scheduled to start in a few days. Meanwhile, Notre Dame assistant coach Gene Ronzani persuaded Fischer to come to Notre Dame for a quick

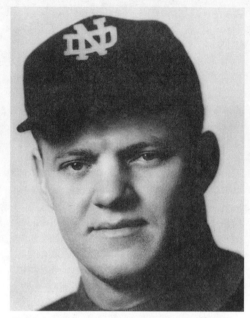

Outland Trophy–winner Bill "Moose" Fischer was an outstanding lineman and 1983 inductee into the College Football Hall of Fame. He was also a two-time All-Pro and later an assistant coach at Notre Dame.

visit—one that would last four years. Fischer enrolled in classes and began to practice with the football team. It turned out well for everyone, except, presumably, Eliot and anyone else involved with the Illinois program.

Fischer played a lot at tackle as a freshman and became a starting guard as a sophomore. He remained in the starting lineup for three seasons, during which time Notre Dame did not lose a football game, compiling a 26–0–2 record. Notre Dame also won national championships during Fischer's sophomore and junior seasons. As a senior, the two-time consensus All-American and Outland Trophy winner (awarded to the nation's top interior lineman) led the team in minutes played, with 300 in 1947. During his time on the team, Notre Dame beat Illinois twice, 7–0 in 1945 and 26–6 in 1946.

The Chicago Cardinals selected Fischer in the first round of the NFL draft. He played five seasons, twice being named All-Pro. Then he went back to his college to work under head coach Terry Brennan, from

1954 to 1958. In 1983 he was inducted into the College Football Hall of Fame.

FLANAGAN, CHRISTIE
Halfback (1925–27), 6'0", 170 lbs.

You've heard of the Four Horsemen, the immortalized offensive backfield that played for Notre Dame in 1924, but what about the Lone Horseman? Legendary sportswriter Grantland Rice, who coined the moniker for the more famous quartet, came up with an offshoot for Flanagan, of Port Arthur, Texas, two years later. When Flanagan scored on a 70-yard run to give Notre Dame a 7–0 victory over Army, Rice was at work again. In the same report he said that Flanagan was "harder to hold down than a Broadway bankroll." With the compliments came a plethora of comparisons. This didn't seem to bother Flanagan, who had a career-high 731 yards on 188 carries on a 1927 7–1–1 Notre Dame team. He was also selected a first-team All-American.

Flanagan's success came after a rather inauspicious beginning. The first uniform he was issued included worn pads, a jersey, pants meant for a much bigger man, and mismatched cleats (one size nine, the other size ten). He then made the mistake of pointing out his footwear problem to head coach Knute Rockne, who simply found it funny. It was just a bit of hazing for a freshman player. All it took for Flanagan to earn a new pair of shoes was to perform well in a drill against the varsity, which he did a few weeks later. When he was a sophomore, in 1925, Flanagan was the team's starting halfback and led the team in rushing with 556 yards on 99 carries, and in scoring with 45 points. The following season he averaged 7.9 yards a carry (68 carries for 535 yards) and was named a second-team All-American, as the team went 9–1.

Flanagan left Notre Dame with two shoes the same size and a ranking of fourth on the school's all-time rushing list. Despite playing only three years of varsity football, he was still eighteenth after the 2000 season. He did not play professional football.

CAREER STATS

Year	Att.	Yards	Avg.	TDs
1925	99	556	5.6	7
1926	68	535	7.9	4
1927	118	731	6.2	4
Total	285	1,822	6.4	15

FLANIGAN, JIM
Defensive tackle/Linebacker (1990–93), 6'2", 276 lbs.

It took a switch from linebacker to defensive tackle to jump-start Flanigan's career. Flanigan, from Sturgeon Bay, Wisconsin, was named state Player of the Year his senior year of high school. His first two college seasons were rather unspectacular as a backup linebacker, but then he was moved forward to defensive tackle as a junior. He started the final twenty-three games of his college career, often coming up with big plays. The one-time *Sports Illustrated* cover boy recorded 8 tackles in a 31–24 upset over top-ranked Florida. He also had 10 tackles in a 17–0 victory over Purdue. During Flanigan's senior season, Notre Dame was 11–1 and beat Texas A&M, 24–21, in the Cotton Bowl.

Obviously, Flanigan didn't suffer from the *Sports Illustrated* jinx, which has been blamed for ruining numerous sports careers. The Chicago Bears picked him in the third round of the 1994 NFL draft, and he was still with the team through the 2000 season.

FOLEY, TIM
Offensive tackle/Center (1976–79), 6'5", 265 lbs.

After playing football at Cincinnati's Roger Bacon High School, Foley was a starting tackle on Notre Dame's 11–1 national championship team in 1977. He also received his share of individual honors. Foley was named an honorable mention All-American in 1978, his junior year. The three-year starter earned first-team All-American status in 1979, as Notre Dame went 7–4. Foley went on to play for the Baltimore Colts in 1981.

FOUR HORSEMEN, THE

Quarterback Harry Stuhldreher, left halfback Jim Crowley, right halfback Don Miller, and fullback Elmer Layden made up one of the best offensive backfields in the history of college football. They had played together since 1922, when Fighting Irish head coach Knute Rockne put the quartet together as sophomores. It wasn't until October 19, 1924, however, when legendary sportswriter Grantland Rice's report on Notre Dame's 13–7 victory over Army at the Polo Grounds appeared in the *New York Herald Tribune*, that they were immortalized. Rice summarized the game and college football's most famous backfield with the most famous passage in sportswriting history:

"Outlined against a blue, gray October sky the Four Horsemen rode again. In dramatic lore they are known as famine, pesti-lence, destruction, and death. These are only aliases. Their real names are: Stuhldreher, Miller, Crowley, and Layden. They formed the crest of the South Bend cyclone before which another fighting Army team was swept over the precipice at the Polo Grounds this afternoon as 55,000 spectators peered down upon the bewildering panorama spread out upon the green plain below.

"A cyclone can't be snared. It may be surrounded, but somewhere it breaks through to keep going. When the cyclone starts from South Bend, where the candle lights still gleam through the Indiana sycamores, those in the way must take to storm cellars at top speed. Yesterday the cyclone struck again, as Notre Dame beat Army 13 to 7, with a set of backfield stars that ripped and crashed through a strong Army defense with more speed and power than warring cadets could meet."

Rice had done his part, and it was time

The Four Horseman consisted of (left to right) halfback Don Miller, fullback Elmer Layden, halfback Jim Crowley, and quarterback Harry Stuhldreher.

for George Strickler, who was Rockne's student publicity aide, to turn the two paragraphs into history. Strickler, who would later become the sports editor of the *Chicago Tribune*, came up with an idea for one of the most famous photographs of all time. When the team returned to South Bend, he had the four players pose, in uniform, on four horses borrowed from a nearby stable, and the image was sent out across the wire to every state in the land. The Four Horsemen, none taller than 6 feet or heavier than 162 pounds, were a reality.

"At the time, I didn't realize the impact it would have," Crowley was later quoted as saying. "But the thing just kind of mushroomed. After the splurge in the press, the sports fans of the nation got interested in us along with other sportswriters." Notre Dame finished the season 10–0 and, after a 27–10 victory over Stanford in the 1925 Rose Bowl, the Irish were crowned national champions. "Our record helped, too," Crowley said. "If we'd lost a couple, I don't think we would have been remembered."

In their three years together (1922–24), Notre Dame compiled a 27–2–1 record, including the school's two hundredth win, against Georgia Tech (34–3) on November 1, 1924. All four players—Crowley, Layden, Miller, and Stuhldreher—were consensus All-Americans and have been inducted into the College Football Hall of Fame.

FRY, WILLIE
Defensive end (1973, 1975–77),
6'3", 242 lbs.

Fry had made a name for himself before he made it to South Bend, and all he did was build on his sterling reputation while he was there. At Northside High School in Memphis, Tennessee, he was an all-state and All-American football player as a senior, led his basketball team to the state final, and was a

member of the varsity tack team. In the classroom he was equally impressive. Fry was a member of the National Honor Society, senior class president, and winner of the Outstanding High School Student Award.

At Notre Dame he appeared in every game as a freshman second-string defensive end, as Notre Dame won the national championship in 1973. He missed the next season because of injuries, but was back, and starting, in 1975. He made 78 tackles that year, good for fifth on the team. In 1976, Fry was named captain, the first junior to be so honored since Bob Olson in 1968. He made 77 tackles that year and was accordingly named a second-team All-American. During his senior campaign, Fry had 47 tackles as Notre Dame went 11–1 and won another national championship ring, while Fry was again named a second-team All-American.

FURJANIC, ANTHONY JOSEPH
Linebacker (1982–85), 6'2", 228 lbs.

The only thing that slowed down Chicago native Tony Furjanic, a four-year letter winner, was a knee injury. He was a special-teams player as a freshman, and by the following season he was the first team's middle linebacker. He proved to be durable and capable. Furjanic played 318 minutes, tops on the team, and made 142 tackles, more than twice as many as any of his teammates. He missed all but six games as a junior because of a torn knee ligament, but came back with a vengeance in 1985, his senior season. Furjanic again led the team with an amazing amount of tackles, 147, and played a lot of minutes, a team-leading 327. He was also named an honorable mention All-American. The Buffalo Bills selected him in the eighth round of the 1986 draft, and he remained in western New York until 1988. He also played part of the 1988 season for the Miami Dolphins.

GANDY, MIKE
Offensive guard (1998–2000),
6'4", 315 lbs.

Gandy used his size and strength to start his final two seasons at Notre Dame. Injuries kept him out of the lineup for the 1996 and 1997 seasons, but he used his extra season of eligibility to be a leader on the Fighting Irish offensive line, leading all active players in 2000 in career playing time.

Gandy, who went to Garland High School in Texas, had broken a bone just above his ankle before the 1997 Pittsburgh game and did not play again until his sophomore season in 1998, when he played in all eleven games and took a starting position against LSU when Jerry Wisne was injured. Gandy would not relinquish that spot for the rest of his college career, starting every game at right guard for the Irish in 1999, logging 340:24. Gandy followed up with an outstanding senior season, scoring the number three rank among offensive guard prospects, according to the *Sporting News*.

The Chicago Bears made the third-team All-American the first of six Fighting Irish players to be selected in the 2001 National Football League draft when they used their third-round pick (sixty-eight overall) on the big lineman.

GANN, MIKE
Defensive tackle (1981–84), 6'5", 256 lbs.

Gann, who was born in Stillwater, Oklahoma, and achieved prep All-American status while playing his high school ball in Lakewood, Colorado, made the Notre Dame varsity and lettered as a freshman. In 1982, his career took a detour when he hurt his

knee and had to undergo surgery, but after a successful rehabilitation he was back in the starting lineup the following season—he still had eleven years of football left in him. In 1983, he played 274 minutes and made 52 tackles. As a senior, Gann placed third on the team in tackles, with 60, and was named a second-team All-American. The Falcons selected him in the second round of the 1985 NFL draft, and he played for Atlanta for nine seasons.

GATEWOOD, TOM
Split end (1969–71), 6'2", 208 lbs.

For two seasons, Gatewood and Joe Theismann combined to give Notre Dame one of the deadliest aerial attacks in college football history. The two were likely the smartest combination in the game, too, as they were both Academic All-Americans. Gatewood, from Baltimore, Maryland, was a sophomore when he was first named a starter, and that's when he first hooked up with Theismann, a junior. That year Gatewood was Notre Dame's top receiver and also one of the best pass catchers in the country. He played 277 minutes, caught 47 balls for 743 yards, and scored 8 touchdowns.

His junior season, 1970, was even better. Gatewood was the second-leading receiver in the country, with 77 receptions for 1,123 yards—both are still school records—and 7 touchdowns. He was also third on the team in points with 48. After the season, he caught a touchdown pass in the first quarter of Notre Dame's 24–21 victory over the University of Texas in the Cotton Bowl, but had to leave the game early with a hamstring injury. Gate-

Two-time All-American Tom Gatewood was quarterback Joe Theismann's favorite target.

down catches per game, with .6, and in a six-way tie for the most touchdowns in a game (3 against Purdue on September 26, 1970). He is behind only Jim Seymour in receptions in a game (12 against Purdue in 1970), pass receptions per game (5.2), pass reception yards per game (112.3 in 1970), and for a career (76.1). Derrick Mayes, with 22, is the only receiver with more touchdown grabs than Gatewood, who had 19. Gatewood is also third on the career yardage list for a receiver, with 2,283.

Gatewood was drafted by the New York Giants in the fifth round of the 1972 NFL draft. He did not play much and was out of the league after two seasons.

CAREER STATS

Year	Rec.	Yards	Avg.	TDs
1969	47	743	15.8	8
1970	77	1,123	14.6	7
1971	33	417	12.6	4
Total	157	2,283	14.5	19

GIBBONS, TOM
Safety/Cornerback (1977–80), 6'1", 181 lbs.

Once he made his way into the starting lineup as a sophomore, Gibbons was a dependable and consistent defensive back. In his three seasons as a starter his statistics were nearly identical (46, 48, and 41 tackles). Only 7 tackles separated his best season from his worst, and he had 3 interceptions twice and 2 once. Gibbons, from Alexandria, Virginia, was also a first-team Academic All-American as a senior, and made the second team as a sophomore and junior. He didn't make the grade by taking fluff courses, either. He graduated in 1981 with a degree in engineering.

wood was a consensus All-American after the season and an Academic All-American.

Gatewood was a team captain in 1971; he still put up numbers, despite Theismann's graduation. He caught 33 balls for 417 yards for 4 touchdowns and was named a first-team All-American. He again was named an Academic All-American and won scholarships from the NCAA and National Football Foundation. Before he left school, Gatewood certainly left his mark on the school's record book. He is first or second all-time in ten receiving categories and third in another. His 157 catches for a career is still the school standard. Gatewood is the leader in touch-

CAREER STATS

Year	Tackles	Int.	Yards
1977	5	1	38
1978	46	3	48
1979	48	3	74
1980	41	2	55
Total	140	9	215

GIBSON, OLIVER
Defensive tackle/Nose tackle (1990–94),
6'3", 275 lbs.

Gibson's college career got off to a slow
start, but he continued to improve, and his
final game at Notre Dame turned out to be
his best. He had 7 tackles in a 24–21 loss to
Colorado in the 1995 Fiesta Bowl.

USA Today named him the high school
Defensive Player of the Year for his play as a
senior at Romeoville High School in Illinois,
where he was captain of both the basketball
and football teams. Gibson only played three
games as a college freshman because of an injury. He ended up receiving red-shirt status
from the NCAA and called the year a wash.
In 1991, he played eleven games at tackle
and end and showed sparks of life, an indication that he was going to be a player to be
reckoned with.

By his senior season, Gibson was the
first string's starting nose tackle, and in 1994
he finished fourth on the team in tackles,
with 59, and the honors rolled in. He was the
recipient of the Lineman of the Year Award
of the Moose Krause Chapter of the National
Football Foundation and Hall of Fame and
won the Nick Pietrosante Award, named in
honor of the late Fighting Irish fullback who
died of cancer in 1988. His award goes to the
player who exemplifies the courage and spirit
that was a trademark of Pietrosante. The
Pittsburgh Steelers selected Gibson in the
fourth round of the 1995 draft. He played
there until moving to the Cincinnati Bengals
in 1999.

GIPP, GEORGE
Halfback (1917–20), 6'0", 180 lbs.

George Gipp had the stuff legends were
made of. He was a small-town kid whose
college coach discovered him while he was
just goofing around with a football on campus, and ended up being one of the best players in the country and a standout performer
on offense, defense, and special teams. And
he was Notre Dame's first-ever All-American.

Gipp is, however, better known for his
tragic death at age twenty-five than his
tremendous football aptitude. He was a senior
at Notre Dame when he came down with
strep throat. Two weeks after being named an
All-American he died, but not before, as legend would have it, addressing head coach
Knute Rockne from his death bed: "I've got
to go, Rock. It's all right. I'm not afraid.
Sometime, Rock, when the team is up against
it, when things go wrong and the breaks are
beating the boys—tell them to go in there
with all they've got and win just one for the
Gipper. I don't know where I'll be then, Rock.
But I'll know about it, and I'll be happy."

That's the way that Hollywood remembered the event. The scene was immortalized in an idealistic film called *Knute
Rockne, All-American.* Future president of the
United States Ronald Reagan portrayed Gipp
as a strapping, clean-cut young man. In real
life, however, Gipp was not the most disci-
plined of Rockne's disciples. He was more interested in hanging out in pool halls than in
going to class. He wanted to transfer out of
Notre Dame twice and was once nearly ex-
pelled, but remained in school thanks to a
string-pulling effort by Rockne.

Rockne saved the Gipper speech until
1928. On November 10 of that year, Notre
Dame boasted a 4–2 record. Ravaged by injuries, they were about to face powerhouse
Army at Yankee Stadium. During Rockne's
stirring pregame speech he said, "The day before he died, George Gipp asked me to wait
until the situation seemed hopeless—then
ask a Notre Dame team to go out and beat
Army for him. This is the day, and you are
the team." The Fighting Irish went on to
beat the Cadets, 12–6. After scoring a touchdown, halfback Jim Chevigny reportedly
hollered, "That's one for the Gipper!"

Gipp came to Notre Dame from Lau-
rium, Michigan, looking to graduate and
maybe play on the baseball team. One day he
was playing around with a football, drop-
kicking it an extremely long way. Oppor-
tunistic assistant (at the time) coach Rockne
eyed the young talent and convinced him to

give football a chance. As the team's starting halfback, Gipp led the team in rushing for three consecutive seasons, compiling a career total of 2,341 yards, a record that stood for half a century. Almost eighty years after his senior season, Gipp is still eighth on Notre Dame's all-time list. Each season his average gain per carry rose, and was a phenomenal 8.1 when he was a senior. He also passed for 1,769 yards in his career as a *halfback*.

As a defender, Gipp was also an all-star. He was a tough competitor and tough tackler who reportedly never allowed a man he was guarding to catch a pass. With Gipp on the field, Notre Dame was on a roll, amassing 27 wins against only 2 losses and 3 ties. Gipp was among the first class of inductees into the College Football Hall of Fame in 1951.

CAREER STATS

RUSHING

Year	Att.	Yards	Avg.	TDs
1917	63	244	3.9	0
1918	98	541	5.5	6
1919	106	729	6.9	7
1920	102	827	8.1	8
Total	369	2,341	6.3	21

PASSING

Year	Att.	Comp.	Yards	TDs	Pct.
1917	8	3	40	1	.375
1918	45	19	293	1	.422
1919	72	41	727	3	.569
1920	62	30	709	3	.484
Total	187	93	1,769	8	.497

GLADIEUX, BOB
Halfback (1966–68), 5'11", 185 lbs.

Gladieux exhibited the same nose for the end zone in college that made him a high school standout. During the three years he played at Louisville High School the team went 28–1–1, and he led the state of Ohio in scoring in 1964, his senior season.

As a collegian, Gladieux played more

and contributed more in each of his three varsity seasons. As a sophomore, in 1966, he gained 111 yards rushing and caught 12 passes for 208 yards. He also had a total of 5 touchdowns. The following season his rushing total was 384, his receiving total was 297, and he scored 7 touchdowns. His best season was as a senior, when he rushed for a team-high 713 yards and was second on the team in yards receiving, with 442. He also scored 12 rushing touchdowns and 2 receiving touchdowns while tying Bob Kelly's 1944 single-season scoring record with 84 points. The two men are tied for tenth on the school's all-time list of top scorers for a season. For his career, Gladieux scored 26 touchdowns at Notre Dame—20 by ground and 6 (2 each season) by air.

The Boston Patriots selected Gladieux in the eighth round of the NFL draft. He played for Boston, later the New England Patriots, and the Buffalo Bills. During his four seasons in the league, Gladieux gained 239 yards on 65 rushing attempts, and 252 yards on 25 receptions. He did not score any touchdowns.

CAREER STATS

RUSHING

Year	Att.	Yards	Avg.	TDs
1966	27	111	4.1	3
1967	84	384	4.6	5
1968	152	713	4.7	12
Total	263	1,208	4.6	20

RECEIVING

Year	Rec.	Yards	Avg.	TDs
1966	12	208	17.3	2
1967	23	297	12.9	2
1968	37	442	11.9	2
Total	72	947	13.2	6

GOEDDEKE, GEORGE
Center (1964–66), 6'3", 228 lbs.

It's not always easy for a center to stand out on a football team, but when you play a lot of minutes and are a key contributor to one of the best teams in Notre Dame history, it becomes easier. After one season of backing up Norm Nicola, Detroit native Goeddeke became a starter his junior season. He spent 206 minutes on the field and would have played more had he not missed two games after he had his appendix taken out. Goeddeke was back in the starting lineup as a senior, when Ara Parseghian's Fighting Irish were 9–0–1 (a two-game improvement on the previous season), and Notre Dame won its first consensus national title since 1949. Goeddeke was one of twelve Notre Dame players to earn All-American status for the season. He was a third-round NFL draft pick of the Denver Broncos in 1967, and spent his entire six-year career in the Mile High City.

All-American linebacker Bob Golic ranks second all-time in career tackles at Notre Dame and went on to a fourteen year career in the NFL.

GOLIC, BOB
Linebacker (1975–78), 6'3", 244 lbs.

If you wanted someone tackled, Bob Golic was the right guy for the job. Golic and Bob Crable share the school record for tackles in a game, with 26. Golic made his hits in a 28–14 loss to Michigan in 1978. He is also second, behind Crable, in tackles for a career, with 479, and he led the team with 146 tackles, then a school record, in 1977.

A talented two-sport star from Willowick, Ohio, Golic was Notre Dame's first multiple-sport All-American since "Moose" Krause (1933). He had prepped for Notre Dame at St. Joseph's High School, where he was an all-state football player and state heavyweight wrestling champion. His wrestling record was 67–4–2, including a 28–0–1 record his senior year. Golic's three-year wrestling record in college was 54–4–1, and he finished in the top four in the heavyweight division of the NCAA tournament twice—third in 1978 and fourth in 1977.

Golic is best known, however, for football, the marquee sport at Notre Dame. He was upgraded to starting middle linebacker during his freshman season and finished fourth on the team in tackles, with 82. The following season he tied Ken Dike for second on the team, with 99 tackles. In 1977, playing mid-

dle guard, he set a single-season record with 146 tackles and won second-team All-American status. Notre Dame won the national championship that season after a 38–10 victory over the University of Texas in the Cotton Bowl. Golic, making 17 tackles and stuffing Heisman Trophy winner Earl Campbell, was the game's MVP. In each game that season Golic had at least 10 tackles, including 18 in a 16–6 victory over Michigan State.

In his senior season, Golic upped his personal record with 152 tackles, which was 8 behind fellow linebacker Steve Heimkreiter, who had also led the team in 1976. Golic, a tri-captain, was a consensus All-American. In addition to his 479 tackles at Notre Dame, he also intercepted 6 passes and recovered 2 fumbles.

The New England Patriots selected Golic in the second round of the 1979 NFL draft. His fourteen-year career included four years in New England and stops in Cleveland, where he played for the Browns from 1982 to 1988, and in Los Angeles, where he was a member of the Raiders from 1989 to 1992. After his retirement from pro football, Golic became an NFL commentator and studio analyst for television.

GOLIC, MIKE
Linebacker/End (1981–84), 6′5″, 257 lbs.

Bigger isn't always better, especially when it comes to Golics. Three years after his brother Bob graduated as one of the fiercest linebackers in Notre Dame history, younger brother Mike hit the scene. He was 2 inches taller and 13 pounds heavier than his older brother but did not generate the same outstanding statistics. After arriving in South Bend from Willowick, Ohio, he did, however, have his fair share of success and was even named an honorable mention All-American and defensive Most Valuable Player by his teammates in 1983, his junior season. That was Golic's first season as a starter, and he was third on the team in sacks, with 4 for -35 yards, and fourth on the squad in tackles, with 59. Like his brother, Golic was named captain as a senior, but he missed two games with injuries and ended up with just 25 tackles.

The Houston Oilers selected Golic in the tenth round of the NFL draft, and he stuck around the league for a decade. He played for the Oilers from 1985 to 1987, for the Philadelphia Eagles from 1988 to 1992, and for the Miami Dolphins in 1992. After he retired from the league he became a television broadcaster and color commentator for NFL games.

GOMPERS, BILL
Halfback (1945–47), 6′1″, 175 lbs.

Despite the fact that he attended Notre Dame at the same time as Emil Sitko, one of the best running backs in Fighting Irish history, Gompers got his chances. Sitko may have led Notre Dame in rushing for four consecutive seasons (1946–49) but Gompers's blocking was at least part of the reason for his success. Notre Dame was named national champion by at least three organizations, and the team went 17–0–1 when Sitko and Gompers shared the backfield.

The first guy that Gompers played behind was Elmer Angsman in 1945. Angsman led the team in rushing, with 616 yards on

87 carries. Gompers, from Bridgeville, Pennsylvania, was a second-string sophomore and carried the ball 36 times, gained 185 yards, and scored 3 touchdowns. The following season Angsman graduated, but in came Sitko. Gompers was a key element in the 8–0–1 season that led to a national title his junior year. He gained 279 yards on 51 carries and scored 3 more touchdowns. As a senior, Gompers made the most of his opportunity to play. He only carried the ball 20 times, but averaged 6.8 yards a carry and finished with 136 yards and a touchdown. He played for the Buffalo Bills of the All-America Football Conference in 1949.

GRASMANIS, PAUL
Nose guard/Defensive end (1990–92), 6′2″, 279 lbs.

A tough, emotional player, Grasmanis achieved what he did through hard work. He entered Notre Dame from Jenison, Michigan, with six other freshmen and began to make an impact as a sophomore. He missed three early-season games with an ankle injury but came on strong, playing nose guard, in the last seven games of the season, setting himself up for a shot at the starting spot the next year.

Grasmanis was a starter as a junior, but was moved to the outside by head coach Lou Holtz, who made him a defensive end. Grasmanis made 49 tackles in 10 games. As a senior he was moved back to nose guard and became the full-time starter. He played 243:40 and made a career-high 69 tackles, 13 of which (including 10 solo hits) came in a 35–17 victory over Navy. He earned honorable mention All-American honors. The Chicago Bears selected him in the fourth round of the NFL draft. He played in the NFL for the St. Louis Rams and the Cincinnati Bengals, his current team, in 1999.

GREEN, MARK
Flanker/Tailback (1985–88), 6′0″, 184 lbs.

For Green, along with a change in coaches, from Gerry Faust to Lou Holtz, came a change in position. Playing for Faust as a freshman, Green, from Riverside, California, played flanker and caught 9 passes for 116 yards and ran the ball 5 times for 64 yards. In came Holtz the following season, and Green was moved to tailback. He led the team with 406 yards rushing and scored 2 touchdowns in addition to catching 25 passes for 242 yards.

His junior season was his best. Again he led the team in rushing, with 861 yards on 146 carries, and he scored 6 touchdowns, and caught 13 passes for 98 yards. His play earned him honorable mention All-American honors. As a senior Green was named captain, and played more minutes than any other running back on the squad. Quarterback Tony Rice hit the scene that year and took over the team's rushing lead, with 700 yards. Green was third on the team, with 646. He also scored 7 rushing touchdowns and caught 155 yards worth of passes, numbers good enough to make him an honorable mention All-American.

Green's 1,977 yards were also enough to keep him at twelfth place on the school's all-time rushing list. The Chicago Bears selected him in the fifth round of the 1989 NFL draft. He spent four years playing in the Windy City.

CAREER STATS

RUSHING

Year	Att.	Yards	Avg.	TDs
1985	5	64	12.8	0
1986	96	406	4.2	2
1987	146	861	5.9	6
1988	135	646	4.8	7
Total	382	1,977	5.2	15

RECEIVING

Year	Rec.	Yards	Avg.	TDs
1985	9	116	12.9	0
1986	25	242	9.7	0
1987	13	98	7.5	0
1988	14	155	11.1	0
Total	61	611	10.0	0

GREENEY, NORM
Guard (1930–32), 5'11", 190 lbs.

Cleveland native Greeney first tasted team success as a third-string guard on Notre Dame's national championship team of 1930. The next season, his junior year, he became a second-team player. He finally made the starting lineup as a senior. By the end of his run he was a more-than-adequate performer, but was often overshadowed by linemates such as All-Americans "Moose Krause" and Joe Kurth.

Greeney played three seasons in the professional ranks. He was a member of the Green Bay Packers in 1933, and then played for the Pittsburgh Steelers for two seasons. From there he entered the coaching ranks with the Newsboy Union Skippies.

GROOM, JERRY
Center/Linebacker (1948–50),
6'3", 215 lbs.

Two-platoon football helped Groom, and in turn the Notre Dame Fighting Irish. The two-way star (at linebacker and center) from Dowling High School in Des Moines, Iowa, was twice named all-state. In his sophomore season at Notre Dame, Groom was a backup center. The following season brought two-platoon football, and Groom became a linebacker and went down as one of the best defensive players in school history. His play was rewarded in 1994 with an induction into the College Football Hall of Fame.

NCAA rules forced Groom to play on the freshman team in 1947. The next year he backed up Bill Walsh at center. Finally, in 1949, his third year in South Bend, he was moved to middle linebacker and named the starter. He helped the Fighting Irish go 10–0 while they won their third consensus national title in four years. The next year Notre Dame crash-landed to Earth with a 4–4–1 record, but Groom, the captain, was a standout. He played both linebacker and center, was a consensus All-American, and was invited to play in the East-West Shrine Game.

Groom's Notre Dame career almost didn't happen. He was all but ready to commit to the University of Iowa, but he held off his decision until he had a chance to hear what Notre Dame head coach Frank Leahy had to say. Leahy was the speaker at Groom's senior banquet, and the coach was familiar with the player's skill. Leahy, no master salesman, had the luck of selling the Irish tradition and a campus that a high school kid could love. Groom only promised to make a visit to the South Bend campus, but that was all it took. Those were good times at Notre Dame. The football team had won the 1947 national championship, and it didn't look as if the run would end any time soon. Groom was all for being part of history.

After Notre Dame, Groom was a first-round draft pick of the Chicago Cardinals in the 1951 NFL draft. He played professionally for Chicago until 1955.

GRUNHARD, TIM
Guard/Center (1986–89), 6'3", 292 lbs.

Head coach Lou Holtz liked Grunhard's attitude. He looked at the big lineman from Chicago as a throwback. Grunhard

All-American guard Tim Grunhard helped clear the way for the Notre Dame backfield to amass an amazing 287.7 yards per game in 1989.

played a lot of minutes, earned four letters, and was twice named an All-American. His best season was his final college campaign. In 1989 he was on the field for almost 300 minutes as Notre Dame averaged a whopping 287.7 yards rushing a game, and Grunhard earned All-American honors. Grunhard, who started twenty-four games during his four college seasons, was also named an honorable mention All-American as a junior. The Kansas City Chiefs picked him in the second round of the 1990 NFL draft, and as of 2000 he was still on their roster.

GUGLIELMI, RALPH
Quarterback (1951–54), 6'0", 185 lbs.

Quarterback Guglielmi may not be a household name like Joe Montana or Joe Theismann, but that doesn't mean he didn't have a stellar career in South Bend. He had come to Notre Dame from Columbus, Ohio, after leading Grandview High School to the Central Ohio football championship. After playing behind John Mazur as a freshman, Guglielmi started his final three seasons in South Bend. He still ranks as the school's twelfth-leading passer through the 2000 season, with 3,037 career yards (he completed 209 of 436 passes). In 1952, his first as a starter, Guglielmi completed 61 of 142 passes for 683 yards and 4 touchdowns as the Fighting Irish finished 7–2–1 and third in the final Associated Press poll. He threw for 792 yards for a 9–0–1 Notre Dame team in head coach Frank Leahy's final season.

In 1954, in came a new head coach, Terry Brennan, and Guglielmi helped get him off to a great start. Notre Dame was 9–1 in 1954 and Guglielmi, who played in both the East-West Shrine Game and the College Football All-Star Game (in which he was named Most Valuable Player), earned consensus first-team All-American honors by completing 68 of 127 passes for 1,160 yards and 6 touchdowns.

Guglielmi, who threw 18 touchdown passes in his college career, is tied with Rick

All-American quarterback Ralph Guglielmi's three-year starting record was 25-3-2 at Notre Dame.

Mirer for the school record of consecutive games with a pass completion (34). He also rushed for 200 yards and 12 touchdowns and had 10 career interceptions. The Washington Redskins selected him in the first round of the 1955 NFL draft. Two of his teammates were selected later in the first round—tackle Frank Varrichione by the Pittsburgh Steelers and halfback Joe Heap by the New York Giants. Before entering the business world, Guglielmi played for four teams in a nine-year NFL career. The quarterback was a member of the Redskins in 1955 and 1958 to 1960, and also played for the St. Louis Cardinals in 1961, the New York Giants in 1962 and 1963, and the Philadelphia Eagles in 1963. In 2001, Guglielmi became the thirty-ninth Notre Dame alum to be inducted into the college Football Hall of Fame.

CAREER STATS

Year	Att.	Comp.	Pct.	Yards	TDs
1951	53	27	.509	438	0
1952	142	61	.429	683	4
1953	113	52	.460	792	8
1954	127	68	.535	1,160	6
Total	435	208	.478	3,073	18

HAINES, KRIS
Split end (1975–78), 6'0", 181 lbs.

Haines, a starting split end on Notre Dame's 1977 national championship team, was a heck of a running back in high school. He came to Notre Dame from Sidney, Ohio, in 1975, the same year that head coach Dan Devine debuted. Although he didn't catch a single pass, Haines did earn a letter. As a senior, three years later, he led the squad in receiving, with 32 catches for 699 yards, and he was fourth on the team in scoring, with 30 points.

In between he moved his way up the ranks at Notre Dame. As a junior he grabbed 28 passes for 587 yards for a healthy average of 21 yards per reception. Notre Dame was named the top school in the land for the season, and the poised play of Haines was a factor. He caught a 27-yard pass from quarterback Rusty Lisch to set up the winning score in a 19–9 victory over Pittsburgh the first week of the season. He also had 5 receptions for 120 yards in a 31–24 victory over Purdue in the third week.

The Washington Redskins selected Haines in the ninth round of the 1979 draft. He played for one season in Washington before moving on to Chicago to play three seasons for the Bears.

HANRATTY, TERRY
Quarterback (1966–68), 6'1", 200 lbs.

Hanratty came to Notre Dame with impressive credentials. He was a prep All-American at Butler High School in Pennsylvania. He more than lived up to the hype, and did so virtually the first time he took a snap from center.

In his sophomore year, Hanratty took over the helm of the Fighting Irish offense and led the team to a 9–0–1 record and a national championship under Ara Parseghian. In training camp, Hanratty beat out Coley O'Brien, but then missed two games, including the 10–10 tie against Michigan State, with a shoulder injury. In eight games he completed more than half his passes (78 of 147 attempts) for 1,247 yards. He also rushed for 124 yards and 5 touchdowns, and was sixth in the voting for the Heisman Trophy.

That was just a sneak peek at what was ahead. Not only would Hanratty be in the running for the Heisman each of the next two seasons, twenty years later he still holds numerous records and is one of the most prolific and accurate passers in Fighting Irish history. He had a fine time hooking up with multiple-record-holding receiver Jim Seymour, and completed more than half his passes in all three years as a starter.

Hanratty's shoulder was healed in time for his junior season, and he completed 110 of 206 pass attempts for 1,439 yards and 9 touchdowns. He ran for 7 more touchdowns, was named an honorable mention All-American, and finished ninth in the voting for the Heisman. As a senior, Hanratty was better than ever. He completed nearly 60 percent of his passes (116 of 197 attempts) for 1,466 yards and a career-high 10 touchdowns, and also rushed for 586 yards, scoring 16 more touchdowns. He was a consensus All-American, the Monogram Club's Most Valuable Player, and finished third for the prestigious Heisman.

Hanratty, who graduated as the school's all-time leader in pass completions, is still atop the chart for pass attempts in a game— 63 in a 28–21 loss to Purdue in 1967 (he completed 29). Both his 28.1 pass attempts and 16.6 completions per game in a season are still school records. With a career average 21.2 pass attempts per game, Hanratty trails only Ron Powlus, who averaged 22 throws a game. He is also second behind Powlus in career average of pass completions per game at 11.69 (compared with Powlus's 12.68), and in career passing yards per game with 159.7 (compared with Powlus's 172.7). He trails only Joe Theismann in passing yards in a game (366 versus Purdue in 1967 compared with 526 for Theismann) and in passing yards per game (146.6 to Theismann's 252.9 in 1970). Hanratty is also third all-time in pass completions in a game (29 versus Purdue in 1967) and completion percentage for a season (.598 in 1968). His 550 career pass attempts (he completed 304) and 4,152 career yards are both fifth on the list.

The Pittsburgh Steelers grabbed Hanratty in the second round of the 1969 NFL draft. He played with the Steelers for seven seasons, including the 1975 Super Bowl. He also played for the Tampa Bay Buccaneers in 1976. During his NFL career, which spanned eight seasons, Hanratty completed 165 of 431 passes for 2,510 yards.

CAREER STATS

Year	Att.	Comp.	Pct.	Yards	TDs
1966	147	78	.531	1,247	8
1967	206	110	.534	1,439	9
1968	197	116	.588	1,466	10
Total	550	304	.553	4,152	27

HARDY, KEVIN
Defensive tackle/Defensive end (1964–67), 6'5", 270 lbs.

Hardy's best sport at Notre Dame may have been football, but it certainly wasn't his only one. The big, bruising lineman from Oakland, California, didn't even suit up for a game of organized football until his junior year in high school, but he was the first Notre Dame player in nineteen years to win letters in three sports. As a freshman, Hardy aver-

aged 2.3 points for the Notre Dame basketball team, which went on to the NCAA tournament, and he played on the varsity baseball team. As a junior, Hardy showed that he wasn't just a good hitter on the football field. As a right fielder he led the baseball team with a .398 batting average his senior season.

In football, Hardy was the starting right tackle in his freshman season, though he missed most of his sophomore year with an injury. He was back on the first team as a junior, earning All-American honors. As a senior he emerged as one of the best defensive linemen in the nation. Playing both tackle and end, he was again named All-American.

The New Orleans Saints used the seventh overall pick in the 1968 NFL draft to grab Hardy. He played for the San Francisco 49ers in 1968, the Green Bay Packers in 1970, and the San Diego Chargers in 1971 and 1972.

HARPER, JESSE
Head coach (1913–17)

Harper played for a college football legend before becoming one himself. The cattle rancher's son from Papaw, Illinois, played at the University of Chicago for Amos Alonzo Stagg, for whom the Division III football championship is named. Six years after graduating, at the tender age of twenty-nine, Harper showed Notre Dame that he was ready to take over the program—and it almost came at the Fighting Irish's expense. In 1911, Harper was coaching Wabash and almost pulled a major upset, but Notre Dame barely held on to win, 6–3. Two years later, Harper was working in South Bend.

Harper's first Notre Dame team went 7–0, and the program beat national power Army to become a team of prominence. On November 1, 1913, the small Catholic school accepted $1,000 to go to West Point to take on the powerhouse Cadets. Notre Dame quarterback Gus Dorais and end Knute Rockne shocked the sports world by using the forward pass as a set play rather than a gimmick or desperation play. The game plan worked, as Notre Dame beat a flummoxed Army, 35–13.

The use of the pass proved that football was a game of skill as well as a game of physical strength, and the sport was changed forever. Harper was extremely innovative in other ways, too. The following season he and Rockne, who had graduated after his 1913 season and was now an assistant coach, came up with the Notre Dame shift. The team would drive defenses crazy by lining up in a standard T formation and then shift into one of three other formations right before the ball was snapped. He also opened up the schedule to play teams such as the University of Texas, Yale, Princeton, and Army, further raising the school's identity.

Harper coached five seasons at Notre Dame, compiling an exceptional record of 34–5–1. He was also the coach of the baseball, basketball, and track teams, and was the athletic director. In 1918 he stepped aside, making room for Rockne at the top, and went into the family cattle business. Harper retired from football at the age of thirty-three and moved to a 20,000-acre ranch in Sitka, Kansas. In 1931, after Rockne died in a plane crash, Harper came back to Notre Dame for a two-year stint as athletic director.

Harper, a slight halfback (5-foot-10, 155 pounds) missed most of his college career with injuries. His sophomore and junior years were all but lost, but he did help Chicago to a 7–0 record as a senior. He graduated from college in 1906, and Stagg led him into coaching. His first post was at Alma College in Michigan, which went 10–4–4 during three seasons under Harper. His next stop was Wabash College in Indiana, which was 15–9–2 during Harper's tenure. Wabash won its first four games in 1910 by an incredible margin of 118–0 before canceling the rest of its season due to the death of a player during a game against St. Louis. From there Harper went to Notre Dame, and his next stop in college football was the Hall of Fame, which inducted him posthumously in 1970.

CAREER RECORD

Year	W	L	T
1913	7	0	0
1914	6	2	0
1915	7	1	0
1916	8	1	0
1917	6	1	1
Total	34	5	1

HARRISON, RANDY
Free safety (1974–78), 6'1″, 207 lbs.

With only four years of eligibility, Harrison did the near impossible at Notre Dame—he earned five letters. He started two games and played 32 minutes, which was good enough to earn a letter, before breaking his forearm in his junior season. The NCAA, however, allowed him to play an additional season. As luck would have it, he fractured a rib and missed four games of his fourth of five seasons. At Notre Dame Harrison got off to a quick start. He had 57 tackles as a freshman and 54 as a sophomore before he broke his arm the following season. The Hammond, Indiana, native was healthy for his fifth season, but was not in the starting lineup. Joe Restic beat him for the spot, but Harrison still played enough to earn his fifth letter, and made 22 tackles and an interception.

HART, LEON
Right end/Fullback/Wide receiver (1946–49), 6'4″, 245 lbs.

Hart may have been one of the best players in the history of college football. Imagine if he had played in cleats that fit.

Hart was a stellar football, baseball, basketball, and track performer at Turtle Creek High School, in Pennsylvania. He was a blue-chip prospect who turned down many offers, including one from the nearby University of Pittsburgh, to join head coach Frank Leahy in South Bend. Hart was a large man for his time, and when he showed up for his first practice in 1946 he requested size fourteen shoes. Equipment manager John MacAllister

In Heisman Trophy-winner Leon Hart's four seasons at Notre Dame the team went 36-0-1 and won three national championships.

heard him correctly, but handed Hart a pair of size thirteen shoes. Hart pointed out the error, and the gruff MacAllister shot back, "Nobody that wore size fourteens was ever any good—so you're wearing thirteens." Sure enough, Hart wreaked havoc on the opposition for four seasons with his feet crammed in under-sized cleats. His feet would finally get relief when he entered the professional ranks. That was just one of the many true tales about the big man.

Hart, one of only two linemen ever to win the Heisman Trophy (the other was Yale's Larry Kelly in 1936), was one of the last of the great two-way football players. Notre Dame did not lose one game during Hart's four seasons, compiling a jaw-dropping record of 36–0–1, and the Fighting Irish won three national championships. On offense he was a fullback and wide receiver, and did his job admirably. He was an outstanding blocker with soft hands, but he was far more accomplished on defense. Of course, Hart was big, and along with his size came strength. He was also surprisingly quick and agile and attacked the football. No player was more responsible for those great years at Notre Dame than

Hart. He was a first-team All-American in 1947, 1948, and 1949; in the latter two years he was a consensus pick. After his senior year Hart won two awards—the Heisman Trophy and the Maxwell Award—which recognized him as the nation's top player.

Hart's scope ranged beyond college football. He beat out National League Most Valuable Player Jackie Robinson and Sam Snead (who won both the Masters and PGA Championship in golf) to win Male Athlete of the Year from the Associated Press. Not bad for a guy with sore feet.

Hart graduated with a degree in mechanical engineering, but the drafting table was put on hold for seven years while he continued his football success. The Detroit Lions selected him in the first round of the 1950 NFL draft. He was a member of three championship teams in Detroit, and as one of the last players to play on both sides of the line of scrimmage, he was named an All-Pro on offense and defense in his second season. In 1957, Hart retired from the game and was elected into the College Football Hall of Fame in 1973.

HAYES, DAVE
End (1917, 1919–20), 5'8", 160 lbs.

Hayes's football career at Notre Dame appeared as if it would last just one season. He made the team as a walk-on in 1917 and overcame the handicap of a small frame (5-foot-8, 160 pounds) with an outstanding first few days of practice to become a starting end. He then went off to serve in the Army during World War I, and a bullet shattered his left leg. There was doubt whether Hayes would ever walk again, and a return to football seemed out of the question.

Hayes, from Hartford, Connecticut, made it back to South Bend for the 1919 season. He was not only back on the football team, he was back in the starting lineup by the second game of the season. Second-year coach Knute Rockne directed his charges that season to a 9–0 record. Hayes also played in 1920, another 9–0 Notre Dame season.

The miraculous comeback was not the first time Hayes had beaten the odds. He was a New England prep school kid who worked his way through prestigious Phillips Exeter Academy. In 1916 he graduated and headed off to South Bend—broke. He was not a known athlete, but that didn't stop him from stopping by the office of university president Father Matthew J. Walsh. The gutsy kid not only told the president that he wanted to go to Notre Dame, but that he wanted to play football for Knute Rockne. Walsh must have liked Hayes's attitude, because he offered him a scholarship, and the kid got to live both dreams. Hayes had to help pay for his "scholarship" by waiting tables in a local restaurant, above which he lived. He went on to play two seasons of professional football for the Green Bay Packers before retiring.

HEAP, JOSEPH LAWRENCE
Halfback (1951–54), 5′11″, 180 lbs.

Heap, a three-time Academic All-American, was one of ten children. Back in

During 1954, versatile halfback Joe Heap was the top scorer, kick returner, and receiver as well as second on the team in rushing.

Abita Springs, Louisiana, he was a standout on the football and track teams at Holy Cross High School. The football team won the New Orleans city championship in his junior and senior seasons—1949 and 1950—and Heap was an all-state player in his senior year.

In 1954, his senior year at Notre Dame, the Fighting Irish had a record of 9–1 under first-year head coach Terry Brennan. In his third season as a starter, Heap was a versatile weapon. The halfback was the team's leading scorer, with 48 points, and top receiver, with 18 receptions for 369 yards, and also the leader in kickoff returns, with 7 for 143 yards. He was also second on the team in rushing, with 110 carries for 594 yards.

The New York Giants picked Heap in the first round of the 1955 NFL draft. He played one season for the team.

HEARDEN, THOMAS
Running back (1924–26), 5′9″, 160 lbs.

"Red" Hearden had a fruitful career at Notre Dame, both athletically and academically. As a sophomore from Green Bay, Wisconsin, he was a reserve on Knute Rockne's 10–0 national championship team in 1924. He started the next season, in which the team was 7–2–1, and was a cocaptain in 1926, when the team finished 9–1.

Hearden played for the Green Bay Packers in 1927 and 1928, and for the Chicago Bears in 1928, but eventually he went into football coaching, starting off at St. Norbert's High School in West DePere, Wisconsin, and moving his way up the ranks as an assistant coach for Marquette University, the University of Wisconsin, and the Green Bay Packers. He retired in 1957 due to poor health.

HEAVENS, JEROME
Fullback (1975–78), 6′0″, 204 lbs.

Heavens was a potent combination of size, speed, and dependability. Along with quarterback Joe Montana and running back Vagas Ferguson, he was part of an offensive combination that gave opposing defenses fits.

Heavens hit the Notre Dame scene from East St. Louis, Illinois, in 1975, and, as a freshman, was a starter and the school's leading rusher, with 129 carries for 756 yards and 5 touchdowns. He also caught 8 passes for 64 yards and made 1 tackle. During the third game his sophomore season was shortened when he sustained a knee injury. Nevertheless, Heavens still managed 204 yards on 54 carries, plus 2 receptions for 22 yards. He was back in the starting lineup the following season, during which Dan Devine's team went 11–1 and captured the national championship. He narrowly missed a 1,000-yard season and would have had one if he were not stopped for a loss in the season finale, a 48–10 drubbing of Miami. He finished as the team's leading rusher with 994 yards on 229 runs from scrimmage, and was third on the team in receiving, with 12 catches for 133 yards. In 1978, as a senior, he had 728 yards and 4 touchdowns on 178 carries and caught 13 passes for 113 yards. In Notre Dame's 35–34 come-from-behind Cotton Bowl victory over Houston, he rushed 16 times for 71 yards and made 4 receptions for 60 yards.

Heavens finished his college career with 2,682 yards rushing and 15 touchdowns. Heavens also caught 35 passes for 332 yards. His total surpassed the great George Gipp and made him the school's all-time leading rusher. He ranks fourth on the list, two spots behind former teammate Ferguson. Despite the 3,014 yards of total offense, he never made an All-American team, and was only a ninth-round draft pick of the Chicago Bears in 1979. He did not play in the NFL.

CAREER STATS

Year	Att.	Yards	Avg.	TDs
1975	129	756	5.9	5
1976	54	204	3.8	0
1977	229	994	4.3	6
1978	178	728	4.1	4
Total	590	2,685	4.5	15

HECK, ANDY
Offensive tackle/Tight end (1985–88), 6'7", 258 lbs.

The 1988 national championship team was a young squad to achieve such an accomplishment. Heck, from Annandale, Virginia, was one of only two seniors to start on that team. His move to the offensive line to shore up a unit that had been depleted by injury certainly helped the team reach its goals of an undefeated season and national championship under head coach Lou Holtz. After his resounding success at his new position, one could only wonder what his career would have been had he played up front for four seasons.

Heck had been a tight end for the first three years of his career in South Bend. Then, faced with the dilemma of needing depth at offensive tackle, Holtz moved Heck to the line during the spring drills after his junior year. Heck turned out to be a fine blocker; he started all twelve games that season and shared the team mark of 256:16 of field time with center Mike Heldt. Heck's teammates honored him with the Nick Pietrosante Award for spirit and courage. He was also a consensus All-American. The Seattle Seahawks used the fifteenth pick in the 1989 NFL draft to select him. Heck played in Seattle until 1993, and as of 1998, played for the Chicago Bears for five seasons before moving to the Washington Redskins in 1999.

HEENAN, PAT
End (1959), 6'2", 190 lbs.

After tearing up the intramural ranks for three years in South Bend, Heenan decided to do head coach Joe Kuharich a favor and lend his services to the Notre Dame varsity. Through his junior year, he was an all-campus end in the recreational league but had never played a minute of intercollegiate ball. Heenan had experienced football at its highest level, however. During his time as a high school student in Detroit, Michigan, he worked as an assistant to Detroit Lions trainer Hugh Burns.

In his senior year of college, Heenan decided to give the college team a whirl. He not only made the team as a walk-on (an improbable task), he was the team's starting end (a nearly impossible task). A natural athlete, Heenan was the team's second-leading receiver, with 12 catches for 198 yards and a touchdown. On defense he made 28 tackles. He was not selected in the NFL draft, but did play a season for the Washington Redskins.

HEIMKREITER, STEVE
Linebacker (1975–78), 6′2″, 228 lbs.

Heimkreiter's career at Notre Dame was abbreviated because of injuries in his freshman and junior seasons. But he did make the most of his healthy time, racking up an incredible amount of tackles. The fact is, if Heimkreiter, from Cincinnati, Ohio, had had four healthy seasons, he may very well have become the school's all-time leader in tackles.

Stuck in the middle of a fine run of linebackers whose careers overlapped (including Bob Golic and Bob Crable), Heimkreiter was limited to 42 minutes his freshman year. He was a starting outside linebacker the next year and played nearly 220 minutes, leading the team with 118 tackles. Heimkreiter's junior year was mixed. He missed three entire games because of injuries but still recorded 98 tackles (third behind Golic and defensive end Ross Browner). As a senior, it all came together for Heimkreiter. He had 160 tackles, breaking Golic's year-old record of 146 (Golic had 152 in 1978). Crable has held the record since 1979, when he made 187 tackles. Heimkreiter finished his career with 398 tackles, third on the school's all-time list through 2000. Ahead of him are only fellow linebackers and teammates Crable, with 521, and Golic, with 479.

The Baltimore Colts selected Heimkreiter in the eighth round of the 1979 NFL draft, and he played for them in 1980.

HELDT, MIKE
Center (1987–90), 6′4″, 267 lbs.

Heldt, of Tampa, Florida, was a mainstay and the anchor of Notre Dame's offensive lines at the end of the 1980s. After playing backup to Chuck Lanza as a freshman, Heldt started three years at center, a total of 37 consecutive games. As a sophomore he shared the team's playing-time lead, of 256:16, with fellow offensive lineman Andy Heck. In 1989 he started every game as a junior, and for his efforts was named an honorable mention All-American. As a senior, Heldt was back in his familiar position, and was second on the team in playing time (slightly behind quarterback Rick Mirer), with 298:27. Again, Heldt was an All-American. In 1991, he was a tenth-round draft pick of the San Diego Chargers. His National Football League career consisted of two seasons (1992 and 1993) with the Baltimore Colts.

HELWIG, JOHN
Guard/Linebacker (1948–50), 6′2″, 194 lbs.

Helwig was a man for three seasons at Notre Dame. If he wasn't playing football, he could probably be found performing for the track and field team during the indoor or outdoor seasons. He had attended Los Angeles's Mt. Carmel High School, where he set a scholastic shot put record.

In 1948, Helwig earned his first letter as a backup guard on the football team. The next year, during a temporary switch to two-platoon football, he became a starting linebacker. He was on the first squad in 1949 when Frank Leahy's team went 10–0 and won the national championship, and he was again a starting linebacker as a senior. Amazingly, football may not have been Helwig's best sport at Notre Dame. He set indoor and outdoor school records in the shot put. In the eleventh round of the 1950 NFL draft he was drafted by the Bears, and played for them from 1953 to 1956.

HENTRICH, CRAIG ANTHONY
Kicker/Punter (1989–92), 6'1", 197 lbs.

Hentrich came to Notre Dame from Marquette High School in Alton, Illinois, with a fabulous reputation. In addition to kicking and punting, Hentrich also played safety and quarterback. At Notre Dame, he was a versatile kicker and as effective as a punter as he was as a placekicker. He holds the school record for punting average (44.1 yards) and extra points (177) and extra-point percentage (.983), as he missed just 3. With 294 career points, Hentrich is second in all-time scoring at Notre Dame. His 39 field goals tied Dan Reeve's 1977 mark for second in school history behind John Carney, who made 51 three-pointers in 1986. He set the school's single-season record for punting average as a freshman (44.6 yards) and broke it the following year when his kicks averaged 44.9 yards. Also as a freshman, Hentrich kicked 8 field goals and made 44 of his 45 extra-point attempts, for 68 points.

As a sophomore, the four-year letter winner nailed all 41 of his extra-point attempts and 16 of his 20 field goals for a kicker's-record 89 points. Hentrich missed two games with a knee injury as a junior, but that hardly slowed down this stat machine. He attempted only 8 field goals (but made 5), and set a school record with 48 extra points, not missing any. In 1991 his punting was down to 42.9 yards per kick.

Hentrich had successful knee surgery to repair a torn ligament and was alive and kicking by the fall of his senior season. He averaged 43.8 yards per punt, and made 10 of 13 field goals and 44 of 46 extra points (his first misses since his freshman year). He finished with 74 points and was twice honored as an honorable mention All-American (as both a punter and kicker). After Notre Dame, Hentrich was selected in the eighth round of the 1993 NFL draft by the New York Jets. He punted with the Green Bay Packers from 1994 to 1997, and joined the Tennessee Oilers in 1998.

CAREER STATS

KICKING

Year	FG	PAT	Points
1989	8–15	44–45	68
1990	16–20	41–41	89
1991	5–8	48–48	63
1992	10–13	44–46	74
Total	39–56	177–180	294

PUNTING

Year	Punts	Yards	Avg.	Long
1989	26	1,159	44.6	66
1990	34	1,526	44.9	63
1991	23	986	42.9	61
1992	35	1,534	43.8	62
Total	118	5,205	44.1	66

HERING, FRANK
Quarterback (1896); Head coach (1896–98), 5'9", 154 lbs.

Hering was Notre Dame's first paid football coach. In three seasons, from 1896 through 1898, the South Bend resident (who was also the school's first basketball coach) led Notre Dame to a 12–6–1 record.

Hering, who also came up with the idea of Mother's Day, played end and quarterback for Chicago in 1893 and 1894, moved to Bucknell in 1895, and finally to Notre Dame the following year, when he served as both coach and captain. He was a confident and poised leader and was a master at taking advantage of his opponent's weaknesses. His team ripped the South Bend Commercial Athletic Club 46–0, and the next year many of those kids showed up at Notre Dame to play for the coach. Notre Dame spread 15 touchdowns among nine players (none of whom were named Frank Hering) in a 82–0 victory over Highland Views. The next year he became the first player to stay on as coach.

He was so influential that Knute Rockne named an award after him. The Hering Award is presented to the most outstanding and most improved players who participate in spring workouts. Rockne devised the award to encourage participation in the off-season practice sessions.

HO, REGGIE
Kicker (1987–88), 5'5", 135 lbs.

Ho didn't try out for the Notre Dame football team until his junior year. He wanted to get his academics in order before taking on the responsibility of Division I athletics. He made the team as a walk-on but kicked only 1 extra point. The following year, however, Ho led the team in scoring, with 59 points. The former soccer player and placekicker at St. Louis High School in St. Louis made 9 of 12 field goals and 32 of 36 extra points for Notre Dame as a senior. He kicked 2 extra points and a 32-yard field goal to lead Notre Dame past West Virginia in the 1989 Fiesta Bowl, clinching a 12–0 season and a national championship for head coach Lou Holtz and his team.

Ho graduated with a grade point average of 3.7 and was named a second-team Academic All-American after his senior season. He chose medical school over an additional year of football eligibility.

HOFFMAN, FRANK
Guard/Tackle (1930–31), 6'2", 224 lbs.

A late start in football didn't stop Hoffman from contributing to the Fighting Irish gridiron program. The Seattle, Washington, native's introduction into the game was as a sophomore in South Bend, when he successfully made the team as a walk-on. As a junior, Hoffman earned his first letter as a reserve guard, as Notre Dame went 10–0 and won the 1930 national title. Head coach "Hunk" Anderson moved "Nordy" to right guard for his senior season. He made the first team and made himself into one of the nation's best linemen, repeatedly playing through injuries and earning All-American honors.

Hoffman was more than just a big lug on the football team. He was an accomplished pianist, and in his day was one of the best shot putters in Notre Dame history. After leaving Notre Dame he went on to great things, one of which was induction into the College Football Hall of Fame. In professional life, he became head of the United Steel Workers legislative office, executive director of the Democratic Senatorial Campaign Committee, and sergeant at arms of the United States Senate.

HOGAN, DON
Halfback (1962), 5'11", 185 lbs.

Hogan, from Chicago, Illinois, was on his way to an outstanding career at Notre Dame, but tragedy struck him and his family. After a stellar sophomore season, Hogan was in a car accident during Christmas break. In the wreck, his sister was killed and his hip was crushed. Hogan did try to make it back on the field, but he just couldn't do it. He then wrote a heroic farewell letter to the squad that went down as proof of his determination and courage when everything seemed to be going against him.

Reggie Ho (lifted up by Pete Graham in a victory embrace) was the kicker on the 1988 national championship team. (Bill Panzica)

In 1962, as a first-year varsity sophomore, Hogan led the team in rushing as the starting right halfback, with 454 yards and 3 touchdowns on 90 carries. He was also second in receiving, with 12 catches for 146 yards, and kickoff returns, with 9 for 206 yards. He also made a 2-point conversion and 15 tackles.

HOLLOWAY, JABARI
Tight end (1997–2000), 6′3″, 260 lbs.

Holloway, who prepped at Sandy Creek High School in Tyrone, Georgia, was a tremendous asset to the Fighting Irish offense throughout his career by combining a large frame that led to a nice target and many receptions to go along with exceptional blocking ability. His 16.9 yard-per-catch average for his college career proved he was a load to pull down after catching the ball.

Holloway was one of only six freshmen to earn a letter in 1997 as he played in eleven games, starting six, including the Independence Bowl against LSU. For the season, he caught 8 passes for 144 yards and a touchdown. By his sophomore season, Holloway was Notre Dame's full-time starter at tight end, coming off the bench only against USC when the Irish went with a three-receiver look. He finished second on the team with 15 catches for 262 yards. Holloway also scored 2 touchdowns.

As a junior, Holloway started all twelve of Notre Dame's games and caught 12 passes for 189 yards and 3 touchdowns. He scored an additional touchdown by falling on the ball in the end zone against USC with 2:40 to play in the game, giving Notre Dame a 1-point victory. Holloway was a Football News honorable mention All-American.

Holloway, who makes up for his less-than-ideal height with tremendous leaping ability, was named one of four Irish captains during his senior season, along with fellow tight end Dan O'Leary. He added 6 receptions and 97 yards to bring his career totals to 41 catches for 692 yards. He was selected by the New England Patriots in the fourth round of the 2001 National Football League draft (119 overall). Two rounds later, Holloway was joined in the draft by O'Leary, who was selected by Buffalo with the 195th selection.

HOLOHAN, PETE
Flanker (1978–80), 6′5″, 228 lbs.

Head coach Dan Devine recruited Holohan to play quarterback—but it didn't work out. He didn't throw passes for the Notre Dame varsity. He caught them.

It should come as no surprise that Holohan was such an adaptive athlete. As a senior at Liverpool High School in New York, he was the first kid in state history to earn all-state honors in both football and basketball. Football was his dominant sport, as he also gained prep All-American honors. In 1978, after a year on the Notre Dame junior varsity, he was moved to flanker as a sophomore. An injury to Tom Domin during the team's training camp opened up a spot for Holohan on the first team, and the impressive athlete took advantage of it. He caught 20 passes for 301 yards as a sophomore, 22 passes for 386 yards as a junior, and 21 passes for 296 as a senior.

In the 1981 NFL draft, Holohan was selected in the seventh round as a tight end by the San Diego Chargers. He turned out to be a steal, outlasting many players picked ahead of him over a twelve-year career. He played for the Chargers (1981–87), the Los Angeles Rams (1988–90), the Kansas City Chiefs (1991), and the Cleveland Browns (1992). He finished his pro career with 363 receptions for 3,981 yards and 16 touchdowns.

CAREER STATS

Year	Rec.	Yards	Avg.	TDs
1978	20	301	15.1	1
1979	22	386	17.5	0
1980	21	296	13.2	1
Total	63	983	15.6	2

HOLTZ, LOU
Head coach (1986–96)

Lou Holtz's association with Notre Dame goes back to his grade school days. The Sisters of Notre Dame taught him at St. Aloysius High School in the 1940s. When the kids left class for lunch, recess, or at the end of the day, they did so to the tune of the Notre Dame Victory March. The Follansbee, West Virginia, native grew up in East Liverpool, Ohio, and became a student of the football program. He would read newspaper accounts of the team and tune in to games on the radio. Those were high times at Notre Dame during the Frank Leahy era, and Notre Dame was a dominant force, winning more than 85 percent of its games. Holtz was a young Catholic school student in the Midwest, and Notre Dame seemed like heaven.

About forty years later Holtz got to live his dream, as he was named the twenty-seventh head coach in Notre Dame history. He had his work cut out for him. It was a long and circuitous route to the top, as Holtz bounced around college and pro football for twenty-six years before finding his way to South Bend. During the Gerry Faust era, which produced a 30–27 record from 1981 to 1985, Notre Dame had fallen off its perch in the highest echelon of college football.

The Notre Dame head coaching job not only carries a great deal of prestige, it is also packed with high-stakes pressure. It is considered by some to be one of the hardest jobs, if not *the* hardest job, in sports. Holtz was more than up for the challenge. He was armed with the smarts and the energy to bring Notre Dame back to national prominence, and by the end of his second season his mission was complete.

From 1987 to 1995, Notre Dame went to nine consecutive January bowl games, including seven on New Year's Day. His 132 games coached ranks first on Notre Dame's all-time list, and his one hundred victories trails only Knute Rockne's 105. Three times during his tenure, Notre Dame did not play cream-puff schedules to get the Fighting Irish back in the win column, but played the toughest schedule in college football. Under his watch, Notre Dame was 32–20–2 against teams in the Associated Press Top Twenty-Five.

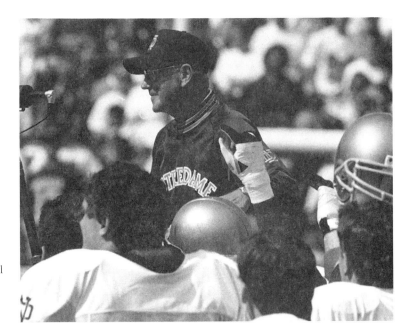

The Notre Dame football team celebrates one of a hundred victories with coach Lou Holtz. (Bill Panzica)

The team's ascent was rapid. In 1986, Notre Dame went 5–6 but showed signs of improvement, as five of the losses were by a total of 14 points. The next year Tim Brown won the Heisman Trophy and led the Fighting Irish to an 8–4 record, with wins over Michigan, Michigan State, and USC. Notre Dame was still playing on the first day of 1988, but lost to Texas A&M, 35–10, in the Cotton Bowl. Holtz was named one of four finalists for the Football Writers Association of America Coach of the Year Award.

His third season in South Bend was also his best. Notre Dame went 12–0 to win the national championship, and Holtz was named Coach of the Year by the Football Writers Association of America. The Fighting Irish clinched the national title with a 34–21 victory over West Virginia in the Fiesta Bowl. Notre Dame had also beaten number one Miami (of Florida), 31–30, in the season's sixth game. It was the only national championship the team would win under Holtz.

The next year Notre Dame was the consensus preseason pick to win it all. The Fighting Irish steamrolled through the regular season, winning all of its first eleven games and taking out Big Ten champ Michigan and Pac Ten champ USC. Miami's 27–10 victory in the final game of the season, however, was sweet revenge for the previous season's loss. On January 1, Notre Dame was back in Miami to beat Colorado, 21–6, in the Orange Bowl. By season's end, though, Notre Dame had dropped one notch and finished second in the final Associated Press poll.

Notre Dame dropped to 9–3 and 10–3 the next two seasons. In 1992, Notre Dame was 10–1–1, and the following year, 1993, the Irish won eleven of twelve games, including the Cotton Bowl, 24–21, over Texas A&M. In 1994, Notre Dame barely eked out a winning season, going 6–5–1.

The year 1995 was particularly rough for Holtz. It began with a 17–15 loss at home to Northwestern, which was a perennial pushover, but that year won its conference title. Holtz missed one game when he had to undergo neck surgery and coached another from a box above the stadium to avoid further injury. He only went down to spend the game's final minutes on the sideline. The Fighting Irish finished the season with a 9–3 record, which upped Holtz's ten-year total to 92–27–2, giving him the most victories over ten seasons of any coach in the program's history. Before stepping down, he added eight more victories in his final season to reach the milestone of one hundred wins. His only explanation for his exit was that "it just feels right." Less than a week later he was replaced by his defensive coordinator, Bob Davie.

CAREER RECORD

Year	W	L	T	Bowl
1986	5	6	0	No bowl appearance
1987	8	4	0	Cotton, L, Texas A&M, 10–35
1988	12	0	0	Fiesta, W, West Virginia, 34–21*
1989	12	1	0	Orange, W, Colorado, 21–6
1990	9	3	0	Orange, L, Colorado, 9–10
1991	10	3	0	Sugar, W, Florida, 39–28
1992	10	1	1	Cotton, W, Texas A&M, 28–3
1993	11	1	0	Cotton, W, Texas A&M, 24–21
1994	6	5	1	Fiesta, L, Colorado, 24–41
1995	9	3	0	Orange, L, Florida State, 26–31
1996	8	3	0	No bowl appearance
Totals	100	30	2	5–4

*Notre Dame won the national championship.

Before he came to Notre Dame, Holtz coached at the University of Iowa, William and Mary, the University of Connecticut, Ohio State University, North Carolina State, the University of Arkansas, the University of Minnesota, and in the NFL for the New York Jets. His career record was 216–95–8 when he left Notre Dame, and he ranks eleventh in victories among all NCAA Division I-A coaches. Eventually he became the ninth person to be named an honorary alumnus of the University of Notre Dame. He was bestowed the honor on April 27, 1990, joining Ara Parseghian, Gerry Faust, and basketball coach Richard "Digger" Phelps. He will have a chance to add to his record beginning in the 1999 season. After working in the broadcast booth in 1997 and 1998, Holtz was ready to go back to the sidelines and accepted the head coaching job at the University of South Carolina for a reported $1 million a season.

HORNUNG, PAUL
Quarterback/Fullback (1954–56),
6'2", 205 lbs.

As a senior, Paul Hornung, from Louisville, Kentucky, accomplished the near impossible. He played for one of the worst teams in Notre Dame history and was named the best college football player in the nation.

Out of high school, Hornung was considered more of a prospect for basketball than for football. As a sophomore at Notre Dame, he scored 6.1 points per game for the hoop team. On the football team he was a backup fullback who carried the ball just 23 times, gaining 59 yards. He also threw 19 passes and completed 5 for 36 yards.

In his junior year, Hornung played primarily at quarterback. He completed 46 of 103 passes for 743 yards and 9 touchdowns, and rushed for 472 yards and 6 touchdowns. On defense, Hornung intercepted 5 passes, including 2 in a 21–7 victory over fourth-ranked Navy, a game in which he also rushed for 1 touchdown and passed for another. It was just another day on the gridiron for the soon-to-

Heisman Trophy–winner Paul Hornung went on to an outstanding career in the pros with the Green Bay Packers and was inducted into both the College and Pro Football Halls of Fame.

be All-American. In another game, a 17–14 victory over Iowa, he threw a game-tying touchdown pass and kicked the game-winning field goal. He also passed for 354 yards in a season-ending loss to USC.

He was even better his senior season, although the team wasn't. Notre Dame was 2–8 in 1956, and whatever success they had could be attributed to Hornung. He finished second in the country in total offense, with 1,337 yards; he rushed for 7 touchdowns, passed for 3 others, and kicked 14 extra points. He was responsible for more than half of the entire team's offense. Hornung was a consensus All-American and is the only player from a losing team to win the Heisman Trophy. What makes his performance even more incredible is that he played the last part of the season with two dislocated thumbs.

In 1957, Hornung was a first-round draft pick of the Green Bay Packers. His first two years in the NFL were not exactly stellar. He was bounced around from quarterback to fullback to halfback to tight end, and it stunted his development as a player. When legendary coach Vince Lombardi took over the team in 1959, however, he found a permanent home for Hornung at left halfback. He also let Hornung handle the place-kicking chores.

Hornung appreciated the stability, and from that point onward was one of the most prolific scorers in the league. In 1960, he scored an NFL-record 176 points—15 touchdowns, 15 field goals, and 41 extra points—and rushed for 671 yards. He served in the army in 1961 but was given leave on Sundays to suit up for Green Bay, and played well enough to be named NFL Player of the Year. For the second consecutive season he led the league in scoring. This time it was 146 points, including 19 in a 37–0 victory over the New York Giants in the NFL Championship Game.

The Hornung story then took a couple of bad turns. He missed most of the 1962 season with injuries, and was suspended by Commissioner Pete Rozelle the following year due to gambling allegations. He was back in 1964 and scored 107 points. Health problems forced him to retire in 1966.

Hornung proved to be a tough and smart NFL player who could block, run, catch, and kick. In nine NFL seasons he rushed for 3,711 yards on 893 carries and caught 130 passes for 1,480 yards. He finished with 760 points on 62 touchdowns, 66 field goals, and 190 extra points. In 1985 he was inducted into the College Football Hall of Fame, and one year later he was bestowed the same honor by the Pro Football Hall of Fame. Hornung is now a businessman who handles TV color commentary for college football games.

CAREER STATS

PASSING

Year	Att.	Comp.	Pct.	Yards	TDs
1954	19	5	.263	36	0
1955	103	46	.447	743	9
1956	111	59	.531	917	3
Total	233	110	.472	1,696	12

RUSHING

Year	Att.	Yards	Avg.	TDs
1954	23	59	6.9	2
1955	92	472	5.1	6
1956	94	420	4.5	7
Total	209	951	5.0	15

HOWARD, JOE
Split end (1981–84), 5'9", 171 lbs.

Howard did not let the fact that he was just 5-foot-9 and 171 pounds slow him down. He made the most out of his stay in South Bend, using his speed to play for both the football and basketball teams. The Clinton, Maryland, native got off to a quick start for the football team. As a freshman he cracked the starting lineup midway through the season and caught 17 passes for 463 yards. He was a big-play threat, averaging 27.2 yards a catch. In his first campaign he finished with 3 touchdowns, including a record 96-yard connection with quarterback Blair Kiel in a 35–3 rout of Georgia Tech.

Howard continued to contribute as a sophomore, catching 28 passes for 524 yards and 2 touchdowns. As a junior he grabbed 27 passes for 464 yards and 2 touchdowns and led the squad in punt returns, with 28 for 202 yards. In his junior season, Howard helped the Fighting Irish beat Boston College, 19–18, in the Liberty Bowl. (A few days after the December 29 game, the basketball coach invited Howard onto the team as a walk-on. He started eleven games at point guard and scored 5.5 points a game; his teammates voted him the most inspirational player.)

Injuries interrupted the first half of Howard's senior season, but he still had an effective year, with 13 receptions for 212 yards. He also averaged 7.5 yards on punt returns. Howard's 19.6 yards per reception is fourth on the school's all-time list for a career, and a testament to his status as a big-play receiver. Howard's size caught up with him in the NFL draft, but many teams were probably sorry they did not take a flyer on the fleet receiver, who forged a six-year NFL career. From 1986 through 1988 he played for the Buffalo Bills, and then played for the Washington Redskins from 1989 through 1991.

CAREER STATS

Year	Rec.	Yards	Avg.	TDs
1981	17	463	27.2	3
1982	28	524	18.7	2
1983	27	464	17.2	2
1984	13	212	16.3	0
Total	85	1,663	19.6	7

HUARTE, JOHN
Quarterback (1962–64), 6′0″, 180 lbs.

It would have been generous to consider Huarte even a remote candidate for the Heisman Trophy as he entered his senior season. Injuries limited him to 8 passes as a sophomore and 42 as a junior. A coach who believes in a player, however, can make a big difference, and Ara Parseghian helped Huarte win the coveted Heisman award.

Parseghian was brought in to turn around a Notre Dame program that had gone 2–7 in 1963. He put the ball in Huarte's hands, and when it wasn't in his hands it was either in the air or in receiver Jack Snow's hands. That year Huarte, who had an odd yet extremely accurate sidearm passing motion, completed 114 of 205 passes for 2,062 yards and 16 touchdowns. Snow caught 60 of those balls for 1,114 yards, second best in the NCAA. Notre Dame went 9–1 that season, and if it had not been for a 20–17 upset by USC in the season finale, Parseghian would have started off his rebuilding effort with a national title. Huarte beat out the University of Tulsa's Jerry Rhome for the Heisman and was also the United Press International Player of the Year and a consensus All-American. Huarte, who set twelve school records as a senior, was the first in an impressive line of quarterbacks for Parseghian, a list that also

Heisman Trophy–winning quarterback John Huarte set twelve school records in his senior season.

included Terry Hanratty, Joe Theismann, and Tom Clements.

The Philadelphia Eagles and New York Jets selected Huarte in the sixth round of the draft. Huarte chose New York, which, in retrospect, was probably the wrong choice. The Jets had also signed a flamboyant quarterback from the University of Alabama named Joe Namath, who was offered $400,000, twice the contract Huarte received. Namath became the American Football League's Rookie of the Year, while Huarte spent most of his first year on the taxi squad. The opportunity he received in his last year of college wasn't there his first year in the pros.

Huarte was released by the Jets in 1966 and wandered for eight seasons around the NFL and AFL as a backup, playing in Boston,

Philadelphia, Kansas City, Chicago, and Minnesota. He also played for Memphis of the World Football League. Huarte's entire professional career consisted of 19 completions on 48 passes for 230 yards and 1 touchdown. He retired in 1975.

CAREER STATS

Year	Att.	Comp.	Pct.	Yards	TDs	INT
1962	8	4	.500	38	0	0
1963	42	20	.467	243	1	0
1964	205	114	.556	2,062	16	11
Total	255	138	.541	2,343	17	11

HUFF, ANDY
Running back (1969, 1971–72),
5'11", 212 lbs.

Toledo, Ohio, native Huff was a dependable blocker and runner, especially in short-yardage situations for Ara Parseghian. He ran for 304 yards as a second-string halfback in his sophomore season, which was also the first year he earned a letter. After missing the 1970 season because of shoulder surgery, Huff returned as the Fighting Irish's starting fullback his junior season, 1971. He carried the ball 68 times and gained 295 yards and scored 2 touchdowns. As a senior, Huff was Notre Dame's second-leading rusher, with 567 yards on 124 carries. He also scored a team-high 60 points and was named offensive Most Valuable Player by the National Monogram Club.

HUFFMAN, DAVE
Center/Tackle (1975–78), 6'5", 245 lbs.

Once the ball is snapped, it's not always easy to pick out the center on a football team. He's often buried beneath a pile of wide bodies, but Dave Huffman came up with a plan that would make it easy for his mother to find him in these scrums. Huffman wore red elbow pads, which helped her pick him out of the crowd.

Huffman was a prep All-American at Dallas's Thomas Jefferson High School and went on to play alongside his brother, Tim,

at Notre Dame in 1977 and 1978. He began his Notre Dame career as a tackle but was shifted over to center in his sophomore season, during which he won the starting job. In 1977, he was the anchor of the offensive line that helped Notre Dame score 382 points and chalk up 4,840 yards of total offense en route to a national championship. During the season he played 308 minutes and may not have gotten the credit from the casual fan that quarterback Joe Montana, running back Jerome Heavens, and tight end Ken MacAfee did, but his play didn't go unnoticed. He was an exceptional blocker on runs as well as pass plays. A versatile athlete, he would also line up in a double tight end formation opposite MacAfee, and once caught a pass for 16 yards.

The next season he was just as good. He threw one memorable block that sprung Montana for a score in a 26–17 victory over Pittsburgh. Huffman, linebacker Bob Golic, and Montana were the three key elements in Notre Dame's 9–3 season, which earned the Fighting Irish a season-ending rank of seventh according to the Associated Press. Huffman was a consensus All-American, and Minnesota selected him in the second round of the 1979 NFL draft. He played center, guard, and tackle for twelve years for the Vikings before retiring in 1990 to become a broadcaster.

HUFFMAN, TIM
Guard/Tackle (1977–80), 6'5", 265 lbs.

Tim Huffman never rose to the heights that his All-American brother Dave did, but he still held a starting position on the offensive line for three seasons. Tim and Dave, both from Dallas, played together for a few minutes in 1977, Tim's freshman season, but the next year they played nearly the entire season together, Tim at guard, Dave at center. Tim started ten games as a junior, but injuries severely limited his play as a senior. The Green Bay Packers selected him in the ninth round of the 1981 NFL draft, and he played guard and tackle with the franchise until 1985.

HUGHES, ERNIE
Guard/Defensive end (1974–77),
6'3", 248 lbs.

Ernie Hughes, from Boise, Idaho, was a quick, strong lineman with outstanding technique who made a lot of noise at Notre Dame once he was moved from defense to offense. The Enforcer, as he was known, played defensive end as a freshman and made 4 tackles in 13 minutes of play.

The following season, first-year head coach Dan Devine moved Hughes over to the offensive line, where he started at guard for three seasons. He played 322 minutes his sophomore season, and even made more tackles (5) than he did as a freshman on defense. He also recovered a fumble. Hughes was named Offensive Player of the Game after a 31–30 victory over Air Force. The next year Hughes played 318 minutes and added 2 tackles and 2 fumble recoveries to his total.

Then, in 1977, he was part of something special. Notre Dame went 11–1 and won the national championship. Hughes was a second team All-American, and a big part of the 38–10 Cotton Bowl victory over Texas. He cleared the way for Jerome Heavens and Vagas Ferguson, both of whom rushed for more than 100 yards, and put the clamps down on Outland Trophy winner Brad Shearer, who made only one tackle.

The San Francisco 49ers selected Hughes in the third round of the 1978 NFL draft. He played there in 1978 and 1980, and then became a member of the New York Giants from 1981 to 1983.

HUNTER, AL
Halfback (1973, 1975–76), 5'11", 190 lbs.

Because he was suspended for his sophomore season, Hunter was limited to three seasons of play at Notre Dame. A blue-chip prospect and prep All-American out of J. H. Rose High School in Greenville, North Carolina, Hunter had speed that made many college scouts salivate.

A moody player with blazing speed (he was clocked at 9.3 seconds for the 100-yard dash and 21.4 seconds in the 220-yard dash in high school), he made up for lost time in his senior season when he gained a team-leading 1,058 yards on 233 carries and scored 12 touchdowns. His 78 points also led the Fighting Irish. He was third in receiving, with 15 catches, and returned 12 kickoffs for 241 yards. However, he was not higher than honorable mention on any All-America team.

Hunter began his career at Notre Dame as a second-string halfback, rushing for 150 yards on 32 carries and scoring 3 touchdowns as Notre Dame won the 1973 national championship under head coach Ara Parseghian. He also returned a kickoff for a score in Notre Dame's 24–23 victory over the University of Alabama in the Sugar Bowl. In 1975, after his 1974 suspension for having a female in his dorm room after curfew, Hunter rejoined the squad, and won the starting left halfback position, where he was second on the team in rushing. His 558 yards trailed only Jerome Heavens's 756 for the season. Hunter also scored 48 points. His best outing was against USC, when he rushed for 82 yards and a touchdown and passed for a 2-point conversion.

Hunter finished his career at Notre Dame with 1,766 yards (twentieth in the school's history), and also scored 23 touchdowns. The Seattle Seahawks selected him in the fourth round of the 1977 NFL draft. He played in Seattle for four seasons.

CAREER STATS

Year	Att.	Yards	Avg.	TDs
1973	32	150	4.7	3
1975	117	558	4.8	8
1976	233	1,058	4.5	12
Total	382	1,766	4.6	23

HUNTER, ART
Tackle/End/Center (1951–53), 6'3", 226 lbs.

The Akron, Ohio, native played a different position in each of his three college seasons, but the third position he played was a charm. He was strong, fast, and excelled at all three spots, drawing comparisons with tight end and lineman Dave Casper.

Hunter won his first letter as a sophomore center. In his junior year, he played right end and finished the season as the third-leading receiver among the Fighting Irish with 16 receptions for 246 yards and a touchdown. As a senior, Hunter finally found his best college position. He played offensive tackle, logged a tremendous 423 minutes of a possible 600, and recovered 3 fumbles, including 1 for a touchdown. His play earned him a spot in the East-West Shrine Game as well as consensus All-American status.

Hunter was one of three Notre Dame players to be selected in the first round of the 1954 NFL draft. Right halfback Johnny Lattner went to Pittsburgh, fullback Neil Worden went to Philadelphia, and Hunter went to Green Bay. He played center in the pros and was a member of the Packers in 1954; then, from 1956 to 1959, he went to Cleveland to play for the Browns. His career continued as a member of the Los Angeles Rams from 1960 to 1964, and he wrapped up his professional tour the following season with the Pittsburgh Steelers.

HUNTER, TONY
Tight end/Wingback/Split end (1979–82), 6'5", 226 lbs.

Hunter was Ohio's prep football player of the year in 1978 and was reunited with his high school coach at Notre Dame. Gerry Faust, who had coached Hunter at Cincinnati's Moeller High School, replaced Dan Devine as the Fighting Irish's coach in 1981, Hunter's junior season. The deep threat started seven games at split end his freshman season and caught 27 passes for 690 yards and

2 touchdowns. His 25.6-yards-per-catch average as a freshman was a single-season school record.

Hunter was an exceptional blend of size and speed, and he used it to lead Notre Dame in receiving the ensuing three seasons. He became the starting split end in 1980 and led the team in receiving, with 23 catches for 303 yards. He also rushed the ball 5 times for 52 yards. In 1981, reunited with Faust, Hunter played tight end, split end, and wingback. Again he was the team's leading pass catcher, with 28 receptions for 397 yards and 2 touchdowns. He also carried the ball 27 times for 68 yards and a touchdown.

By 1982, Hunter had become as good a blocker as a receiver, and he settled in to what was probably his natural position: tight end. As a starter, he was Notre Dame's leading receiver for the third consecutive season, with 42 catches for 507 yards, and was named a first-team All-American. As of 2000, he was the team's sixth all-time receiver, with 120 receptions for 1,897 yards.

The Buffalo Bills selected Hunter twelfth overall in the 1983 NFL draft. He played with the Bills in 1983 and 1984, and with the Los Angeles Rams from 1985 through 1987. In his NFL career, Hunter caught 134 passes for 1,501 yards and 9 touchdowns.

CAREER STATS

Year	Rec.	Yards	Avg.	TDs
1979	27	690	25.6	2
1980	23	303	13.2	1
1981	28	397	14.2	2
1982	42	507	12.1	0
Total	120	1,897	15.8	5

ISMAIL, RAGHIB RAMADAN
Flanker/Split end (1988–90),
5'10", 175 lbs.

"Rocket" Ismail could have relied only on his incredible 4.12 40-yard-dash speed to be a college standout, but the fleet-footed receiver also had moves to juke defenders and the guts to go across the middle of the field. Ismail was stunningly quick off the line, and he was not only tough to catch, he had the leg strength to break tackles in the event that he was caught. He put all of those skills together to play three All-American years at Notre Dame and nearly won the Heisman Trophy as a senior.

Ismail was born in Newark, New Jersey, and moved to Wilkes-Barre, Pennsylvania, after the death of his father. He went on to become one of the best prep athletes in Pennsylvania history. As a tailback, the blue-chip prospect rushed for 4,494 yards and 62 touchdowns in three years on the varsity football team at Meyers High School. He also won a state track and field championship in the 100 meters, long jump, and 400-meter relay.

Ismail weighed only 175 pounds and was too small to play tailback in college, but he certainly had the jets to play split end. That is where he would start half the games as a freshman, on a 12–0 team that won the national championship under head coach Lou Holtz. That season Ismail was clocked at 4.33 in the 40-yard dash. When he later worked out for NFL scouts, he would cut .21 off that time. Ismail caught 12 passes for 331 yards, intimidating defenses with a 27.6-yards-per-catch average. He also led the nation by averaging 36.1 yards on 12 kickoff returns.

That season he scored 4 touchdowns and was named an honorable mention All-American.

In 1989 Holtz moved Ismail to flanker to take advantage of his versatility, and Ismail performed incredibly well. For the season, he caught 27 passes for 535 yards, returned 20 kickoffs for 502 yards and 2 scores, averaged 7.5 yards on 64 carries for a total of 478 yards and 2 touchdowns, and returned 7 punts for 113 yards and another touchdown. He capped the season, in which Notre Dame went 12–1, with a Most Valuable Player performance in a 21–6 victory over the University of Colorado in the Orange Bowl. Ismail was named a consensus All-American; by the end of the season he had another distinction. He became the first college player to run back two kickoffs for touchdowns in two different games. As a freshman he scored twice on kickoffs against Rice University, and did it again as a sophomore against Michigan.

Ismail came back for his junior year in 1990 and devastated opposing defenses. He started at flanker and played a little tailback on a 9–3 Notre Dame team. He caught 32 passes for 699 yards and 2 touchdowns, rushed the ball 67 times for 537 yards (for 8.0 yards per carry) and 3 touchdowns, returned 14 kickoffs for 336 yards and a touchdown, and ran back 13 punts for 151 yards. A consensus first-team All-American, Ismail was named Player of the Year in 1990 by the Walter Camp Foundation and the *Sporting News*. Brigham Young quarterback Ty Detmer was the only player to finish ahead of Ismail in Heisman Trophy voting. Penn State coach Joe Paterno, who must have felt burned losing the local product, called Ismail "one of the three or four best players ever to play college football."

CAREER STATS

RECEIVING

Year	Rec.	Yards	Avg.	TDs
1988	12	331	27.6	2
1989	27	535	19.8	0
1990	32	699	21.8	2
Total	71	1,565	22.0	4

RUSHING

Year	Att.	Yards	Avg.	TDs
1988	No rushing attempts			
1989	64	478	7.5	2
1990	67	537	8.0	3
Total	131	1,015	7.7	5

KICKOFF RETURNS

Year	Ret.	Yards	Avg.	TDs
1988	12	433	36.1	2
1989	20	502	25.1	2
1990	14	336	24.0	1
Total	46	1,271	27.6	5

PUNT RETURNS

Year	Ret.	Yards	Avg.	TDs
1988	5	72	14.4	0
1989	7	113	16.1	1
1990	13	151	11.6	0
Total	25	336	13.4	1

ALL-PURPOSE YARDS

Year	Yards
1988	836
1989	1,628
1990	1,723
Total	4,187

Ismail's final college numbers, even without a senior year, were staggering. He amassed 4,187 all-purpose yards, and his 22.0 yards per reception is a Notre Dame career record. He also holds the record for touchdowns on kickoff returns, with 5. His 85-yards-per-kick-return average against Rice in 1988 also stands as a school record. And despite foregoing his final season of eligibility to enter the professional ranks, Ismail is near the top of the Fighting Irish record book in several return categories. He is second behind Tim Brown in kickoff return yards for a career (1,271) and kick return yards for a career (1,607). His 192 yards on three kickoff returns against the University of Michigan in 1989 trails only Paul Castner, who ran back 4 kickoffs for 253 yards against Kalamazoo in 1922. Ismail is third in kickoff return yards for a season (502), kickoff returns for a career (46), and fourth in kick return yards for a season (615). Had Ismail stayed for a fourth season, he would have likely held those and many other records.

Ismail decided to move on to the pros after his junior season and signed with the Toronto Argonauts of the Canadian Football League. After tearing up the Canadian league for two seasons, he came back to the United States and signed with the Los Angeles Raiders. In 1993, his first season in the NFL, he led the AFC in kickoff returns. He played for the Raiders until 1995, when he was traded to the Carolina Panthers. He joined the Dallas Cowboys in 1999.

IZO, GEORGE
Quarterback (1957–59), 6'2", 210 lbs.

Izo, from Barberton, Ohio, was Notre Dame's starting quarterback for a year and a half. In the 1958 season he came off the bench to lead the Fighting Irish in a 29–22 comeback victory over Purdue. That performance secured him the starting position during the rest of Terry Brennan's final season as coach. Izo led the team in passing, with 60 completions for 1,067 yards and 9 touchdowns. He also was a key defender, with 21 tackles and a team-high 4 interceptions. The next year, playing for first-year coach Joe Kuharich, Izo split time at quarterback with Don White and completed 44 of 95 passes for 661 yards and 6 touchdowns.

The Chicago Cardinals of the NFL and New York Titans of the AFL made Izo a first-round draft pick. He bounced around football for six seasons, playing for the Cardinals, the Washington Redskins, the Detroit Lions, and the Pittsburgh Steelers.

JACKSON, JARIOUS
Quarterback (1996–99), 6'1", 228 lbs.

Jackson waited three years to get his chance behind the center at Notre Dame after an All-American career and being ranked as the sixth-ranked quarterback by *Bluechip Illustrated* and number ten by *SuperPrep* out of Tupelo High School in Mississippi. The wait was well worth it for both Jackson and the Fighting Irish as he started his final two seasons and left school after breaking several records, many set by his predecessor, Ron Powlus. Jackson was also a tremendous team leader, acting as only the third sole captain of the Fighting Irish in thirty-two years—Rodney Culver (1991) and Mike Kovaleski (1986)—were the others.

Jackson played sparingly behind Powlus during his first two seasons and attempted 32 passes, completing 18 for 327 yards and 4 touchdowns. Taking the helm of the offense as a junior, Jackson proved ready to pick up where Powlus left off. Jackson, the only quarterback on the roster with game experience, finished the season thirteenth in the nation in passing efficiency (149.5), connecting on 104 of 188 passes for 1,740 yards, 13 touchdowns and only 6 interceptions. Jackson also rushed for 441 yards and 3 touchdowns. However, his season was not without a major setback. Enjoying his most productive game of the season against LSU, throwing for a career-high 276 yards and 2 touchdowns and rushing for 80 yards, Jackson brought the Irish from behind for a 39–36 victory. But, when taking an intentional safety to end the game, Jackson sprained the medial collateral ligament in his right knee, forcing him to miss the season finale against USC, a 10–0 loss that kept Notre Dame out of the Bowl Championship Series. Jackson, whose injury did not require surgery, was back on the field for the 1999 Gator Bowl, in which he completed 13 of 24 passes for 150 yards in the Irish loss.

Jackson didn't show any ill effects from his knee injury during his senior season. He set Notre Dame records including passing yards in a season (2,753), surpassing the mark Joe Theisman set in 1970 (2,429), and total offense (3,217), again topping Theisman's 1970 standard (2,820). Jackson, whose junior season was the sixth best for total offense (2,101) in school history, also broke records for pass attempts (316) and completions (184) in a season, previously held by Powlus (298 and 182, respectively). Jackson finished second to Kevin McDougal in career pass efficiency rating and fourth, behind only Powlus, Steve Beuerlein, and Rick Mirer, in career passing yards (4,820), third in touchdown passes (34) and second in career pass completion percentage (.571). The fourth-ranked quarterback in Notre Dame history was subsequently named one of fifteen semifinalists for the '99 *Football News* Offensive Player of the Year. Jackson, an honorable mention All-American and the Notre Dame National Monogram Clubs MVP, played in the All-Star Gridiron Classic.

The Denver Broncos picked Jackson in the seventh round of the 2000 National Football League draft.

CAREER STATS
PASSING

Year	Att.	Comp.	Pct.	Yards	TDs
1996	15	10	.667	181	3
1997	17	8	.471	146	1
1998	188	104	.553	1,740	13
1999	316	184	.582	2,753	17
Total	536	306	.571	4,820	34

RUSHING

Year	Att.	Yards	Avg.	TDs
1996	11	16	1.5	0
1997	8	36	4.5	3
1998	113	441	3.9	3
1999	140	464	3.3	7
Total	272	957	3.5	13

JEWETT, HARRY
Fullback/Halfback (1887–88)

The speedy Jewett scored Notre Dame's first-ever touchdown in a 26–6 loss to Michigan in 1888, earning a write-up from legendary scribe Grantland Rice who in the 1920s would coin the "Four Horsemen" nickname for Notre Dame's awesome backfield: "Jewett secured the ball, and by a magnificent run made [a] touchdown in Ann Arbor ground . . . [his] play was an elegant one and it caught the fancy of the crowd who were evidently pleased to see the Michigan team's [shutout] record broken."

That was not the only loss for the Chicago native that day. Jewett was at one time reported to be the world record holder in the 100-yard dash. That set up a match the same day against Michigan's fastest runner, James Duffy. Duffy won the race by a hair; Jewett's time was 11 seconds on a predigital stopwatch.

JOHNSON, ANTHONY
Fullback (1986–89), 6'0", 220 lbs.

A local product from South Bend, Johnson was a rugged, dependable, and mentally tough player who laid some monster blocks and was a key member of Notre Dame's 1988 national championship team. He was, however, far from the most celebrated player on the team, which included Tony Rice, Ricky Watters, and Raghib Ismail. In clearing the way for teammates to score in the red zone, Johnson strapped on the pads every week and did what was necessary.

As a freshman in 1986 he started five games at fullback, and on 80 carries gained 349 yards and scored 5 touchdowns. He also caught 6 passes for 53 yards. He was a full-time starter as a sophomore, and led the team with 11 touchdowns. He rushed for 366 yards on 78 carries, caught 4 passes for 110 yards, and returned 2 kickoffs for 55 yards.

During the undefeated national championship season of 1988 he carried the ball 69 times for 282 yards and 5 touchdowns. He also grabbed 7 passes for 128 yards and returned 2 kickoffs for 27 yards. The next year, as a senior, Johnson was a tri-captain who gained 515 yards on 131 carries and again scored 11 rushing touchdowns. He also caught 8 passes for 85 yards and 2 touchdowns, and led the team with 78 points. He earned honorable mention All-American honors and the Nick Pietrosante Award for courage, dedication, and spirit.

Johnson's four-year college career netted 1,512 yards on the ground. His 32 rushing touchdowns ties him for third all-time with Vagas Ferguson (in 1985, Allen Pinkett had 49, and in 1983 Louis "Red" Salmon had 36). Johnson is also fourth in overall touchdowns.

The Indianapolis Colts selected Johnson in the second round of the 1990 NFL draft (he was thirty-sixth overall). He played with the Colts until 1993, for the New York Jets in 1994, the Chicago Bears in 1995, and then joined the Carolina Panthers in 1996, coming into his own in the 1997 season, when he led the team in rushing, with 1,120 yards. His 1,312 yards from scrimmage also set a record for the fledgling franchise. His 1998 statistics were not nearly as spectacular (136 yards on 35 carries) but Johnson has been a solid contributor, and at press time was still on the Panthers's roster.

CAREER STATS

RUSHING

Year	Att.	Yards	Avg.	TDs
1986	80	349	4.4	5
1987	78	366	4.7	11
1988	69	282	4.1	5
1989	131	515	3.9	11
Total	358	1,512	4.2	32

RECEIVING					CAREER STATS				
Year	Rec.	Yards	Avg.	TDs	Year	Rec.	Yards	Avg.	TDs
1986	6	53	8.8	0	1995	0	0	0	0
1987	4	110	27.5	0	1996	25	449	18.0	2
1988	7	128	18.3	0	1997	42	596	14.2	2
1989	8	85	10.6	2	1998	43	692	16.1	6
Total	25	376	15.0	2	Totals	110	1,737	15.7	10

JOHNSTON, MALCOLM
Split end (1995–98), 6'5", 215 lbs.

Johnson improved each year he was in South Bend. After red-shirting his freshman season, and playing a mere 20:50 spread out over eleven games his first season on the varsity, Johnson caught his first of 110 college passes as a sophomore, the first of three consecutive seasons he would lead the Fighting Irish in yards receiving. The three-year college starter came to Notre Dame from Gonzaga College Prep High School in Washington, D.C., where he earned two letters each in football and track.

After playing sparingly as a red-shirt freshman, Johnson gained the most receiving yards on Notre Dame with 449 and was second in receptions with 25, only two behind Pete Chryplewicz in 1999 as a sophomore. His annual improvement continued for the next two seasons. As a junior, Johnson again led Notre Dame with 596 yards receiving. He had 42 catches, and was part of a powerful one-two punch with Bobby Brown, giving the Fighting Irish their first pair of 40-reception receivers in school history. As a senior, Johnson again achieved gains over the previous season with 43 catches for 692 yards and career-high 6 touchdowns, which came in six consecutive games, making it the longest streak in Fighting Irish history. This time he was clearly the number one receiver on the team as the second-leading receiver had just 15 receptions. The Pittsburgh Steelers selected Johnson in the fifth round of the 1999 National Football League draft. Johnson, who joined Jerry Wisne and Mike Rosenthal as fifth-round selection in the 1999 draft, later moved on to play for the New York Jets.

JOHNSTON, MIKE
Kicker (1980–83), 5'11", 185 lbs.

Maybe there's something in the mighty Genesee River, because Rochester, New York, grows good kickers for Notre Dame. Mike Johnston came to Notre Dame as an unknown commodity. He kicked only 2 field goals during his prep career at Rochester's Cardinal Mooney High School. College teams were not exactly stumbling over one another to fight for his services, but Notre Dame alumnus Bob Thomas, an Academic All-American kicker from Rochester, suggested Johnston to the Notre Dame coaching staff, and they gave him a shot as a walk-on.

Johnston's rise to the top was slow. He didn't even get a scholarship until his junior year. As a freshman, he handled kickoffs and made 1 extra point. As a sophomore, he again was in charge of kickoffs; Harry Oliver kicked the field goals and extra points during those two seasons. Then, in 1981, as a junior, Johnston had his best year of football ever. His "apprenticeship" was over, and he finally received a scholarship to play football. He immediately proved that he'd learned some tricks from Oliver, setting a single-season Notre Dame record by making 19 of 22 field goals. (Oliver, who'd kicked 18 field goals in 1980, was the reigning record holder, but John Carney, who kicked 21 field goals on 28 attempts in 1986, was the record holder as of 2000. Carney went on to score 87 points in 1986 on 24 extra points and 21 field goals.)

Johnston also made all 19 extra point attempts, for a total of 76 points, a Notre Dame record at the time. That kind of accuracy earned him honorable mention All-American status. He made all 33 of his extra points as a senior, but he was a bit off in the field goal category, making just 12 of 21. He never played in the NFL.

JOYCE, EDMUND

Edmund Joyce never played a down of football for the Fighting Irish. He never served as coach, either. That's not to say, however, that the Reverend Edmund P. Joyce was not an instrumental figure in Notre Dame football, and a titanic figure in the school and all of its athletic programs during his nearly four-decade tenure at the university.

Joyce was born in Honduras (his father worked for the United Fruit Company), and attended high school in Spartanburg, South Carolina. He was a sports fanatic who, when picking a college to go to, was lured to Notre Dame in part because of his interest in Knute Rockne's football program (now *that's* recruiting). He attended the school from 1933 to 1937, and his only relationship with the athletic department was getting cut from the varsity basketball team as a freshman. That, he would say later, was one of the biggest disappointments in his life.

Joyce studied for the priesthood at Holy Cross College in Washington, D.C. Twenty-two years after graduating he returned to South Bend, and on June 3, 1949, he was ordained in Sacred Heart Church on the Notre Dame campus. He didn't leave the university until he retired on May 31, 1987, twenty-three days after a double-domed athletic complex where the basketball and hockey teams play was renamed the Edmund P. Joyce Athletic and Convocation Center.

In between, Joyce helped reshape the school and its athletic program. His first position was that of assistant vice president of business affairs. Within a year he was promoted to acting vice president. He went off to study for a year in Oxford, and in 1952 returned to receive another promotion to executive vice president.

For thirty-five years Joyce was ostensibly the school's chief executive officer, working in the shadows of university president Reverend Theodore Hesburgh. He crunched

the numbers and oversaw the completion of more than forty new buildings. Meanwhile, under his reign, the endowment increased more than fortyfold, from about $9 million to $400 million. The annual operating budget of the ultrasuccessful private university, which Joyce was in charge of, ballooned to $175 million, which included expenses for intercollegiate athletics.

Rockne may have been long gone, but Joyce was still a booster of the Fighting Irish football program. During the relatively low seasons in the 1950s and 1960s, he was quick to assure fans and alumni that varsity sports were still a very important part of Notre Dame, both financially and for purposes of esteem. This was not to say that Joyce would turn his back so that the athletes—even the nonhockey players—could skate through college. He set a strict and rigid academic standard for all of the school's athletes, and appointed mechanical engineering professor and fencing instructor Mike DiCicco to a third position—full-time academic advisor.

DiCicco did not report to coaches. He reported directly to Joyce and had the power to suspend players from games or practice if they did not meet the university's academic requirements. Joyce wanted anyone wearing a Notre Dame uniform to perform at the highest level on the field and in the classroom. These standards of excellence have been met by very few Division I-A collegiate programs.

Joyce was always outspoken on issues of academic integrity within the NCAA, and was well respected for it. He served as secretary treasurer of the College Football Association and received the Distinguished American Award from the National Football Foundation. He holds several honorary degrees, including one from Notre Dame.

JURKOVIC, MIRKO
Guard/Defensive tackle (1988–91),
6'4", 289 lbs.

Jurkovic began his Notre Dame career as a defensive tackle and finished it as one of the best offensive linemen in the country. The immovable object from Calumet City, Illinois, was one of just two freshmen to earn a letter in 1988, playing 48 minutes on the national championship team as a backup defensive tackle. The next season he switched to the other side of the ball and began a three-year tour at offensive guard. He played 69 minutes at that position as a sophomore behind senior Tim Grunhard. The following season, after Grunhard moved on, the position was Jurkovic's. He played more minutes during his senior season than any other Fighting Irish offensive player, and the team's offense was ranked eleventh in the nation.

Jurkovic's play was definitely noticed. He made several top All-American teams, and was also named the Notre Dame Lineman of the Year by the Moose Krause Chapter of the National Football Foundation and Hall of Fame. The Chicago Bears selected him in the ninth round of the 1992 NFL draft, and he played one season with the team.

JUZWIK, STEVE
Halfback (1939–41), 5'9", 185 lbs.

Juzwik was an all-around player for head coaches Elmer Layden and Frank Leahy. He was a good defender, a good kicker, and a fleet halfback who could take a hit.

Juzwik, from Chicago, was a backup halfback in 1939. His most memorable play was a 32-yard run to set up Notre Dame's touchdown in a 7–0 victory over Northwestern. He was Notre Dame's leading rusher in 1940, with 71 carries for 407 yards. He also gained 89 yards on pass plays and scored 7 touchdowns, including an 84-yard interception return. He made 1 extra point to raise his team-leading point total to 43.

In his senior season, Leahy's first, Juzwik flourished. He was freshman quarterback and future Heisman Trophy–winner Angelo Bertelli's favorite target, catching 17 passes for 305 yards. Juzwik also ran the ball 101 times for 386 yards, scored 8 touchdowns, and made 13 of 19 extra points. He returned 23 punts for 290 yards, returned a kickoff for 20 yards, and returned 3 interceptions for 39 yards. The busy season resulted in 1,040 total yards for Juzwik.

The Washington Redskins selected him during the nineteenth round of the 1942 draft. He played with them for one season and then moved to the All-American Football Conference, playing with Buffalo in 1946 and 1947 and for the Chicago Rockets in 1948.

KADISH, MIKE
Defensive tackle (1969–71), 6'5", 249 lbs.

Kadish came to South Bend from Grand Rapids, Michigan, with every intention of playing on offense, but a few days before the season opener he was moved from the offensive line to defense, where he would eventually earn accolades for his play as a tackle.

In his first varsity season, Kadish learned the ropes by playing next to All-American Mike McCoy. He started at defensive tackle and made 68 tackles, including 6 for losses of -27 yards. He also had an interception and broke up a pass. He was on his way toward a spectacular career but would first suffer a setback.

Kadish injured his knee during training camp before the 1970 season and missed the season's first four games. But he started the final seven and made 47 tackles. He also tackled opposing players for losses 4 times, for -15 yards, and recovered a fumble. Right after Notre Dame's Cotton Bowl victory over Texas, doctors operated on his damaged knee. After a successful rehabilitation, he set out to become one of the best linemen in the country, and succeeded. Kadish led the team with 97 tackles and was a first-team All-American. He broke up 6 passes and nailed opposing players for losses 8 times, for -40 yards. His career total was 212 tackles, including 18 for -82 yards; he also broke up 7 passes, intercepted 1, and recovered a fumble.

The Miami Dolphins selected Kadish in the first round of the NFL draft, but he spent all of his nine seasons in the NFL with the Buffalo Bills.

KELL, PAUL ERNEST
Tackle (1936–38), 6'2", 209 lbs.

Kell wasn't recruited to play football at Notre Dame by a coach; he was talked into attending the school by a future teammate. Kell was an all-state tackle at Niles High School in Princeton, Illinois. Niles played Benton Harbor High School, which featured a future All-American end named Earl Brown. Brown had already announced his intention to go to Notre Dame and convinced Kell to do the same. Brown ended up having the better career in South Bend, but Kell was no slouch. He was a three-year letter winner and a starter as a senior. The Green Bay Packers selected him in the sixth round of the 1939 NFL draft, and he played two seasons for the franchise.

KELLEY, MIKE
Tackle/Center (1981–84), 6'5", 266 lbs.

After a year and a half of pain and frustration, Kelley, from Westfield, Massachusetts, finally got a chance to show his talent. His freshman year was lost to a back injury he suffered during preseason workouts. Then he missed half of the next season with a knee injury, but in 1982 Notre Dame had a healthy Kelley on its offensive line. He started eleven games at tackle, but the next year he was the starting center for twelve games and was named an honorable mention All-American and the team's offensive Most Valuable Player by his teammates. He had another outstanding season in 1984, when he earned second-team All-American honors.

The Houston Oilers selected Kelley in

Notre Dame A–Z   107

the third round of the 1985 NFL draft. He played in Houston for three seasons and in Philadelphia for another.

KELLY, BOB
Halfback (1943–44), 5'10", 182 lbs.

It didn't take an act of Congress, but an act of a congressman, before Bob Kelly was able to play at Notre Dame. He was ready to accept an appointment to West Point but had second thoughts, and late in the game decided to go to Notre Dame. This was in 1943, during World War II, when there was stiff competition for talented athletes ready to move on to college. Many players were off fighting the war, so those who were available, such as Kelly, who was coming off an all-state season at Leo High School in Chicago, were highly coveted.

It's no shock that Army head football coach Earl "Red" Blaik was livid at losing Kelly. He threatened to end the Army–Notre Dame series if Kelly were allowed to go to Notre Dame. Enter Kelly's dad, Edward A. Kelly, a U.S. congressman, who made a few phone calls. Soon his son was off to South Bend.

Because of the plethora of players off to war, Kelly and all other freshmen were ruled eligible by the NCAA during that time. In his first season, Kelly played backup halfback to Julie Rykovich and helped Notre Dame to a 9–1 season and a national championship. Kelly was blessed with breakaway speed, and he had the good fortune to learn the ropes from Heisman Trophy–winning quarterback Angelo Bertelli and All-American halfback Creighton Miller. To rub salt into the wound of its longtime rival, Notre Dame shut out Army 26–0 in 1943, and Kelly rushed for 27 yards on 11 carries. He caught 2 touchdown passes in a 25–6 victory over Northwestern, and also rushed for a score in a 14–13 win over Iowa Pre-Flight.

In 1944, as a sophomore, Kelly played for Ed McKeever, who held down the fort at Notre Dame while head coach Frank Leahy

served in the navy. Kelly led the team in rushing (681 yards on 136 carries), scoring (84 points), punt return average (10.8 yards per return), and kickoff return average (26.6 yards per return). He was the team's Most Valuable Player and a member of a Notre Dame starting lineup that averaged only nineteen years of age.

The navy called Kelly into active duty in 1945. He was back on campus in 1946 but was unable to make the team because many talented players who had been away fighting returned, giving Notre Dame one of its most talented teams ever. Players who had been gone as many as four seasons were back as members of the Fighting Irish.

Despite his 1946 season, the Green Bay Packers still selected Kelly in the eighth round of the 1947 draft. He played for the Los Angeles Dons of the All-American Football Conference in 1947 and 1948, and for the Baltimore Colts in 1949.

KELLY, JIM
End (1961–63), 6'2", 215 lbs.

During his college career, Jim Kelly caught passes from Daryle Lamonica and John Huarte, two of Notre Dame's most famous quarterbacks. The Clairton, Pennsylvania, native played both offensive and defensive end and excelled at both.

In his first varsity season, Kelly, a backup right end, caught 9 passes for 138 yards and scored 2 touchdowns. He also made 26 tackles and recovered a fumble. As the starting right end in 1962, Kelly caught a school record 41 passes for 523 yards and 4 touchdowns. He set a record for catches in a single game, with 11 (for 127 yards and 3 touchdowns) in a 43–22 victory over the University of Pittsburgh. On defense he made 21 tackles, broke up a pass, and recovered a fumble. He finished in a three-way tie (with Daryle Lamonica and halfback Joe Farrell) for the school scoring lead, with 24 points. Kelly did all of that in 349 minutes of playing time, fifth on the team, and was named a first-team All-American.

As a senior Kelly was moved to left end, where he hooked up with quarterbacks Huarte (who would win the 1964 Heisman Trophy), Frank Budka, and Sandy Bonvechio. It was an ugly season, as the Fighting Irish finished 2–7 in head coach Hugh Devore's final year, but Kelly still led the squad with 18 receptions for 264 yards and 2 touchdowns. He was third on the team in points, with 12, and on defense he made 21 tackles, broke up 2 passes, and intercepted another.

The prep All-American was also showered with accolades as a college senior; he was named to several first-team All-American squads. Kelly finished his Notre Dame career with 68 catches for 925 yards and 8 touchdowns. He was the first player selected in the second round of the 1964 draft, by the Pittsburgh Steelers (NFL) and Boston Patriots (AFL). Kelly played for Pittsburgh in 1964, and for Philadelphia in 1965 and 1967.

CAREER STATS

Year	Rec.	Yards	Avg.	TDs
1961	9	138	15.3	2
1962	41	523	12.8	4
1963	18	264	14.7	2
Total	68	925	13.6	8

KELLY, LUKE
Tackle/Guard (1908–11), 5'9", 185 lbs.

The 1911 edition of the Notre Dame football team featured Knute Rockne, Gus Dorais, Alfred Bergman, and Ray Eichenlaub—Notre Dame legends all—but the player considered the best on the squad was a solidly built, tough lineman from Boston named Kelly who penetrated enemy territory, blocked kicks, and caught passes.

A freshman starter, Kelly began his career as a left tackle and scored a touchdown in an 88–0 drubbing of Chicago Physicians & Surgeons. He also fell on a loose kick in the end zone for another score in an 11–0 victory over Indiana, a game in which he pulled in a rare (for the time) 15-yard pass reception. In

a 58–4 romp over Ohio Northern, Kelly blocked a kick near the opponent's end zone that was recovered by Art Smith for a score.

The following two seasons, Kelly backed up at right guard. In 1910, he made his way into Marquette's line and popped the ball carrier hard enough to force a fumble, which he recovered for a touchdown in a 5–5 tie (in the early history of the game touchdowns were worth only five points). Kelly was back in the starting lineup his senior season and was named the team captain. He played right tackle and blocked a kick to preserve a 0–0 tie against the University of Pittsburgh, and caught a 5-yard pass against Marquette University in another scoreless game. He was named second-team All-Western.

KELLY, TIM
Linebacker (1968–70), 6'1", 225 lbs.

Kelly, who was an all-state linebacker at Ohio's Springfield Catholic Central High School, didn't take long to make an impact on the Notre Dame defense. By the time he was a sophomore in South Bend he was a starter and placed second on the team in tackles, with 80. As a junior he placed third on the team, with 71 tackles, and led all linebackers in minutes played, with 225:15.

His final year was his best. Kelly, a senior cocaptain, had 99 tackles. The only player with more tackles was linebacker Bob Olson, who had 129 stops. Kelly was named defensive Most Valuable Player by the National Monogram Club. He played in the College Football All-Star Game in 1971, and was a fifth-round draft choice of the Boston Patriots. He did not play professionally.

KERR, BUD
End (1937–39), 6'1", 194 lbs.

Kerr was a surprise success story at Notre Dame. Not only was he not recruited by the Fighting Irish out of high school, he barely played at Newburgh Free Academy in New York. He earned one letter at the school and spent more time playing trumpet in the band than he did football on the field.

The blessing for Kerr was that he had to work for four years after high school to save up for college. During that time he became more serious about football while playing for the Newburgh town team. He played running back and got the attention of many college scouts, but his friends talked him into going to South Bend.

Kerr began attending the school in the fall of 1936, made the varsity the following year, and earned his first letter as a junior, backing up All-American Earl Brown at the end position. Although he was the starting left end his senior season, remarkably, he didn't catch a single pass. Nevertheless, his play earned him a spot on almost every major All-American team.

KIEL, BLAIR
Quarterback/Punter (1980–83),
6'1", 206 lbs.

Kiel owns the distinction of being the first four-year starter at quarterback for the Fighting Irish since Gus Dorais held the position seven decades earlier. He was a solidly built quarterback with the ability to throw the ball downfield, but he was best with short, precise passes. He was also a strong-legged punter.

Kiel was a prep All-American at East High School in Columbus, Indiana, and immediately beat out Tim Kogel for the starting quarterback position his freshman year in South Bend. During that season, Kiel completed 48 of 124 passes for 531 yards and played more minutes (250) than any first-year quarterback since Dorais in 1910. He also punted 66 times for 2,649 yards (a 40.1-yard average) and ran the ball 71 times for 148 yards and 3 touchdowns.

As a sophomore in 1981 Kiel showed across-the-board improvement. He completed 67 of 151 passes for 936 yards and 7 touchdowns (he also had 10 interceptions). He rushed 31 times for 53 yards and a touch-

down, and punted 73 times for 2,914 yards. He played his best ball as a junior the next year, completing 118 of 219 passes (a .539 completion rate, which, at the time, was fourth in school history) for 1,273 yards and 3 touchdowns. He rushed 19 times for -8 yards and a touchdown and punted 77 times for 3,267 yards (a 42.4-yard average). He also completed 9 consecutive passes in a 27–10 victory over Navy.

Kiel book-ended the season with his two best games. He completed 15 of 22 passes for 141 yards in a 23–17 opening-week victory over the University of Michigan, and ended with an 11–19, 151-yard performance against Boston College in a 19–18 Liberty Bowl win. He was about to etch his name in the Notre Dame record book as the program's top passer by supplanting Terry Hanratty, but his time at the helm was cut short by the arrival of Steve Beuerlein in 1983. After starting three games as a senior, Kiel was replaced by the gifted freshman after throwing 5 interceptions in losses to Michigan State and the University of Miami during the second and third weeks of the season. He finished the year with 64 completions for 910 yards and 7 touchdowns, 3 more than Beuerlein, and punted 43 times for a 39.6-yard average.

Kiel finished his career with 297 completions of 609 passes (fourth on the school's all-time list) for 3,650 yards and 17 touchdowns (plus 5 rushing) and 32 interceptions. As of 2000, he was ranked sixth on the school's all-time passing list. When Kiel finished his career, his 609 attempts were a school record, and his 297 completions were second only to Terry Hanratty, who had 304. Kiel's punting average of 40.67 was fifth on Notre Dame's list as of 2000. The kicks traveled a total of 10,534 yards, but that can be considered a backhanded compliment. If the offense he led had been better he would not have had to kick so often: over his four years at Notre Dame, the teams went a mediocre 27–17–2.

The Tampa Bay Buccaneers selected Kiel in the eleventh round of the NFL draft.

He played for Tampa Bay in 1984, for Indianapolis in 1986 and 1987, and for Green Bay from 1988 to 1991.

CAREER STATS

PASSING

Year	Att.	Comp.	Pct.	Yards	TDs
1980	124	48	.387	531	0
1981	151	67	.444	936	7
1982	219	118	.539	1,273	3
1983	115	64	.557	910	7
Total	609	297	.488	3,650	17

PUNTING

Year	No.	Yards	Avg.
1980	66	2,649	40.1
1981	73	2,914	39.9
1982	77	3,267	42.4
1983	43	1,704	39.6
Total	259	10,534	40.67

KILEY, ROGER
End (1919–21), 6'0", 180 lbs.

Kiley was an all-around athlete who was able to run pass routes as they were drawn up but also had an unspoken bond with George Gipp, and was able to ad lib when necessary. During his three years at Notre Dame the team went 28–1.

The Chicago native's college career began in 1919 as a backup to left end Bernie Kirk, the team's leading receiver, but the next year Kiley won the starting left end spot, and he and Gipp were a potent combination. He caught a 38-yard pass from Gipp in a win over Valparaiso, a 35-yard pass for a touchdown against Army, and another touchdown pass in Gipp's last game. The speedy Kiley was named an All-American that year. The following season he was again a starter and was named a first-team All-American. He scored a touchdown in a win over DePauw, and in the third game of the season, against the University of Iowa, he blocked and re-

covered a kick in the first half. On the first play from scrimmage he caught a pass (1 of 5 he snared that day) from halfback John Mohardt for the lone Irish score. Despite his heroics, Notre Dame lost the game, 10–7, the only blemish on an otherwise perfect season.

Besides his All-American football status, Kiley was also the captain of the Notre Dame basketball team, and as a senior, he played second base for its baseball team. Kiley played professionally for the Chicago Cardinals in 1923, but left the game to practice law. He worked his way up to being an appellate court judge in Illinois.

"KILLER BEES" BACKFIELD, THE
(See individual entries under Lee Becton, Jerome Bettis, Reggie Brooks, and Jeff Burris.)

KINDER, RANDOLPH SAMUEL
Running back (1993–96), 6'1", 204 lbs.

It didn't take long for Randy Kinder, from East Lansing, Michigan, to show that he belonged on the collegiate level. As a freshman, in just his third game at Notre Dame, he rushed for 94 yards on 12 carries in a 36–14 victory over his hometown college, Michigan State. That season, as a backup to tailback Lee Becton, Kinder ran for 537 yards on 89 carries for a superb average of 6 yards per rush.

As a sophomore in 1994, Kinder started five games and ran the ball 119 times for a team-high 702 yards (a 5.9-yards-per-carry average), but his season was cut short when he tore a ligament in his right knee and was forced to miss the Fiesta Bowl.

Kinder was back and running on two good knees when the 1995 season began. He played in ten games, and again led the team with 809 yards on 143 carries (a 5.6-yard average) and rushed for 9 touchdowns. He also caught 8 passes for 75 yards and a touchdown. He played in seven games as a senior and finished with 254 yards on 53 carries for a career total of 2,302 yards on 404 carries (again, a 5.6-yard average). Kinder was also an All-American sprinter for the track team. He played professional football for the Philadelphia Eagles and Green Bay Packers.

KIZER, NOBLE
Guard (1922–24), 5'8", 165 lbs.

Kizer, from Plymouth, Indiana, was one of "the Seven Mules," who cracked open defenses and cleared the way for the Four Horsemen to gain legendary status in college football. Kizer originally attended Notre Dame with the intention of playing basketball, but Rockne lured him away to the gridiron. He was a prototypical example of Rockne's "watch-charm guard": small, very quick, smart, and extremely tough. Rockne taught these players angles and leverage and how to use an opponent's momentum to get them out of the way. Kizer was the team's starting right guard in 1923 and again in 1924, when Notre Dame took the national championship.

KLEINE, WILLIAM WALTER
Defensive tackle (1983–86), 6'9", 274 lbs.

Wally Kleine is one in a long line of tall and athletic Kleines. His cousin, Joe, for instance, is a 7-foot basketball center who played at the University of Arkansas and moved on to a long career in the National Basketball Association. Wally, though, was a football player, a tight end at Midland High School in Texas, who was moved to defensive tackle in South Bend.

Kleine turned out to be a nightmare for opposing quarterbacks, penetrating the offensive line for sacks and using his reach to bat down passes. None of that happened, however, until his sophomore season, because he missed his freshman year due to arthroscopic surgery on both knees. He was back in 1983, and despite playing only 25 minutes, he made 5 tackles, a sack, and forced a fumble.

In 1984, Kleine was a full-time starter and played 230 minutes. He made 48 tackles (11 for -25 yards) and 2 sacks. He also caused 3 fumbles and recovered 3 others. That performance helped him win the Hering Award as the team's most improved player during subsequent spring workouts. But Kleine's knees got scoped again before his junior season and he missed four games. He finished with 36 tackles (6 for -25 yards) and 5 sacks. He also caused 2 fumbles.

In 1986, as a senior, Kleine was at his best. He led all defensive linemen in field time (224:34) and tackles (74, 8 for -24 yards). He also had 5 sacks and broke up 3 passes. His performance as a senior earned him second-team All-American status. He finished his career with 163 tackles (26 for -80 yards), 13 sacks, 6 fumbles forced, 3 recovered, and 4 passes defended. The Washington Redskins selected him in the second round of the 1987 NFL draft, but he did not play professionally.

KNAPP, LINDSAY
Offensive tackle (1989–92), 6'6", 271 lbs.

By the time he was a junior in 1991, Knapp was one of the anchors on Notre Dame's offensive line. He certainly did his part to help the program, which had one of the top offenses in college football that season.

Knapp, who came to Notre Dame after an All-American high school career in Deerfield, Illinois, played in six games as a freshman. By his junior season he started all twelve games for the Irish. He repeated twelve starts during his senior season and was named first-team All-American and the Notre Dame Lineman of the Year by the Moose Krause Chapter of the National Football Foundation and Hall of Fame. Knapp was also a winner in the classroom. He won the State Farm–Mutual Broadcasting Student-Athlete of the Year Award in 1992, and graduated with a degree in economics and a 3.249 grade point average.

The Kansas City Chiefs selected Knapp in the fifth round of the 1993 NFL draft. He played in Kansas City from 1993 to 1995, and also for the Green Bay Packers from 1995 to 1997, the season the Packers won the Super Bowl.

KOKEN, MIKE
Halfback (1930–32), 5'9", 168 lbs.

Koken, from Youngstown, Ohio, was an all-around threat for Notre Dame. He had outstanding speed, a strong arm, and a leg made for kicking. Koken was a backup at left halfback for the 1930 national championship team, the last to be coached by Knute Rockne. He was again a reserve left halfback in 1931, but his other contributions were more valuable. For instance, he had 3 touchdowns and 4 extra points in a 63–0 victory over Drake. He finally cracked the starting lineup as a senior on a team that went 7–2. In a 42–0 win over Carnegie Tech, Koken scored on a 58-yard run, gained a total of 116 yards, completed a 31-yard pass, and kicked 2 extra points. He played one season of pro football for the Chicago Cardinals.

KOSIKOWSKI, FRANK
End (1946–47), 6'0", 202 lbs.

Kosikowski arrived at Notre Dame with a well-earned reputation for speed: as a Milwaukee schoolboy, he had set a state record in the 200-yard dash. When he left, his resumé included two national championship seasons at the college level.

He came to South Bend after serving in the navy, where he played for the Fleet City navy team, which won the 1945 Armed Services Championship. His first year at Notre Dame, 1946, Kosikowski played behind Jack Zilly and Heisman Trophy–winner Leon Hart at end. That team, and the one Kosikowski played for the following season, both won national championships. During Kosikowski's run, Notre Dame's record was 17–0–1. He went on to play for the Buffalo Bills and Cleveland Browns of the All-American Football Conference in 1948.

KOVALESKI, MIKE
Linebacker (1983–86), 6'2", 218 lbs.

In 1986, Mike Kovaleski became the first Fighting Irish player since Rocky Bleier, in 1967, to serve as a solo captain of the foot-

ball team. During that season, he made 88 tackles.

Kovaleski, from New Castle, Indiana, made 62 tackles as a freshman and had his best season as a sophomore. The four-year starter proved he had a nose for the ball with a team-leading 108 tackles in 1984, a season during which he had many nagging injuries. He went on to make 95 tackles as a junior. He finished his college career with 335 tackles and 1 sack. He also broke up 9 passes, intercepted another, and forced 4 fumbles.

KOVATCH, JOHN
End (1939–41), 6'3", 181 lbs.

John Kovatch was already a resident in good standing in South Bend before he worked his way into the Notre Dame starting lineup. He was an all-around student at Washington High School, where he was senior class president, valedictorian, and a star on both the basketball and football teams. A big-time defender in high school, Kovatch caught only 1 pass during his final prep season.

In college he became a decent receiver, but it was on defense that he made it onto the first team for the final three games of his collegiate career. The Washington Redskins selected Kovatch in the eleventh round of the 1942 NFL draft. He played in the nation's capital in 1942 and 1946, and for the Green Bay Packers in 1947.

KOWALKOWSKI, SCOTT THOMAS
Linebacker/Defensive end (1987–90),
6'2", 230 lbs.

Kowalkowski was the second member of his family to play professional football; his father Bob had played for the Detroit Lions and Green Bay Packers.

The Farmington Hills, Michigan, native started during his final two seasons in South Bend, earning honorable mention All-American status at two different positions. In 1989, he played defensive end and then moved to linebacker the following season. Kowalkowski, who had 107 tackles in his college career, was one of the most durable players of that era: he was the only football player at the school to play in every game from 1987 to 1990. After his final campaign, he was invited to play in the 1991 Senior Bowl.

The Philadelphia Eagles selected Kowalkowski in the eighth round of the 1991 National Football League draft. He played in the City of Brotherly Love until 1993, and then truly followed in his father's footsteps by signing as a free agent with the hometown Detroit Lions in 1994. He became one of Detroit's best special-teams players and was eventually named captain of the unit.

KRAUSE, "MOOSE" (EDWARD WALTER KRAUCIUNAS)
Tackle (1931–33); Athletic director (1949–80), 6'3", 217 lbs.

Before he went to high school there wasn't even a Moose Krause. There was an Edward Walter Krauciunas, the son of Lithuanian immigrants, who worked in his family's butcher shop when he was a kid. The young boy's mother wanted him to appreciate the arts, so she made sure that he took violin lessons.

But genes pointed Krause in the direction of sports, and just a few years after answering to two different names than the ones he was born with, he became the first Fighting Irish athlete to be named All-American in both football and basketball. Edward was 6 feet tall and weighed 175 pounds by the time he entered high school, and that's when people started calling him Moose. It was a name that stuck with him until he passed away on December 10, 1992. Norm Barry, Moose's football coach at DeLaSalle Institute in Chicago, took care of his last name. He could neither spell nor pronounce Krauciunas, so he shortened the surname to Krause. That was not a problem for Moose, who went on to become one of the finest all-around athletes in the city, captaining the football, basketball, and baseball teams. He was an allstate player in football and basketball, and led the Meteors to two national Catholic basketball championships.

Krause was due for a career of heavy manual labor until Notre Dame legend Knute Rockne rescued him. He was working in the stockyards when Barry set up a meeting for the boy and Rockne, who liked what he saw both in size and attitude. Krause was offered a scholarship to play football at Notre Dame in exchange for working in the university dining room. Clearing a few dirty plates was like a vacation compared to the grunt work of the stockyards, so Krause was in heaven.

Krause's size was important to Rockne. A change in NCAA rules had all but obliterated "the Notre Dame Shift," and speed and quickness had to make way for size and strength. Freshmen were ineligible to play when Krause entered school, so he never got to play an official game for Rockne, whose last year as head coach was 1930. He did catch the coach's eye in his first year on campus, though, when he put the varsity quarterback hard on the turf during a practice scrimmage. Krause practiced one spring and one fall for Rockne and heard many of his lectures, which helped bridge the gap between the Rockne and "Hunk Anderson" eras. He took what he learned all the way into the 1980s, when he finished a thirty-two-year tenure as athletic director in South Bend.

It was for Anderson that Krause played three seasons of standout tackle, often being double- and triple-teamed. He left a legacy of iron-man durability: as a junior, Krause played an astounding 521 of a possible 540 minutes. As a senior, Krause broke his jaw in the first play of an All-Star game but still remained on the field for all but 4 minutes. He also made All-American in his senior season.

That was nothing compared to the basketball career he put together. He was the team's starting center, earning All-American honors in 1932, 1933, and 1934. He also may have changed the way the game was played. Krause was big and solid for a football player; imagine, then, the havoc he wreaked on the basketball court. He was like a wall that opposing players couldn't move or get through; many think the 3-second rule, whereby a player cannot stand in the foul lane for more than 3 seconds, was instituted as a direct result of his physical dominance.

Led by Krause, the Fighting Irish basketball team was 54–12, and he established a school record with 547 career points. He was also a spring athlete. He played baseball and threw the javelin and discus for the Fighting Irish track and field team. Krause not only hit football players and baseballs, he also hit the books. He graduated cum laude with a degree in journalism.

His postcollege path could have led to professional sports; instead it led him back to campus. He was offered a tryout with the Chicago Cubs and a job with the Chicago Bears of the NFL, but decided to take the posts of basketball coach and athletic director at St. Mary's College in Minnesota. For a little extra cash, he put together a barnstorming hoop team that played teams such as the Harlem Globetrotters.

Krause stayed in Minnesota for six years and then moved to Worcester, Massachusetts, to work at Holy Cross College and also play semipro basketball, the top game in the country. In 1942, almost nine years after he graduated college, Krause was back in South Bend. Frank Leahy had hired him as an assistant football coach. The next year he added head basketball coach to his duties. In February 1944, Krause took a hiatus from Notre Dame to serve in the Marine Corps as an air-combat intelligence officer.

Krause was discharged in 1946 and went directly back to Notre Dame to work with both the football and basketball programs. Running the basketball program completely filled his plate, so he decided to resign from his football post. In 1947, Krause was a one-sport—basketball—man.

Two years later Krause got the call he had coveted. He was named athletic director at Notre Dame, and resigned as basketball coach after compiling a respectable career record of 98–48. He ran the athletic department with the utmost integrity. He was hard but fair, and he loved the school's athletics. Always charming, smart, and full of energy, Krause excelled at raising money and smoothing over differences. He hired dozens

of coaches and oversaw the construction of the Joyce Athletic and Convocation Center.

Krause was inducted into the Basketball Hall of Fame in 1976. He died sixteen years later, but his name is immortal at Notre Dame. Since 1986, the Moose Krause Chapter of the National Football Foundation has presented the Moose Krause Lineman of the Year Award to honor a Fighting Irish front-liner.

On September 17, 1999, the day before a home game against Michigan State, Krause was honored again, this time with the dedication of a bronze sculpture of him sitting on a bench in front of the Joyce Center and looking at Notre Dame Stadium.

KRIMM, JOHN
Cornerback (1978–81), 6'2", 190 lbs.

Krimm was a three-year starter at cornerback for Dan Devine and Gerry Faust. He had all the tools to succeed—speed, range, and hitting ability. By the time he was done at Notre Dame he'd made 116 tackles and snared 4 interceptions.

Born in Philadelphia and raised in Columbus, Ohio, Krimm earned all-state prep honors in both football and track. After his three years of solid work with the Fighting Irish, the Saints were impressed enough to use a 1982 third-round NFL draft pick for Krimm. He played only two seasons with the Saints before retiring from pro football.

KUECHENBERG, BOB
Offensive tackle/Defensive end (1966–68), 6'2", 245 lbs.

Kuechenberg, from Hobart, Indiana, was a fine lineman, and he proved his talent on both sides of the line of scrimmage. In 1966, he was a starting offensive tackle on a national championship team that scored 362 points (the second-most of any Ara Parseghian–coached team) and provided great protection for quarterback Terry Hanratty.

The next year Parseghian decided to better utilize Kuechenberg's athleticism and switched him to defensive end in the third game of the 1967 season. Kuechenberg responded by making 32 tackles and deflecting

4 passes during the remainder of the year. As a senior in 1968, he followed up with 44 tackles (8 for losses). He also broke up 2 passes and recovered 2 fumbles and was named the defensive MVP by the National Monogram Club.

The Philadelphia Eagles selected Kuechenberg in the fourth round of the 1969 NFL draft, but he spent his entire fourteen-year pro career playing guard and tackle for the Miami Dolphins, playing alongside fellow Notre Dame alum Nick Buoniconti. The Dolphins made it to four Super Bowls during that time and won two. Kuechenberg was also a member of the Dolphins' undefeated team in 1972.

KUHARICH, JOE

Guard (1935–37); Head coach (1959–62), 6'0", 193 lbs.

It's ironic that Joe Kuharich is the only coach in Notre Dame football history to compile a losing record. He grew up in South Bend, was literally touched by Knute Rockne, and went on to become a standout player in both college and the pros. He succeeded on the high school, college, and professional level—except at Notre Dame, where, in four seasons, the Fighting Irish had a 17–23 record. Under Kuharich, Notre Dame had three 5–5 seasons and one disastrous 2–8 campaign. Coaching the team was his dream job, but it ended up as a nightmare.

As a kid in South Bend, Kuharich would wander by Cartier Field, fantasizing about being on the other side of the fence. One afternoon Rockne saw him and took him by the hand to watch the team practice. The young boy promised himself that he would be one of those players. He got the most out of his 150-pound body at Riley High School. His lack of heft did not stop him from playing the line. It did, however, stop Notre Dame head coach Elmer Layden from offering the slender athlete a scholarship when he arrived on campus. That was okay; Kuharich let his play do the talking and put on some muscle to become a productive member of the squad.

On the field, Kuharich fit right in. He gained 25 pounds as a freshman and another 20 during his college career, during which he

earned three letters and started two seasons at right guard. He stayed on to serve as a graduate assistant at Notre Dame before moving to Albany, New York, in 1939, to take the head coaching job at Vincention Institute.

After a year it was time to put on the pads again, and Kuharich played the 1940 and 1941 seasons for the Chicago Cardinals (this was two years after Pittsburgh had selected him in the tenth round of the 1938 draft). He then served in the navy for four years during World War II, and came back to wrap up his playing career with the Cardinals in the fall of 1945.

Kuharich's next stop was Pittsburgh, where, in 1946, he took a job as an assistant coach with the Steelers. In 1947 he went to the University of San Francisco, where he served as an assistant for a season before landing the head coaching spot with the Dons. Under Kuharich they went 26–14 in four seasons, which included a 9–0 year (1951). Kuharich's record at USF earned him a return trip to Chicago, where he would coach the NFL Cardinals during the 1952 season before becoming an independent scout.

In 1955, Kuharich was back on the sidelines as an assistant coach with the Washington Redskins. The following season he was designated head coach and led a great turnaround in the nation's capital. Washington had won just three games the year before Kuharich took over, but were 8–4 in his first season. The success earned him NFL Coach of the Year honors. He remained in Washington until December 1958, when he got the call he wanted: he was offered the head coaching job at his alma mater.

NOTRE DAME COACHING RECORD

Year	W	L
1959	5	5
1960	2	8
1961	5	5
1962	5	5
Total	17	23

This story didn't end in storybook fashion. After four subpar seasons and a .425 winning percentage, Kuharich left to become the supervisor of NFL officials for two years. From

1964 to 1969 he served as head coach and general manager of the Philadelphia Eagles.

KUNZ, GEORGE
Defensive tackle/Tight end/Offensive tackle (1966–68), 6′5″, 240 lbs.

After an inauspicious start at Notre Dame, Kunz, from Arcadia, California, settled in to become one of the best linemen in the school's history, making the starting unit at right defensive tackle in his sophomore season. That wasn't just any Notre Dame team: Coach Ara Parseghian's 1966 team went 9–0–1 and took the national championship. Unfortunately, Kunz was injured in the second game of the season, a 35–7 victory over Northwestern, and missed the rest of the year. At the beginning of his junior season he was moved to tight end, where he caught 7 passes for 101 yards in the first two games of the sea-

George Kunz was an All-American tackle at Notre Dame who went on to play for ten seasons in the NFL.

son. Then Parseghian began to tinker with his lineup, moving Bob Kuechenberg from offensive tackle to defensive end, which opened up a hole that Kunz was called on to fill.

It was a smooth transition for Kunz, who spent the rest of his career at tackle. As a senior in 1968 he was a cocaptain and earned consensus All-American status. Kunz was also an Academic All-American and won a postgraduate scholarship from the NCAA and the National Football Foundation. The Atlanta Falcons used the second overall pick in the 1969 NFL draft to select him. Kunz played ten seasons in the NFL—1969 to 1974 in Atlanta, and 1975 to 1977 and 1980 in Baltimore.

KURTH, JOE
Tackle (1930–32), 6′2″, 197 lbs.

Joe Kurth combined quickness, strength, and technique to become an excellent lineman for Knute Rockne and "Hunk" Anderson. In 1930, after transferring from his hometown college, the University of Wisconsin in Madison, Kurth became the first sophomore to start on a Notre Dame national championship team. He also saved that undefeated season: in the opener he made a touchdown-saving open-field tackle in a 20–14 victory over SMU. He was an especially good defender, but he also made many big blocks on long touchdown runs throughout the season.

By his junior season, Kurth was considered one of the best linemen in college football. And one thing you could not question was his toughness. He ignored doctor's orders to skip a game against the University of Pittsburgh. The Fighting Irish won, 25–12, thanks in part to a strong defensive effort by the injured Kurth. He subsequently spent three days in the hospital, but was back in the starting lineup the next week to beat Carnegie Tech, 19–0. For his efforts, Kurth earned first-team All-American honors. He played more excellent football as a senior, and was a unanimous first-team All-American selection. He later played in the East-West Shrine Game and two seasons professionally with the Green Bay Packers.

LAMBEAU, EARL
Fullback (1918), 5'10", 188 lbs.

"Curly" Lambeau may have only played one year of football at Notre Dame, but he learned enough to be one of the pioneers of the professional game. Lambeau, from Green Bay, Wisconsin, was a starter at fullback alongside George Gipp on the first team coached by Knute Rockne. He scored a touchdown in a 26–6 victory over Case Tech and two in a 67–7 shellacking of Wabash. He may have played in the shadows of Gipp, but Lambeau, the only freshman to win a letter in 1918, did his part as a good blocker and short-yardage rusher. His college career ended abruptly when he contracted a case of tonsillitis and withdrew from school.

Lambeau took a job at the Indian Packing Corporation in Green Bay, but he just couldn't leave football behind. He talked to the bosses at Indian Packing about sponsoring a football team, and the company came through with $500. Lambeau took the cash, bought uniforms and equipment, and started selecting players. The Green Bay Packers were born. By 1921, the Packers were in the American Professional Football Association and Lambeau was a player and coach. It was only five years earlier that Rockne (along with quarterback Gus Dorais) had popularized the forward pass. It proved to be such an effective offensive weapon that Lambeau brought it to the APFA, which in 1922 would become the National Football League. In that era of grind-'em-out ground games, Lambeau's frequent use of the forward pass was an exciting innovation, and it helped usher in the era of modern football.

Eight years later, Lambeau retired as a player to coach full-time, and he put together a powerhouse team. He certainly knew how to identify talent: he signed players such as linemen Mike Michalske and Cal Hubbard and running back Johnny McNally, all of whom were future NFL Hall of Famers. Those three stars were the cornerstones of a Packer franchise that won league titles in 1929, 1930, and 1931. In a four-year span the Packers went 34–7. They also won NFL championships under Lambeau in 1936, 1939, and 1944.

Things got tough in the post–World War II era, and in 1951 Lambeau resigned from the franchise he founded and built. He subsequently coached the Chicago Cardinals and Washington Redskins before retiring in 1955 with a career record of 229–134–22. His winning percentage of .623 is seventh on the NFL's all-time list. Lambeau, who passed away on June 1, 1965, was inducted into the Professional Football Hall of Fame in 1963.

LAMONICA, DARYLE
Quarterback/Defensive back/Punter (1960–62), 6'2", 205 lbs.

A strong-armed quarterback with good mobility and outstanding leadership abilities is not enough to lead a college football team to victory. If it were, Notre Dame would have done better than 12–18 during Daryle Lamonica's three years of varsity football.

The four-sport star from Clovis High School in Fresno, California, had earned all-state football honors as a senior. Despite throwing for just 1,363 yards and 8 touchdowns in college, Lamonica went on to have a long and prosperous professional career, with nearly 20,000 yards passing and 164 touchdowns.

In 1960, Lamonica took over the quarterback position George Izo vacated, but he wasn't the team's leading passer. George Haffner, who completed 30 of 108 passes, was. Lamonica was just 15 for 31 for 242 yards and 5 interceptions. In the final days of one-platoon football, Lamonica's versatility came in handy. He averaged 37.4 yards per punt and made 33 tackles, broke up 2 passes, and intercepted another as a defensive back. He was also the team's second-leading scorer, with 18 points. The following season, as a junior, Lamonica split time with Frank Budka and completed 20 of 52 passes for 300 yards, 2 touchdowns, and 4 interceptions. He also rushed 44 times for 135 yards and 3 touchdowns, averaged 38.4 yards per punt, and made 29 tackles and had 2 interceptions on defense.

In 1962, Lamonica finally gave the South Bend fans a glimpse of what his future would be. As a full-time starter, he had a primary target in the form of All-American receiver Jim Kelly, who had 41 receptions, and Lamonica completed half of his 128 passes for 821 yards, 6 touchdowns, and 7 interceptions. He also ran 74 times for 145 yards and 4 touchdowns. His time on defense was limited, so Lamonica had only 3 tackles, 1 interception, and 1 pass defended. But he punted a career-high 49 times for an average of 36.5 yards per kick. After the season he was named a third-team All-American.

Lamonica was selected in the twelfth round of the 1963 NFL draft by Green Bay of the NFL and Buffalo of the AFL. In 1967, after four years with the Buffalo Bills, he was traded to the Oakland Raiders, where he blossomed. In his first year playing in the Bay Area, Lamonica not only led the Raiders to the AFL championship, he was named AFL Player of the Year. The following season he led the Raiders to the Super Bowl, where they lost to the Green Bay Packers. For that season Lamonica completed 220 of 425 passes for 3,228 yards and 30 touchdowns. The next year his Raiders were back in the AFL title game, and he was again the AFL Player of the Year after completing 221 of 426 passes for 3,302 yards and 32 touchdowns. After the 1974 season Lamonica retired, but not before throwing for 10.88 miles

and 164 touchdowns. During his twelve-year career, he connected on 1,288 of 2,601 passes for 19,154 yards.

CAREER STATS

Year	Att.	Comp.	Pct.	Yards	TDs
1960	15	31	.484	242	0
1961	20	52	.384	300	2
1962	64	128	.500	821	6
Total	99	211	.426	1,363	8

LANZA, CHARLES LOUIS
Center (1984–87), 6'2", 270 lbs.

Chuck Lanza's Notre Dame career got off to a slow start. The big lineman from Germantown, Tennessee, enrolled in the university in the fall of 1983 but missed his entire freshman season with injuries. He played the following four years, earning a letter in each. Each year his contributions were greater than the previous one. As a sophomore in 1985 he played 80 minutes as a second-string center. In 1986, he won the starting job and was named an honorable mention All-American. In 1987, he was a first-team All-American and was also the recipient of the Lineman of the Year award from the Moose Krause Chapter of the National Football Foundation and Hall of Fame. The Pittsburgh Steelers selected Lanza in the third round of the 1988 NFL draft, and he played for the franchise until 1990.

LARKIN, MIKE
Linebacker (1981–82, 1984–85), 6'1", 210 lbs.

Cincinnati's Larkin may not have been the biggest and strongest linebacker in Fighting Irish history, but he was certainly one of the fastest. The brother of Cincinnati Reds star Barry Larkin, he played his best ball as a sophomore. After making 10 tackles, 1 sack, and 1 fumble recovery as a freshman in 1981, he earned a starting spot for his sophomore season. He was second best on the team in tackles with 112 (more than half his career total of 201), 1 behind linebacker Mark Zavagnin.

Injuries either slowed or stopped him the rest of his time at South Bend, and he would never again achieve his sophomore numbers. He missed the entire 1983 season with a twice-broken arm. In 1984 he was expected to start again at outside linebacker but missed most of the season with a knee injury, and he finished with just 39 tackles. The following year he made 40 tackles and 5 sacks.

LARSON, FRED "OJAY"
Center (1918, 1920–21), 6'1", 190 lbs.

Larson, of Calumet, Michigan, was tough beyond description. Playing for Knute Rockne and blasting open holes for George Gipp, he was the team's starting center in 1918 and also in 1920, when he contributed to a 9–0 record. In a 27–17 victory over Army that season, Larson showed his grit when he played most of the second quarter with torn muscles and a partially dislocated hip. Unfortunately, he lost his letter by playing in a semi-pro game. After college he played for the Chicago Bears in 1922, the Milwaukee Badgers in 1923 and 1924, the Green Bay Packers in 1925, and the Chicago Cardinals in 1929.

LATTNER, JOHN
Right halfback (1951–53), 6'1", 190 lbs.

To put John Lattner's career in perspective, the Notre Dame player he is most often compared with is the legendary George Gipp. Both were ultraversatile backs who could beat you in any number of different ways by running, passing, catching, returning, or even defending. No one part of Lattner's game was so good that defenders could key on it, but the sum total was good enough to beat them. As a senior, the Chicago native did not lead his own team in any statistical category, but he still won the Heisman Trophy as college football's top player.

Lattner was a consistent rusher who could be counted on to average 5 yards a carry by season's end. That was his average as a sophomore, and the following two seasons his average dipped ever so slightly, to 4.9 yards.

In 1951, his first season with the varsity, he was a second-string right halfback. He rushed 68 times for 341 yards and 6 touchdowns, caught 8 passes for 157 yards, completed a pass for 23 yards, returned 10 punts for 91 yards, and on defense he led the team in turnover recoveries with 5 interceptions and 4 fumble recoveries. Included in his 401 of a possible 600 minutes of playing time, despite being an offensive backup, were 26 punts for a 32.4-yard average.

In 1952, his junior year, he rushed for 732 yards and 5 touchdowns, caught 17 passes for 252 yards and a touchdown, completed 2 passes, returned 7 punts for 113 yards, returned 3 kickoffs for 45 yards, recovered 3 fumbles, had 4 interceptions, and punted 64 times for an average of 36.6 yards. Lattner was a consensus All-American, won the Maxwell Award as college football's top player, and was fifth in the Heisman Trophy voting.

Lattner's senior season was, if you can believe it, even more impressive. He played 421 minutes and rushed for 651 yards and 9 touchdowns, caught 14 passes for 204 yards

Heisman Trophy–winning halfback John Lattner was a versatile player who amassed 3,250 all-purpose offensive yards, a record that stood for twenty-six years. He also was an All-American, a two-time Maxwell Award winner, and an inductee into the College Football Hall of Fame.

and a touchdown, completed a pass, returned 8 kickoffs for 321 yards and 2 touchdowns, and returned 10 punts for 103 yards. On defense he had 4 interceptions, recovered a fumble, and punted 29 times for a 35-yard average.

Then the honors started to roll in. He probably needed an extra suitcase to bring home the hardware. He was a consensus All-American, won his second consecutive Maxwell Award, and nipped Minnesota's Paul Giel for the Heisman Trophy. Lattner, who was Coach Frank Leahy's fourth and final recipient of the prestigious honor, received 1,850 points in the voting to Giel's 1,794. Notre Dame was 9–0–1 that season and was named national champion by every major organization but the Associated Press and United Press International. Those two organizations named the unbeaten University of Maryland the top team in the land.

Lattner finished with 3,250 yards of total offense, which stood as a school record for twenty-six years, until Vagas Ferguson topped it in 1979. Coincidentally, in that same year, Lattner was inducted into the College Football Hall of Fame.

The Pittsburgh Steelers selected Lattner in the first round of the NFL draft, and he played one season in Pittsburgh before entering the military. He suffered a severe knee injury in a service game and was never able to play again.

CAREER STATS

RUSHING

Year	Att.	Yards	Avg.	TDs
1951	68	341	5.0	6
1952	148	732	4.9	5
1953	134	651	4.9	9
Total	350	1,724	4.9	20

RECEIVING

Year	Rec.	Yards	Avg.	TDs
1951	8	157	19.6	0
1952	17	252	14.8	1
1953	14	204	14.6	1
Total	39	613	15.7	2

KICKOFF RETURNS

Year	Ret.	Yards	Avg.	TDs
1951	None			
1952	3	45	15.0	0
1953	8	321	40.1	2
Total	11	366	33.3	2

PUNT RETURNS

Year	Ret.	Yards	Avg.	TDs
1951	10	91	9.1	0
1952	7	113	16.1	0
1953	10	103	10.3	0
Total	27	307	11.4	0

INTERCEPTIONS

Year	Int.	Yards
1951	5	66
1952	4	58
1953	4	4
Total	13	128

LAUTAR, JOHN
Guard (1934–36), 6'1", 184 lbs.

Lautar's father was a coal miner in West Virginia, where John graduated from Moundsville High School at the age of sixteen. He immediately went to work, accepting a position in the engineering department of a glass-manufacturing company. He saved his money and went to South Bend to enroll in Notre Dame's engineering department.

Although he hadn't played organized football until his senior year of high school, Lautar also went out for Notre Dame's football team. He not only made the squad, he eventually became an All-American. He was on the freshman team in 1933 and moved up to the varsity level the following season. He was a starter in 1935 and became the team captain in 1936 when Bill Smith, who held the post, relinquished it because of season-ending surgery. Notre Dame was 6–2–1 that year, and Lautar was named a first-team All-American.

LAW, JOHN
Guard (1926–29), 5′9″, 163 lbs.

Law was a prototypical lineman of the Rockne era. He was tough and quick, despite being relatively small for the position. Hailing from Yonkers, New York, Law was the smallest player in Notre Dame's entire starting lineup. Still, he played four years of varsity ball, earning three letters. He started his final two seasons and was the captain of the 1929 national championship team, which went 9–0. Law played one year of pro ball for the Newark Bears, who were members of the first American Football League. He then went into coaching, serving at Manhattan College and then Sing Sing prison in Ossining, New York.

LAYDEN, ELMER
Running back/Quarterback/Punter
(1922–24); Head coach (1934–40),
5′11″, 162 lbs.

Known as the Quiet Horseman, Elmer Layden had an association with Notre Dame that spanned nearly twenty years, and he left behind a legacy of quality football as both a player and a coach. During his three seasons on the Notre Dame varsity the team compiled a record of 27–2–1. In his seven seasons as coach, Notre Dame was a tremendous 47–13–3.

Layden was the biggest and fastest of the Four Horsemen (which included Don Miller, Jim Crowley, and Harry Stuhldreher), the most famous, and quite possibly the best backfield in college football history. He was capable of running a 10-second 100-yard dash and was also the team's best defensive player and punter.

Layden arrived in South Bend from Davenport, Iowa, in 1921 at the tender age of eighteen. The following season he saw time at left halfback and quarterback on a team that won eight games and lost and tied one apiece. Layden saw time as a starter, rushing for 453 yards on 80 carries (an average of 5.7 yards a carry). Some of his highlights were an interception that preserved a 0–0 tie against

Army, a touchdown reception from Stuhldreher in a 19–0 victory over Carnegie Tech, and a touchdown pass thrown to Miller.

In 1923, the 162-pound Layden was the team's starting fullback, and he proved that he was up to the challenge. He gained 420 yards on 102 carries and scored 5 touchdowns, and also caught 6 passes for 78 yards and 2 scores. On defense he broke open a game in which Notre Dame beat Princeton, 12–0, with an interception and subsequent 40-yard touchdown return. Two weeks later, by averaging 48 yards per kick, he kept Purdue stuck in its own territory in a 34–7 Fighting Irish victory. The squad's only loss that season was to Nebraska, 14–7, a week later, and it finished at 9–1.

In the third game of the 1924 season, Layden and the rest of the quartet became living legends. He scored a touchdown in the 13–7 victory over Army at Brooklyn's Polo Grounds, and also picked off a pass at midfield to set up the eventual game-winning drive. The nickname Four Horsemen was coined by sportswriter Grantland Rice in his report on the game in the October 19, 1924, edition of the *New York Herald-Tribune*. Rice was comparing the four football players to the biblical Four Horsemen of the Apocalypse (Famine, Pestilence, War, and Death) when he likened Layden and his teammates to "famine, pestilence, destruction, and death" for their opponents.

Layden was part of a unique team that year. Notre Dame was 10–0, and outscored opponents 285–54 (including a 27–10 victory over Stanford in the Rose Bowl) en route to its first consensus national title. Layden chipped in with his usual season, rushing for 423 yards on 111 carries and 5 touchdowns. The consensus All-American also threw a 65-yard touchdown pass to Crowley. Layden might have played his best game in the Rose Bowl. He scored 3 touchdowns: one on a 3-yard plunge, one on a 78-yard interception return, and another on a 70-yard interception return with 30 seconds left to play in the game. His booming punts also kept Stanford mired in its own territory.

After he graduated, Layden returned to

Iowa in 1925 to practice law and coach football at a small school called Columbia College in Dubuque. After two seasons, eight victories, five losses, and two ties, Layden moved to Pittsburgh to coach Duquesne University, where he also served as athletic director. In seven seasons, he led Duquesne to a formidable 48–16–6 record (.728). In 1933, his Duquesne team not only beat the University of Miami 33–7, in the Festival of Palms Game, an early version of the Orange Bowl, it also stuck crosstown rival and national powerhouse Pittsburgh with a 7–0 loss.

That was enough to earn him a call from South Bend. Layden fit the Fighting Irish like a glove. He was a favorite son, owner of a gifted football mind, an organized administrator, a guy who could work a crowd from a podium, and certainly not the least of the factors that made Layden attractive to Notre Dame was the fact that he was a staunch Irish Catholic. Before a disastrous 3–5–1 season under Heartley "Hunk" Anderson was completed, Layden was named the sixteenth football coach in the school's history. He would also replace Jesse Harper as athletic director.

Layden turned the ship around instantly, wining three of his first four games as coach and leading the Fighting Irish to a 6–3 record in 1934. That turned out to be his worst season as coach. He led Notre Dame to a 19–0 victory over the University of Minnesota on November 12, 1938, which was the school's three-hundredth win. The team won all of its other ten games that season and was named national champion by several organizations, but not the Associated Press. Despite his outstanding seven-season record of 47–13–3 (.769), Notre Dame never won a consensus national championship during his tenure.

Layden left in a huff after the 1940 season, during which the team won seven of its nine games. When his contract expired he was only offered a one-year extension, which he refused to sign. To put this in perspective, his previous contract extension had been for five seasons. He departed South Bend for a high-paying job as commissioner of the National Football League, a post he held for five

years. He was inducted into the College Football Hall of Fame in 1951.

CAREER STATS

Year	Att.	Yards	Avg.	TDs
1922	80	453	5.7	0
1923	102	420	4.1	5
1924	111	423	3.8	5
Total	293	1,296	4.5	10

NOTRE DAME COACHING RECORD

Year	W	L	T
1934	6	3	0
1935	7	1	1
1936	6	2	1
1937	6	2	1
1938	8	1	0
1939	7	2	0
1940	7	2	0
Total	47	13	3

LEAHY, BERNIE
Halfback/Fullback (1929–31),
5'10", 175 lbs.

"The other Leahy" had a fine career at Notre Dame. Bernie Leahy was not as famous as Frank, who played tackle and later coached the Irish, and the two were not related. The two were teammates, however, on Knute Rockne's 1929 undefeated national championship team, on which Bernie Leahy was a reserve. The Chicago native won his first letter the following season as a halfback, and was moved to fullback in 1931 when head coach "Hunk" Anderson took over the program. Frank Leahy had graduated the previous year, and Bernie saw considerable playing time. In 1932, he played his lone season of professional football for his hometown Chicago Bears.

LEAHY, FRANK
Tackle (1928–30); Head Coach (1941–43, 1946–53), 5'11", 183 lbs.

Even though he was a good player, Leahy is mainly remembered in South Bend for his outstanding coaching, which was second only to Knute Rockne, from whom he learned. You could almost say that Frank Leahy learned to coach football through osmosis.

His three-year playing career abruptly came to an end when he tore cartilage in his knee a week before he was set to start at tackle in the 1930 season. Leahy had also been a tackle the two previous years, including on the 1929 national championship team. After the injury, Leahy spent the season on the sidelines with head coach Knute Rockne, observing his techniques, and Rockne loved having a pupil at his side. The time spent with Rockne piqued Leahy's interest in becoming a coach himself some day.

After the season, Rockne invited Leahy to join him at the Mayo Clinic in Rochester, Minnesota, where Rockne was to have his phlebitis treated. He suggested that Leahy come along and have his knee examined, and the two shared a hospital room for a week. Rockne talked football Xs and Os and Leahy sopped it all up like a sponge. He would put it to good use. His .855 winning percentage (87–11–9) at Notre Dame trails only Rockne's .881 in college football history. Like his mentor, Leahy was an innovator, and brought the audible and pro defensive sets to the college game.

Upon his graduation from college in 1931, Leahy embarked on his coaching career, beginning as a line coach at Georgetown University. The following season he took a job at Michigan State working for Jim Crowley, one of the famed Four Horsemen. The next year Crowley moved on to accept a position at Fordham University and took Leahy with him. From 1935 to 1938, Leahy made a name for himself at Fordham, where he coached the "Seven Blocks of Granite," one of whom was Vince Lombardi. That fearsome front line thrust Fordham into national prominence. Fordham lost only two games in those four years.

After six years at Fordham, Leahy was ready for his own program, and in 1939 he took the helm at Boston College. In two years the Eagles went 20–2, including a 19–13 victory over the University of Alabama in the Sugar Bowl, which earned him a trip he wanted to take—a one-way ticket

to South Bend to coach the Fighting Irish.

Notre Dame was 8–0–1 in Leahy's first year, and two years later, in 1943, won the first wire-service national championship in program history. During World War II, Leahy had to leave to serve two years in the navy, but upon his return in 1946 he picked up right where he'd left off. The 1946 team outscored its opponents, 271–24, on its way to an 8–0–1 record, beginning a string of four seasons without a defeat and national championships in 1947 and 1949. By 1949, Leahy's postservice record was an astounding 36–0–2.

The 1950 season was an aberration. The team went 4–4–1, but it was back to its winning ways in 1951 with a 7–2–1 record. The Fighting Irish were third in the final Associated Press poll in 1952, and second in 1953, Leahy's last year, when they were undefeated (9–0–1). He fittingly won his final game as coach, 40–14, over SMU. Leahy's health forced him to quit coaching at the end of the 1953 season. During the fourth game, a 27–14 victory over Georgia Tech, he collapsed at halftime. At the time he was only forty-five years old and had only been a head coach for eleven seasons, but his successes—six undefeated seasons, thirty-six All-Americans, and twelve future inductees into the College Football Hall of Fame—are undeniable. He capped off a stellar career when he was inducted into the College Football Hall of Fame in 1970.

CAREER RECORD

Year	W	L	T
1941	8	0	1
1942	7	2	2
1943	9	1	0*
1946	8	0	1
1947	9	0	0*
1948	9	0	1
1949	10	0	0*
1950	4	4	1
1951	7	2	1
1952	7	2	1
1953	9	0	1
Total	87	11	9

*Notre Dame won national championships.

LEHMANN, JOSEPH ROBERT
Guard (1961–63), 6'0", 215 lbs.

Bob Lehmann, from Louisville, Kentucky, was an overachiever who made up for his lack of physical size with a strong will and an excellent work ethic. He played at the same high school, Flaget, as Notre Dame legend Paul Hornung. As for Lehmann, he played behind All-American Nick Buoniconti as a sophomore in 1961, making 41 tackles in 258 minutes. In 1962, as a junior, he became one of the team's top linemen, an excellent blocker on offense, and an even better defender. He was third on the team—behind guard Jim Carroll and center Ed Hoerster—with 367 minutes played and was second on the team in tackles, behind Hoerster, with 61.

Lehmann was named captain the following spring and played well despite leading a 2–7 team. He trailed only Bill Pfeiffer in tackles, with 95, and led the squad with 361 minutes played. He was a first-team Academic All-American and a second-team All-American. After college, Lehmann's size finally caught up with him. He was not selected until the seventeenth round of the draft (by the New York Jets) and never played on the professional level.

LEMEK, RAY
Guard/Tackle (1953–55), 6'1", 205 lbs.

Lemek came to Notre Dame after starring in four sports at Heelan High School in Sioux City, Iowa, where he was the football and basketball captain as a senior. He played football for Ed Simonich, who was a Notre Dame fullback in the late 1930s and recommended his alma mater to his top player. In South Bend, Lemek started at left guard as a sophomore and played all but 9 minutes in the season opener, a 28–21 victory over the University of Oklahoma. He played 347 minutes that season and would not relinquish his starting role until the second-to-last game of his junior season, when he blew out his knee.

The following season, despite missing spring practices, Lemek was back; he was named team captain and won back his starting spot at right tackle. He was a terror to opposing offenses. While playing for both Frank Leahy and Terry Brennan, he forced many turnovers and had a great nose for the ball. The Washington Redskins selected Lemek in the nineteenth round of the 1956 NFL draft. He proved his doubters wrong by lasting eight seasons in the NFL, the first five with the Redskins and the final three with the Pittsburgh Steelers.

LEONARD, JAMES
Guard/Fullback (1931–33), 6'0", 187 lbs.

"Big Jim" Leonard, from Pedricktown, New Jersey, played his very first football at Philadelphia's St. Joseph's Prep. By the time he graduated he was one of the best high school players in the City of Brotherly Love. Leonard played on Notre Dame's freshman team in 1930 and joined the varsity as a reserve fullback along with first-year head coach "Hunk" Anderson the following season. As a junior he spent time at fullback again before switching to offensive guard as a senior. That season Leonard showed his toughness, as he played six entire games without sitting out one play.

After leaving Notre Dame, Leonard played four seasons as a quarterback for the Philadelphia Eagles before retiring in 1937. He then went into coaching, taking an assistant's position with the Eagles before taking over the program at St. Francis College in Loretto, Pennsylvania.

LEOPOLD, BOBBY
Safety/Linebacker (1976–79), 6'2", 217 lbs.

Leopold, from Port Arthur, Texas, may have had only 6 interceptions during his entire three-year college career, but he made the most of them. He set a school record by returning 3 of them for scores. He was a bruising hitter and energetic player who could cover the pass as well as the run. He had 180 career tackles, despite struggling with knee and ankle injuries. The San Francisco 49ers selected him in the eighth round of the 1980 NFL draft, and he played his entire four-year pro career with the franchise, including the 1982 Super Bowl.

LEWIS, AUBREY
Halfback (1955–57), 6'0", 185 lbs.

Lewis, from Montclair, New Jersey, was Paul Hornung's fleet-footed sidekick. In his day, the world-class sprinter was the fastest player ever to suit up for the Notre Dame football team. An obvious threat to break into the open field, Lewis was also a standout defender.

Lewis was a backup left halfback in 1955 and rushed 56 times for 222 yards and 2 touchdowns. He also caught a 32-yard scoring pass, returned 4 kickoffs for 91 yards, and on defense made 4 interceptions. As a junior he was better across the board. In his best season, Lewis played 286 minutes and rushed 59 times for 292 yards, caught 11 passes for 170 yards and a touchdown, returned 6 kickoffs for 167 yards (27.8 yards per return), and ran back 5 punts for 46 yards. Defensively, Lewis picked off 3 passes and recovered a fumble. But Lewis was only a shadow of himself as a senior. He rushed only 11 times for 20 yards, and caught only 2 passes for 96 yards and a touchdown. The Chicago Bears selected him in the tenth round of the 1958 NFL draft, but he did not play as a pro.

LIND, HARRY NORMAN
Fullback (1960–62), 6'0", 195 lbs.

"Mike" Lind played during a down period for the Notre Dame football program, but he certainly did his job before injuries limited him to 21 minutes on the field as a senior in 1962. Lind came to Notre Dame from Calumet High School in Chicago, where he was an all-city running back in 1957. He was Notre Dame's starting fullback as a sophomore in 1960, his first year on the varsity, during which Notre Dame won just two of ten games. Lind was one of the team's few bright spots: he rushed for 167 yards on 53 carries and made 17 tackles. As a junior, he was the team's

second-leading rusher, with 450 yards on 87 carries, trailing only Angelo Dabiero, who ran for 637 yards. He was second in scoring, with 24 points, and caught 4 passes and made 31 tackles. The following season Lind was elected captain of the 1962 team before injuries cut his playing time to almost nothing.

Lind was not selected in the NFL draft, but he had a six-year career in the league with the San Francisco 49ers (1963–64) and the Pittsburgh Steelers (1965–68) during which he ran the ball 221 times for 661 yards and 8 touchdowns.

LINS, GEORGE
Center/Guard/Fullback/Halfback/End (1896–1901), 6'0", 185 lbs.

Obviously there were different, more lenient, rules regarding eligibility in the 1800s. That's why Lins, from Wilmington, Illinois, shares a Notre Dame school record that will never be broken: he played for the team for six years. It's a record he tied, following teammate Jack Mullen, who was on the squad from 1894 to 1899.

In his six years on the Notre Dame football team, Lins played at center, guard, fullback, halfback, and end. For those of you scoring at home, that's five positions. He also played for four different coaches, which might have something to do with his adaptive nature. Then again, he played as many as three positions in one season. There were no computers back in those days and records are somewhat spotty, but some accounts have Lins playing forty-eight games in his career, which is coincidentally what a four-year player would play today.

The fleet-footed player with good blocking skills began his career as a backup center in 1896. The following season he was the team's starting left guard and also played some at center, including a 0–0 tie against Rush Medical in the season opener. He was the left guard in a 62–0 victory over Chicago Dental Surgeons, in which teammate John Farley rushed for more than 400 yards. Most of the scores in that game came on runs of more than 50 yards. His third starting position was right halfback, and he scored 2 touchdowns in one game.

In his third season, Lins was the starting right halfback and was called on to run the ball in short yardage situations. He had his best game with more than 80 yards rushing in a 52–0 victory over Michigan State. During season number four, Lins scored on a 6-yard run in a 29–5 victory over Englewood High School. In a 12–0 victory over Northwestern, he ran the ball once for 4 yards. Then, with three games left on the schedule, Lins quit the team for no known reason.

He came back, however, for a fifth season in 1900 and made an immediate impact. He was the team's starting left end and scored on a 95-yard touchdown run from the fullback position in the season-opening 55–0 loss to Goshen. He also scored on a 10-yard run in a 64–0 drubbing of South Bend Howard Park. His strong running near the goal line helped Notre Dame preserve a 5–0 win (touchdowns were scored at 5 points at that time) over Rush Medical. Finally, in 1901, Lins was the starting left end and also a reserve left halfback, and he scored the only touchdown in a 5–0 shutout of Beloit College.

LISCH, RUSTY
Quarterback (1976–77, 1979), 6'4", 210 lbs.

Lisch can make an interesting claim: he beat out Joe Montana for a starting position on the Notre Dame football team. He also completed more than half his passes and amassed 2,272 yards during his three-year career.

Lisch, from Belleville, Illinois, was Rick Slager's backup quarterback in 1976, but in the summer of 1977 head coach Dan Devine announced that Lisch, not Montana, would be the starting signal caller for the 1977 season. Before the season ended, though, Montana had won the position and led the 11–1 Fighting Irish to a national title. Lisch completed 51 of 94 passes for 568 yards and 2 touchdowns during the season, but it was Montana who won the quarterback battle, completing 99 of 189 passes for 1,604 yards. Lisch elected to sit out the 1978 season, and

it was a good thing because Montana was back, and better than ever. Lisch came back and led the team in 1979, occupying the starting position from beginning to end. He completed 108 of 208 passes for 1,437 yards and 4 touchdowns. On the negative side, he chucked 10 interceptions.

The St. Louis Cardinals selected Lisch in the fourth round of the NFL draft. He played with the Cardinals from 1980 to 1983, and with the Chicago Bears in 1984. His career totals were 55 of 115 attempts for 547 yards, 1 touchdown, and 11 interceptions.

CAREER STATS

Year	Att.	Comp.	Pct.	Yards	TDs
1976	41	16	.381	267	2
1977	94	51	.543	568	2
1978	Did not play				
1979	208	108	.519	1,437	4
Total	343	175	.510	2,272	8

LIVINGSTONE, ROBERT EDWARD
Halfback (1942, 1946–47), 6'0", 168 lbs.

Bob Livingstone was a real speed burner who was a threat to break a big play every time he was on the field, be it by any of the three Rs: running, receiving, or returning. He had come to Notre Dame after playing football at Hammond High School in Indiana, where he earned all-state honors in 1940.

In 1942, Livingstone was the starting left halfback in head coach Frank Leahy's new T formation. He hooked up with quarterback Angelo Bertelli for scores in a 27–0 victory over Stanford and a 28–0 shutout of Iowa Pre-Flight. He also scored a rushing touchdown in a 27–20 victory over Northwestern.

Livingstone then missed the following three seasons while serving in the army, but he returned to South Bend in 1946. During that season he ran for 191 yards on 40 carries as Terry Brennan's backup at left halfback on the Fighting Irish's 8–0–1 national championship squad. The following season Notre Dame was 9–0, and Livingstone again helped the team to a national championship. He ran for 242 yards on 45 carries while scoring 4 touchdowns, and he grabbed 4 passes for 78 yards.

Livingstone played four seasons of pro ball for four different teams in two different leagues. He was a member of three teams that were in the All-American Football Conference: the Chicago Rockets in 1948, the Chicago Hornets in 1949, and the Buffalo Bills in 1950. The following year he moved over to the NFL to play for the Baltimore Colts—his final year as a pro.

LONGO, TOM
Defensive back (1963–65), 6'1", 195 lbs.

Longo came to Notre Dame with a reputation for throwing passes, but in college he made his name by defending them. He was a quarterback both in high school in Lyndhurst, New Jersey, and on Notre Dame's freshman team, but with future Heisman Trophy winner John Huarte entrenched in the quarterback slot for two more seasons, it made sense to move Longo. That gave head coach Ara Parseghian a defensive back who combined the speed to stick with receivers and the hitting ability to make them think twice about catching the ball.

Longo switched to the backfield before his sophomore season in 1963, and he became one of the Fighting Irish's top defenders. He played in special defensive situations as a sophomore and made 17 tackles and had 2 interceptions. The next year, while Huarte was winning the Heisman and Parseghian was leading the team to a 9–1 record in his first season, Longo led all defensive backs in tackles, with 72, while starting at right cornerback. He intercepted 4 passes, shared the team lead by breaking up 10 passes, and also recovered a fumble. As a senior, Longo again led all defensive backs in tackles, with 73. He also intercepted 4 passes, broke up two others, and recovered another fumble. The NFL's Philadelphia Eagles and the AFL's Oakland Raiders selected Longo in the fourteenth round of the draft. He played for the New York Giants in 1969

and 1970, and for the St. Louis Cardinals in 1971.

LUHN, HENRY
Halfback (1887)

All of the touchdowns, wins, championships, and accolades that have become part of Notre Dame's storied history can be traced back to one man: Henry Luhn, the first coach, captain, and halfback at the university.

In March 1887, Luhn called a meeting in Brownson Hall to start the ball rolling for a football program. Fifteen students showed up. Sure, there were obstacles: Luhn had no football, and there was no field, no uniforms, and no opponents. Two weeks later the first football arrived at the school, and the campus literary society raised money to buy white cotton uniforms, if only eleven of them.

The first field was near Sorin Hall, which is about 100 yards south of the Golden Dome. The sidelines were marked by rocks and the end zones by trees. Eventually two poles were put up for practice kicks. Practices were held with the original fifteen men who displayed enough interest to show up for the meeting, and innocent bystanders who happened upon the practices and were snookered into participating. The final team was cut down to eleven because that was how many uniforms they had.

There was a practice game in April, and the first official contest, an 8–0 loss at home against the University of Michigan, took place on November 23. It was the only game of the first season. From this humble beginning, Henry Luhn's enthusiasm for football would be echoed by Notre Dame players and fans for succeeding generations with an all-encompassing ardor he hardly could have imagined.

LUJACK, JOHNNY
Quarterback/Punter/Defensive back (1943, 1946–47), 6'0", 180 lbs.

Johnny Lujack is one half of the answer to the following question: Who are arguably the two best quarterbacks ever to play for the same college team at the same time?

Lujack replaced Heisman Trophy–winner Angelo Bertelli, and (after serving in the navy during World War II), he won college football's top individual prize as well. Lujack, from Connellsville, Pennsylvania, combined a strong arm, outstanding mobility, fiery intensity, and natural leadership abilities to become quite possibly the best quarterback ever to play at Notre Dame. He was a tough defender and also a fine kicker.

Lujack backed up Bertelli on the 1943 national championship team, which won nine of ten games. Six games into the season, though, Bertelli left school to enlist in the Marine Corps. Lujack stepped up and helped Notre Dame win three of its final four games en route to the national title.

In his first start, a 26–0 victory over Army, Lujack threw for 2 touchdowns, ran for a third, and intercepted a pass. For the season, it was Lujack, not Heisman Trophy winner Bertelli, who led the Fighting Irish in passing. Lujack was 34 for 71 for 525 yards and 4 touchdowns. He also rushed for

Heisman Trophy–winning quarterback John Lujack was a two-time All-American and led Notre Dame to three national championships.

191 yards on 46 carries. Lujack was absent from South Bend in 1944 and 1945 while he served in the navy during World War II. In 1946 he returned to the campus and began the second act of a spectacular career. Lujack ran the offense out of the T formation and completed 49 of 100 passes for 778 yards and 6 touchdowns. He also rushed for 108 yards on 23 carries with another touchdown, handled the team's punting duties, and was a stellar defensive back who tied for the team lead with 3 fumble recoveries. Lujack's most memorable play of the year occurred when he stacked up Army fullback Doc Blanchard on a scoring run to preserve a scoreless tie. At the time, Army was ranked first in the nation and Notre Dame second. By the end of the year, the teams flip-flopped spots, and Notre Dame, at 8–0–1, won the national crown. Lujack was a consensus All-American and runner-up in the Heisman voting to Army's Glenn Davis.

Lujack was back for more in 1947. He passed for 777 yards, 9 touchdowns, and 8 interceptions, and rushed for 139 yards and another score. He was again a consensus All-American, and this time won the Heisman and was named the Associated Press Male Athlete of the Year, while the Fighting Irish were again undefeated at 9–0 and won another national title.

The Chicago Rockets selected Lujack in the sixteenth round of the 1947 All-American Football Conference draft. He ended up playing four years in the NFL, all for the Chicago Bears. During that short stint, Lujack was a two-time Pro Bowl participant and led the Bears in scoring four times. In 1949, he set an NFL record by passing for 458 yards and 6 touchdowns against the Chicago Cardinals.

In 1952, Lujack retired from the pro ranks to return to South Bend as the backfield coach in 1952. As a fitting reward for a spectacular career, he was inducted into the College Football Hall of Fame in 1960.

CAREER STATS

PASSING

Year	Att.	Comp.	Avg.	Yards	TDs
1943	71	34	.479	525	4
1946	100	49	.490	778	6
1947	109	61	.559	777	9
Total	280	144	.514	2,080	19

RUSHING

Year	Att.	Yards	Avg.	TDs
1943	46	191	4.2	0
1946	23	108	4.7	1
1947	12	139	11.6	1
Total	81	438	5.4	2

LUKATS, DICK
Halfback (1930, 1932–33), 6′0″, 180 lbs.

After a year as a backup at left halfback for head coach Knute Rockne and a season lost to a broken leg, Lukats, from Perth Amboy, New Jersey, earned a starting spot in 1932 for "Hunk" Anderson. He was a consistent runner, a solid blocker, and a versatile athlete. In one game, a 42–0 victory over Carnegie Tech, he completed two 21-yard passes and another for 25 yards on a sustained touchdown drive, and then laid out eight opponents with a block to spring a teammate for a touchdown on a punt return. For the season, he led the team in passing (13 completions of 28 attempts), with 252 yards and 2 touchdowns.

Lukats again started as a senior and scored the winning touchdown in a 13–12 season-ending victory over Army, and he led the team in rushing, passing, and scoring for the year. He ran for 339 yards on 109 carries, completed 21 of 67 passes for 329 yards, and scored 2 touchdowns. He also intercepted 2 passes.

LYGHT, TODD
Cornerback (1987–90), 6′1″, 184 lbs.

Lyght arrived at Notre Dame as a receiver, and left the school as one of the best defensive backs in the nation. He had size, speed, outstanding coverage skills, and could track down a pass with the best of them. He was a member of an athletic family—his father, sister, and brother all competed at the college level—and after an All-American prep career at Luke M. Powers High School, in Flint, Michigan, he fit right into the college game. In 1987 he logged more starting time than any other freshman, playing in all twelve games, in which he made 29 tackles and intercepted a pass. He also forced a fumble and broke up 2 passes.

As a sophomore, Lyght was a full-time starter at cornerback; he made 36 tackles and broke up 9 passes for the 12–0 national championship team. He led the team in tackles, with 6, in the 34–21 Fiesta Bowl victory over the University of West Virginia. After the season he was an honorable mention All-American. In 1989, his junior year, Lyght's superlative play made him a finalist for the Jim Thorpe Award, which honors the top defensive back in the nation. He had 47 tack-

All-American cornerback Todd Lyght was one of the best defensive players in Notre Dame history and became one of the best in the NFL. (Bill Panzica)

les and 8 interceptions (including 1 returned for a touchdown), and broke up 6.5 passes. Logging more time than any other player on Notre Dame's defensive unit, he started his twenty-fourth consecutive game and was a unanimous first-team All-American.

Expectations were high for Lyght as a senior. The *Sporting News* named him "the best player in college football" in its season preview issue, and he had another good season, although not as good as his junior year. He missed two games with a hamstring injury and made 49 tackles, had 2 interceptions, and broke up 2 passes. He was a consensus All-American and again a semifinalist for the Thorpe Award. The Los Angeles Rams selected Lyght fifth overall in the 1991 NFL draft. He later moved with the franchise to St. Louis and became one of the best cornerbacks in the league, making the Pro Bowl on numerous occasions. After ten years with the Rams, starting 137 of 143 games, including being a member of the victorious team in Super Bowl XXXIV, Lyght signed with the Detroit Lions as an unrestricted free agent in April 2001.

LYNCH, DICK
Halfback (1955–57), 6'0", 185 lbs.

Lynch, from Bound Brook, New Jersey, is best known for one play at Notre Dame. During his senior season, he scored the lone touchdown to beat the University of Oklahoma 7–0 on the road, ending the Sooners's forty-game winning streak. The multitalented player was one of Notre Dame's top offensive weapons in 1957.

Lynch's first two seasons of varsity college football were not spectacular. He was a backup at right halfback both seasons. As a sophomore he carried the ball 24 times for 124 yards and a touchdown. As a junior he rushed 14 times for only 10 yards, caught 5 passes for 54 yards, and returned 2 kickoffs for 54 yards.

As a senior, in addition to his 3-yard touchdown run with 3:50 to play against Oklahoma, Lynch was first on the Fighting

Irish in punt returns, kickoff returns, and receiving (with 13 passes for 128 yards). He was also second on the team in rushing and scoring. His 287 yards on 77 carries were second to Nick Pietrosante's 449 yards on 90 carries, and his 30 points trailed only Monty Stickles's 32. On defense, Lynch made 28 tackles from his defensive backfield position. For his career at Notre Dame, he gained 888 total yards and scored 6 touchdowns.

As it turned out, Lynch was a much better professional player. The Washington Redskins selected him in the sixth round of the 1958 NFL draft. He played in the nation's capital for one season before moving on to the New York Giants for eight more.

LYNCH, JIM
Linebacker (1964–66), 6'1", 225 lbs.

As a freshman at Notre Dame, Lynch had to sit on the sidelines with an injury as the varsity football team suffered through a 2–7 season. But the next year he and new head coach, Ara Parseghian, were key figures in Notre Dame's return to national prominence.

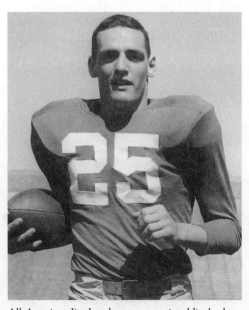

All-American Jim Lynch was a sensational linebacker who played on a national championship team, received the Maxwell Award, won a Super Bowl ring as a pro, and was inducted into the College Football Hall of Fame.

Lynch, from Lima, Ohio, was the captain of the football team in high school and on the roster of the baseball and basketball squads. His older brother, Tom, was the captain of the U.S. Naval Academy football team. Lynch, one of the best linebackers in Fighting Irish history, was the complete package. He could hit, run, move, and attack the football, and he was a smart player. As a 210-pound sophomore, he started in six games and played 117 minutes, making 41 tackles and breaking up a pass before a knee injury ended his season.

By the fall of 1965 Lynch was back at full strength, and starting his second season at outside linebacker. He was the team's defensive leader and signal caller as the Fighting Irish allowed a stingy 73 points all season and only a minuscule 2 yards per rush. Lynch led the team in tackles with 108, broke up 3 passes, intercepted another, and was named a second-team All-American.

As a senior, Lynch played even better. He was the team captain as Notre Dame went 9–0–1 and won a national championship, the school's first consensus title in seventeen years. They posted six shutouts that season, including three in a row—against Army, North Carolina, and Oklahoma—and held all ten of their opponents to a miserly 38 points. Lynch made 106 tackles, intercepted 3 passes, broke up 2 others, and recovered a fumble. For Lynch, the honors came fast and furious, as he made the first squad of every major All-America team. He also became the fourth Notre Dame player to win the Maxwell Award as college football's top player, and he earned first-team Academic All-American honors. He finished his Notre Dame career with 255 tackles and 4 interceptions.

The Kansas City Chiefs selected Lynch in the second round of the 1967 draft, and he played all eleven of his NFL seasons in Kansas City, helping to lead the franchise to the 1970 Super Bowl title. Another honor bestowed on Lynch, alongside his NFL championship ring, was his induction into the College Football Hall of Fame in 1992.

MacAfee, Ken
Tight end/Split end (1974–77),
6'4", 251 lbs.

Ken MacAfee was a prototypical tight end. He was tall and solid, fast enough to play end, and was an excellent receiver who could get open, often offering an outlet to quarterbacks Tom Clements and Joe Montana.

The Brockton, Massachusetts, native was a two-time prep All-American and was twice named all-state. He caught 10 passes in each of his final two seasons to set a school record, and he was on the varsity golf, track and field, and basketball teams while making the dean's list.

MacAfee began his college career in 1974 as a big split end until an injury opened up a spot at tight end, where he would make his name and become a three-time All-American. In his first year he caught 14 passes for 146 yards. As a sophomore, MacAfee moved into the starting lineup and led the Fighting Irish in receiving, with 26 receptions for 333 yards and 5 touchdowns, good enough for first-team All-American honors. In 1976, he again led the team in receiving, with 34 catches for 482 yards and 3 touchdowns. Among his many highlights were scoring the team's only touchdown in a 31–10 season-opening loss to eventual national champion Pittsburgh, and ripping up his father's alma mater, the University of Alabama. He played one of the best games of his career in the 21–18 victory over the Crimson Tide, for which his father, Ken Sr., was a wide receiver. The voters noticed his play, and MacAfee was a consensus All-American.

MacAfee kept getting better. His 1977 senior season was his best, with 54 receptions

Three-time All-American tight end Ken MacAfee was a favorite target of quarterback Joe Montana.

for a team-high 797 yards, and he scored 6 touchdowns for the 11–1 team that was named national champions. He grabbed 4 passes for 45 yards in Notre Dame's surprise 38–10 victory over the University of Texas in the Cotton Bowl. He was a consensus All-American and finished third in the voting for the Heisman Trophy, which was won that season by Texas running back Earl Campbell.

MacAfee stands fifth on Notre Dame's all-time receiving list, with 128 catches for 1,759 yards. The San Francisco 49ers selected him as the seventh overall pick in the 1978 NFL draft. In the same draft, defensive tackle Ross Browner was selected eighth by the Cincinnati Bengals, and defensive back Luther Bradley was chosen eleventh by the Detroit Lions. MacAfee played two seasons for the 49ers before retiring from the game.

CAREER STATS

Year	Rec.	Yards	Avg.	TDs
1974	14	146	10.4	1
1975	26	333	12.8	5
1976	34	483	14.2	3
1977	54	797	14.8	6
Total	128	1,759	13.7	15

MacDonald, Tom
Defensive back (1961–63), 5′11″, 180 lbs.

MacDonald, of Downey, California, was virtually a one-way player during the final seasons of single-platoon football. As a crafty defensive back he proved to be one of the best pass defenders in Fighting Irish history, and he still ranks among the leaders in more than one interception category.

MacDonald was a third-string halfback as a sophomore in his first varsity season. He carried the ball twice for 3 yards, returned 4 punts for 3 yards, and, more important, made the first of many interceptions. As a junior, in 1962, MacDonald set a school record with 9 interceptions (it was broken ten years later by Mike Townsend, who picked off 10 passes). He also ran the ball 10 times for 14 yards and caught a pass for no gain, and he made 29 tackles, broke up 5 passes, and returned 2 kickoffs for 30 yards. In his senior year, MacDonald, as a defensive specialist, led the team with 5 interceptions, broke up 6 passes, and was sixth in tackles, with 47, and tops in punt returns, with 8 for 56 yards. He also recovered a fumble.

MacDonald finished his career at Notre Dame with 15 interceptions, the school record for players with only three years of eligibility. Luther Bradley has since surpassed him, with 17 in four years of football. The Washington Redskins picked MacDonald in the fifteenth round of the NFL draft, but he did not play in the league.

CAREER STATS

Year	Int.	Yards	Avg.	TDs
1961	1	23	23.0	0
1962	9	81	9.0	0
1963	5	63	12.6	1
Total	15	167	11.1	1

Mack, Bill
Halfback (1958–60), 6′0″, 175 lbs.

If he weren't so injury prone in college, "Red" Mack would have been an all-time Notre Dame asset. He was a quick and talented running back from Allison Park, Pennsylvania, who was a starting left halfback as a sophomore and averaged almost 6 yards per rush. He missed the first two games of his junior season with a knee injury and was never quite the same player again. He had the knee surgically repaired after the 1959 season and was only able to play two games as a senior.

Pittsburgh of the NFL and Buffalo of the AFL selected him in the tenth round of the 1961 draft. He showed what Notre Dame missed out on by lasting six seasons in the pro ranks, playing for Pittsburgh from 1961 to 1963 and in 1965, Philadelphia in 1964, and Atlanta and Green Bay in 1966.

Maggioli, Achille
Halfback (1943–44), 5′11″, 180 lbs.

Mainly because of World War II, "Chick" Maggioli played for three different college football teams, and won titles at two of them. He was from Mishawaka, Indiana, and began his college career at Indiana University, where he made the football team as a walk-on. In 1943 he joined the Marine Corps Officers Training Program and was transferred to Notre Dame. He made the football team as a reserve halfback, and the team went 9–1 and won its first national championship for head coach Frank Leahy. The following year, with Leahy serving his country, Maggioli became a starter for interim coach Ed McKeever.

Before the end of the 1944 season, Maggioli was called for active duty. At war's end, he enrolled at the University of Illinois. Not only did he finish his degree there, he also helped the Illinois football team win the 1956 Big Ten championship. The Buffalo Bills of the All-American Football Conference drafted Maggioli in 1948. He played one season for the Bills, and one for the Detroit Lions and one for the Baltimore Colts in the NFL. After retiring from the pro ranks he was inducted into the Indiana Football Hall of Fame.

MAHALIC, DREW
Linebacker (1972–74), 6'4", 222 lbs.

Mahalic was often one step ahead of the opponent's offense. He had a quarterback's mentality, which allowed him to anticipate on defense and utilize his range and hitting ability. The Farmington, Michigan, native was a topnotch quarterback in high school, earning state prep Player of the Year honors. Head coach Ara Parseghian, however, switched him to linebacker when he got to Notre Dame, and he thrived at his new position.

The three-year starter led the entire team in field time by playing 287:31 his sophomore year. Mahalic finished the season with 77 tackles and 2 interceptions, one of which he ran back for a touchdown. He also broke up a pass. As a junior he made 59 tackles, recovered a fumble, intercepted a pass, and broke up another. Those statistics are impressive if you take into account the fact that the Notre Dame offense dominated games: the Fighting Irish outscored opponents 358–66 during the season, winning all eleven games and a national championship. In the Sugar Bowl, Mahalic recovered an Alabama fumble that set up Eric Penick's winning touchdown run on the following play. Notre

Dame won the game 24–23 to clinch the championship. During his senior year in 1974, the only player who made more tackles than Mahalic, who had 117, was linebacker Greg Collins, with 144. Six of Mahalic's hits resulted in losses; he also recovered a fumble, intercepted a pass, and broke up four others.

Mahalic finished his career with 253 tackles, and he was selected in the third round of the 1975 NFL draft by the Denver Broncos. He played one season for the San Diego Chargers and three more for the Philadelphia Eagles.

MARTIN, DAVE
Linebacker (1965–67), 6'0", 210 lbs.

At the linebacker position, Martin made up for a lack of size and experience with intelligence and outstanding reaction time. He was a fullback at Bishop Miege High School in Shawnee Mission, Kansas, though at Notre Dame he was a three-year starting linebacker who had 70 tackles as a sophomore. The next season, he was a key contributor to Notre Dame's 9–0–1 record and first national title in seventeen years. He made 62 tackles, recovered 2 fumbles, and in the season finale ran back an interception for a 33-yard touchdown in 51–0 drubbing of USC. He also had 71 tackles as a senior, which placed him fourth on the team.

The Philadelphia Eagles selected Martin in the sixth round of the 1968 NFL draft, but he played the 1968 season with the Kansas City Chiefs and the next for the Chicago Bears.

MARTIN, JIM
End/Tackle (1946–49), 6'2", 204 lbs.

Martin had a good reason to keep football in perspective, not that it affected his play. The Cleveland native was a bona fide war hero. He won a Bronze Star as a member of the Marine Corps before moving on to Notre Dame, where he played for a program that didn't lose any games.

All-American lineman Jim Martin played for undefeated Notre Dame teams that went 36-0-2 and won three national championships. He also won the George Gipp Award, played thirteen years in the NFL, was named to the Pro Bowl, and was inducted into the College Football Hall of Fame.

During the four years that Martin was at Notre Dame, the team had an undefeated record of 36–0–2 and won three national championships (1946, 1947, and 1949). Martin, who played on both sides of the ball, was a great lineman who combined quickness, strength, courage, and determination. He played end on defense and tackle on offense his entire college career. He started seven games at left end as a freshman and recovered 3 fumbles as Notre Dame went 8–0–1 and won the national championship. The following season the Fighting Irish went 9–0 and won another title; Martin rushed 10 times for 86 yards and a touchdown and caught 13 passes for 170 yards.

Martin's junior season included several personal highlights. He blocked a punt, which fullback John Panelli ran back for a 70-yard touchdown in a 28–27 season-opening victory over Purdue. He also caught a 13-yard touchdown pass in a 44–13 romp over Nebraska, and finished the season with 14 receptions for 98 yards and a touchdown.

Martin was a cocaptain his senior year, during which Notre Dame outscored its opponents 360–86 and only had one close game—a 27–20 season-ending victory over SMU. The Fighting Irish's perfect season earned them another national crown, and Martin was named a first-team All-American. He also won the George Gipp Award, which is handed out every year to the school's finest athlete.

The Cleveland Browns selected Martin in the second round of the 1950 NFL draft. He played one season for the Browns before being traded to the Detroit Lions, for whom he played a dozen seasons. Among his honors was a Pro Bowl appearance in 1962 and an induction into the College Football Hall of Fame in 1995.

MARX, GREG
Defensive tackle (1970–72), 6'5", 265 lbs.

Marx, from Redford, Michigan, broke his arm in 1969 and missed the entire season, but he more than made up for it with three fine seasons that accounted for his college career.

In 1970, he started at left tackle and quickly became an integral part of a very strong front four. He made 82 tackles, 8 for losses, and broke up 2 passes. In 1971, as a junior, he played more than 230 minutes at right tackle and made 85 tackles, second-best on the team. Twelve of his stops resulted in losses for Notre Dame's opponents, and he broke up 3 passes. After the season he was named a first-team Academic All-American. He was a cocaptain on the 1972 team and again ranked second in tackles, this time with 96, including a team-high 6 for losses. He also broke up a pass and was named to every prominent All-American team.

Marx's scholarly skills earned him a postgraduate scholarship from the NCAA and the National Football Foundation. The all-around student athlete was on the rosters of both the Hula Bowl and the College Football All-Star Game in 1973. The Atlanta Falcons selected him in the second round of the 1973 NFL draft, making Marx the first Fighting Irish player to be picked that year. He played only one season in Atlanta.

MASTRANGELO, JOHN
Guard (1944–46), 6'1", 210 lbs.

Mastrangelo was kept home from World War II because of weak eyesight, but became one of Notre Dame's most honored and valuable players both during and after the war. After earning four varsity football letters at Vandergrift High School in Pennsylvania, the lifelong fan of Knute Rockne naturally gravitated toward Notre Dame.

Mastrangelo was one of the first football players to wear contact lenses during a game, and earned letters in both of his first two years as a reserve lineman. A starter in 1945, he led the team to a record 7–2–1. His amazing performance as an open-field blocker and his fervor as a player earned him first-team All-American honors. When the war ended, coach Frank Leahy took over from interim coach Hugh Devore, and the team ranks filled with returning soldiers; Mastrangelo, however, remained the starting left guard. In his senior year he helped lead Notre Dame to an undefeated season, and the Irish finished first in the final Associated Press poll.

In 1947, Mastrangelo was a second-round draft pick of the Pittsburgh Steelers for whom he played two seasons. He later played for the New York Yankees of the All-American Football Conference in 1949, and the New York Giants in 1950.

MAYES, DERRICK
Split end (1992–95), 6'1", 204 lbs.

By the time he left South Bend, Mayes was Notre Dame's all-time leader in receiving yards, with 2,512, and touchdown receptions, with 22. His 129 catches ranked him fourth all-time.

Mayes came to Notre Dame from Indianapolis, Indiana, after being named to *USA Today*'s high school All-America team in 1991. He went right to work. As a freshman, his first 3 receptions were for touchdowns, and he finished the season with 10 catches for 272 yards while playing behind Lake

Dawson, who moved to flanker the following season. Mayes, who just about doubled his freshman output with 24 receptions for 512 yards, shared the split-end spot with Clint Johnson. He also scored 2 touchdowns. In one game, a 41–39 loss to Boston College in the final regular-season game of the year, he nearly outdid his entire freshman output with 7 receptions for 147 yards. It was Notre Dame's only loss of the season.

The starting position was all Mayes's during his junior year, and he made good use of it, becoming one of the nation's top receivers. He led the team with 47 receptions (including a team-leading 11 for touchdowns) for 847 yards. He earned honorable mention All-American honors and was named Most Valuable Player by the Monogram Club.

There was no letdown for Mayes in his senior season. As one of five Notre Dame captains, he again led the team in receptions with 48 for 881 yards. He had a career-high 8 catches in a season-opening 17–15 loss to Northwestern, and 7 grabs in a 35–28 victory over Purdue a week later. He finished his career with 6 receptions for 96 yards in a 31–26 Orange Bowl loss to Florida State and was named the Fighting Irish's Most Valuable Player. He achieved second-team All-

Two-time Monogram Club MVP Derrick Mayes holds the Notre Dame records for receiving yards and touchdown receptions. (Don Stacy)

American honors. The Monogram Club again named him its MVP, and he was a semifinalist for the Fred Biletnikoff Award, which is presented to the top receiver in the country.

The Green Bay Packers selected Mayes in the second round of the 1996 NFL draft. He was a member of the Packers Super Bowl championship team in 1997 and with their Super Bowl–losing team of 1998. Mays moved to the Seattle Seahawks in 1999.

CAREER STATS

Year	Rec.	Yards	Avg.	TDs
1992	10	272	27.2	3
1993	24	512	21.3	2
1994	47	847	18.0	11
1995	48	881	18.4	6
Total	129	2,512	19.5	22

MAYL, EUGENE
End (1921–23), 6'1", 177 lbs.

If it weren't for "Moose" Mayl and the rest of the Seven Mules, we may have never heard of the famed Four Horsemen. The Mules were the silent partners in one of the most explosive backfields in college football, and end Mayl was one of them. They didn't get the headlines, but they got the job done. Mayl, from Dayton, Ohio, was a starter at right end in his senior year. He was also a member of the Notre Dame basketball team. He played one season in the NFL, 1924, for the Dayton Triangles.

MAZUR, JOHN
Quarterback (1949–51), 6'2", 198 lbs.

Plymouth, Pennsylvania, native Mazur spent two seasons as a backup quarterback for the Fighting Irish before he got to show off his own strong arm and leadership abilities properly. As a sophomore and junior he sat behind Bob Williams, who led the team to a 10–0 record and a national championship in 1949. In limited action, Mazur connected on 2 of 5 passes for 36 yards. He was quite an

efficient fellow, since he was credited with 2 touchdown throws. He saw more action as a junior and completed 13 of 24 passes for 166 yards, 2 touchdowns, and an interception.

In 1951, the wait was finally over for Mazur, and the team was his. He turned things around. After four unbeaten seasons, Notre Dame had been 4–4–1 in 1950. With Mazur leading the offense, the Fighting Irish went 7-2-1. He completed 48 of 110 passes for 645 yards, 5 touchdowns, and 12 interceptions. He also scored 3 running touchdowns.

MCAVOY, TOM
End (1905), 5'10", 160 lbs.

McAvoy, from Corning, New York, started for one season at Notre Dame and then was nowhere to be found. It was a very good year for the smallish end, as he sprung loose for some long gainers in the school's 5–4 season. His 60-yard scoring run was the most memorable play in a 28–0 victory over Michigan State. He scored 3 touchdowns, including a 110-yard run, and made 2 conversions in a 142–0 victory over American Medical College. McAvoy's 25-yard run was the longest from scrimmage in a 22–5 loss to Indiana, and he ran back a kickoff for 60 yards in a 22–0 shutout over Bennett Medical College of Chicago.

MCCOY, MIKE
Defensive tackle (1967–69), 6'5", 274 lbs.

McCoy was an imposing physical presence who fit into the Notre Dame scheme instantly. His size and reach, which came in handy to deflect passes at the line of scrimmage, was coupled with amazing quickness. McCoy, who had been the captain of the city championship wrestling team and an all-state football player at Cathedral Prep in Erie, Pennsylvania, won the Hering Award as the team's top lineman during his first set of spring practices. That fall he split time with All-American tackle Kevin Hardy and had 43 tackles, 2 for losses, and intercepted a pass.

As a junior, McCoy was a full-time starter and made more tackles (72) than any other lineman, placing him third on the team overall. Eight of his stops were for losses, and he broke up 7 passes. In his senior year, McCoy evolved into one of the country's top linemen. He had 88 tackles, including 10 for losses, intercepted a pass, and broke up 7 others.

He was a unanimous first-team All-American, the Associated Press Lineman of the Year, and finished sixth in the voting for the Heisman Trophy. In his three-year varsity career, McCoy made 203 tackles and then played in the College All-Star Game. The Green Bay Packers took him as the second overall pick in the 1970 NFL draft. He spent six seasons in Green Bay, two seasons with the Oakland Raiders (1977–78), nearly two with the New York Giants (1979–80), and the rest of the 1980 season with the Detroit Lions.

McDONALD, DEVON
Defensive end/Outside linebacker
(1989–92), 6'4", 241 lbs.

McDonald was a big-play defensive lineman who was able to penetrate the opponent's line and get to their quarterback. That was, of course, when his knees were okay. McDonald was born in Kingston, Jamaica. His family later moved to Paterson, New Jersey, where he and his twin brother Ricardo, who went on to play for the University of Pittsburgh, were the top jocks at John F. Kennedy High School.

McDonald missed his entire freshman year of college because of his knee problems, and recuperation from off-season arthroscopic knee surgery forced him to miss the first three games of his sophomore season. He started four games at defensive end and played 132:27. In that time he had 8 solo tackles, 26 assists, and 4 sacks. In 1990, as an outside linebacker who started two games, McDonald had 23 solo tackles, 15 assists, and a sack. He finally became a full-time starter at outside linebacker in 1991. In 297:22 on the

field he had 29 solo tackles, 31 assists, 2 sacks, and 11 other hits for losses, and he was named an honorable mention All-American.

Because of his early-career injuries, McDonald was afforded a fifth year of eligibility by the NCAA, and went on to have his best season. He made 30 tackles, 17 assists, a team-leading 8.3 sacks, and another 4.5 tackles for losses. He played 247:57, forced a fumble, and broke up a pass, and was again named an honorable mention All-American. He was also named defensive Most Valuable Player in Notre Dame's 28–3 Cotton Bowl victory over Texas A&M, when he made 10 tackles, 4 for -22 yards.

McDonald finished his college career with 90 solo tackles, 114 assists, 15.3 sacks, and another 25.5 tackles for losses. The Indianapolis Colts selected him in the fourth round of the 1993 NFL draft. He played three seasons for the franchise before moving on to play for the Arizona Cardinals for a year.

McDONALD, PAUL
Fullback/Halfback (1907–08), 6'0", 180 lbs.

Before Knute Rockne and Gus Dorais came on the scene, there was Paul McDonald of Columbus, Ohio. He was not as heralded as the other two, but he certainly was as versatile. McDonald was solidly built and had explosive speed that lent itself to big plays on offense. He was also the team's kicker, passed the ball with some success, and was one of Notre Dame's top defenders, making Notre Dame's first-ever interception in an 8–4 victory over Wabash in 1908. In 1907, he scored on plays of 40, 50, 60, and 75 yards during a 6–0–1 season for Notre Dame.

The following year, as Notre Dame went 8–1, McDonald scored on two 65-yard runs, including 1 in a 3-touchdown performance in a 64–0 victory over Franklin. He also kicked 3 conversions in the game. He scored 3 touchdowns and a conversion in a 58–4 drubbing of Ohio Northern and scored 2 touchdowns in an 88–0 shellacking of Chicago Physicians and Surgeons.

McDougal, Kevin
Quarterback (1990–93), 6'2", 194 lbs.

If McDougal had gone to another school, he might have been a four-year starter, but at Notre Dame he had to wait his turn behind All-American Rick Mirer. When Mirer finally left school after the 1992 season, McDougal, from Pompano Beach, Florida, got his chance and more than made up for lost time. His 1993 season was a good career in one year, and he set many passing marks that may never be broken.

In his first three seasons, McDougal played a total of 49:05 in parts of fifteen games. As a senior he led the Fighting Irish to an 11–1 record. They were one play away from a national championship before falling to Boston College, 41–39, in the season finale. For the season, McDougal played

237:46 as the team's starting quarterback, completing 98 of 159 passes for 1,541 yards, 7 touchdowns, and 5 interceptions. He also ran the ball 55 times for 85 yards and 4 scores. He finished his career with an excellent outing against Texas A&M in the Cotton Bowl, where he was 7 for 15 for 105 yards, and ran for a touchdown on a 19-yard option in the 24–21 victory.

McDougal's career stats hold up pretty well. He completed 112 of 180 passes (.622 percent, a school record) for 1,726 yards, 10 touchdowns, and 6 interceptions. He also rushed 71 times for 159 yards and 6 touchdowns. His senior-year completion percentage of .616 (98 completions of 159 attempts) is still a single-season record, and he is the career leader in completion percentage (.622). His quarterback efficiency rating of 154.41 eclipsed Mirer's mark of 138.9, and his 9.58 yards per pass attempt is a school record for a career. Only John Huarte averaged more yards per pass attempt in a season (10.1 to McDougal's 9.69), and only Mirer's career interception avoidance percentage (.0329) is stingier than McDougal's (.0333).

Quarterback Kevin McDougal is the Notre Dame career leader in yards per pass completion (9.58), completion percentage (.622), and quarterback efficiency rating (154.41). (Bill Panzica)

McGill, Mike
Linebacker (1965–67), 6'2", 222 lbs.

A knee injury during McGill's junior year may have slowed him down, but it definitely didn't stop his progress. McGill, who was a four-sport star at Bishop Knoll High School in Hammond, Indiana, enrolled at Notre Dame in 1964. He became a starting linebacker on the varsity in 1965, his first year on the squad, and played 217 minutes, placing third on the team in tackles, with 88. After blowing out his knee in 1966, in a 38–0 drubbing of Oklahoma in the fifth game of Notre Dame's 11–0–1 national championship season, McGill came back as a senior. His final season turned out to be his best. He made it back onto Notre Dame's starting lineup and made 93 tackles, which was second on the team to Bob Olson, who had

98. His efforts earned him first-team All-American honors.

The Minnesota Vikings selected McGill in the third round of the 1968 NFL draft. He played in Minnesota for three seasons, and then moved to the St. Louis Cardinals for two years before retiring after the 1972 season.

MCGLEW, HENRY
Quarterback/End (1900–1903),
5'8", 170 lbs.

"Fuzzy" McGlew played alongside Notre Dame's first All-American, Louis "Red" Salmon, and was a major contributor to the early days of Notre Dame football. He was known for solid defense and the ability to break big plays. McGlew, from Chelsea, Massachusetts, limited his mistakes and never fumbled the football—an extraordinarily impressive achievement considering the fact that he handled the ball so much and that football was a much more mistake-prone game in those days.

In 1900, McGlew was a backup quarterback and replaced Salmon in a 55–0 season-opening victory over Goshen. In 1901, he won the team's starting quarterback position. In a 2–0 loss to Northwestern, he recovered a blocked punt and saved a touchdown with an open-field tackle. After Notre Dame topped Indiana, 18–5, he was referred to as the state's best quarterback by the Hoosiers's coach.

McGlew was back as the starting quarterback in 1902 and had runs of 80, 65, and 40 yards, plus a touchdown, in a 92–0 annihilation of American Medical College. In 1903, McGlew again earned a spot on the first team, but this time he played left end as Notre Dame had an incredible season. The team went 8–0–1 and piled up eight shutouts while outscoring its opponents, 292–10. McGlew scored a touchdown and covered a lot of ground in a 52–0 stomping of American Medical and played great on special teams in a 28–0 shutout of Missouri Osteopaths. Salmon would boot punts and McGlew would virtually beat the ball downfield, giving receivers no room to run.

MCGOLDRICK, JIM
Guard (1936–38), 5'11", 175 lbs.

McGoldrick followed the Notre Dame football team while growing up in Philadelphia, Pennsylvania. When he saw Philadelphia's Tom Conley, an All-American and captain, lead Notre Dame to a 60–20 victory over the University of Pennsylvania, he knew whose footsteps he wanted to follow in. It didn't hurt that McGoldrick, who played football and hockey and was on the crew team of West Catholic High School, was the son of an Irish immigrant. The selection of Notre Dame was automatic, and McGoldrick got to feel at home in South Bend, playing for line coach Joe Boland, a Philadelphia native.

McGoldrick was a three-year letterman who saw his playing time jump considerably from his sophomore to his junior season. He made up for his slightness with a gutsy perseverance; that quality made him a starter and captain as a senior. He led Notre Dame to an 8–1–1 record and a number five ranking in the final Associated Press poll, and he was named a second-team All-American.

MCGUIRE, GENE
Center/Tackle (1988–91), 6'4", 286 lbs.

Gene McGuire's start at Notre Dame was a slow one. He saw limited action his first two seasons. Although the Panama City, Florida, native made his way onto the starting lineup in his third season at South Bend, his momentum was halted during the third game of the season (a 37–11 victory over Purdue) when a knee injury forced him to get arthroscopic surgery. After the operation the rugged lineman only missed two games, and was back on the field to help Notre Dame place among the nation's top offensive teams. As a senior, McGuire was shifted over to center and was a starter in every game; after the season he was named an honorable mention All-American. The New Orleans Saints selected him in the fourth round of the 1992 NFL draft. He played in New Orleans in 1992 and 1993, for the

Green Bay Packers in 1995, and for the Miami Dolphins in 1995 and 1996.

McKeever, Ed
Head coach (1944)

McKeever was asked to act as interim coach in 1944, when Notre Dame head coach Frank Leahy was called for active duty by the navy. McKeever was the obvious choice. He was Leahy's top assistant, knew the personnel, and would keep things running at the previous level.

Leahy and McKeever had known each other since 1938. The two men met at a coaching clinic in Lubbock, Texas. Leahy, who was an assistant at Fordham, lectured on line play. McKeever, a native of San Antonio, was working at Texas Tech as a coach and spoke about backfield play. The two immediately hit it off. One year later, Leahy got the head coaching job at Boston College and hired McKeever to be his backfield coach. Leahy was hired at Notre Dame in 1941, and McKeever turned down a promotion in Boston to take the ride back to South Bend, where he had played freshman ball in 1930.

Three years later, with Leahy off to fight in World War II, McKeever's loyalty was rewarded with his selection as interim coach and athletic director. He led Notre Dame to an 8–2 record, which included three wins to start the season by a combined score of 152–0. Notre Dame was ranked in the top ten in the final polls.

McKeever earned himself another season as interim coach and athletic director. Initially he accepted, but eventually he turned the job down. At the postseason football banquet, University President Father J. Hugh O'Donnell spoke glowingly about the school's tradition of excellence. He went on and on about Leahy's teams of the early 1940s, but by most accounts, he barely mentioned McKeever and his 1944 team. McKeever was reportedly hurt and soon accepted an offer to coach at Cornell University.

Two years later McKeever took the head football post at the University of San Francisco, and in 1948 he entered the pro ranks as the head coach of the Chicago Rockets of the All-American Football Conference. By 1949 he was back in college as an assistant coach at Louisiana State University. He became the general manager of the Boston Patriots of the American Football League in 1960.

McKenna, Jim
Quarterback (1935), 5'10", 169 lbs.

McKenna was an early Rudy Ruettiger (the man whom the inspirational movie *Rudy* about an unlikely Notre Dame football hero was based on). The slight St. Paul, Minnesota, native was not even on Notre Dame's traveling squad, but when the undefeated Fighting Irish journeyed to Columbus to meet undefeated and heavily favored Ohio State, McKenna decided he needed to be there. He snuck onto the team train, was hidden in a berth by his teammates, and made it to Columbus. All he wanted to do was see the game, but he was caught by head coach Elmer Layden in the locker room. McKenna had another problem. He didn't have a ticket to the sold-out game. Layden liked the kid's determination and let him suit up and watch the game from the sideline.

McKenna was only supposed to watch—that is, until Layden ran out of substitutes. McKenna found himself in what (in the fiftieth year of college football) the Associated Press called "the game of the century." In a stirring 18–13 game, Notre Dame came back from a 13–0 deficit and executed the game-winning play with 32 seconds left in front of 81,000 stunned Buckeye fans.

At that time, coaches were not allowed to call in plays from the sideline; only an entering quarterback could bring in a play. Enter McKenna, Layden's only healthy remaining quarterback. The play was 57–1, a crossing pattern for two receivers. With about a half of a minute to go, the Irish were down 13–12 but were threatening on the Buckeye's 19-yard line. McKenna joined the huddle and called the play. The halfback option pass from Bill Shakespeare to end Bill Millner was successful, and the last of Notre Dame's three fourth-quarter touchdown plays.

That was the end of McKenna's college football career, and he did not play professional football, but at least he had one shining moment when he helped his team win an important game.

MEHRE, HARRY
Center (1919–21), 6'1", 190 lbs.

Mehre came to Notre Dame from Huntington, Illinois, with the intention of playing basketball, but after one conversation with head football coach Knute Rockne he was on the gridiron as a member of the football team. That conversation, which began with Rockne's astute assessment of Mehre's physical stature and segued into a sales pitch, changed the course of the young man's life.

Mehre began his college football career as a backup halfback on the freshman team. The next season, 1919, he made the varsity team and was switched to center. He earned a letter as a junior and was a full-time starter as a senior. Mehre was lucky enough to be a part of one of Notre Dame's all-time great runs. During his three varsity seasons, Notre Dame was an astounding 28–1.

After he graduated from Notre Dame, Mehre played two seasons of professional football for the Minneapolis Marines and then embarked on a career as a college football coach. In 1924, he took a job as an assistant coach at the University of Georgia. Four years later he was promoted to head coach and, over a ten-year span, led Georgia to a respectable 59–34–6 record. He left Georgia in 1938 to take a similar position at the University of Mississippi, where his teams went an outstanding 31–8–1.

MELINKOVICH, GEORGE
Halfback/Fullback (1931–32, 1934), 6'0", 180 lbs.

Melinkovich's career at Notre Dame spanned three coaching regimes. He was recruited by Knute Rockne and then played for

both "Hunk" Anderson and Elmer Layden. In his first varsity season, Melinkovich, from Tooele, Utah, was thrust into the starting fullback position after starting halfback Nick Lukats broke his leg. It was Anderson's first year as well, and the two helped Notre Dame achieve a 6–2–1 record.

In 1932, Melinkovich stepped up and led the team in rushing (88 carries for 503 yards) receiving (7 catches for 106 yards), scoring (48 points), and kickoff return average (41.0 yards). He was named a first-team All-American by many organizations. He missed the entire 1933 season with a kidney ailment, but was back on campus in 1934. Layden, who took over the program in 1934, found himself a man short at the halfback position, so Melinkovich became his starting right halfback. The versatile backfield player with speed, power, and soft hands had another great season. He led Notre Dame in rushing (73 carries for 324 yards) and scoring (36 points), as Layden kicked off his phenomenal coaching career with a 6–3 record.

MELLO, JIM
Fullback (1942–43, 1946), 5'11", 185 lbs.

Mello's wartime service in the navy was book-ended by two national championships at Notre Dame, but it was after his football-playing days were over that Mello did his most important work—training special athletes in Olympic competition.

Mello was a backup fullback in 1942 and Notre Dame's starter at the position in 1943, when the Fighting Irish went 9–1 and won the national title. He was second on the team in rushing, with 137 carries for 714 yards, and he scored 5 touchdowns. The ballplayer from West Warwick, Rhode Island, spent the next two years in the navy, where he played for Paul Brown at the Great Lakes Naval Training Station and was named to the All-Service team. He returned to Notre Dame in 1946 and won back his starting position. He may not have been as heralded as quarterback Johnny Lujack or halfback Emil Sitko, but Mello was certainly an integral part of the

8–0–1 team that won the national crown. He rushed 61 times for 307 yards and 6 touchdowns and caught 2 passes for 40 yards. During his two years as a starter, he ran for 1,021 yards and 11 touchdowns on 198 carries.

Mello had a recurring knee injury that cut short his professional career. He did play parts of five seasons with the Los Angeles Rams, Chicago Cardinals, Chicago Rockets, and Detroit Lions, but was forced to retire from football in 1951 and embarked on a career as a physical education teacher and administrator. He spent several years as the head of physical education at the Mansfield Training School, a facility for mentally retarded individuals in Mansfield Depot, Connecticut. His approach turned out to be the basis for the Special Olympics. In 1985, Mello received the Notre Dame Alumni Association's Harvey G. Foster Award, which honors former athletes who have gone on to do significant work in civic endeavors or university achievement.

METZGER, BERT
Guard (1928–30), 5'9", 149 lbs.

When it came to linemen, Knute Rockne was willing to sacrifice size for quickness and guts. Bert Metzger certainly tested, and proved, that theory. Even Rockne questioned Metzger's ability, to which the polite young man simply stated, "Yes sir, I'm small, but I'm rough"—rough enough to be a unanimous All-American selection after his senior season.

Metzger, who went to high school at Loyola Academy in Chicago, was equally impressive on defense and offense, where he opened holes for Notre Dame running backs Marchy Schwartz, Marty Brill, and Joe Savoldi. At just 149 pounds, often more than 100 pounds lighter than the man he was lined up against, Metzger was so fast that he would spring into action and use his leverage to neutralize a defender virtually as soon as the ball was snapped.

He was a backup at right guard in 1928 and 1929, when a tale that showed Metzger's

determination unfolded after the fourth game of the 1929 season. Notre Dame was playing at Carnegie Tech, and a running back named Bull Karcis was making mincemeat out of the Fighting Irish defense, plowing through the line for 10-yard run after 10-yard run. Metzger spoke up and asked for a chance to shut down Karcis. Despite his size, Rockne and line coach "Hunk" Anderson liked his bravado and figured it was worth the chance. Metzger, the smallest player on the field, performed as promised, and Notre Dame won the game, 7–0. When he was named a starter the following week, Metzger had finished his ascent from the tenth team to the first team and was a starter for the final year and a half of his college career. He and the 1929 team would go on to a 9–0 season and win a national championship.

The 1930 season was the final one for both Metzger and Rockne, and it resulted in a 10–0 season, another national championship, and first-team All-American status for Metzger. To cap off a topnotch career, Bert Metzger was a 1982 inductee into the College Football Hall of Fame.

MILLER, CREIGHTON
Halfback (1941–43), 6'0", 187 lbs.

Miller was the last in a long line of Millers to attend Notre Dame. This included his father Harry, a starting running back from 1907 to 1909; his uncle Walter, a blocking back for George Gipp; his uncle Don, who was one of the legendary Four Horsemen; his uncle Ray, who played left end behind Knute Rockne; his uncle Gerry, who was a reserve on the topnotch teams of the early 1920s; and his older brother Tim. Creighton himself was a great high school athlete from Wilmington, Delaware, but attempts by other schools to recruit him proved to be futile. "My father didn't ask me what college I wanted to attend," he was quoted as saying, "he told me what time the train left for South Bend."

Even though he had a shaky start with head coach Frank Leahy, Miller followed in the family tradition. It helped that he pos-

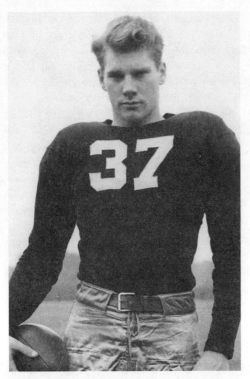

All-American halfback Creighton Miller, who came from a long line of fine Fighting Irish athletes, played on the 1943 national championship team and was inducted into the College Football Hall of Fame.

sessed the versatility of another all-time Irish standout, George Gipp, and enough speed to earn a letter sprinting for the track team. Things didn't always go well for Miller at Notre Dame. A routine physical indicated that he had high blood pressure, and he was instructed by doctors to avoid strenuous exercise indefinitely. Miller told Leahy of his diagnosis and that he would not be able to participate in spring workouts. Leahy was a no-nonsense coach who did not tolerate anything but 110 percent effort, and the slightest suggestion of laziness infuriated him; he didn't even trust a doctor's diagnosis as an excuse. Leahy voiced the opinion that Miller might not be of the stock to survive at Notre Dame. In 1941, Miller still made the team as a backup halfback, and carried the ball 23 times for 183 yards and a touchdown. He also caught a 40-yard pass and punted 4 times for an average of 49 yards. He made it onto the

starting lineup in 1942 and had a few highlights: one was a 68-yard touchdown run in a 13–13 tie against a highly favored Great Lakes All-Service team.

A war was on, and Miller decided to enlist in the army in the spring of 1943. His army physical confirmed that he really did have hypertension, and he spent six weeks in a military hospital before receiving his discharge. He returned to Notre Dame, and with this latest news, Leahy was finally convinced that Miller was not concocting his ailment, so the two reached an agreement. Miller was to practice and practice hard, but if he felt tired or got dizzy he could rest. This was a major concession for Leahy. Miller and Notre Dame went on to have a great season in 1943. Notre Dame was 9–1, and Leahy won his first national championships, thanks in large part to Miller.

Miller became only the second Notre Dame runner to compile more than 900 yards. He led the team with 911 yards on 151 carries and scored 13 touchdowns. He also led the team with 6 interceptions, 7 punt returns for 151 yards, and 4 kickoff returns for 53 yards. He was a consensus All-American and fourth in voting for the Heisman Trophy, finishing three slots behind his teammate, quarterback Angelo Bertelli.

The Brooklyn Tigers used a second-round draft pick to select Miller in 1944, but he opted instead to go to Yale Law School. In recognition of his outstanding accomplishments, Miller was inducted into the College Football Hall of Fame in 1976.

MILLER, DON
Halfback (1922–24), 5'11", 160 lbs.

Don was not only the best of five Miller brothers from Defiance, Ohio, to play football at Notre Dame, he was also the best (statistically) of the quartet that were dubbed the Four Horsemen. Miller led the Horsemen in receiving 3 times, in rushing twice, and in scoring once.

Indeed, he almost didn't go to Notre Dame at all, but a hard sell by head coach

Knute Rockne eventually won him over, and Miller decided to follow in the footsteps of three of his brothers to South Bend. Harry "Red" Miller was an All-American in 1909; Ray, who was eventually elected the mayor of Cleveland, played backup to Rockne; and Walter was a starting fullback in 1917. His fourth brother, Gerry, played at the same time as Don and was a backup.

Rockne, usually taciturn when it came to public praise of his players, was quick to call Miller the best open-field runner he ever coached. Miller had the speed to turn the corner, and he averaged 6.8 yards per carry during his career, still a school record. During his sophomore season, Miller emerged as a starter. He was second on the team—behind Jim Crowley's 566 yards—with 472 yards and 3 touchdowns on 87 carries. He was also a feared kick returner, running back one kickoff for a 95-yard score, and he caught 6 passes for 144 yards and a touchdown.

As a junior, in 1923, Miller emerged as the team's leading rusher, with 698 yards on 89 carries and 9 touchdowns. He also caught 9 passes for 149 yards and a touchdown, had an interception, and returned 4 punts for 69 yards and one kickoff for 15 yards. He was the only member of the crew soon to be named the Four Horsemen to earn first-team All-American honors.

In 1924, Miller was the starting right halfback on the undefeated national championship team, the first consensus title in school history. He rushed for 763 yards on 107 carries and scored 5 touchdowns, caught 16 passes for 297 yards and 2 touchdowns, made 2 interceptions, and returned a kickoff for 20 yards. This time, however, things evened up, as Miller was the only Horseman not to make first-team All-American.

Miller graduated from Notre Dame second on the all-time rushing list, behind only George Gipp. At the beginning of the 2001 season, his total of 1,933 yards on 283 carries still ranked fourteenth all-time. Miller also played varsity basketball at Notre Dame, and he was the president of his college senior class. He graduated in 1925 with a law degree, and

after a year of playing professionally for the Providence Steam Roller he embarked on his career as a lawyer-football coach. He worked as an assistant at Georgia Tech and Ohio State in the fall months, and the rest of the year at his firm, Miller, Hertz, and Miller, in Cleveland. As the business took off he phased out coaching. In 1941, President Franklin D. Roosevelt appointed Miller as U.S. district attorney for northern Ohio. Later he became national president of the United States Attorney's Association, and was inducted into the College Football Hall of Fame in 1970.

CAREER STATS

RUSHING

Year	Att.	Yards	Avg.	TDs
1922	87	472	5.4	3
1923	89	698	7.5	9
1924	107	763	7.1	5
Total	283	1,933	6.8	17

RECEIVING

Year	Rec.	Yards	Avg.	TDs
1922	6	144	24	1
1923	9	149	16.5	1
1924	16	297	18.6	2
Total	31	590	19.0	4

MILLER, HARRY
Halfback (1906–09), 6'0", 175 lbs.

"Red" Miller, from Defiance, Ohio, was the first of the long line of football Millers who attended Notre Dame. He was the first of five brothers to play football at the school. Not the least of his contributions to the program was two sons, one of whom was All-American Creighton Miller, who was the last of the Millers to play for the team.

Red was not the best known of the family to attend the school, but he was one of the best backs of his day. He was a four-year starter and led the team to a 7–0–1 record in 1909, when he earned third-team All-American honors.

Harry was followed by brother Ray, who was eventually elected the mayor of

Cleveland after playing backup behind left end Knute Rockne; Walter, a starting fullback in 1917; Gerry, a reserve in the early 1920s; and Don, one of the fabled Four Horsemen.

MILLER, MICHAEL
Flanker (1991–94), 5'7", 160 lbs.

Michael Miller made up for his small stature with two of the fastest feet ever to attend Notre Dame. His blazing speed, which was clocked at 10.32 seconds for the 100-meter dash in high school, made him a threat every time he stepped onto the field. He was a high school All-American in Sugarland, Texas.

His diminutive size, however, prevented him from doing much rushing from the backfield in college, but he dazzled fans as a wide receiver and kick returner. As a sophomore, Miller scored on a 70-yard pass from quarterback Rick Mirer in a 42–7 opening-game victory over Northwestern. He averaged upward of 30 yards per kickoff return that season as well. The next season he led all Fighting Irish receivers with a 21.7-yards-per-reception average, and he scored a touchdown on a 56-yard punt return in a 36–14 win over the University of Michigan.

Miller made it into the starting lineup for six games as a senior, but lost his spot when a hamstring injury slowed him down. He seemed well on his way to an All-American season on opening night, when he caught 7 passes for 142 yards and a touchdown in a 42–15 victory over Northwestern. The Cleveland Browns selected Miller in the fifth round of the 1995 NFL draft, but he did not play pro ball.

MILLNER, WAYNE
End (1933–35), 6'0", 184 lbs.

Millner, of Salem, Massachusetts, was responsible for two extremely memorable plays in Notre Dame football history. That they happened to lead the Fighting Irish to come-from-behind victories made them even more impressive.

Millner, a member of both the college (inducted in 1990) and professional (1968) football Halls of Fame, led Notre Dame in minutes played each of his three seasons on the varsity. He became a starter during the second game of his varsity career, when he blocked an Army punt late in the fourth quarter and fell on the ball in the end zone for a touchdown as the Fighting Irish defeated the Cadets, 13–12, in a season-ending victory. It was one of the few bright spots for Notre Dame, which went 3–5–1 that season. As a senior, Millner caught the game's final touchdown pass from halfback Bill Shakespeare in an 18–13 victory over heavily favored Ohio State, in the game dubbed the Game of the Century. He was named a consensus All-American and competed in the College Football All-Star Game.

The Boston Redskins selected him in the eighth round of the 1936 draft. He moved with the franchise to Washington, D.C., the following season as the Redskins toppled the Chicago Bears 28–21 in the NFL Championship Game. Millner caught 2 touchdown passes (of 55 and 78 yards) from Sammy Baugh. He played in Washington until 1941, and returned in 1945 for one more season after serving in the navy. Millner then worked as an assistant coach to Frank Leahy at Notre Dame and became the head coach of the Philadelphia Eagles in 1952.

MINOR, KORY
Outside linebacker (1995–98),
6'1", 245 lbs.

A four-year starter at Notre Dame, Minor came to the school after being named *USA Today's* Defensive Player of the Year in 1994, winning the Bobby Dodd Award as national prep lineman of the year from the Atlanta Touchdown Club, and making several All-American teams at Bishop Amat High School in LaPuente, California. As a freshman, Minor, who had blazing quickness, was the team's only regular freshman starter and he was on the first team in ten of eleven games, including the 1996 Orange Bowl against Florida. As a sophomore, Minor was third on the team with 8 sacks and led the team by forcing 3 tackles. During his junior year, Minor was only one of three defensive players to start all thirteen games and led the squad with 3.5 sacks, which ironically was his lowest total in his four seasons, in which he amassed 22.5 sacks. Minor was an honorable mention All-American as a junior, which set the stage for his senior season when he was a tri-captain and had 12 quarterback hurries, more than twice as many as any other Irish player, and 5 sacks. He played in the Senior Bowl.

The San Francisco 49ers selected Minor in the fifth round of the 1999 National Football League draft.

MIRER, RICK
Quarterback (1989–92), 6′2″, 217 lbs.

Mirer was born to play quarterback, and he began his career shortly thereafter. The son of a Goshen, Indiana, high school coach, Mirer threw his first football not long after he took his first steps.

He competed in the national Punt, Pass and Kick competition when he was just eight, and took those skills, plus his strong and extremely accurate arm, with him to high school, college, and the pros. After an All-American high school career, he sat behind quarterback Tony Rice his first year at Notre Dame and learned the position. He did well when called on, completing half of his 30 passes for 180 yards. The next season the position was all Mirer's, and the drop-back quarterback began a career that would see him set a school record for career touchdown passes, with 41. Ron Powlus has since broken the record, with 52 touchdown strikes. As of the end of the 2000 season, Mirer still has three of the top ten seasons (third, eighth and tenth) of total offense in school history.

As a sophomore, Mirer was the full-time starter and played more minutes than any other offensive player. He completed 110 of 200 passes for 1,824 yards and 8 touchdowns, earning honorable mention All-American status.

His junior season was his best. He completed 132 of 234 passes for 2,117 yards and 18 touchdowns (at the time a record, but broken by Powlus in 1994 when he threw for 19 scores). He also ran for 306 yards on 75 carries

and scored 9 touchdowns on the ground, setting school marks for points and total yards for a season. His 2,423 yards in total offense trails only Jarious Jackson, who had 3,297 in 1999, and Joe Theismann, who chalked up 2,813 in 1970. Mirer connected on 14 of 19 passes for 154 yards and 2 touchdowns in Notre Dame's 39–28 Sugar Bowl victory over the University of Alabama. His heroics again won him honorable mention All-American status.

For his senior season, Mirer was named captain and set a career record for total offense (6,691 yards), which was later topped by Powlus, with 7,479. He completed 120 of his 234 passes, finishing his college career with four seasons of .500 or better passing accuracy. He passed for 1,876 yards and 15 touchdowns and rushed for 158 yards and 2 more touchdowns. Mirer was named second-team All-American, and while he was only a finalist for the Johnny Unitas Golden Arm Award, he won the Most Exemplary Player Award from the Downtown Athletic Club and *Street and Smith's.*

Mirer's record as a winning quarterback was 29–7–1 (797). As of 2000, he ranks second—that's right, to Powlus—in consecutive games with a completed pass (34 for

Quarterback Rick Mirer set numerous passing records while at Notre Dame and is still ranked in the top three in many statistical categories. (Bill Panzica)

Mirer, 44 for Powlus) and lowest interception percentage in a career (.0329 to .0278). He is also second, behind Steve Beuerlein, in completion percentage for a game (12 of 14, .857, in a 45–21 victory over Purdue in 1991), and he is fourth in passing yards for a season (2,117 in 1991) and third for a career (5,997).

Mirer was the second player taken in the 1993 NFL draft. The Seattle Seahawks selected him after the New England Patriots used the first pick on quarterback Drew Bledsoe. Despite setting an NFL rookie record for passing yards, with 2,833 in 1993, his career is a bit of a disappointment through six seasons. He played four seasons in Seattle, and finished up third in franchise history in attempts (1,258), completions (678), yards (7,548), and touchdowns (36). He was then traded to the Chicago Bears, along with a fourth-round draft pick, for the eleventh overall selection in the NFL draft. He was subsequently picked up by the Green Bay Packers and followed that with stints with the New York Jets and San Francisco 49ers.

CAREER STATS

PASSING

Year	Att.	Comp.	Pct.	Yards	TDs
1989	30	15	.500	180	0
1990	200	110	.550	1,824	8
1991	234	132	.564	2,117	18
1992	234	120	.513	1,876	15
Total	698	377	.540	5,997	41

RUSHING

Year	Att.	Yards	Avg.	TDs
1989	12	32	2.7	0
1990	98	198	2.0	6
1991	75	306	4.1	9
1992	68	158	2.3	2
Total	253	694	2.7	17

MOHARDT, JOHNNY
Halfback (1918–21), 5'11", 170 lbs.

Had he come along at another time or played at another school, Mohardt might

have gone down as one of the best college football players ever. His misfortune was that he played on some of the best Notre Dame teams in history and in the same backfield as the great George Gipp.

Mohardt was a versatile athlete from Gary, Indiana, who could throw, catch, and run the ball well. In 1921, after two years of blocking for Gipp, he got the starting nod and showed what he could do. Mohardt led Notre Dame in rushing, with 781 yards on 136 carries, in passing, with 995 yards and 9 touchdowns on 53 of 98 attempts, and in scoring, with 72 points. With 9 passing touchdowns and 72 other points, he personally accounted for 126 of Notre Dame's 375 total as the team outscored its opponents a walloping 375–41. Mohardt was named a second-team All-American after leading his team to a 10–1 record in his final year. He graduated cum laude and played professional football for the Chicago Cardinals and Chicago Bears. He also played professional baseball for the Detroit Tigers.

For Mohardt, however, there was more to life than playing ball. He used his pro income to put himself through Northwestern University Medical School. He received a fellowship from the Mayo Clinic in Rochester, Minnesota, and was a resident there in 1931, when Notre Dame coach Knute Rockne came in for treatment of his phlebitis. Unfortunately, the coach met an untimely end in a plane crash a few weeks later. In 1933, Mohardt opened a private medical practice in Chicago and went on to have a distinguished career in medicine with the Army Medical Corps and later the Veterans Administration.

MONAHAN, BILL
Halfback/Fullback (1897–99),
5'8", 150 lbs.

Bill Monahan was a powerfully built back who packed a lot into his 5-foot, 8-inch frame. He was listed at 150 pounds, though some reports list him as low as 140. He was referred to as a "scientific player" for his intelligent play, but he was also a heck of a runner. Monahan, from Chicago, was a starting right halfback in 1897. He was the second-best running back in the game in which John Farley ran for 464 yards—in the 62–0 victory over Chicago Dental Surgeons, Monahan ran for more than 106 yards on 18 carries and scored a touchdown.

Despite his size, Monahan was Notre Dame's starting fullback in 1898. His best game was a 110-yards-plus performance in a 5–0 victory over Illinois, during which he ran the ball 10 consecutive times up the middle for 60 yards. He also scored 3 short-yardage touchdowns into the belly of Michigan State's defense in a 53–0 shutout. He was overshadowed by other players and finished his career as a backup fullback.

MONOGRAM CLUB

Every Notre Dame athlete who earns a varsity letter is admitted into the Notre Dame National Monogram Club. Among its many activities, the Monogram Club each year presents a Most Valuable Player Award, which is determined by a vote of team members. A partial list of past winners includes: Terry Hanratty, Bob Kuechenberg, Joe Theismann, Dave Casper, Ken MacAfee, Greg Collins, Joe Montana, Bob Golic, Vagas Ferguson, Bob Crable, Dave Duerson, Allen Pinkett, Tim Brown, Tony Rice, Raghib Ismail, Jerome Bettis, Rick Mirer, and Derrick Mayes.

MONTANA, JOE
Quarterback (1975, 1977–78), 6'2", 191 lbs.

Montana actually played his best football before and after he attended Notre Dame. It's difficult to believe that Montana, a gifted All-American football player and three-sport star in high school on his way to becoming one of the best quarterbacks in the history of professional football, completed just 1 of 6 passes on the junior varsity in South Bend.

Montana was one of seven signal callers to arrive on campus in 1974. He turned down a basketball scholarship from North Carolina State, was a champion high-jumper in high school, and was also named to the *Parade* magazine All-America football team. The versatile athlete out of Monongahela, Pennsylvania, was outplayed, however,

and was quickly demoted to the junior varsity, where he continued to struggle.

Montana began to find his stride as a sophomore, surprising some observers with his nerves of steel. He got a second chance to make a first impression as the team switched head coaches, and new coach Dan Devine had a chance to evaluate Montana without preconceived ideas about his play. Montana replaced injured starter Rick Slager during the third game of the season, and, astonishingly, led the Fighting Irish to a 31–7 win over Northwestern. Off the bench, Montana brought Notre Dame back two other times before a broken finger in the eighth game ended his season.

Injuries continued to plague Montana, who missed the entire 1976 season with a separated shoulder. The third game of the season continued to be pivotal for him. His college career began to flourish in 1977, when he came in to relieve starting quarterback Ray Lisch during the third game of the season and turned a 24–14 deficit into a 31–24 victory over Purdue. He started the next game, a 16–6 victory over Michigan State, and the next twenty games after that one. "The Comeback Kid" completed 99 of 189 passes for 1,604 yards and 11 touchdowns that year, earning him honorable mention All-American honors. The Fighting Irish were undefeated in his nine starts, which included a 38–10 drubbing of number one–ranked Texas in the Cotton Bowl. As a senior, Montana capped off a 9–3 season with another All-American honorable mention. He had his best year statistically by completing 141 of 260 passes for 2,011 yards and 10 touchdowns (he was only the third Notre Dame passer to top 2,000 yards in a season).

The NFL scouts still underrated Montana, who was selected by the San Francisco 49ers in the third round of the 1979 draft, eighty-second overall. Montana proved the naysayers wrong. His sixteen-year NFL career is one of the best ever. He led the 49ers to four Super Bowl wins, passed for 40,551 yards and 273 touchdowns, led the league in completion percentage 5 times, was named NFL MVP twice, won three Super Bowl MVPs, and was named the Associated Press Male Athlete of the Year in 1989 and 1990. He was traded to the Kansas City Chiefs in 1993 but did not have the high-caliber supporting cast he enjoyed in San Francisco and retired after the 1994 season.

CAREER STATS

Year	Att.	Comp.	Pct.	Yards	TDs
1975	66	28	.424	507	4
1976	Missed the season with a separated shoulder				
1977	189	99	.524	1,604	11
1978	260	141	.542	2,010	10
Total	515	268	.520	4,121	25

MORIARTY, LARRY
Fullback (1980–82), 6'2", 223 lbs.

Moriarty was as old, if not older, than the members of the senior class when he arrived in South Bend. Injuries and illnesses cut short his high school career, and he took a three-year hiatus before emerging at hometown Santa Barbara City College in California, where he played for a football team ranked in the national top ten.

Moriarty came to Notre Dame as one of the relatively few transfer students in the school's history—and he was ready to play. He was extremely strong and could bench press 485 pounds, more than twice his weight. He was a backup fullback in 1980, gaining 78 yards on 3 carries. The following year he was again a backup fullback and carried the ball 20 times for 94 yards and a touchdown. Moriarty broke into the starting lineup as a senior, carrying the ball 88 times for a total of 520 yards and 5 touchdowns. He left school as one of the all-time leaders in yards per carry, averaging 5.9.

Moriarty continued to make up for lost football time in the pros. The Houston Oilers selected him in the fifth round of the 1983 NFL draft, and he played the first four years of his nine-year professional career for the franchise. He also played with the Kansas City Chiefs from 1986 through 1991.

MORSE, JIM
Halfback (1954–56), 5'11", 175 lbs.

Morse, of Muskegon, Michigan, started three seasons at halfback for the Fighting Irish and combined his speed and hands with slick moves that often made something out of nothing on broken plays. He started at right halfback in 1954, his sophomore season. That year he proved his all-purpose abilities, with 345 yards and 2 touchdowns on 68 rushing carries, 15 receptions for 236 yards and 3 scores, 5 kickoff returns for 166 yards, and 4 punt returns for 31 yards.

As a junior halfback, he switched to the right side. He ran the ball 92 times for 404 yards and 3 touchdowns, caught 17 passes for 424 yards and 3 more scores, returned 5 kickoffs for 88 yards and 6 punts for 26 yards, and intercepted 2 passes.

It was business as usual during Morse's senior season, although his responsibilities seemed to grow as a receiver and shrink as a rusher. He led the team with 20 receptions for 442 yards and a touchdown, completed 5 of 7 passes for 68 yards, carried 48 times for 148 yards, and returned 4 kickoffs for 72 yards and 1 punt for 12 yards. His totals at Notre Dame were 2,443 yards gained and 12 touchdowns.

The Green Bay Packers selected Morse in the thirteenth round of the NFL draft, but he did not play in the pros.

MOYNIHAN, TIM
Center (1926–29), 6'1", 195 lbs.

Tim Moynihan was a four-year varsity player and three-time letterman at Notre Dame. While playing for head coach Knute Rockne, the Chicago native rose through the ranks to become team captain during his senior year when the Fighting Irish went 9–0 and won the national crown.

After he graduated, Moynihan caught on as an assistant coach in South Bend. He later held similar positions at the University of Texas and Denver University. Three years after he graduated from college, Moynihan gave professional football a whirl, playing the 1932 and 1933 seasons with the Chicago Cardinals.

MULLEN, JACK
End (1894–99), 5′8″, 155 lbs.

Just like the multidimensional George Lins, Mullen, from Iona, Minnesota, put in a school-record six seasons on the Notre Dame football team. He also has the lone distinction of being the only three-time captain of the most storied team in college football history and the only player to start in the same position for five seasons.

Mullen was a fearless sort who started at right end during his final five campaigns and was the team's captain from 1897 to 1899. He was one of the players to leave the field in protest of a bad call in a 4–0 loss to Chicago Physicians & Surgeons in 1896, but he could boast of many livelier highlights during his extended college career. Among them were a 90-yard touchdown run in a 46–0 romp over South Bend Commercial Athletic Club and a touchdown in an 82–0 trouncing of Highland Views, both in 1896.

The following season was Mullen's first as captain. In 1898, he was again named team captain and scored a touchdown and ran for more than 50 yards in a 53–0 drubbing of Michigan State. Mullen was still at it in 1899, when he ran for 70 yards on 10 carries in a season-opening 29–5 victory over Englewood High School. Mullen must have realized that his college career was almost finished when the right end let several of his teammates serve as game captains that season for valuable experience.

MURPHY, GEORGE
End (1940–42), 6′0″, 175 lbs.

Murphy, a hometown schoolboy from South Bend, had a solid career at Notre Dame. He was a backup right end in 1940 and became a starter the following season, finishing with 13 receptions for 130 yards and 2 blocked punts. In 1942, Murphy again started at right end and was elected team captain, hooking up with quarterback Angelo Bertelli on scoring plays. He went on to become a longtime assistant coach for the Fighting Irish.

MUTSCHELLER, JIM
End (1949–51), 6′1″, 198 lbs.

Mutscheller's first full varsity season was 1949, when Notre Dame, under head coach Frank Leahy, went undefeated and won a national championship. Though only a backup, he contributed his share: the Beaver Falls, Pennsylvania, native intercepted a pass to ensure a season-ending 27–20 victory over SMU. Mutscheller, who played behind Bill Wightkin at left end, was primarily a defensive end, but that year he did catch 2 passes for 27 yards.

The next season Mutscheller got the starting nod and led the team with a school record 35 receptions (topping former teammate Leon Hart), and 426 yards (surpassing Wightkin). He also scored 7 touchdowns and led the Fighting Irish in points, with 42. He was named captain for his senior season and was again the team leader, with 20 receptions for 305 yards and 2 touchdowns. Mutscheller went undrafted but still had an eight-year NFL career, all with the Baltimore Colts.

End Jim Mutscheller played on the 1949 national championship team, later set several school records, and was named captain for his senior season. He had an eight-year NFL career with the Baltimore Colts.

NIEHAUS, STEVE
Defensive end/Defensive tackle (1972–75), 6'5", 260 lbs.

Because of knee injuries, this Cincinnati kid missed about half of his first two seasons at Notre Dame. Still, in the three years that he did play, his large presence was felt and he made 290 tackles, 25 for losses totaling 128 yards.

Niehaus had it all—size, strength, speed, and a killer instinct. With the exception of Alan Page, Niehaus was the best defensive lineman to play under head coach Ara Parseghian. He was a starter at tackle from his first game as a freshman in 1972. After five games, though, his knee gave out and he needed surgery. In half a season, Niehaus made 47 tackles, about 10 a game. He was back in 1973 to play tackle for the 11–0 national championship team. Again he missed the latter chunk of the season due to knee surgery, but in 1974, his junior year, he lasted the entire campaign. Parseghian moved him outside to end, and he responded by finishing third on the team, with 95 tackles, 13 for -82 yards. He also broke up 2 passes and recovered a fumble, and was named a first-team All-American for his efforts.

Niehaus returned in 1975 to claim a starting defensive end position for the second consecutive season. He led the team in tackles, with 113, and was a consensus first-team All-American, landing on the squad of every major organization and finishing twelfth in the voting for the Heisman Trophy. The Notre Dame National Monogram Club named him its defensive Most Valuable Player for the season. The Seattle Seahawks selected him second overall in the 1976 NFL draft. He played three seasons for the Seahawks and one for the Minnesota Vikings.

NIEMIEC, JOHN
Halfback (1926–28), 5'8", 170 lbs.

Niemiec, from Bellaire, Ohio, waited in the wings, playing behind All-American Christy Flanagan, until his senior year in 1928. That season Niemiec, one of the best passers on the team, carved his niche in history and was involved in one of the most talked-about moments in Notre Dame gridiron lore. It was Niemiec who threw the 45-yard desperation option pass to Johnny "One-Play" O'Brien in front of 78,188 people at Yankee Stadium to lift Notre Dame past Army, 12–6. That was the famous "Win One for the Gipper" game.

Before that season, during which Niemiec started at left halfback and threw for several touchdowns, his career included a few other highlights. In 1926, his sophomore year, he caught the game-winning touchdown pass in a 6–0 victory over Northwestern. He also caught the game winner in a 13–12 win over USC. During his junior season he led the team in passing, with 14 completions in 33 attempts for 187 yards. Before he won one for the Gipper, Niemiec won the Navy game, 7–0, with a touchdown pass, and nailed extra points to help secure other victories.

NOVAKOV, DAN
Tackle/Center (1969–71), 6'2", 225 lbs.

Novakov, of Cincinnati, Ohio, was a bright spot in Notre Dame's 21–7 loss to the University of Texas in the Cotton Bowl following the 1969 season. He played a great game at offensive tackle for the Fighting Irish, and was moved inside by head coach Ara Parseghian to fill the void left by the graduation of All-American center Mike Oriard. Novakov would start at the position for his final two seasons. In 1970, he helped Notre Dame win ten of eleven games and exact revenge on Texas in the Cotton Bowl with a 24–11 victory. He was named offensive Most Valuable Player by the Monogram Club following his senior season.

O'CONNOR, WILLIAM
End (1944–47), 6′4″, 215 lbs.

"Zeke" O'Connor was just seventeen years old when he first won a starting job on the Notre Dame football team. With so many college athletes off fighting in World War II in the 1940s, the NCAA altered its eligibility rules and opened up varsity football to freshmen. O'Connor was one of the beneficiaries. At first it looked as if his two top college choices were USC and Army, the two schools that most actively recruited him. When Fighting Irish head coach Hugh Devore entered the sweepstakes, however, things changed: O'Connor's father and high school coach were impressed and pointed the young man from Fort Montgomery, New York, in the direction of South Bend.

At Mount St. Michael High School, O'Connor was a three-sport standout; he was an all-state basketball player and also led the school to an All-Catholic title in football. He graduated high school in January 1944, packed his bags, and went out to Notre Dame, where he immediately enrolled in classes and joined the basketball team. The following fall, the seventeen-year-old was a starter on a varsity football squad with most of its players fighting in the war.

In 1945, O'Connor joined the navy and played for the Great Lakes Naval Training Center team. The following year he returned to Notre Dame, but with so many mature players returning from service, he couldn't make the grade. Notre Dame was a combined 17–0–1 in 1946 and 1947, winning a national championship each year. O'Connor, however, did not earn a letter either season.

The Buffalo Bills of the All-American Football Conference selected O'Connor in the fourth round of the 1948 AAFC draft. He played for the Bills in 1948, for the New York Yankees of the All-American Football Conference in 1949, and the Cleveland Browns in 1951. He went on to become a star with the Toronto Argonauts in the Canadian Football League.

O'LEARY, DAN
Tight end (1997–2000), 6′3″, 260 lbs.

O'Leary, a two-time All-State selection while playing for St. Ignatius High School in Cleveland, Ohio, which won the state championship his senior season, brought the receiving ability of a split end and rapidly improving blocking skills to the tight end position at Notre Dame.

He showed up in South Bend in 1996, but didn't see any action until the 1997 football season when he found the Fighting Irish in need of a tight end due to the graduation of Pete Chryplewicz and his backup Kevin Carretta. O'Leary was the starter heading into the season and played in six games, starting two, before shoulder and ankle injuries kept him out of six games. He did make it back on the active roster in time to play as a reserve in the 1997 Independence Bowl versus LSU. For the season, O'Leary made 6 catches for 81 yards. As a sophomore, O'Leary played in all twelve games and started one. He made only 3 receptions for 32 yards and recorded his first college touchdown. O'Leary was also the long snapper on special teams as a sophomore and junior, which was his best receiving season statistically. He caught 13 passes for 183 yards and 2 touchdowns. O'Leary, one of four team captains as a senior, led all 2000 Notre Dame receivers in playing time and formed a terrific tight end tandem with Jabari Holloway, also a captain. O'Leary caught 10 passes for 87 yards and a touchdown in his final campaign.

The Buffalo Bills selected O'Leary in the sixth round of the 2001 National Football League draft, using the 195th overall selection. He joined Holloway (fourth round, 119 overall to the New England Patriots). He became the second sixth-rounder from Notre Dame to go to Buffalo in the draft. The Bills had selected Tony Driver with the 175th pick.

OLIVER, HARRY
Kicker (1980–81), 5'11", 185 lbs.

It took two years of refining his skills on the junior varsity football team before Oliver, out of Moeller High School in Cincinnati, moved up to the varsity at Notre Dame. When he finally made it to the big team, he proved more than capable. He made 18 of 23 field goals and 19 of 23 extra points in head coach Dan Devine's final season in South Bend. Oliver's total of 73 points as a junior was just two short of the school record set by Dan Reeve in 1977. He had a strong leg and twice made field goals of more than 50 yards; he ranked third in the NCAA, with an average of 1.64 field goals a game, and was named a third-team All-American.

In his senior year, Oliver, a left-footed, soccer-style kicker, was reunited with his high school coach Gerry Faust, who took over the helm at Notre Dame in 1981. Faust's Moeller High School teams had won three consecutive state championships while Oliver was doing the kicking. For his final season he made 28 of 30 extra points, but struggled on 3-pointers, missing 7 of 13 attempts.

OLSON, BOB
Linebacker (1967–69), 6'0", 226 lbs.

Olson made the most of his three years on the Notre Dame varsity football team. He led the team in tackles each season and was a team cocaptain during the latter two.

The hard-hitting inside linebacker

from Superior, Wisconsin, jumped right in as a sophomore. His team-leading tackle total was 98, 6 of which were for losses. He also broke up 5 passes and recovered a fumble. As a junior, Olson made 129 tackles, which was the highest total for a Notre Dame player in five seasons. Eight of the hits were for losses, and he also broke up 3 passes.

Olson continued to improve, and as a senior he made a school record (at the time) 142 tackles (10 for losses), intercepted a pass, broke up another, and recovered a fumble. He was named Outstanding Defensive Player in Notre Dame's 21–17 loss to the University of Texas in the Cotton Bowl following the 1969 season. The National Monogram Club tabbed him Notre Dame's Most Valuable Player, and he earned second-team All-American honors. The Boston Patriots selected Olson in the fifth round of the 1970 NFL draft, but he did not play professionally.

O'MALLEY, JIM
Linebacker (1970–72), 6'2", 221 lbs.

O'Malley spent two seasons as a starting middle linebacker at Notre Dame, and combined his speed with his ability to level ball carriers. He was an all-state player at Chaney High School in Youngstown, Ohio, but during his sophomore season in South Bend his role was strictly backup, and he made 12 tackles. As time went on, he overcame chronic knee problems to be a major contributor for the Fighting Irish. O'Malley broke into the starting lineup in 1971 and, despite limited playing time (126 minutes), he made 72 tackles. As a senior, O'Malley led Notre Dame in tackles, with 122. The Denver Broncos selected him in the twelfth round of the 1973 NFL draft. He played in the Mile High City from 1973 to 1975.

ORIARD, MIKE
Center (1968–69), 6'3", 221 lbs.

Oriard not only beat the odds by making the Notre Dame football team as a walk-on, he worked his way up to starter and cocaptain and did so much with the opportunity that he was named an All-American and parlayed it into a professional career.

Oriard, who snapped the ball to both Terry Hanratty and Joe Theismann, earned his first letter in 1968 when he played backup to Tim Monty. He took over the position on a starting basis during his next, senior, season. He and linebacker Bob Olson were named cocaptains and Notre Dame went 8–2–1, with Oriard being named a second-team All-American. The Spokane, Washington, native also took advantage of the educational opportunities in South Bend and won academic scholarships from the NCAA and the National Football Foundation.

Graduate school, however, would wait; Oriard had more football to play. The Kansas City Chiefs selected him in the fifth round of the 1970 NFL draft, and he spent four seasons with the team. Eventually he went back to school, and not just to study. He became a professor of literature at Oregon State and wrote an autobiographical book about football entitled *The End of Autumn*.

PAGE, ALAN
Defensive end (1964–66), 6'5", 238 lbs.

Page enrolled in college in 1963, which was the same year that the Pro Football Hall of Fame was opened in his hometown of Canton, Ohio. He returned to Canton in 1988, a quarter of a century later, to be inducted into the shrine.

Page started three years at Notre Dame at defensive end, playing at an All-American level each season. He did not have the dimensions of a classic lineman. He was taller and narrower than most, but he was fast and agile and strong and durable. Page was one of the finest athletes ever to don a Notre Dame uniform in any sport, and he achieved excellence both in the classroom and on the football field.

After tearing up opponents on the freshman team, Page hit the varsity scene and laid claim to the starting defensive end position that he would keep for three seasons. As a sophomore he made 41 tackles, recovered 2 fumbles, and scored a touchdown on a 57-yard runback of a blocked punt. In 1965, he made 30 tackles, batted down a pass, and recovered 2 fumbles. Page came on strong during his senior season, and people noticed. He made 63 tackles and broke up a pass, and he was part of a stellar defense that allowed just 38 points in its 9–0–1 national championship season. Page was one of four consensus All-Americans to play on the squad, and he was named a first-team All-American.

Page competed in the 1967 College Football All-Star Game and was one of three Fighting Irish linemen to be selected in the first round of the 1967 NFL draft. The Min-

nesota Vikings used the fifteenth pick to grab him. The New York Jets had selected offensive guard Paul Seiler three picks earlier, and offensive guard Tom Regner, who also played some defensive tackle in college, went to the Houston Oilers eight slots after Page.

Page's career makes the term *iron man* seem inadequate. He played fifteen years in the trenches in the NFL and never missed a game. The Vikings moved him inside to tackle, and his quickness made him a tough matchup for far-less-mobile offensive linemen. He could not win a contest of brute force against the behemoth opponents, but he could get around them and outsmart them.

His best professional season was in 1971. He made 109 tackles and had 10 assists and was the first defensive player ever to win the Associated Press Player of the Year award. After eleven complete seasons Minnesota released Page, who had helped them to four league or conference championships. The coaching staff did not like the fact that he had begun to use long-distance running in his training regimen and let his weight drop to 225 pounds, so they cut him from the roster in 1978. The next stop for Page's incredible career was Chicago, where he would play for the Bears until he retired in 1981. Page, a nine-time All-Pro, started 238 professional games, made 1,431 tackles and 164 sacks, and recovered 24 fumbles.

After his football-playing career was over, Page turned his athletic drive toward marathon running and made his living as an attorney (he had gone to law school while playing professional football). Page was appointed as a justice to the Minnesota Supreme Court in 1992. In 1993, he was inducted into the College Football Hall of Fame.

PALUMBO, SAM
Tackle (1951–54), 6'1", 208 lbs.

Palumbo played four seasons of varsity football at Notre Dame. It was during a brief time when two-platoon football was the rage and bodies were needed. Freshmen were also eligible, so Palumbo stepped right in to a starting spot.

Palumbo, who graduated from Collinwood High School in Cleveland, started at defensive tackle in 1951 and 1952 in South Bend. In 1953, two-platoon football was again phased out, and Palumbo fell behind left tackle Frank Varrichione on the team's depth chart. The following season Varrichione was moved over to the right side and Palumbo was back on the first team. The Cleveland Browns selected him in the fourth round of the 1955 NFL draft. He played for Cleveland in 1955 and 1957, the Green Bay Packers in 1957, and the Buffalo Bills in 1960.

PANELLI, JOHN
Fullback (1945–48), 5'11", 185 lbs.

Rocco Panelli played on three undefeated teams for head coach Frank Leahy, two of which won national championships. Panelli, from Morristown, New Jersey, came to Notre Dame in 1945, two years after Heisman Trophy–winning quarterback Angelo Bertelli left the program. It was watching Bertelli, however, that lured Panelli to South Bend.

Panelli was a big-play fullback and was apt to break a long gain off a lateral—a play he worked to perfection with Johnny Lujack and Frank Tripucka. During his freshman season he played behind Frank Ruggerio at fullback. He showed promise, rushing for 115 yards on just 18 carries and scoring 2 touchdowns. In 1946, he was again a backup fullback, and the team went 8–0–1 and won a national championship. It was the first of four undefeated teams for Leahy. The backfield was loaded that season: Jim Mello and Corwin Clatt were both at the fullback position, Emil Sitko and Terry Brennan patrolled the halfback position, and Lujack was the quarterback. Still, Panelli made the most of his playing time, rushing 58 times for 265 yards and 4 touchdowns.

In 1947, Panelli made his way onto the starting team and rushed 72 times for 254 yards and 4 touchdowns. He also caught 3 passes for 38 yards, and the Fighting Irish went 9–0 and won their second consecutive national championship. His best season was clearly his senior campaign, as Notre Dame went 9–0–1. Panelli rushed 92 times for 692 yards and scored 8 touchdowns (both totals were second on the team behind Sitko, a consensus All-American).

The Detroit Lions selected Panelli in the second round of the NFL draft, and the New York Yankees of the All-American Football Conference chose him in the second round of their draft. He opted for the NFL and played for the Lions in 1949 and 1950. Then he played for the Chicago Cardinals from 1951 through 1953.

CAREER STATS

Year	Att.	Yards	Avg.	TDs
1945	18	115	6.4	2
1946	58	265	4.6	4
1947	72	254	3.5	4
1948	92	692	7.5	8
Total	240	1,326	5.5	18

PARSEGHIAN, ARA
Head coach (1964–74)

Ara Parseghian could not have come to Notre Dame at a better time. By 1964 the program had sunk to unprecedented depths under head coaches Joe Kuharich (the only man to compile a losing record at the school) and Hugh Devore, whose team had won only two games in 1963.

Parseghian proved to be an immediate antidote to all the losing. His first team went 9–1 and probably would have won the national championship were it not for a 20–17 loss to USC in the final game of the season. The 180-degree turnaround was enough to earn Parseghian national College Coach of the Year honors.

Unlike Knute Rockne or Elmer Layden, there is no questioning whether Parseghian was a better player or coach: his on-field endeavors were respectable but not outstanding. He attended his hometown campus, Akron University, and played during the 1941 season. Then he left school to enlist in the navy. After his tour in World War II, Parseghian went to Miami University in Ohio and won the starting halfback spot. He played two seasons for the Cleveland Browns of the All-American Football Conference before injuries ended his career.

Parseghian started his stellar coaching career in 1950, when he went back to Miami to work as an assistant coach for Woody Hayes. Hayes moved on to Ohio State the following year, and Parseghian was promoted to the head slot. His teams went 39–6–1 in five seasons and won all nine games in 1955. In 1956 Northwestern came calling. Despite the fact that Northwestern was often overmatched on the field talent-wise, mainly due to its tough academic standards, Parseghian led the team to a 56–8–3 record. In that record were four victories in four meetings against Notre Dame.

Hey, if you can't beat him, hire him! After an outstanding start at 9–1, then a 7–2–1 record in 1965, Notre Dame went 9–0–1 in 1966 and the program was named consensus national champions for the first time in seventeen years. The only blemish on the record was a 10–10 tie against number two Michigan State on the road. A week after that contest, Notre Dame finished its season against USC. The Fighting Irish left nothing to chance, with a 51–0 drubbing of the Trojans. That year Parseghian's team possessed a great deal of talent. The offense featured quarterback Terry Hanratty, split end Jim Seymour, and halfback Nick Eddy. The defense featured standouts such as defensive end Alan Page and linebacker Jim Lynch.

The Fighting Irish simply annihilated its opponents by a combined score of 362–38.

Parseghian, whose Notre Dame teams had a combined winning percentage of .836, engineered three undefeated seasons, and only one team (1972) lost as many as three games. He also brought Notre Dame back into bowl play. The school had competed in the 1925 Rose Bowl, defeating Stanford, 27–10, but shortly thereafter the administration, concerned that bowl competition interfered with academic schedules, decided against further bowl participation. That was it for postseason play until 1970, when Parseghian's squad lost to the University of Texas, 21–17, in the Cotton Bowl. The Fighting Irish beat Texas in the same bowl, 24–11, the following year.

After two good but not great seasons— 8–2 in 1971 and 8–3 in 1972—Parseghian's charges stormed through an 11–0 campaign in which Notre Dame scored 358 points to 66 for its opponents. There was one more hurdle: the Sugar Bowl against top-ranked Alabama, which was also undefeated. Notre Dame took the game, 24–23, on a 19-yard field goal by Bob Thomas with 4:26 to play.

Notre Dame followed that magical season with a 10–2 year. That would be all for Parseghian, whose final game was a 13–11 victory over Alabama in the Orange Bowl, after which his players carried him off the field. Parseghian was an intense perfectionist who always gave his all, demonstrating drills during practice and working the sidelines like a madman. The stress was exhausting and it finally took its toll: Parseghian admitted himself into a hospital for rest. At the time, he said that he was surprised that the committee selecting the next coach did not seek his counsel. When Parseghian finally got a letter, it read that the committee wished him a speedy recovery "by a 4-to-3 margin."

Parseghian left coaching with a twenty-four-year mark of 170–58–6 (.739) and was inducted into the College Football Hall of Fame in 1980. He worked as a broadcaster for ABC from 1975 to 1981, and for CBS from 1982 to 1988.

NOTRE DAME COACHING RECORD

Year	W	L	T	Bowl Game
1964	9	1	0	No bowl appearance
1965	7	2	1	No bowl appearance
1966	9	0	1	No bowl appearance
1967	8	2	0	No bowl appearance
1968	7	2	1	No bowl appearance
1969	8	2	1	Cotton, L, Texas, 17–21
1970	10	0	1	Cotton, W, Texas, 24–11
1971	8	2	0	No bowl appearance
1972	8	3	0	Orange, L, Nebraska, 40–6
1973	11	0	0	Sugar, W, Alabama, 24–23
1974	10	2	0	Orange, W, Alabama, 13–11
Total	95	16	5	3–2

PATULSKI, WALT
Defensive end (1969–71), 6′5″, 235 lbs.

Patulski was a starter from the second he was eligible to play varsity football at Notre Dame. From the first game of his sophomore season until the final game of his senior year he was a fixture at defensive end. A lot was expected from him after a high school All-American career at Christian Brothers Academy in the Syracuse, New York, suburb of Liverpool. The recruiting war for his services was fierce. Notre Dame won, and Patulski didn't disappoint them.

In 1969 he made 54 tackles, 6 for losses. He also broke up 3 passes and recovered 2 fumbles. He needed shoulder surgery between his sophomore and junior years, but was ready to play by the fall. Patulski made 58 tackles, 17 for a team-leading -112 yards, recovered 2 fumbles, and broke up a pass during his second varsity season, earning honorable mention All-American honors. Patulski served as cocaptain in 1971 and finished third on the team in tackles, with 74, including a

team-high 17- for -129 yards. He was an integral part of a defense that was ranked third against the run and fourth overall in the nation. He also broke up 6 passes, recovered a fumble, and returned a blocked punt for 12 yards. Patulski won the Lombardi Trophy, a granite block trophy awarded to the best lineman in college football, and was named Lineman of the Year by United Press International. He was a consensus first-team All-American, making the top team of every major organization. Patulski started every game from 1969 to 1971 and finished his college career with 186 tackles, 40 for losses.

The Buffalo Bills used the first overall pick in the 1972 NFL draft on Patulski. To illustrate the talent he played alongside on the Fighting Irish defense, two of his teammates, defensive back Clarence Ellis (drafted fifteenth by the Atlanta Falcons) and defensive tackle Mike Kadish (drafted twenty-fifth by the Miami Dolphins) were also first-round picks. Injuries cut into his professional career a great deal. He played in Buffalo from 1972 through 1975, then missed the next season with a knee injury and joined the St. Louis Cardinals in 1977. He missed the 1978 season with a back injury and retired in 1979.

PENICK, ERIC
Halfback (1972–74), 6′1″, 209 lbs.

Cleveland native Penick was on his way to stardom at Notre Dame, but a knee injury during his senior year cut his college career short. Penick was a backup right halfback in 1972, but he still led the team in rushing with 727 yards and 5 touchdowns on 124 carries. As a junior, Penick proved his ability to make big plays. He had an 85-yard touchdown run in a 23–14 victory over sixth-ranked USC, and also scored the winning touchdown against top-ranked Alabama in Notre Dame's 24–23 Sugar Bowl victory. Both plays were considered keys to the Fighting Irish's 11–0 season and national championship. The two plays were not all that Penick did as a junior. As a starter he gained 586 yards and scored 7 touchdowns on 102 carries. In 1974, the knee injury all but wiped out his senior season. Penick rushed only 12 times for 14 yards.

PENZA, DON
End (1951–53), 6'1", 200 lbs.

Penza played for St. Catherine's High School in his hometown of Kenosha, Wisconsin. In 1950, he entered Notre Dame and over the next few years moved his way up the depth chart, making the first team as a junior and acting as captain of the undefeated 1953 team, which went 9–0–1 for head coach Frank Leahy in Penza's senior season. Penza was the fourth-leading receiver for the Fighting Irish and an above-average defensive player, and he earned second-team All-American honors. The Pittsburgh Steelers selected him in the eighteenth round of the 1954 NFL draft. He did not play professionally.

PERGINE, JOHN
Linebacker (1965–67), 6'0", 215 lbs.

As it turned out, all Pergine needed was playing time to be a major factor in Notre Dame's success. As a sophomore out of Norristown, Pennsylvania, where he played quarterback, Pergine played only 42:47 and made only 15 tackles in his first varsity college season. The following year he became a starter and played 261:55, the most on the team. He played the first half of the season at inside linebacker and the second half, after Mike McGill was lost to injury, on the outside. He finished the season with 98 tackles (second on the team behind consensus All-American Jim Lynch) and 5 interceptions. The Fighting Irish were 9–0–1 and won their first national championship in seventeen years. Pergine himself was an honorable mention All-American.

The 1967 season may not have been as spectacular for Pergine or the Fighting Irish, but both had fine years. Pergine remained at outside linebacker, where he led the team in interceptions, with 4, and was third, in tackles, with 89, and he was named a second-team All-American. The Los Angeles Rams

selected him in the eleventh round of the 1968 NFL draft. He played for the Rams from 1969 through 1972, and for the Washington Redskins from 1973 through 1975.

PETERSON, ANTHONY
Linebacker (1990–93), 6'0", 223 lbs.

Peterson came to Notre Dame from Monongahela, Pennsylvania, the same hometown as future Hall of Fame quarterback Joe Montana. The starting inside linebacker was the team's top tackler in his junior year and was expected to be a dominant force for the Fighting Irish defense in 1993, his senior season. He undoubtedly would have if an injury-prone knee hadn't disrupted his career. He suffered a torn knee ligament in the season opener against Northwestern and missed more than a month, but made it back for the sixth game of the season, against Pittsburgh. On the third play of the game Peterson tore cartilage in the same knee, but he underwent arthroscopic surgery and made it back in time to help the Fighting Irish top Texas A&M, 24–21, in the Cotton Bowl.

The San Francisco 49ers selected Peterson, questionable knee and all, in the fifth round of the 1994 NFL draft. He played with the franchise from 1994 to 1996 and spent a season with the Chicago Bears before returning to play for San Francisco. He joined the Washington Redskins two years later, in 2000.

PETITBON, JOHN
Halfback/Safety (1949–51), 6'0", 185 lbs.

New Orleans native Petitbon found instant success when he joined the Notre Dame varsity football team as a sophomore in 1949. He was there just in time to enjoy the final of four consecutive undefeated seasons for head coach Frank Leahy (10–0 and a national championship). He only carried the ball 3 times on offense and lost 9 yards in the process, but on defense he was a starting safety who made 3 interceptions, including one he ran back for a 43-yard score during a 32–0 victory over seventeenth-ranked USC.

The next year was Leahy's worst as coach by far. Notre Dame barely escaped a losing season with a 4–4–1 record. The outcome was not the fault of Petitbon, whose responsibilities practically doubled. During the 1950 season he started at both left halfback and safety. He rushed 65 times for 388 yards and 3 touchdowns, caught 18 passes for 269 yards and 2 scores, and finished the year with 30 points, second-best on the team. He also returned a punt for 14 yards and 2 kickoffs for 69 yards. On defense he made 1 interception.

During his senior season, Notre Dame (7–2–1) was back to its winning ways. Petitbon rushed 48 times for 227 yards and 4 touchdowns, caught 8 passes for 105 yards, and returned 14 punts for 189 yards and 3 kickoffs for 115 yards (averaging 38.3 yards per return). He also intercepted 2 passes on defense.

The Dallas Texans selected Petitbon in the seventh round of the 1952 draft. He played for Dallas in 1952, the Cleveland Browns in 1955 and 1956, and the Green Bay Packers in 1957.

PETITGOUT, LUKE
Offensive tackle (1995–98), 6'6", 300 lbs.

After earning his starting stripes at Notre Dame at the outset of his junior season, Petitgout blossomed into a star at Notre Dame and was the first of three Fighting Irish linemen to be selected in the 1999 National Football League draft. Entering Notre Dame as a tight end and guard, Petitgout had played in only three games at guard as a second-year freshman and seven at tackle as a sophomore, for a combined 70 minutes. The ironically named Petitgout, who was a high school All-American tight end and defensive end at Sussex Central High School in Georgetown, Delaware, then started twenty-one of the twenty-three games he played at tackle in as a junior and fifth-year senior, playing more than 300 minutes his final season.

The New York Giants selected Petitgout with the nineteenth pick of the first round of the 1999 NFL draft. Petitgout, who

still plays with his former Irish line mate Mike Rosenthal (whom the Giants picked in the fifth round), was a member of the Giants Super Bowl team in 2001.

PHELAN, JIM
Quarterback/Kicker (1915–17),
5'11", 182 lbs.

Head coach Jesse Harper got a lot out of Phelan, who could beat an opponent in one of four ways: passing, running, kicking, and defending. Phelan, from Portland, Oregon, started the 1915 season as a reserve. He scored one touchdown and threw for another in a season-opening 32–0 victory over Alma College. The next week he was in the starting lineup and threw several short passes in a 34–0 victory over Haskell. He also played a big part in a 6–0 victory over the University of South Dakota: he ran back a punt to South Dakota's 20-yard line, and Notre Dame got the game's only score on the ensuing play. Phelan also had an all-around great game in a 41–0 drubbing of Creighton University. He scored 2 touchdowns, intercepted a pass, completed another, kicked a conversion, rushed for 48 yards, and returned a punt for 21 yards. He also scored a touchdown in a 36–7 win over the University of Texas.

In 1916, he was named the team's starting quarterback from the outset and he led the team to 293 points during the season, compared with only 30 for Notre Dame's opponents, or rather opponent. The Fighting Irish, 8–1 that season, shut out every rival with the exception of perennial powerhouse Army, which won their meeting, 30–10.

Phelan got off to a good start in 1917, scoring the season's first touchdown in a 55–0 victory over Kalamazoo. He scored two more times in that game, and then nearly beat Wisconsin single-leggedly. Phelan tried to drop-kick a 61-yard field goal, but it hit the crossbar, preserving a 0–0 tie. Unfortunately, that would be all for Phelan's college football career. He was drafted into the armed forces for World War I and sent to Camp Taylor in Louisville, Kentucky.

PHILBROOK, GEORGE
Guard/Tackle/Punter (1908–11),
6′3″, 225 lbs.

Philbrook was a devastating blocker who also had great size to go along with outstanding speed and hands for a man playing in the first decade of the century. The Olympia, Washington, native was a versatile athlete, and certainly one of the best Notre Dame players in his, and some would argue any, era.

In 1908, Philbrook was used mainly as a punter; in 1909 he became a starter at left guard. In addition to his blocking chores, he rushed for a touchdown in a victory over Olivet, scored on a 50-yard pass play against Rose Poly, and recovered a fumble against Michigan State. He also scored twice against Miami University in Ohio, and scored once against Wabash, which was coached by future Notre Dame coach Jesse Harper. Philbrook was named to the All-Western team that year.

Philbrook was moved to left tackle in 1910 and fashioned a miraculous play in a 51–0 victory over Butchel of Akron, Ohio. He was supposed to run a "tackle around end" play, but fumbled the ball. He quickly scooped it up and rambled 75 yards for a score, shaking off three defenders in the process. He was back as a starting left tackle in 1911, but was used only against major schools. Since there were only two that season—the University of Pittsburgh and Marquette University—Philbrook did not see much action. To take advantage of his height, he was used as a pass receiver. He caught 1 ball for 20 yards in a scoreless tie against Pitt.

PIEPUL, MILT
Fullback/Kicker (1938–40), 6′1″, 206 lbs.

Piepul had a great senior year. Not only was he named a second-team All-American, he was also the first running back to be named team captain in fourteen years.

The powerful fullback from Thompsonville, Connecticut (who was also used as a kicker), played third string behind Mario Tonelli and Joe Thesing in 1938. He showed his promise, with 137 yards on 40 carries.

Piepul was upgraded to a starting position in 1939 and made the most of it. Not only did he lead the team in rushing with 414 yards on 82 carries, he also led the team in scoring, with 6 touchdowns. That output led to his captain status as a senior. He also played linebacker and was the team's full-time placekicker. Piepul was the squad's second-leading rusher and top kickoff returner (4 for 122 yards), and was the only Fighting Irish player to be named an All-American. The Detroit Lions selected him in the eleventh round of the 1941 NFL draft. He played one season for the franchise.

PIETROSANTE, NICK
Fullback/Punter (1956–58), 6′2″, 215 lbs.

The passion and spirit of Nick Pietrosante is embodied in an award given each year since 1988 to the Notre Dame player who "best exemplifies the courage, loyalty, teamwork, dedication, and pride of the late Irish All-American fullback" who died of cancer on February 6, 1988.

Pietrosante came to Notre Dame University after attending Notre Dame High School in New Haven, Connecticut. He played sparingly as a sophomore in South Bend, gaining 27 yards on 8 carries as a backup fullback, but in 1957 he made the starting lineup and led the team in rushing, with 449 yards on 90 carries (5.0 yards per carry). He also scored 2 touchdowns, caught 4 passes (for 5 yards), intercepted a pass, recovered 2 fumbles, broke up 2 passes, made 37 tackles, and averaged 39.6 yards on 39 punts. His performance was rewarded by third-team All-American honors.

Pietrosante was even busier as a senior in 1958. Again he led the team in rushing (117 carries for 556 yards and 4 touchdowns). He also caught 10 passes for 78 yards, was third on the team in scoring, with 26 points, made 44 tackles, broke up 3 passes, returned a kickoff for 17 yards, and punted 26 times

All-American fullback Nick Pietrosante is remembered for his courage, loyalty, teamwork, dedication, and pride, which are honored every year with the presentation of the Nick Pietrosante Award to the Notre Dame player who best exemplifies those qualities.

for a 33.7-yard average. Pietrosante was invited to play in the East-West Shrine Game and was named a first-team All-American. The Detroit Lions selected him in the first round of the 1959 draft. He played in the Motor City from 1959 to 1965 and finished his career with a two-year stint in Cleveland.

PILNEY, ANDY
Halfback (1933–35), 5'11", 175 lbs.

Pilney was a star athlete and president of the poetry club at Chicago Technical High School. He never started a game at Notre Dame, but always made a contribution. Never was that more evident than on November 2, 1935. It was "the Game of the Century" at heavily favored and unbeaten Ohio State, and Notre Dame scored 3 touchdowns in the

fourth quarter to beat the Buckeyes, 18–13. Pilney, a backup halfback, returned a punt 47 yards to Ohio State's 13-yard line and completed a pass to set up the first score. During the second scoring drive he completed 3 passes for 75 yards and had a 32-yard run, which set up Bill Shakespeare's game-winning touchdown pass to end Wayne Millner with 32 seconds to play. That year, Pilney's senior season, he also threw for a touchdown and ran for a second in a 27–0 shutout of the University of Wisconsin and connected on both touchdown passes in a 14–0 victory over Navy.

Pilney hit the varsity scene as a backup left halfback in 1933, and he scored the game's only touchdown in a 7–0 victory over Northwestern. It was far from a great season for the Fighting Irish, who went 3–5–1, and Pilney's touchdown was just one of the team's 5 for the season. He also led the team in punt returns (9 for 124 yards). In 1934, Pilney was again a backup left halfback. He threw for a touchdown in a 19–0 victory over Wisconsin and gained 46 yards on 11 carries in a 13–0 victory over Carnegie Tech.

The Detroit Lions selected Pilney in the third round of the 1936 NFL draft, but he decided to forego a pro career for a life in coaching.

PINKETT, ALLEN
Tailback (1982–85), 5'9", 181 lbs.

The diminutive Pinkett was not only fast and had great balance, shifty moves, and good hands, he was also extremely strong. He had the leg drive to extend runs, and his upper body was solid. He could bench press 385 pounds, more than twice his weight, and he was extremely durable, starting thirty-six consecutive games. He was a three-time college All-American, and until Autry Denson surpassed his mark in 1998, Notre Dame's all-time leading rusher.

Pinkett came to South Bend after an All-American career at Park View High School in Sterling, Virginia, and wasted no time making his presence felt. As a freshman

Pinkett was generally used as a backup (he started only one game), but he still gained 532 yards on 107 carries and scored 5 touchdowns. He also caught 9 passes for 94 yards and returned 14 kickoffs for 354 yards and a touchdown.

Pinkett became a full-time starter the next year, and had the best sophomore season of any Fighting Irish running back, leading the team in both rushing and receiving. He gained 1,394 yards and scored 16 touchdowns on 252 carries and caught 28 passes for 288 yards and 2 touchdowns. He also completed a pass for 59 yards and scored on a 2-point conversion. He capped the season (in which he was named first-team All-American) with 111 yards and 2 touchdowns on 28 carries in a 19–18 Liberty Bowl victory over Boston College. In just his second season in South Bend, Pinkett began to rewrite the Notre Dame record book. He set a single-season record for touchdowns (18), points (110), and 100-yard rushing games (9). He was only 43 yards behind Vagas Ferguson's single-season rushing mark.

Pinkett's junior year was nearly as amazing statistically. He gained 1,105 yards on 275 carries and scored 17 touchdowns. He also caught 19 passes for 257 yards and another score. In a 27–20 loss to SMU in the Aloha Bowl, he gained 136 yards on 24 carries and became Notre Dame's top postseason rusher. Those achievements earned him honorable mention All-American status.

Pinkett kept rolling along as a senior. He gained 1,100 yards on 255 carries, becoming the first Notre Dame running back to have three consecutive 1,000-yard seasons. He scored 11 touchdowns and caught 17 passes for 135 yards. He was eighth in the voting for the Heisman Trophy, earned first-team All-American honors, and was Notre Dame's Most Valuable Player for the third consecutive season.

Pinkett not only finished his career with a record 4,131 yards rushing, he also set marks for career touchdowns (53), rushing touchdowns (49), rushing yards per game (96.1), carries (889), and points (320). The Houston

Oilers grabbed him in the third round, sixty-first overall, of the 1986 NFL draft. He played six seasons with the franchise.

CAREER STATS
RUSHING

Year	Att.	Yards	Avg.	TDs
1982	107	532	5.0	5
1983	252	1,394	5.5	16
1984	275	1,105	4.0	17
1985	255	1,100	4.3	11
Total	889	4,131	4.6	49

RECEIVING

Year	Rec.	Yards	Avg.	TDs
1982	9	94	10.4	0
1983	28	288	10.3	2
1984	19	257	13.5	1
1985	17	135	7.9	0
Total	73	774	10.6	3

PLISKA, JOE
Halfback (1911–14), 5'10", 172 lbs.

Chicago native Pliska was part of a powerful backfield at Notre Dame and one of the players to help the team emerge as a national power when Jesse Harper took over the program in 1913.

Pliska started during his sophomore, junior, and senior seasons and was a major contributor, though he was often lost in the shadows of end Knute Rockne and quarterback Gus Dorais. As a freshman Pliska was a backup right halfback in 1911. He scored 3 touchdowns (and kicked 3 conversions) against St. Bonaventure, and also scored touchdowns against Ohio Northern, St. Viator, and Loyola. In 1912, Pliska took over the starting right halfback spot. He scored a career-high 4 touchdowns in a 74–7 romp over Adrian and added 3 others in a 47–7 drubbing of St. Louis University. He also scored in the first three minutes in a season-ending 69–0 romp over Marquette University in head coach John L. Marks's final game.

As a junior, Pliska again won the starting right halfback position. He ran for 3 touchdowns against both Ohio Northern and Alma and in a 35–13 victory against Army, during which Notre Dame popularized the forward pass, he caught 2 passes from Dorais and scored 2 touchdowns. Pliska was back for more in 1914. He scored on three long plays against Alma, returned a punt for 65 yards and made a conversion kick, and gained more than 100 yards and scored on runs of 60 and 35 yards in his second-to-last game, a 48–6 victory over Carlisle. He finished his college career with a touchdown in a 20–0 victory over Syracuse University. For one year he played professional football for the Hammond Pros.

POLISKY, JOHN
Tackle (1925–27), 5'7", 192 lbs.

Polisky entered Notre Dame at a tough time to break into the lineup. The 1924 team had won all ten of its games and a national championship. "Bull" Polisky was a Pittsburgh native but graduated from St. Edward's High School in Austin, Texas. The stocky, outgoing tackle managed to catch the eye of head coach Knute Rockne as a freshman but didn't make his mark until the 1925 season, when he won the starting position that he kept for the next three years. He was a second-team All-American as a senior.

After his playing career was over, Polisky stayed around to work under Rockne until 1928 when he finished up his law degree. He played for the Chicago Bears before opening a law office in Whiting, Indiana, but couldn't stay away from football for long. He took a job as an assistant coach at Rice University in Houston and later at Creighton University, where he worked for another Notre Dame graduate, All-American Marchy Schwartz.

POTTIOS, MYRON
Center/Guard/Linebacker (1958–60), 6'2", 220 lbs.

Pottios, from Van Voorhis, Pennsylvania, was one of the few bright spots during a

Myron Pottios was the only Notre Dame All-American in 1960; he went on to have a thirteen-year career in the NFL, including a Super Bowl championship with the Washington Redskins.

subpar period in the history of Notre Dame football. During his three years on the varsity team, while playing for Terry Brennan and Joe Kuharich, Notre Dame was 13–17.

Pottios hit the scene in 1958, winning the starting center spot. The following season, when he was a junior, he played right guard and linebacker. Through three games he led the team with 24 tackles, but he injured his knee in the fourth game of the season, a 19–0 loss to Michigan State, and was finished for the year. Pottios underwent off-season surgery to repair ligament damage and then was named captain of the 1960 team, which went 2–8 (the worst record in Notre Dame's modern history). He started at both left guard and linebacker, led the team in tackles, with 74, and also blocked a kick. He won the game ball used in the season finale, a 17–0 victory over USC in which the Trojans rushed for only 74 yards. Pottios was the only Notre Dame All-American in 1960, but he was a first-teamer. He finished his college career with 130 tackles, an interception, and a fumble recovery.

Pittsburgh, of the NFL, and Oakland, of the AFL, selected Pottios in the second round of the 1961 draft. His thirteen-year professional career included stops in Pittsburgh (1961, 1963–65); Los Angeles, where he played for the Rams (1966 to 1970); and Washington Redskins (1971 to 1974), where he played on the 1973 Super Bowl team.

POWLUS, RON
Quarterback (1994–97), 6'2", 222 lbs.

Powlus entered Notre Dame in 1993 with an ambitious goal—to win the starting spot vacated by All-American Rick Mirer. Although he didn't achieve that goal, Powlus left Notre Dame as, statistically, the best quarterback in the school's history—better than Joe Montana, Joe Theismann, and Mirer.

Powlus played for one of the best high school teams in the country and, more specifically, best in quarterback country: Berwick High School in Pennsylvania. He led Berwick to a 37–5 record in three seasons as a starting quarterback. When he was a senior Berwick was undefeated, won the Pennsylvania state championship, and was ranked number one nationally. Powlus threw for more than 2,900 yards and tossed 31 touchdowns. He also ran for 677 yards and 20 touchdowns, earning national prep Player of the Year from *USA Today* and *Parade* magazine. In three seasons, with 445 completions of 791 attempts for 7,339 yards and 62 touchdowns, he showed the ability he would bring to Notre Dame. He also rushed for 1,679 yards and 45 touchdowns.

Football pundit Beano Cook predicted that he would win two Heismans, but during training camp before his freshman season, Powlus suffered a broken collarbone. The injury was later aggravated during an October practice, effectively ending his freshman season; he watched from the sidelines most of the year as Kevin McDougal became the starting signal caller.

Powlus and his extremely accurate arm were back in time to prepare for his sophomore season. He was named the starter in summer camp, and went on to lead the team to a 6–5–1 record. He completed 18 of 24

passes for 291 yards and 4 touchdowns in his first start, a season-opening 42–15 victory over Northwestern. He finished the season with 119 completions of 222 attempts for 1,729 yards, 9 interceptions, and a school record 19 touchdown tosses.

Powlus started the first ten games of the 1995 season before injury—a broken wrist—struck again. He went down in a 58–21 victory over Navy and missed the regular season's final game and the Orange Bowl. Lou Holtz's Notre Dame team improved to 9–3 that year, and Powlus completed 124 of 217 passes for 1,853 yards and 12 touchdowns. He had a metal rod implanted to stabilize his wrist, and by the start of the 1996 season he was ready to take aim at the Notre Dame record book.

Powlus was named a tri-captain that year and showed no ill signs from the broken wrist. He had his best season, with 133 completions of 232 passes for 1,942 yards, 12 touchdowns (giving him the career record of 43, 2 more than Mirer), and just 4 interceptions. Entering his final season, Powlus already held nine school records and was second all-time in two other categories.

The NCAA granted Powlus an extra year of eligibility because of his lost first season. He started and played in all thirteen games, again as a tri-captain. That season he completed more passes than any other team in the school's history. He set single-game highs with 43 attempts and 293 passing yards, and also set a single-game mark for consecutive completions with 14 against Michigan. He finished the season with 182 completions in 298 attempts for 2,078 yards, 9 touchdowns, and 7 interceptions.

If you look at the top of the quarterback rankings in the Notre Dame record book you will see the name Powlus numerous times. He is the record holder for touchdowns in a game (4, three times), consecutive pass completions (14), single-season pass attempts and completions (298 and 182 in 1997), touchdown passes (19 in 1994), total offensive attempts (409 in 1997), and interception avoidance (.0172 in 1996). His 31 passes completed in a single game (against Purdue in 1997) is second only to Joe Theismann's 33 against USC in 1970.

Powlus also set career marks in passes attempted (969), completions (558), consecutive games with a completion (44), passing yards (7,602), touchdown passes (52), total offensive attempts (1,201), yards (7,479), interception avoidance percentage (.0278), and most games with 200 yards passing (15). He is also second in completion percentage for a season. In 1997, he connected on .611 of his passes (McDougal's mark was .616 in 1993).

The Tennessee Oilers signed Powlus as a free agent, but he did not make the team. He later landed on the roster of the Detroit Lions.

CAREER STATS

PASSING

Year	Att.	Comp.	Pct.	Yards	TDs	Int.
1994	222	119	.536	1,729	19	9
1995	217	124	.571	1,853	12	7
1996	232	133	.573	1,942	12	4
1997	298	182	.611	2,078	9	7
Total	969	558	.575	7,602	52	27

POZDERAC, PHIL
Tackle (1978–81), 6'9", 270 lbs.

Pozderac, from Garfield Heights, Ohio, won a starting offensive tackle position during his junior season in 1980. He had size, strength, and toughness, and he showed a great deal of durability as well. He started all twelve games and played a team-high 315 minutes, making the most of the opportunity after playing behind All-American Tim Foley during his first two seasons. He was again a starter in 1981.

The Dallas Cowboys selected Pozderac in the fifth round of the 1982 NFL draft. He played six seasons with the franchise before retiring in 1987.

PRITCHETT, WESLEY ANDREW
Linebacker (1985–88), 6'6", 251 lbs.

Atlanta native Pritchett was a giant linebacker whose emotional style of play rubbed off on his teammates. He won a starting spot as a junior and made 70 tackles. The following season Pritchett led the Fighting Irish in tackles, with 112, as the team went 12–0 and won a national championship under head coach Lou Holtz. Pritchett was a second-team All-American, and was invited to play in both the East-West Shrine Game and the Hula Bowl. The Miami Dolphins selected him in the sixth round of the 1989 NFL draft. He played with the Buffalo Bills in 1989 and 1990 and for the Atlanta Falcons in 1991.

PRUDHOMME, EDWARD
Fullback/Halfback (1887–89)

Prudhomme was one of the founders of the Notre Dame football program. The game, like Notre Dame football itself, has changed immensely over the past century, so it's hard to compare Prudhomme to today's stars. He was, however, the first two-time team captain. Prudhomme, a strong player, from Bermuda, Louisiana, started at fullback in 1887 and 1888. On April 20, 1888, he kicked the first-ever conversion in school history in a 26–6 (touchdowns scored only 5 points in the early days of football) loss to Michigan. He also kicked 2 conversions in Notre Dame's first-ever victory that December, 20–0 over Harvard Prep (Chicago). In 1889, he switched over to right halfback, and again acted as captain. After graduation, Prudhomme went back home to Louisiana and was elected to the state legislature.

PUPLIS, ANDY
Quarterback (1935–37), 5'8", 168 lbs.

Passing wasn't really a prerequisite for quarterbacks who played for head coach Elmer Layden. He favored versatile athletes, and that's what he had in Puplis, a good rusher, receiver, and kicker who'd been a star athlete at Chicago's Harrison High School. Layden liked the short young man who led the team to identical 6–2–1 records in 1936 and 1937—mainly because he had the knack of calling the right play at the right time.

Puplis began his college career as a backup quarterback in 1935. His highlight that season was a 70-yard punt return in a 27–0 victory over Wisconsin. The following season he was promoted to the first string and led the team in kickoff returns with 5 for 136 yards. As a senior, Puplis was a fearsome rusher. He carried the ball 10 times for 177 yards (a 17.7-yard average), caught 4 passes for 78 yards (a 19.5-yard average), and completed 2 of 4 passes. He also made 2 interceptions, scored 3 touchdowns, and made 6 of 8 extra points. He led the Fighting Irish in scoring, with 24 points, and his total yardage for the season was 569 yards on 46 plays, for an average of 12.4 yards, more than a first down on each play. In 1943 he played for the Chicago Cardinals.

QUINN, STEVE
Center (1965–67), 6'1", 225 lbs.

Quinn, from Northfield, Illinois, only saw backup time on Ara Parseghian's 9–0–1 national championship squad in 1966, but after spring practice the next season he was given the Hering Award for "most improved lineman." He started that season, and the team went 8–2. He wasn't picked in the 1968 NFL draft, but he signed with the Houston Oilers as a free agent and played with them for one year before retiring from pro football.

RASSAS, NICK
Halfback/Defensive back (1963–65),
6'0", 185 lbs.

From walk-on to consensus first-team All-American is a path not taken by many college football players, but Rassas, from Winnetka, Illinois, took that path in South Bend. Despite not being offered a scholarship, Rassas was compelled to go to Notre Dame to follow in his father's footsteps. George Rassas had been a Fighting Irish receiver who graduated in 1940. Nick impressed head coach Hugh Devore enough to make the 1963 team, and later proved himself to be an outstanding defensive asset in the secondary, and a threat to run back interceptions and kicks for scores. As a sophomore he carried the ball only 8 times for 33 yards, caught a 9-yard pass, and made 2 tackles.

It was in 1964, under new coach Ara Parseghian, that Rassas began to make an impact. He earned his first letter as a starting safety and had 51 tackles, broke up 4 passes, and intercepted a pass, which he returned 23 yards. He also ran back 4 kickoffs for 103 yards and led the team in punt returns, with 15 for 153 yards. As an offensive halfback, Rassas caught a 2-yard touchdown pass from John Huarte in a victory over Purdue. He also had another 2-yard reception and ran the ball 3 times for 37 yards. His personal triumph was almost matched by the team's: the squad was undefeated until a season-ending 20–17 loss to USC.

In 1965, as a senior, Rassas stepped up to the top echelon of college football. He was superb on defense, with 53 tackles and 6 interceptions for 197 yards and a touchdown,

and he broke up 3 passes. Rassas may have been even better on special teams. He led the nation in punt returns, with 24 for 459 yards and 3 touchdowns. His 19.1 single-season punt return average and career average of 15.7 were school records until they were broken by Allen Rossum more than thirty years later. Rassas earned first-team consensus All-American honors and was the only Fighting Irish player to compete in the 1966 College Football All-Star Game. He finished his career with 106 tackles, 7 interceptions, and 5 touchdowns, plus 8 kickoff returns for 185 yards and 39 punt returns for 612 yards and 3 touchdowns.

The NFL Atlanta Falcons and the AFL San Diego Chargers selected Rassas in the second round of the 1966 draft. He played three seasons in Atlanta before retiring.

RATTERMAN, GEORGE
Quarterback (1945–46), 6'0", 165 lbs.

Ratterman was one of the most versatile athletes ever to attend Notre Dame. He was enrolled in the navy's V-12 program during World War II, and is one of the few athletes ever to earn four varsity letters in a single school year. As a junior, Ratterman lettered in football, baseball, tennis, and basketball, and made several all-star teams.

In the fall of 1946, Ratterman, from Fort Thomas, Kentucky, played T-formation quarterback at Notre Dame, splitting time with eventual Heisman Trophy winner Johnny Lujack. He connected on 8 of 18 passes for 114 yards as the Fighting Irish went 8–0–1 and won the national title. Lujack may have received the honors in college, but

Ratterman had the better professional career. He was not drafted but still played ten seasons as a pro, in the All-American Football Conference for the Buffalo Bills (1947 to 1949) and the New York Yankees (1950 and 1951), and later for the NFL Cleveland Browns (1952 to 1956).

REEVE, DAN
Kicker (1974–77), 6′3″, 216 lbs.

Reeve, of Bloomington, Illinois, capped a four-year varsity career at Notre Dame by leading a national championship team in scoring in 1977.

As a freshman in 1974, the strong but erratic Reeve made 38 of 40 extra points and 7 of 10 field goals, to score 59 points. The following season he only scored 57 points— 24 of 26 extra points and 11 of 16 field goals—but that was enough to lead the team. As a junior, he showed his leg strength by setting a school record with a 53-yard field goal in a 31–10 loss to the University of Pittsburgh. He made 2 extra points and 2 field goals in a 20–9 victory over Penn State in the Gator Bowl, and made 29 of 33 extra points, but only 9 of 18 field goals, for the season.

The following year was special for Reeve and the rest of the Fighting Irish, who went 11–1 and won the national title. He made 39 of 44 extra points and 12 of 20 field goals to lead Notre Dame with 75 points, his own career high. He also connected on a field goal and 5 extra points in the 38–10 Cotton Bowl victory over Texas. Reeve was not drafted and did not play professional football.

REGNER, TOM
Offensive guard/Defensive tackle (1964–66), 6′1″, 245 lbs.

During his sophomore and first varsity season at Notre Dame, Regner played defensive tackle. He had 68 tackles, fifth on the team and first among linemen, and played 262 minutes. The next year he was switched to offensive guard, though obviously his defensive

All-American Tom Regner played guard for the 1966 Notre Dame football team that went 9–0–1 and won the national championship.

ability wasn't a factor in the change. Head coach Ara Parseghian, however, was right to switch Regner's position, because the gifted athlete from Kenosha, Wisconsin, helped the Fighting Irish to the promised land.

The transition was smooth. Regner played 303 minutes as a junior and was named a second-team All-American. Entering his senior year, he was regarded as one of the top offensive linemen in the country, and he lived up to the hype. Notre Dame went 9–0–1 during the 1966 season and outscored opponents 362–38 en route to a national championship. Regner was a major factor in the success. He made nearly every first-team All-American squad, and was also named a first-team Academic All-American.

To put into perspective the talent that he played alongside at Notre Dame, Regner was selected by the Houston Oilers, twenty-third overall, in the 1967 NFL draft and was the third Fighting Irish player picked.

The New York Jets used the twelfth pick on guard Paul Seiler, and the Minnesota Vikings selected defensive end Alan Page with number fifteen. Regner played his entire six-year career with the Oilers.

REHDER, THOMAS BERNARD
Tackle/Defensive tackle/Tight end
(1984–87), 6'7", 263 lbs.

Rehder, of Santa Maria, California, played almost as many positions as he did seasons at Notre Dame. He played offense and defense, inside and outside, and was big enough and athletic enough to make it work. As a freshman in 1984, he was a backup defensive tackle. The following season he was moved to tight end and started nine games, gaining 182 yards on 13 receptions and scoring a touchdown. Lou Holtz took over as head coach in 1986 and moved Rehder again, this time to offensive tackle. Rehder started eight of eleven games in 1986 and, despite contracting a case of pneumonia that kept him out of spring drills the next year, he started all but one game as a senior.

Holtz's decision lasted well beyond Rehder's Notre Dame career. The New England Patriots selected Rehder in the third round of the 1988 NFL draft, and he played two seasons with the Patriots, one with the New York Giants, and, after missing a season, one with the Minnesota Vikings. He retired in 1992.

REILLY, JIM
Offensive tackle (1967–69), 6'2", 247 lbs.

Reilly was one of the anchors of two of the most explosive offense teams Notre Dame has ever fielded. He played more than 250 minutes a season and was one of the starters when Notre Dame rolled for 4,489 yards of total offense in 1969 and a record 5,105 yards and 330 points in 1970. He also made first-team Academic All-American status in his senior season.

The three-year college starter came to Notre Dame via Hackley Prep in Tarrytown, New York. He was a state champion in the shot put and discus, but chose football in college, as did his brothers Mike, who played at Brown University, and Tom, who played at George Washington University.

The Buffalo Bills selected Reilly in the third round of the 1970 NFL draft. He played in Buffalo for two seasons.

RESTIC, JOE
Safety/Punter (1975–78), 6'2", 190 lbs.

Restic did a lot to keep opponents from scoring during his four-year varsity career at Notre Dame. On defense he was a big-play safety who could hit well and had an uncanny knack of intercepting passes. When Notre Dame's offense sputtered, he kept opponents on their heels with a strong punting foot.

Restic was the son of former Harvard football coach Joe Restic Sr., so it is no surprise that he was also a star quarterback, punter, and defensive back at Milford High School in Massachusetts. As a freshman at Notre Dame, Restic, who joined the team the same year as head coach Dan Devine, was the team's punter and had 40 kicks for 1,739 yards (a 43.5-yards-per-punt average), including a long of 63 yards. He also threw a 10-yard touchdown pass to tight end Ken MacAfee. His average of 51.6 yards per punt in a 31–30 victory over Air Force is still a single-game school record. The following season Restic added starting free safety to his chores and made 54 tackles and 4 interceptions and recovered a fumble. He punted 63 times during the season for 2,627 yards (a 41.7-yard average), including a long of 63 yards, and completed a pass for a 4-yard gain.

Restic, who was a first-team Academic All-American in 1977 and 1978, was one of the top defenders on Notre Dame's 11–1 national championship team in 1977. As the starting free safety, he made 51 tackles and led the team with 6 interceptions. He made 4 tackles before being forced out of Notre Dame's championship-clinching 38–10 Cotton Bowl victory over Texas with a knee injury. During the season he also punted 45 times for 1,713 yards (a 38.1-yard average). His knee was better by the start of the 1978 season, and he again started at free safety. He made 51 tackles, broke up 8 passes, intercepted 3 others, and recovered 2 fumbles. His punting totals for the year were 61 kicks for 2,330 yards (a 38.2-yard average), which included a long of 66 yards.

CAREER STATS

INTERCEPTIONS

Year	Int.	Yards	Avg.
1975	None		
1976	4	92	23.0
1977	6	25	4.2
1978	3	59	19.7
Total	13	176	13.5

PUNTING

Year	Punts	Yards	Avg.
1975	40	1,739	43.5
1976	63	2,627	41.7
1977	45	1,713	38.1
1978	61	2,330	38.2
Total	209	8,409	40.2

RICE, TONY
Quarterback (1987–89), 6′1″, 200 lbs.

Rice was not only a quarterback in college, he was an athlete perfectly suited to coach Lou Holtz's option offense. He was an effective passer, enough of a running threat to freeze defenders, and had the innate sense to pitch the ball at the perfect moment. With Rice as a starter the Fighting Irish were 28–3 which included a 12–0 season in 1988, when Notre Dame won the national championship.

Before coming to Notre Dame, Rice was named a prep All-American while playing at Woodruff High School in South Carolina. He was also the South Carolina Player of the Year after he scored 460 points and achieved 7,000 yards of offense in high school.

Rice enrolled at Notre Dame in 1986 but did not play because of academic problems. He was back on the gridiron in 1987

and took over the offense during the fourth game of the season, when senior Terry Andrysiak broke his collarbone. Rice finished the season with 663 yards and a touchdown passing, and 337 yards and 7 touchdowns rushing. Over the next two seasons, he may very well have been the best quarterback in the college game. Notre Dame went 24–1 during his junior and senior years.

As a junior, Rice, who gained 700 yards and scored 9 touchdowns on the ground, was the first Notre Dame quarterback to lead the team in rushing since Paul Hornung in 1956. He also passed for 1,176 yards and 8 touchdowns. Rice capped the championship season with a stellar Fiesta Bowl. In the 34–21 victory over the University of West Virginia, he completed 7 of 11 passes for 213 yards and ran for 75 yards, which earned him Most Valuable Player honors. After the season he was named an honorable mention All-American.

Rice was named a tri-captain in 1989 and set a school record for rushing yards for

The Fighting Irish were 28–3 with All-American Tony Rice as a starter, including a 12–0 season in 1988 when Notre Dame won the national championship. (Bill Panzica)

a quarterback, with 884. He also ran in 7 touchdowns and passed for 1,122 yards and 2 touchdowns. He completed 5 of 9 passes for 99 yards and ran the ball 14 times for 50 yards in Notre Dame's 21–6 Orange Bowl victory over the University of Colorado. This time he made first-team All-American and won the Johnny Unitas Golden Arm Award, which is presented annually to college football's top quarterback. He finished fourth in the voting for the Heisman Trophy.

Rice ended his college career with 1,921 yards rushing, 2,961 yards passing, and 34 touchdowns. His 4,882 yards of total offense ranks sixth on the school's all-time list. His all-around game actually hurt him in making it to the professional level, as his play as an option quarterback rather than a dropback passer led to him be ignored in the 1990 NFL draft. He ended up going to the Canadian Football League to play for the Saskatchewan Roughriders.

CAREER STATS

PASSING

Year	Att.	Comp.	Pct.	Yards	TDs	Int.
1987	82	35	.427	663	1	4
1988	138	70	.507	1,176	8	7
1989	137	68	.496	1,122	2	9
Total	357	173	.485	2,961	11	20

RUSHING

Year	Att.	Yards	Avg.	TDs
1987	89	337	3.8	7
1988	121	700	5.8	9
1989	174	884	5.1	7
Total	384	1,921	5.0	23

ROBINSON, JACK
Center (1932–34), 6'3", 200 lbs.

Robinson overcame some major health hurdles to become Notre Dame's only All-American during the 1934 season. He grew up in a wealthy family in Huntington, New York, and was named the team's first-string center in 1932, his sophomore season.

Then, while he was home during summer break in June 1933, he discovered a cyst on his right eye. The surgery was far from a complete success and he did not make it back to school, spending most of the year in the hospital. He had a second eye operation in February 1934, and a third during the summer right around the time that his father passed away of a heart attack.

A week before the start of the 1934 season, Robinson returned to the team and, surprisingly, made the starting squad in a matter of weeks. He went on to have a fabulous year, despite the fact that he underwent his sixth eye operation in the middle of the season. The procedure didn't faze Robinson, who was back the next week and was eventually named a consensus All-American.

ROCKNE, KNUTE
End (1910–13); Head coach (1918–30), 5'8", 165 lbs.

Had he not been an exceptional pole vaulter, legendary Knute Rockne, who was born in Voss, Norway, may have only engaged in one year of college football as a reserve and spent the rest of his time at Notre Dame focusing on his other interests—the college newspaper, the flute, professional boxing, chemistry, and drama. As it turned out, Rockne was perhaps the most important figure in the history of the football program.

Rockne, small by football standards, sat on the bench as a freshman at Notre Dame, in 1910. He found that warming the bench was a disheartening experience, and he considered moving on to other endeavors, but gained confidence in his sports abilities by setting a school record in the pole vault (12 feet, 4 inches). He went out for the gridiron team again in his sophomore year and was named a starter. During the summer between his junior and senior years he worked out with quarterback Gus Dorais and perfected the forward pass as an offensive weapon. The forward pass had been in existence in football since 1906, but was used only as a gimmick play or a desperation measure; it certainly wasn't part of the standard offensive repertoire, which at that time consisted mostly of muscling opposing linemen out of the way to run. As a senior, Rockne was named captain and the team went 7–0, largely on the strength of the forward pass. The season included a big win over vaunted Army, 35–13 that brought virtually unknown Notre Dame into national prominence.

Rockne, who graduated magna cum laude, worked himself through school as a chemistry research assistant. After graduation he went on to take classes in the school's graduate chemistry program while also assisting football coach Jesse Harper. Harper retired after the 1917 season, making room for Rockne as head coach. The rest, as they say, is history.

Rockne, who can conservatively be called a legend, compiled the best winning percentage as a coach in the history of college football (an astounding .881), the result of a 105–12–5 record. Only Notre Dame coach Frank Leahy (.864) has come close to that average, and Rockne's record has stood since 1930. Under his charge the 1924 team, featuring the Four Horsemen, won a national championship. Rockne's teams were also named consensus national champions in 1929 and 1930. All told, his teams had five undefeated seasons, and averaged less than one loss a season.

Undoubtedly, Rockne would have won more games and national championships had his life not been cut short by tragedy. On March 31, 1931, he took a commercial flight to Los Angeles to do some promotional work. The plane crashed near Bazaar, Kansas, and everyone aboard was killed.

As a coaching strategist, Rockne was ahead of his time. He promoted the use of the forward pass, and his shift play, which featured four backs in motion, wreaked such havoc on defenses that it was eventually ruled illegal. He was the first coach to take on all comers and travel with his team across the country in search of competition. This created rivalries in both the East and West, and expanded Notre Dame's fan base well beyond

South Bend. Just as he had been involved in numerous extracurricular activities as an undergraduate, Rockne also served at various times as Notre Dame's business manager, athletic director, ticket distributor, and equipment manager. His teams wore lighter pads and more aerodynamic uniforms. He was the subject of the 1940 movie *Knute Rockne, All-American,* and was among the first inductees to the College Football Hall of Fame when it opened in 1951.

COACHING RECORD

Year	W	L	T
1918	3	1	2
1919	9	0	0
1920	9	0	0
1921	10	1	0
1922	8	1	1
1923	9	1	0
1924	10	0	0
1925	7	2	1
1926	9	1	0
1927	7	1	1
1928	5	4	0
1929	9	0	0
1930	10	0	0
Total	105	12	5

ROSENTHAL, MIKE
Guard/Tackle (1995–98), 6'7", 300 lbs.

Rosenthal quickly moved up the depth chart at Notre Dame. He played spot duty in the final ten games of his freshman year and started the final seven games of his sophomore season, but he played more time as a junior than as a freshman and sophomore combined. As the starting strong offensive guard, in his third college season, Rosenthal logged 337:32 (one second less than the team's time leader, offensive tackle Mike Doughty), which followed a freshman season in which he saw 100:14 of action, and a sophomore season in which he played 168:47. The prep All-American who played at Penn High School in Mishawaka, Indiana, made the most of his extended college playing time, as he started all thirteen games of his junior year and was named an honorable mention All-American.

In 1998, while serving as team captain along with Bobbie Howard and Kory Minor, Rosenthal was moved to strong tackle and started every game, clearing the way for many a Fighting Irish yard. After the season he was named a first-team All-American.

He was selected in the fifth round of the 1999 NFL draft by the New York Giants, joining another former Irish lineman, Luke Petitgout, who the Giants selected in the first round. Rosenthal has worked his way into the Giants first team and was a member of the 2001 Super Bowl team.

ROSSUM, ALLEN
Cornerback (1994–97), 5′8″, 179 lbs.

Rossum's versatility is easy to prove because he holds an unusual NCAA record. He has the most career returns for touchdowns, with 9, equally distributed (3 apiece) among interceptions, kickoff returns, and punt returns. Rossum ran the fastest 100 meters in the nation (10.02 seconds) during his senior season at Skyline High School in Dallas, Texas, where he captained the track team all four seasons. As a high school football player he played quarterback, cornerback, wide receiver, free safety, and strong safety. He was dominant on defense, with 265 solo tackles and 315 assists during his prep career, and he made 13 interceptions and recovered 3 fumbles.

In South Bend, Rossum was a two-time NCAA track All-American. In football, he left his mark on the Notre Dame record books, as well as set the NCAA mark for touchdowns on returns. He beat Utah's Erroll Tucker, who had 3 on interceptions returns, 3 on punt returns, and 2 on kickoff returns in 1984 and 1985.

Rossum is first in career punt return average (15.8 yards), first in career punt and kickoff return average (23.5 yards), and single-season punt and kick-off returns for touch-

downs (4 in 1997). He is also tied for first in single-season kickoff returns for touchdowns (2 in 1997) and 3 punts returned for a touchdown (3 in 1996), and he is second in career kickoff return average (30.7 yards). As a junior, Rossum led the nation in punt return average (22.9 yards) and ranked second in playing time on the Fighting Irish defense, with 247:02. He was also the only player in the country to return 3 punts for touchdowns.

Rossum was a captain as a senior, along with Ron Powlus and Melvin Dansby. He ranked fourth in the nation in kickoff return average (28.5 yards) and was one of five Division I players to return 2 kickoffs for touchdowns.

After the football season, Rossum was seventh in the NCAA indoor track and field championship, covering 55 meters in 6.26 seconds. The Philadelphia Eagles selected him in the third round of the 1998 NFL draft. He was the only Notre Dame player to be selected.

CAREER STATS

KICKOFF RETURNS

Year	Ret.	Yards	Avg.	TDs	Long
1995	3	94	31.3	0	38
1996	6	227	37.8	1	99
1997	20	570	28.5	2	93
Total	29	891	30.7	3	99

PUNT RETURNS

Year	Ret.	Yards	Avg.	TDs	Long
1995	None				
1996	15	344	22.9	3	83
1997	12	83	6.9	0	23
Total	27	427	15.8	3	83

INTERCEPTIONS

Year	Int.	Yards	Avg.	TDs
1995	3	105	35.0	2
1996	2	8	4.0	0
1997	2	38	19.0	1
Total	7	151	21.6	3

RETURNS FOR TOUCHDOWNS

KICKOFF RETURNS

99 yards, first quarter, 14:47 left vs. Purdue, Sept. 14, 1996

93 yards, first quarter, 14:43 left vs. Pittsburgh, Oct. 11, 1997

80 yards, fourth quarter, 9:56 left vs. Boston College, Oct. 25, 1997

PUNT RETURNS

57 yards, first quarter, 7:59 left vs. Air Force, Oct. 19, 1996

55 yards, first quarter, 12:42 left vs. Pittsburgh, Nov. 16, 1996

83 yards, second quarter, 5:30 left vs. Pittsburgh, Nov. 16, 1996

INTERCEPTION RETURNS

29 yards, fourth quarter, 0:39 left vs. Texas, Sept. 23, 1995

76 yards, fourth quarter, 0:28 left vs. Washington, Oct. 7, 1995

37 yards. first quarter, 14:42 left vs. Hawaii, Nov. 29, 1997

RUDDY, TIM
Center (1990–93), 6′3″, 286 lbs.

Ruddy was the student athlete personified. His combination of intelligence (he maintained a 4.0 grade point average in high school) and athletic ability (he was all-state at Dunmore High School, which won the Pennsylvania Class A title) made him a prize for any college that could acquire his services. When Ruddy entered Notre Dame, he enrolled in the College of Engineering in the fall of 1990 and maintained a 3.859 GPA while majoring in mechanical engineering.

Ruddy started only two games in his first two college seasons, but that all changed when he was a junior. He became a starter and finished third among offensive players in minutes played. That season, Notre Dame was among the leaders in the country in total offense, rushing, and scoring (409 points), and Ruddy was one of the reasons. Not only did he play well, he maintained a straight-A

average and was a National Academic All-American and the recipient of the 1992 Student-Athlete Award from the Notre Dame Club of St. Joseph Valley.

As a senior, in 1993, Ruddy was the team's starting center for the second consecutive season and was named a tri-captain. He played 298:57, more than any other Fighting Irish player, despite missing a start with a pulled abdominal muscle. Notre Dame finished the season with an 11–1 record and a number two ranking. Ruddy's play earned him first-team All-American recognition. His classroom accomplishments were also duly noted. He was again a first-team Academic All-American, the 1994 Cotton Bowl Scholar-Athlete (incidentally, Notre Dame defeated Texas A&M, 24–21, in the game), and he earned postgraduate scholarships totaling $28,000 from the NCAA and the National Football Foundation.

The Miami Dolphins selected him in the second round (sixty-fifth overall) of the 1994 NFL draft. As of 2000 he was still with the franchise.

RUETTIGER, DANIEL
Defensive end (1975), 5′7″, 184 lbs.

No player has made more out of a 27-second career than Daniel "Rudy" Ruettiger of Joliet, Illinois. A former turbine operator for Commonwealth Edison and an improbable Fighting Irish walk-on, Ruettiger got into one game and inspired a movie about his life. The film in turn led to a career as a motivational speaker.

When he entered Notre Dame, Rudy was too slow, too small, and too old to have any right to think about playing at a college football powerhouse, but all he wanted was a letter, and he got it.

Originally he went to Rockport College on a baseball and wrestling scholarship, served two years in the navy, and then graduated from Holy Cross Junior College. He enrolled at Notre Dame in 1974, at age twenty-six, with the dream of dressing up in blue and gold on a Saturday.

Ruettiger managed to make only the practice squad, but his intensity and tremendous attitude was an inspiration to all of his teammates. Near the end of the season he was given some playing time in a 24–3 victory over Georgia Tech in which he played only 27 seconds, yet he sacked the quarterback for a 5-yard loss. When the game was over, the little man with the big heart was carried off the field on the shoulders of his teammates—the only time a Notre Dame player was so honored.

Screenwriter Angelo Pizzo and director David Anspaugh (of *Hoosiers*) got hold of the story and re-created that scene for the cameras in 1992 during a game against Boston College. Sixty thousand fans gave a riotous ovation when actor Sean Astin, who played the title role, got into a mock game and replicated Rudy's heroics. The film's debut was, of course, in South Bend. It turned out to be a commercial and critical success, and Rudy stretched his brief moment of fame well past 27 seconds.

RUETZ, JOE
Guard/Quarterback (1935–37),
6′0″, 184 lbs.

Ruetz was from South Bend and earned his first letter as a second-team left guard in 1935, when he was a sophomore. The following season head coach Elmer Layden moved him to quarterback out of necessity, but he was back at his original position, left guard, as a senior as Notre Dame, compiling a 6–2–1 record.

While playing guard, Ruetz got to share the offensive line with a rival he had known for years. Ruetz had been a star athlete at South Bend Central High School, and future Notre Dame football coach Joe Kuharich had been his counterpart in both football and track at crosstown Riley High School.

Ruetz had a solid career at Notre Dame and went on to play two seasons of pro ball for the Chicago Rockets of the All-American Football Conference.

RYAN, TIM
Guard/Center/Linebacker (1987–90),
6′4″, 266 lbs.

It would be impressive enough had Kansas City, Missouri, native Ryan simply played three different positions at Notre Dame, but he took versatility to a new level, making All-American in two of the spots.

Ryan started his college career in 1987 as a linebacker. Then, in preseason workouts before Ryan's sophomore year, head coach Lou Holtz moved him to center, where he earned honorable mention All-American honors. In 1989, when he was a junior, Holtz moved him again, this time to guard and he again rated honorable mention All-American status. He started all twelve games as a senior guard; only center Mike Heldt played more time on the offensive line than Ryan.

The Tampa Bay Buccaneers selected Ryan in the fifth round of the 1991 NFL draft. He remained with the team through the 1993 season.

RYDZEWSKI, FRANK
Center (1915–17), 6′1″, 214 lbs.

Chicago native Rydzewski was one of the best offensive linemen in the country in 1917. That was his second season as a starter, and he earned first-team All-American honors. His career at Notre Dame ended the same year as head coach Jesse Harper's. Both went out with a 6–1 record.

Rydzewski played six years of pro football and made the rounds. During his career he played for six different teams, including three in one year—the Cleveland Tigers (1920), the Chicago Tigers (1920), the Hammond Pros (1920, 1922–26), the Chicago Cardinals (1921), the Chicago Bears (1923), and the Milwaukee Badgers (1925).

RYMKUS, LOU
Tackle (1940–42), 6′4″, 218 lbs.

During his formative years it didn't look like Lou Rymkus would ever go to college, let alone have his pick of schools and star on the football team. Rymkus grew up in Carbondale, Illinois, a coal mining town, and the family suffered great hardships when his father passed away. His mother moved the family to Chicago, hoping to find work. Lou almost had to drop out of school to help support the family, but his older brother got a job in a stockyard and his aunt boarded the family. The Rymkuses had some breathing room, and Lou enrolled at Tilden Tech.

The football coach took one look at the 6-foot, 220-pound freshman and knew he had a star player. Football came easily to Rymkus, who made all-state as a sophomore, junior, and senior. At this point, it was certain that he would go to college. The only question was where, and Notre Dame wasn't even in the picture yet. Midwestern universities such as Purdue, Wisconsin, and Northwestern were hot on his trail, but Notre Dame wasn't a suitor until late in Rymkus's

senior season, when a Fighting Irish assistant coach saw him dominate a game in Indiana. Rymkus was invited for a campus visit, and soon thereafter his decision was made. It wasn't that hard a sell: Rymkus was a fan of the Fighting Irish while growing up and had listened to every game on the radio.

Rymkus first made the Notre Dame varsity football team as a backup left tackle in his sophomore year. The following season Frank Leahy replaced Elmer Layden as head coach, but Rymkus's status as a second-string tackle remained unchanged. Then, as a senior, he was shifted to right tackle and won a starting spot. Notre Dame was 7–2–2 in 1942, and Rymkus was named Most Valuable Player by his teammates.

After Rymkus graduated, the Washington Redskins selected him in the fifth round of the 1943 NFL draft. He played for Washington in 1943. Then, after World War II, he returned to football and played six seasons with the Cleveland Browns.

SALMON, LOUIS
End/Halfback/Fullback (1900–1903);
Head coach (1904), 5'10", 175 lbs.

One of the amazing things about Louis "Red" Salmon, from Syracuse, New York, is how long some of the marks he set at Notre Dame stood up. His 36 career touchdowns was the record until Allen Pinkett broke it with 53 in 1985. Salmon's 11.7 points per game in 1903 is still the best all-time, and it's even more impressive to note that Notre Dame's opponents scored a total of only 10 points the entire season (Lake Forest had all of them).

Salmon, who was Notre Dame's first All-American and perhaps its best player until George Gipp played in South Bend, scored 105 points in 1903. That was also a school record until Pinkett broke it with 110 points in 1983. Then, in 1991, Jerome Bettis scored 120. (Touchdowns were worth only five points in 1903. Had they been worth six, Salmon's total, too, would have been 120.)

The team had a 28–6–4 record during the four seasons that Salmon, the captain of the 1902 and 1903 teams, started for Notre Dame. He was so good that by the end of his Notre Dame career, reporters spelled his name correctly. Originally it was spelled phonetically, "Sammon," in newspaper reports.

Records are sketchy from the early days of the program, but Salmon was a scoring machine in college. As a freshman, he started at both left end and halfback. He was a fearless 175-pounder: a great smash-mouth football player, making his name by plowing into the line. He was also a fine punter and kicker. During his senior season, Notre Dame was 8–0–1 and outscored its opponents, 292–10.

Salmon scored 15 touchdowns and kicked 30 extra points for a total of 105 points that year. His selection as a third-team All-American after the season was faint praise.

The following fall Salmon took over as coach of the Notre Dame football program, and despite not having him on the roster, the team was 5–3 in Salmon's only year as coach.

SAVOLDI, JOE
Fullback (1928–30), 5'11", 200 lbs.

Savoldi's college football career was cut short by three games because he secretly married his girlfriend. Secrecy would become a way of life for Savoldi, who served in the Office of Strategic Services (OSS) during World War II.

Savoldi, from Three Oaks, Michigan, made Notre Dame's varsity in 1928 as a sophomore. The following season, as a junior, he led the team in rushing, with 597 yards on 112 carries. His standout career ended in infamy when he was asked to withdraw from school three games before the completion of the 1930 season. Notre Dame had no rules about married students or football players, but the Catholic church, at the time, was against secret marriages and marriages outside of the Church. Notre Dame, of course, was a Catholic university, and although Savoldi was a Catholic, he had embarrassed the school with his secret union. In October 1930 the university asked him to leave the campus.

The Chicago Bears acted quickly and immediately signed Savoldi, but his professional career lasted just a year. He served in the OSS during the war and later became a professional wrestler who went by the name of "The Mystery Man of World War II."

SCANNELL, TIM
Guard (1982–85), 6'4", 278 lbs.

Scannell, from State College, Pennsylvania, started at offensive guard for three years, from 1983 through 1985, his senior year, when he was named a second-team All-American and also served as team captain. He chose two generations of Notre Dame family tradition over attending Penn State. His father was vice president at Penn State, but when it was time for Scannell to pick a school, he chose Notre Dame. There wasn't much his father could say about it—he had been a three-time letterer at end for Notre Dame in the 1950s, and *his* father had been chairman of the physical education department in South Bend for four decades. Tim was just carrying on a family tradition.

SCARPITTO, BOB
Halfback (1958–60), 5'11", 180 lbs.

Scarpitto, from Rahway, New Jersey, was a versatile back for Notre Dame and one of the program's best players in the late 1950s. He led the Fighting Irish in scoring during both his junior and senior seasons (48 points and 30 points). He began his varsity career as a backup running back in 1958. The next season he was the team's leading receiver, with 15 catches for 297 yards. As a senior in 1960, he led the team in kickoff returns, with 10 for 230 yards. He was second on the team in receiving with 8 catches for 164 yards, and third in rushing, with 51 carries for 228 yards.

Scarpitto was a ninth-round pick of the San Diego Chargers in the 1961 draft. He played for the Chargers in 1961, the Denver Broncos from 1962 through 1967, and the Boston Patriots in 1968.

SCHAEFER, DON
Quarterback/Fullback/Kicker (1953–55), 5'11", 190 lbs.

In his first year at Notre Dame, head coach Terry Brennan made a move that not only helped Pittsburgh native Schaefer play up to his potential, it also allowed Brennan to begin his coaching career right where the legendary Frank Leahy left off. He came in and moved Schaefer, who'd been a third-string quarterback the previous season, to fullback.

As a sophomore in 1953, Schaefer was down the depth chart as a quarterback. For the season, he ran 23 times for 100 yards and 2 touchdowns, caught a 42-yard pass, completed 3 of 8 passes for 39 yards, intercepted a pass, and punted the ball 4 times for 138 yards.

In his first year at fullback the change worked, and Schaefer led Notre Dame, which won nine of ten games, with 766 yards on 141 carries (a 5.4-yard average). He also scored 3 touchdowns, caught 3 passes for 60 yards, kicked 22 extra points, intercepted a pass, and recovered a fumble. The following season Schaefer again led the team in rushing, with 145 carries for 638 yards. He also scored a rushing touchdown, caught 6 passes for 36 yards and 2 more touchdowns, returned 2 kickoffs for 27 yards, completed a 24-yard pass, made 16 extra points, and had an interception. Those across-the-board numbers earned him first-team All-American honors, and he also made first-team Academic All-American.

The Philadelphia Eagles selected Schaefer in the third round of the 1956 NFL draft. He played only one season for the franchise.

SCHILLO, FRED
Tackle/Halfback (1892–94, 1896–97), 5'11", 180 lbs.

Schillo, from Chicago, was not only an outstanding player of his time, he was also on the field for much of the time. Between Schillo (who played for five years), George Lins (six years), and Jack Mullen (six years), Notre Dame had a nucleus of players who played seventeen years for the Fighting Irish.

Schillo began his college career in 1892 and started at left tackle. He won the starting left tackle position again in 1893, when he rushed for 89 yards in an 8–6 victory over Albion. In a 28–0 victory over De-LaSalle, he ran for 65 yards and a touchdown. In 1894, Schillo was a backup right tackle. After a year away from the football team, he was back in 1896 and returned to his starting left tackle spot, where he was mainly used in short-yardage situations. Finally, in 1897, his fifth and final year on the Fighting Irish, he started at right tackle.

SCHOEN, TOM
Quarterback/Safety (1965–67),
5′11″, 178 lbs.

Schoen entered Notre Dame in hopes of throwing a lot of passes. By the end of his career, he made his name picking them off. The Euclid, Ohio, native began his college career as a sophomore in 1965. He backed up Bill Zloch at quarterback and completed 13 of 24 passes for 229 yards, 1 touchdown, and an interception. He also ran the ball 35 times for 81 yards, caught a 1-yard pass, and made a tackle.

In 1966, highly touted quarterback Terry Hanratty entered the scene, and Schoen's services at quarterback were expendable. Head coach Ara Parseghian realized that Schoen's athletic ability was too good to waste, so he decided to try him at safety. Schoen's quarterback mentality helped him anticipate plays, and the transition worked. For the season, Schoen made 30 tackles, had 7 interceptions for 118 yards and 2 touchdowns, and led the team in punt returns, with 29 for 252 and a touchdown. Notre Dame went 9–0–1 and won the national championship, and Schoen was named a second-team All-American.

Schoen had another exceptional season as a senior. He led all defensive backs with 52 tackles and 11 passes defended, had 4 interceptions for 108 yards, and recovered a fumble. Schoen also returned 42 punts for 447 yards and a touchdown (he set an NCAA single-game record in punt return yardage, with 167 on 9 returns in a 38–0 victory over the University of Pittsburgh). This time Schoen

was a consensus first-team All-American, and was also picked to play in the East-West Shrine Game.

The Cleveland Browns selected Schoen in the eighth round of the 1968 NFL draft. He played the 1970 season for the Browns and then retired to become a sports manufacturing representative.

SCHOLTZ, BOB
Center (1957–59), 6′2″, 240 lbs.

Scholtz, from Tulsa, Oklahoma, was the starting center on three average Fighting Irish teams in the late 1950s. As a junior, he was third in tackles, with 51, while playing 285 minutes. As a senior, he made a team-leading 85 tackles. The Detroit Lions selected him in the third round of the 1960 NFL draft. He played with the Lions from 1960 through 1964, and the following two seasons with the New York Giants.

SCHRADER, JIM
Center (1951–53), 6′2″, 210 lbs.

After playing one year behind soon-to-be-All-American Art Hunter, Jim Schrader, from Carnegie, Pennsylvania, was Notre Dame's starting center for two seasons. When Hunter moved to end, Schrader took over. The Washington Redskins selected him in the second round of the 1954 NFL draft. He played for the Redskins in 1954 and from 1956 to 1961, and he then continued his ten-year professional career in Philadelphia, where he played for the Eagles from 1962 to 1964.

SCHWARTZ, MARCHMONT
Halfback (1929–31), 5′11″, 167 lbs.

Had there been a Heisman Trophy when "Marchy" Schwartz was playing, he surely would have won at least one. With the exception of George Gipp, Schwartz was the best running back to play for Knute Rockne. Schwartz, an extremely versatile performer, was part of a team that won two national titles, and had twenty-five victories, two losses, and a tie.

Schwartz didn't intend to go to Notre Dame, but as was the case with many other young men, all it took was one speech from Knute Rockne and he was sold. After graduating from St. Stanislaus High School in Bay St. Louis, Michigan, the New Orleans native enrolled at Loyola University. While there he heard Rockne speak at a basketball tournament and decided to transfer to South Bend.

It worked out well for all involved, as Schwartz led the team in rushing, passing, and scoring during his junior and senior seasons. He began his career on the undefeated 1920 national championship team as a backup to Jack Elder at left halfback, and finished the season with 65 carries for 326 yards and 3 touchdowns.

In 1930, Schwartz became not only Notre Dame's starting left halfback, but also one of the most dominant players in college football. He led the team in rushing, with 927 yards on 124 carries (a remarkable 7.5 yards per carry), in points with 54, and, as a *halfback*, he led in passing, completing 17 of 56 passes for 319 yards and 3 touchdowns. Notre Dame won all ten of its games and the first back-to-back national championships in college football. Schwartz, who was a consensus All-American, helped preserve the perfect season with a 54-yard fourth-quarter touchdown run in a 7–6 victory over powerhouse Army in the second-to-last game of the season.

In 1931, Schwartz helped "Hunk" Anderson in his first season as head coach. He led the squad in rushing, with 692 yards on 146 carries and 5 touchdowns, and also led in passing, with 9 completions of 51 attempts for 174 yards and 3 touch- downs. Schwartz, a unanimous first-team All- American selection, finished with 1,945 career yards rushing, which at the time trailed only Gipp. But the Gipper compiled 2,341 yards in four seasons, compared with Schwartz's three seasons. As of 2000, Schwartz ranked as Notre Dame's thirteenth all-time leading rusher.

Schwartz, a 1974 inductee into the College Football Hall of Fame, went into coaching after his playing days were over. He

began as an assistant coach at Notre Dame and then took a similar post at the University of Chicago. He went on to become the head coach at Creighton University and Stanford.

CAREER STATS

Year	Att.	Yards	Avg.	TDs
1929	65	326	5.0	3
1930	124	927	7.5	9
1931	146	692	4.7	5
Total	335	1,945	5.8	17

SCULLY, JOHN
Center/Tackle (1977–80), 6'5", 255 lbs.

Scully, from Huntington, New York, overcame injuries and a position move to become the best center in college football. He began his college career as a backup offensive tackle. Then, as a junior, he was shifted to center and asked to replace All-American Dave Huffman. Given the chance to play, Scully made very few mistakes and started eleven games in his first season at center. He was named a tri-captain the following year and was a consensus first-team All-American who went on to play in the East-West Shrine Game.

The Atlanta Falcons selected Scully in the fourth round of the 1981 NFL draft. He played his entire ten-year career in Atlanta.

SEILER, PAUL
Tackle (1964–66), 6'4", 235 lbs.

Seiler's college football career got off to a slow start. He didn't even earn a letter until his senior season, but he took advantage of his playing time and became an All-American, parlaying that success into a professional career. Seiler was a star lineman at Bishop Garrigan High School in Algona, Iowa, but he did not earn a letter at Notre Dame in his sophomore or junior seasons despite being a second-string tackle.

When Bob Meeker graduated, Seiler slipped right into the left tackle slot. Seiler's performance was far better than you would expect from a guy who had spent most of his first two seasons on the bench. He was a key member of the 1966 Notre Dame team that went 9–0–1, led the nation with 362 points, and won a national championship. He was also one of three All-Americans, including guard Tom Regner and center George Goeddeke, from the Notre Dame offensive line. There were twelve All-Americans on the team.

Seiler was also the first of three Fighting Irish players to be selected in the first round of the 1967 NFL draft. The New York Jets chose him at number twelve. The Minnesota Vikings used the fifteenth pick to grab Alan Page, and Regner went to the Houston Oilers as number twenty-three. Seiler played with the New York Jets in 1967, but missed the team's Super Bowl championship season in 1968 by fulfilling his military obligation. He played with the Jets in 1969, missed the 1970 season with an injury, and then played with the Oakland Raiders from 1971 through 1973. After he left Oakland, he played two seasons in the United States Football League before retiring.

SEVEN MULES, THE

Although they did not garner the accolades received by the Four Horsemen for whom they blocked, the Seven Mules were one of the finest offensive fronts in the history of college football. In alphabetical order they were: Joe Bach, tackle; Chuck Collins, end; Ed Hunsinger, end; Noble Kizer, guard; Rip Miller, tackle; Adam Walsh, center; and John Weibel, guard. In 1924, they led Notre Dame to its first national championship with a 10–0 record under head coach Knute Rockne.

SEYMOUR, JIM
Split end (1966–68), 6'4", 205 lbs.

Three years as a starter and three times as an All-American sums up the college career of Seymour, a silky-smooth deep threat on some exceptional Notre Dame teams. Before he enrolled at Notre Dame, Seymour led his Berkley, Michigan, high school football team

to the Detroit Catholic Championship and also starred in track and basketball. At Notre Dame in 1966, Seymour quickly hooked up with quarterback Terry Hanratty to form what is probably the school's greatest passing combo ever.

Seymour had single games that would have been adequate careers for some receivers. In his very first varsity game, for instance, he caught 13 passes for 276 yards and 3 touchdowns in a 26–14 victory over Purdue. His total of 276 yards remains the school's single-game pass reception record, and the 3 touchdowns is tied for tops. Sophomore Seymour had his best college season that year, as Notre Dame went 9–0–1 and took the national championship. He caught 48 passes for 862 yards and 8 touchdowns and was named to several All-American teams. In 1967, as a junior, he made 37 catches for 515 yards and 4 touchdowns and was named a first-team All-American. As a senior, he made 53 catches for 736 yards and 4 touchdowns to earn first-team All-American status.

During his three seasons of college football, during which the Fighting Irish were 24–4–2, Seymour made 138 catches, second only to Tom Gatewood on the school's all-time list, and also played in the 1969 College Football All-Star Game. Seymour was a first-round draft pick of the Los Angeles Rams (tenth overall) in 1969. He played his entire three-year NFL career with the Chicago Bears and caught just 21 passes for 385 yards.

CAREER STATS

Year	Rec.	Yards	Avg.	TDs
1966	48	862	17.9	8
1967	37	515	13.9	4
1968	53	736	13.9	4
Total	138	2,113	15.3	16

SHAKESPEARE, WILLIAM V.
Halfback/Punter (1933–35), 5'11", 179 lbs.

Bill "the Bard" Shakespeare threw one of the most memorable passes in college football history—the 19-yard touchdown pass to

Wayne Millner with 32 seconds to play to complete Notre Dame's stirring come-from-behind 18–13 victory over favored Ohio State in "the Game of the Century." Despite that successful pass, the halfback was most effective as a punter for the Fighting Irish.

The Staten Island, New York, native was a backup left halfback in 1933. He earned his first letter the following year as a junior and led the team in passing (9 completions of 29 attempts for 230 yards and 2 touchdowns) and kickoff returns (4 for 60 yards). In 1935, Shakespeare proved his versatility. He led the team in rushing, with 374 yards and 4 touchdowns on 104 carries; in passing, with 19 completions of 66 attempts for 267 yards and 2 touchdowns; and kickoff returns, with 5 for 123 yards. He also averaged 40 yards per punt. He kicked one ball that traveled 86 yards (still a school record) in a 9–6 victory over the University of Pittsburgh. Shakespeare was named a first-team All-American his senior year and left school with the career punting record—3,705 yards on 91 attempts.

The Pittsburgh Pirates selected Shakespeare in the first round of the 1936 NFL draft, but he bypassed pro football for a career in business. He was inducted into the College Football Hall of Fame in 1983.

CAREER STATS

PUNTING

Year	Punts	Yards	Avg.
1933	5	266	53.2
1934	41	1,638	40.0
1935	45	1,801	40.0
Total	91	3,705	40.7

SHANNON, DAN
Linebacker/End (1951–54), 6'0", 190 lbs.

Chicago native Shannon was a hard-hitting defender and an accomplished receiver who was a four-year starter for Notre Dame. He began his career in 1951 as a starting linebacker and made some big plays, including 4 fumble recoveries and 2 interceptions. The following season he again started at linebacker and made 2 interceptions and caused a couple of fumbles—one in a 14–3 victory over nineteenth-ranked Texas, and the other, one of the biggest plays of his career, to set up the winning score in a 27–21 victory over fourth-ranked Oklahoma. He also intercepted a pass to stop seventh-ranked USC in a 9–0 season-finale victory. During the season, the Fighting Irish played against six ranked teams and compiled a more-than-respectable 7–2–1 record.

In 1953, one-platoon football was back, and Shannon started at left end. He finished the season with 7 receptions for 138 yards and 2 touchdowns, both in a 14–14 tie against the University of Iowa. Notre Dame finished the season with a 9–0–1 record and ranked second in the nation. The following year, Shannon was reunited with Terry Brennan, who had coached him at Mount Carmel High School. Brennan replaced Frank Leahy at Notre Dame, and his old student helped him make a successful leap to one of college football's top programs.

The season was Brennan's best at Notre Dame. The team went 9–1 and finished fourth in the final Associated Press poll. (Its only loss was during the second game of the season, when nineteenth-ranked Purdue stopped the top-ranked Irish 27–14 in South Bend.) Shannon led Notre Dame in receiving, with 11 receptions for 215 yards and 3 touchdowns. Two of his touchdowns—a 22-yarder and an 18-yarder—came in a 42–7 victory over the University of Pennsylvania. After the season he was named a second-team All-American. The Chicago Bears selected him in the sixth round of the NFL draft, but he never played in the pros.

SHAUGHNESSY, FRANK
End (1901–04), 6'0", 178 lbs.

Shaughnessy, from Amboy, Illinois, was a big-play end for Notre Dame shortly after the turn of the century. He was a backup left end and quarterback as a freshman, and made it into the starting lineup at left end the following year. The 1903 season was a good one for both Shaughnessy and Notre Dame, which went 8–0–1 and outscored its opponents, 292–10. Shaughnessy moved over to right end and scored on a 40-yard run against Michigan State, scored twice in a 52–0 drubbing of American Medical College, and rushed for 140 yards, including a 90-yard touchdown, in a 35–0 victory over Ohio Medical University.

In 1904's season opener against Wabash he ran back a fumble recovery for an 80-yard score, and then gained more than 200 yards rushing, and scored on runs of 45 and 101 yards, as Notre Dame annihilated American Medical, 44–0. He also scored Notre Dame's only touchdown on a 100-yard run in a 24–5 loss to the University of Kansas, and capped his career with a team-leading day of more than 70 yards rushing, including plays of 30 and 25 yards, against Purdue.

SHAW, LAWRENCE
Tackle (1919–21), 6′0″, 185 lbs.

"Buck" Shaw didn't let a lack of experience get in his way. He did, however, get in the way of many defenders who wanted to tackle George Gipp. Despite playing just three high school games of prep ball in Lawrence, Iowa, Shaw was a member of the great offensive lines who cleared the way for Gipp.

Shaw's family moved to Stuart, Iowa, when he was ten. Football had been abolished in the town because of a death on the field. But the sport came back in 1917, when Shaw was a senior in high school, and he played three games. He liked it enough to enroll at Creighton University with hopes of becoming a football star. He played one game before a flu epidemic canceled the rest of Creighton's schedule.

In 1919, Shaw enrolled at Notre Dame and made the football team as a walk-on, second-team left tackle. He became a starter in 1920 and helped the Fighting Irish to a 9–0 record and its first national championship. He blocked a punt for a safety against

Nebraska, recovered a fumble for a touchdown against Purdue, made 2 extra points against Northwestern, and blocked 5 punts during the season.

In 1921, he kicked 7 extra points and deflected a punt in a 56–0 whitewashing of Kalamazoo. For the season he made 38 of 40 extra points. After the season, Rockne, who knew that Shaw could add something to the game of football, told him of a few coaching positions that were available and said he would recommend him. Shaw began his coaching career as an assistant at the University of Nevada, and then took off on a long and winding road. In 1924, he became the head coach at North Carolina State. In 1925, he returned to Nevada as head coach and remained there until 1928. In 1929, he became an assistant at the University of Santa Clara, and seven years later became the school's head coach. Under Shaw, Santa Clara won two Sugar Bowls, sixteen consecutive games, and went eleven of those games without allowing a touchdown.

In 1942, Santa Clara disbanded its football program and Shaw took his acumen to the professional ranks. He was the first head coach of the San Francisco 49ers, a team he guided from 1946 to 1955. In 1956 it was back to school for Shaw, who became head coach of the U.S. Air Force Academy. He stayed there for two years and then returned to the pros to coach the Philadelphia Eagles. His start there was shaky, as the Eagles won just two games in his first season. However, the next year, 1960, they turned it around and went 10–2, winning the divisional title. The Eagles went on to upset Vince Lombardi's Green Bay Packers, 17–13, in the NFL championship game. Shaw announced his retirement shortly after the season, and was inducted into the College Football Hall of Fame in 1972.

SHEEHAN, CLARENCE
Center (1903–06), 6′0″, 190 lbs.

Sheehan, from Grand Ridge, Illinois, was the starting center on Notre Dame's undefeated 1903 team. In 1904, he suffered injuries and was limited to backup duty under Louis "Red" Salmon, who had gone from captain to coach in his first season after graduation. Sheehan was a very good long snapper, but he also had a nose for the ball and didn't mind sacrificing his body to block kicks or smother fumbles. That year he blocked a kick and recovered a fumble to help Notre Dame hang on to a 6–0 victory over the Toledo Medical Association. He was back to his starting position in 1905, and scored on runs of 25 and 50 yards and recovered a kickoff in the end zone—3 of Notre Dame's 27 touchdowns in its astounding 142–0 victory over American Medical College. Two weeks later he blocked an Indiana field goal in a losing effort. In 1906, he recovered a loose kickoff for a touchdown in a season-opening 26–0 victory over Franklin. The next week he recovered a blocked punt in a 17–0 victory against Hillsdale. Later that year he blocked a Michigan State punt in the Spartans's own end zone, which led to the only score in Notre Dame's 5–0 victory.

SILVER, NATE
Quarterback (1902–05), 5′8″, 150 lbs.

Chicago native Silver was a three-year starter at quarterback for Notre Dame. After serving as a backup in 1902, he took over the offense in 1903. Under Silver's direction, Notre Dame scored 292 points, allowed only 10, and went undefeated (8–0–1). He retained his starting status during the 1904 and 1905 seasons. Because of injuries he was forced to play end against the Toledo Athletic Association as a junior, and was an important factor in the 6–0 victory. As a senior he scored 3 touchdowns, which included a 40-yard run and an 80-yard kickoff return, in the 142–0 demolition of American Medical College.

SITKO, EMIL
Running back (1946–49), 5′8″, 175 lbs.

"Red" Sitko was a tightly wound bundle of muscle, and a bundle of joy for head coach Frank Leahy. His acceleration was astound-

ing—he could reach top speed in a matter of steps. If he had a weakness it was that he was quicker than he was fast—he could be caught from behind in the open field, but, then again, he often got into the open field.

After serving in World War II, Sitko, from Fort Wayne, Indiana, enrolled at Notre Dame. He led the team in rushing each of the next four seasons; Notre Dame won three national championships and never lost a game those four years, and Sitko was elected into the College Football Hall of Fame in 1984. While he played with Notre Dame its record was 36–0–2.

Sitko immediately won the right halfback position as a freshman and led the team in rushing, with 346 yards on 54 carries for an average of 6.4 yards per run. He scored 3 touchdowns, caught 3 passes for 55 yards, and made 2 interceptions as Notre Dame won the national championship. In 1947, Sitko was back starting at right halfback, and Notre Dame was back on top of the college game with a second consecutive national title. Sitko did his part, averaging 7.1 yards per rush (60 carries for 426 yards and 4 touchdowns). He also caught 4 passes for 48 yards and returned 2 kickoffs for 52 yards. Not bad numbers for a sophomore playing on a team with the likes of George Connor, Bill Fischer, and Heisman Trophy winner Johnny Lujack.

Sitko finished his college career with two nearly identical seasons and was named a consensus All-American after both. As a junior Sitko led the team with 742 yards on 129 carries and 9 touchdowns. He also caught 7 passes for 70 yards and returned a kickoff for 76 yards. His senior season numbers were a team-leading 712 yards on 120 carries, plus 9 touchdowns. He also caught 2 passes for 15 yards, and returned 4 kickoffs for 89 yards and a punt for 23 yards. That was another national championship season. When it was over, Sitko was eighth in the voting for the Heisman Trophy, seven spots behind winner and teammate Leon Hart, but he did win the Walter Camp Trophy as college football's best player. Sitko finished up at Notre Dame with 2,226 yards, which at the time was second only to George Gipp. As of 2000, he ranks ninth all-time at Notre Dame.

Sitko was somehow overlooked in the NFL draft. He did, however, play in 1950 for the San Francisco 49ers, and in 1951 and 1952 with the Chicago Cardinals.

SKOGLUND, BOB
End (1944–46), 6'1", 198 lbs.

Studies were more important than football to Skoglund. Fortunately for all departments at Notre Dame, he excelled at both. His first time on the bluegrass of Notre Dame Stadium occurred when he was eleven. His brother, Len, was the team's starting wide receiver and, one Saturday, got his little brother the best seat in the house—on the Notre Dame bench. Eight years later he was back on that bench. After starring in football, track, and boxing at Loyola Academy in Chicago, Skoglund decided to follow in his brother's footsteps.

Skoglund was an athletic student as opposed to a student athlete. He even skipped freshman football in 1943, his first year on campus, so that he could get his schoolwork in order. Head coach Frank Leahy was impressed with the young man's priorities on one hand, but not so happy that he was missing out on vital football development. By the middle of his second semester, Skoglund was an A student. His first priority taken care of, he was now ready for some football. He took part in Notre Dame's spring workouts and proved that he could succeed outside of the classroom as well.

Skoglund earned a letter in 1944 as a backup to Zeke O'Connor at left end. The following season he took over the starting spot and led the team in receiving, with 9 catches for 100 yards. In 1946, Notre Dame received an influx of high-class talent in the form of future All-American Jim Martin and soon-to-be Heisman Trophy winner Leon Hart. Understandably, Skoglund saw his playing time diminish.

Due to relaxed wartime eligibility rules, Skoglund could have played another season at Notre Dame, but he chose to complete his degree and signed as a free agent with the Green Bay Packers, for whom he played in 1947. Unfortunately, he died in 1949 from a kidney infection at age twenty-four.

SLAGER, RICK
Quarterback (1974–76), 5'11", 190 lbs.

Slager, from Columbus, Ohio, was one of the quarterbacks who started at Notre Dame for head coach Dan Devine while Joe Montana waited for his chance. In 1974, he was a backup to Tom Clements, and ran the ball 12 times for 82 yards and completed 3 of 8 passes for 39 yards. In 1975, he took over the offense while Montana watched from the sidelines. A tough quarterback with good running ability and an adequate arm, Slager completed 66 of 139 passes for 686 yards, with 2 touchdowns and 3 interceptions. He also ran the ball 27 times for 51 yards and a touchdown. In 1976, he led Notre Dame to a 20–9 Gator Bowl victory over Penn State by completing 10 of 19 passes for 141 yards. As a senior he completed 86 of 172 passes for 1,281 yards, 11 touchdowns, and 12 interceptions. He also rushed 49 times for -78 yards and 2 TDs. He was not selected in the 1977 NFL draft and did not play professionally.

SMAGALA, STAN
Defensive back (1986–89), 5'11", 186 lbs.

The smallish Smagala was the starting cornerback for Notre Dame for three years. The all-city tailback from St. Lawrence High School in Burbank, California, became known for his speed, agility, and his unlikely hitting prowess. The highlight of his college career occurred during the final game of the 1988 regular season, when his scoring 64-yard interception return fueled the Irish's 27–10 victory over USC. That year the team again became the national champion. Smagala was drafted in the fifth round of the 1990 NFL draft by the Los Angeles Raiders, but played for the Dallas Cowboys that year, and then went to the Pittsburgh Steelers for two years.

SMITH, ANTHONY
Split end (1989–91), 6'2", 191 lbs.

Tony Smith, from Gary, Indiana, improved steadily and rapidly during his four seasons in South Bend. He did not make the varsity as a freshman, and then made only 2 receptions as a sophomore, and 15 as a junior. Smith's senior season was his breakout year. He led the Fighting Irish with 42 receptions for 789 yards and 4 touchdowns, and caught 7 passes for 79 yards in Notre Dame's 39–28 victory over the University of Florida in the Sugar Bowl. That year he was also named an honorable mention All-American.

The Kansas City Chiefs selected Smith in the sixth round of the 1992 NFL draft—four rounds and 124 picks after the New England Patriots took teammate Rod Smith. Tony played for Kansas City in 1992.

SMITH, HUNTER DWIGHT
Punter (1995–98), 6'2", 218 lbs.

The two-time all-state punter played wide receiver, running back, quarterback, tight end, and kicker at Sherman High School, in Texas. He also high-jumped 6 feet, 10 inches, and placed sixth in the state track and field meet as a junior and third as a senior.

As a Notre Dame freshman in 1995, Smith averaged only 36.4 yards a punt, but as a sophomore he was twenty-fifth nationally, with a career-best 43.3-yard average. In 1997, "Hunter the Punter" connected on 50 punts for a 42.6-yard average, and as a senior he punted 42 times for 1,750 yards.

In 1998, Smith was the team's punter besides handling the kickoffs. A versatile athlete, he also served as the squad's third-string quarterback for part of the season. His booming leg accounted for a 79-yard punt out of Arizona State's end zone; that was the Fighting Irish's longest punt in sixty-three years, and third-longest of all time. He finished his career with a 41.2-yards-per-punt average, which is second best in school history, behind Craig Hentrich, who averaged 44.1 yards.

Smith was selected in the seventh round of the 1999 draft by the Indianapolis Colts. He remains with the team.

CAREER STATS

Year	Punts	Yds.	Avg.
1995	38	1,382	36.4
1996	44	1,906	43.3
1997	50	2,132	42.6
1998	42	1,750	41.7
Total	174	7,170	41.2

SMITH, IRVIN MARTIN
Tight end (1989–92), 6'4", 246 lbs.

Irv Smith didn't get a chance to start at Notre Dame until his senior season. It was at that point that he demonstrated the skills that earned him *Parade* magazine's High School All-American status at Pemberton Township High School in New Jersey, where he played safety, linebacker, and tight end.

Playing behind All-American Derek Brown for three seasons, Smith only had the opportunity to catch 8 passes in his first three college seasons. He was, however, a superior blocker and a good receiver, so when Smith made it to the first team in 1992, he responded with 20 receptions for 262 yards and 2 touchdowns and logged more field time (257:34) than any other Fighting Irish receiver. He led Notre Dame with 3 catches for 38 yards in its 28–3 Cotton Bowl victory over Texas A&M, and after the season was named a second-team All-American.

The New Orleans Saints chose Smith as the twentieth overall selection in the 1993 NFL draft. He was the fourth Notre Dame player chosen. Quarterback Rick Mirer went to Seattle as the second pick, fullback Jerome Bettis went to the Los Angeles Rams tenth, and cornerback Tom Carter went to the Washington Redskins seventeenth. Smith played five seasons for the Saints, and the 1998 season for the San Francisco 49ers. He was traded to the revived Cleveland Browns in early 1999.

SMITH, JOHN
Guard (1925–27), 5'9", 165 lbs.

Even Knute Rockne made mistakes. The legendary Notre Dame figure supposedly took one look at "Clipper" Smith, a 5-foot-9,

165-pound guard, and informed the prospective player that he was too small to play the game. This is surprising, as Rockne favored small, quick linemen. The appraisal, however, didn't stop Smith from having a standout career and eventually being inducted into the College Football Hall of Fame.

After captaining his high school football team in Hartford, Connecticut, Smith made his way to Notre Dame in 1924 and earned his first monogram as a backup guard in 1925. He became a starter in 1926 and was named team captain in 1927, his senior season. Notre Dame was 7–1–1 that year, thanks in part to the intelligent, quick, and aggressive player whom Rockne didn't think was big enough to make the team. Smith was also a consensus first-team All-American.

Smith graduated in the top 10 percent of his class, and then worked a year as an assistant coach at Notre Dame while completing his law degree. But he eventually chose coaching over law. His first stop was as an assistant coach at Trinity College in his hometown of Hartford. Then he was off to Georgetown before being named head football coach and athletic director at North Carolina State. In 1935, he took over the Duquesne University program, which shocked the nation the following season by defeating vaunted crosstown rival Pittsburgh, 7–0. In Smith's second season Duquesne finished 7–2 and beat Mississippi State, 13–12, in the Orange Bowl. Smith also coached at Villanova before retiring from coaching. He was inducted into the College Football Hall of Fame in 1975.

SMITH, ROD
Defensive back/Flanker (1988–91),
6'0", 186 lbs.

There were few players, if any, ever to wear the Notre Dame blue who were faster than Rod Smith. He came to Notre Dame from St. Paul, Minnesota, with the 1987 Minnesota state championships in the 100 meters, 200 meters, and long jump in hand. He was a member of Notre Dame's track team, but his accomplishments there were dwarfed by his work on the gridiron.

Smith was a flanker during his freshman season, but was shifted to cornerback the following year, and proved to be more effective defending passes than catching them. He started three games in 1989 and four in 1990, his junior season, and made 29 tackles that year. As a senior, Smith played more than 284 minutes, splitting time between cornerback and strong safety. He made 69 tackles, trailing only linebacker Demetrius DuBose, and made 3 interceptions. Smith saved his best performance for last, making a career-high 18 tackles in Notre Dame's 39–28 victory over Florida in the Sugar Bowl after the 1991 season.

In the 1992 NFL draft, the New England Patriots selected Smith in the second round (thirty-fifth overall). He played in New England from 1992 to 1994, and then moved on to play for the Carolina Panthers.

SMITHBERGER, JIM
Defensive back (1965–67), 6'1", 190 lbs.

Smithberger, of Grundy, West Virginia, was part of one of Notre Dame's stingiest defenses. He played defensive back on the 1966 team that allowed just 38 points en route to a 9–0–1 record and a national title. That year the junior played 261 minutes in his first year as a starter and made 54 tackles and 4 interceptions. The following season, he made 41 tackles and 2 interceptions and was credited with breaking up 7 passes. Postseason honors included second-team All-American and first-team Academic All-American status. The Philadelphia Eagles selected Smithberger in the fifth round of the 1968 NFL draft, but he did not play pro football.

SNOW, JACK
End/Flanker/Punter (1962–64), 6'2", 215 lbs.

Quarterback John Huarte may have won the Heisman Trophy in 1964, but it's safe to say that he wouldn't have done it without the stellar play of Snow. Snow arrived in South Bend from Long Beach, California, in 1961 after making all-city as a baseball and football player at St. Anthony's High School. He made the Fighting Irish varsity in 1962 as

All-American receiver Jack Snow was Heisman Trophy–winning quarterback John Huarte's favorite target.

a backup split end, but did not play enough to earn a letter. He finished the season with 4 receptions for 46 yards. He also made an interception and caught a pass for a 2-point conversion. However, in 1963 he began to show signs that he would be a college standout. He played both split end and flanker, and had 6 receptions for 82 yards, second on the team. He averaged more than 38 yards per punt, and made 21 tackles and an interception on defense.

Snow's senior year saw his numbers take a quantum leap. He caught more than half of the successful passes that Heisman Trophy–winner Huarte threw in 1964, and he was the NCAA's second-leading receiver, with 60 catches for 1,114 yards and 9 touchdowns. In the process, he set single-season Notre Dame records for yardage, receptions, touchdowns, and receiving yards. As of 1998, he stood second in yardage, touchdowns, and receiving yards for a game (217 yards on 9 receptions for 2 touchdowns in a season-opening victory over the University of Wisconsin). Snow was understandably a consensus first-team All-American. He also finished just four slots below Huarte in Heisman Trophy voting.

Snow was selected in the first round of the 1965 draft by Minnesota of the NFL and San Diego of the AFL, but he played his entire eleven-year professional career with his hometown Los Angeles Rams. He is one of the franchise's all-time leading receivers, with 340 receptions for 6,012 yards and 45 touchdowns. When Snow retired from football, he became a broadcaster.

SPANIEL, FRANK
Halfback/Fullback (1947–49),
5'10", 184 lbs.

Spaniel, of Vandergrift, Pennsylvania, was a member of two national championship teams during his three seasons on the Notre Dame varsity football team. He was a backup on head coach Frank Leahy's 1947 team, which won all nine of its games and was crowned the top team in the land. Spaniel was a reserve at right halfback and ran the ball 4 times for 13 yards. In 1948, he backed up at fullback and rushed 24 times for 174 yards and a touchdown. He also caught a 3-yard touchdown pass and made 2 interceptions.

In 1949, Notre Dame had a devastating backfield that consisted of Spaniel, Emil Sitko, and Larry Coutre. Spaniel finally broke into the starting lineup and tore apart opposing defenses. From his left halfback position, he was third on the team in rushing, with 496 yards on 80 carries, which averaged out to an impressive 6.2 yards per carry. He also was third on the squad in points, with 42, fourth in receiving (16 receptions for 212 yards and 3 touchdowns), and second in both kickoff and punt return yardage (5 for 70 yards, 3 for 32 yards). In 1949, Notre Dame was 10–0 and won the national championship.

Spaniel was not drafted to play in the NFL, but did play one year, 1950, with the Baltimore Colts and then the Washington Redskins.

STAMS, FRANK
Fullback/Linebacker/Defensive end
(1984–88), 6'4", 237 lbs.

Stams, who was recruited to play at Notre Dame by head coach Gerry Faust, was an outstanding high school running back. He rushed for more than 2,300 yards at St. Vincent–St. Mary High School in Akron, Ohio. During his first two seasons at Notre Dame he found himself in the offensive backfield, and in 1985, his sophomore season, he started at fullback for Faust. Lou Holtz was named coach before the start of the 1986 season and moved Stams to defense, but in 1986 Stams broke his leg during spring practice and missed virtually the entire fall season. He was back in 1987 and played in eleven games as a backup to outside linebacker Darrell "Flash" Gordon.

After one more position switch, to defensive end in 1988, Stams finally found a

All-American defensive end Frank Stams was an integral part of the 1988 national championship team that went 12–0 under coach Lou Holtz. (Bill Panzica)

home. He started all twelve games and brought with him the quickness and agility that had made him an outstanding rusher. On a very good defense he was a force to be reckoned with: he made 51 tackles and had 7 sacks as Notre Dame went 12–0. Holtz had completed his mission: to bring Notre Dame, which was named national champion, back to national prominence. The Moose Krause Chapter of the National Football Foundation named Stams its Lineman of the Year, and he was a consensus All-American.

The Los Angeles Rams selected the brand-new defensive end in the second round of the 1989 NFL draft. He played with the Rams from 1989 through 1991, with the Cleveland Browns from 1992 through 1994, and with the Carolina Panthers in 1995.

STICKLES, MONTY
End/Place kicker (1957–59), 6'4", 225 lbs.

Stickles, of Poughkeepsie, New York, never played on a national championship team at Notre Dame. As a matter of fact, the team only won eighteen games in his three seasons of varsity, but Stickles, a two-time All-American, was one of the best players on some mediocre teams.

Stickles was named a starter at end in 1957, his first varsity season, and led the team in scoring, with 32 points. He scored 3 touchdowns receiving, and made 11 extra points and a field goal. He was Notre Dame's second-leading receiver, with 11 catches for 183 yards. On defense he made a respectable 27 tackles and broke up 2 passes.

Stickles again led the team in scoring in 1958, with 60 points—7 touchdowns, a field goal, and 15 extra points. He had his best year receiving, with a team-leading 20 receptions for 328 yards. He also made 31 tackles, recovered 2 fumbles, and broke up 2 passes, which merited a first-team All-American selection.

In 1959, Stickles caught 11 passes for 235 yards and 2 touchdowns, and kicked 16 extra points and 3 field goals, for a total of 37 points. On defense he made 52 tackles, recovered a fumble, broke up 2 passes, and blocked a kick. Stickles was named a con-

Two-time All-American end Monty Stickles was an outstanding player on some less-than-sterling Notre Dame teams. He went on to have a great pro career with the San Francisco 49ers.

sensus All-American and was invited to play in the East-West Shrine Game and the College Football All-Star Game.

The San Francisco 49ers took Stickles in the first round of the 1960 NFL draft. He played in San Francisco for eight seasons and spent a year with the New Orleans Saints before returning to San Francisco to take a position as a marketing executive with the 49ers.

CAREER STATS

Year	Rec.	Yards	Avg.	TDs
1957	11	183	16.6	3
1958	20	328	16.4	7
1959	11	235	21.3	2
Total	42	746	17.8	12

STONEBREAKER, MICHAEL
Linebacker (1986, 1988, 1990),
6'1", 228 lbs.

Stonebreaker, from River Ridge, Louisiana, had an excellent, if unconventional, career at Notre Dame. He was a two-

time All-American, but only played in even-numbered years. Stonebreaker played in ten games as a freshman. As the season went on, he saw more action, and he made 19 of his 21 tackles in the season's final five games. He was expected to contend for a starting spot in 1987 but missed the season because of academic problems.

The following season, with his grades in order, Stonebreaker was back. He was also one of the best linebackers in the nation and finished the season with 104 tackles, good for second on the team. He was named a first-team All-American by virtually every voting organization in the country, and also finished third in the voting for the Butkus Award, which goes to the country's top linebacker.

The 1989 season was another washout for Stonebreaker, who broke a hip and dislocated a kneecap in a car accident. In 1990 he was ready to play again and led Notre Dame with 95 tackles. Stonebreaker was a consensus first-team All-American and again finished third in the voting for the Butkus Award. The Chicago Bears picked him in the

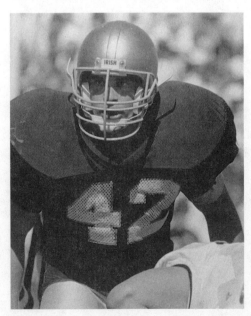

Michael Stonebreaker was a two-time All-American linebacker for Notre Dame.

ninth round of the 1991 NFL draft. He played with the Bears in 1991 and for the Atlanta Falcons in 1993 and 1994.

STROHMEYER, GEORGE
Center (1946–47), 5′9″, 195 lbs.

Strohmeyer had a big mouth, but at least he could back it up. He arrived in South Bend from McAllen, Texas, as an enormously successful six-sport athlete in high school, earning a dizzying twenty-four varsity letters in four years. With no regard for freshman protocol, he announced that he would be the team's starting center. This stunned coaches and angered some of his teammates. His declaration would be bold for any freshman, but at Notre Dame, the school with the most competitive football program in the country, it was flat-out audacious, particularly for someone who stood only 5-foot-9.

The year Strohmeyer made his prediction was a particularly competitive one as well. In 1946, many mature athletes returned after serving in World War II, and the talent pool was overflowing. During training camp, Strohmeyer impressed coaches and angered teammates with outstanding hitting and nonstop talking. He turned out to be a man of his word and outplayed both Bill Walsh, the starting center the previous season, and Art Statuto, a senior who was entering his fourth varsity season. The cocky freshman did indeed start at center in 1946 on one of Notre Dame's best all-time teams. The Fighting Irish went 8–0–1, outscored opponents 271–24, and won the national championship. Strohmeyer made almost every All-American team.

That would be virtually all anyone heard from Strohmeyer at Notre Dame. He showed up out of shape for summer practices in 1947 and Walsh beat him out for the starting center position. He did not return to school in 1948, opting instead for a professional career. That year he played for the Brooklyn Dodgers of the All-American Football Conference, and in 1949 he played for the AAFC's Chicago Hornets.

STUHLDREHER, HARRY
Quarterback (1922–24), 5′7″, 151 lbs.

Stuhldreher was the most feared of the famed Four Horsemen, as well as Knute Rockne's prototypical quarterback. He understood the nuances of the game, had a strong arm and voice, was as tough as they come, and somehow overcame his small size to be a very good blocker. He was also an exceptional punt returner despite unexceptional speed.

Stuhldreher selected Notre Dame mainly because as a child in Massillon, Ohio, he had watched Rockne play for the Massillon Tigers. The memory stayed with him long enough for him to select Notre Dame after graduating from Kiski Prep. Stuhldreher began the 1922 season as a backup quarterback, but in the third-to-last game of the year fullback Paul Castner went down with a hip injury and was replaced by quarterback Elmer Layden. That opened up a spot in the lineup

All-American and College Football Hall of Fame–inductee Harry Stuhldreher was the quarterback in the legendary Four Horsemen backfield and led Notre Dame to a 10–0 season and a national championship.

for Stuhldreher, and the Four Horsemen were born. After Layden, Stuhldreher, Don Miller, and Jim Crowley were assembled in the same backfield, Notre Dame won twenty-two of twenty-three games. It would, however, be two more seasons before legendary sportswriter Grantland Rice coined their moniker.

In his sophomore year, Stuhldreher passed for 68 yards and 3 touchdowns and rushed for 49 yards and 5 touchdowns. He also caught 6 passes for 95 yards and a touchdown, and returned 28 punts for 199 yards and 1 kickoff for 10. In 1923 his numbers were way up. As the starting quarterback, he passed for 205 yards and 3 touchdowns and rushed for 50 yards and 2 touchdowns. He also caught 7 passes for 63 yards, intercepted 3 passes, and led the team in punt returns, with 32 for 308 yards.

Confident to some, arrogant to others, Stuhldreher led Notre Dame to a 10–0 record and a national title in 1924, and he became one of the best-known players in the country during his senior year. He had his best year passing, completing 25 of 33 passes (.757 percent) for 471 yards and 4 touchdowns. He also rushed for 19 yards and 3 touchdowns, caught 5 passes for 52 yards, returned 22 punts for 194 yards and 2 kickoffs for 13 yards, and scored an extra point. Along with Layden and Crowley, he was named a first-team All-American.

The most famous backfield in college football history got its name on October 19, 1924, in Rice's *New York Herald-Tribune* report on Notre Dame's 13–7 victory over Army at the Polo Grounds. Stuhldreher later proved his toughness by playing much of Notre Dame's 27–10 Rose Bowl victory over Stanford with a broken bone in his ankle.

Stuhldreher finished up at Notre Dame with 744 yards and 10 touchdowns passing, 118 yards and 10 touchdowns rushing, 18 receptions for 210 yards and a touchdown, 3 interceptions, 88 punt returns for 701 yards, 3 kickoff returns for 23 yards, and 2 extra points. His grand total on offense was 1,796 yards on 221 attempts for an average

of 8.12 yards. He also was credited with 33 touchdowns.

After he graduated from Notre Dame, Stuhldreher became the head coach at Villanova in 1925. The following season he played professionally for Brooklyn. In 1936, he became the head coach and athletic director at the University of Wisconsin. He retired from coaching in 1947 with a career record of 110–87–15. Stuhldreher then became a businessman and wrote two books and several short stories and nonfiction pieces that appeared in the *Saturday Evening Post*. He was inducted into the College Football Hall of Fame in 1958.

CAREER STATS

PASSING

Year	Att.	Comp.	Pct.	Yards	TDs
1922	15	8	.533	68	3
1923	19	10	.526	205	3
1924	33	25	.757	471	4
Total	67	43	.642	744	10

PUNT RETURNS

Year	Ret.	Yards	Avg.
1922	28	199	7.1
1923	38	308	8.1
1924	22	194	8.8
Total	88	701	8.0

SWATLAND, DICK
Guard (1965–67), 6'2", 235 lbs.

Swatland arrived at Notre Dame from Stamford, Connecticut, in 1963 ready to play, but freshmen were not eligible for varsity football in those days. He missed the following season with an injury and finally made the varsity squad as a reserve offensive guard in 1965. During the subsequent spring practices, Swatland was the recipient of the Hering Award as the most improved lineman. In 1966, he made the starting team and played 227 minutes while Notre Dame went 9–0–1 and won the national championship.

Swatland used his additional year of eligibility to become Notre Dame's best offensive lineman in 1967 and a second-team All-American. The New Orleans Saints selected him in the eighth round of the 1968 NFL draft. He played one professional season, 1968, for the Houston Oilers.

SWEENEY, CHUCK
End (1935–37), 6′0″, 179 lbs.

After graduating from Trinity High School in Bloomington, Illinois, where he starred in both basketball and football, Sweeney worked the summer months as a seaman on a freighter. Not long afterward he stepped ashore and headed off to Notre Dame. Sweeney tried out for the basketball and football teams and played for both during his first two years at school, but then concentrated solely on football. He earned his first letter in 1936 and cracked the starting lineup in 1937, contributing a great deal on both offense and defense. Notre Dame went 6–2–1, and Sweeney was good for many big plays. In a 9–7 victory over Navy, he stopped halfback Allan McFarland in the end zone for the winning safety. His heroics earned him first-team All-American honors.

SWISTOWICZ, MIKE
Halfback/Defensive back (1946–49), 5′11″, 195 lbs.

Despite winning four letters at Notre Dame, Swistowicz, from Chicago, took a while to make an impact on the Notre Dame football team. His play was limited for his first three seasons because of various injuries. He was healthy for the 1949 season, however, and turned out to be one of the team's best defensive players. Swistowicz also ran the ball 11 times for 53 yards to further help the team win all ten of its games and capture the national championship. The New York Bulldogs selected him in the fifth round of the draft. In 1950, he played for the New York Yankees and Chicago Cardinals before retiring from football.

SYLVESTER, STEVE
Tackle (1972–74), 6′4″, 241 lbs.

In 1973, Sylvester opened up gaping holes from his starting right tackle position to help Notre Dame to set a school single-season rushing record, with 3,502 yards. He played more minutes than any other offensive lineman (more than 288), as Notre Dame won all ten of its games and the national title. He was at right tackle in 1974, head coach Ara Parseghian's final season, and Notre Dame went 10–2. Although the Fighting Irish did not defend their title, Sylvester got his due, earning third-team All-American honors.

That was a long way from his humble beginnings in South Bend. The native of Milford, Ohio, and graduate of Cincinnati's Moeller High School (which was coached by future Notre Dame coach Gerry Faust), hardly played in his sophomore season, and had to wait until his third year at Notre Dame to break through.

The Oakland Raiders selected Sylvester in the tenth round of the 1975 NFL draft and Sylvester turned out to be a steal. He played nine seasons for the franchise and ended up with three Super Bowl rings to go with his college championship.

SZYMANSKI, DICK
Center/Linebacker (1951–54), 6′2″, 215 lbs.

Szymanski, of Toledo, Ohio, entered Notre Dame in 1951 and found himself in demand thanks to the fact that two-platoon football was the order of the day. Even freshmen were needed to fill out squads, and Szymanski started at middle linebacker. He pitched in with 3 interceptions and 5 fumble recoveries, and was the starter at right linebacker in 1952. One-platoon football was back the following season, and Szymanski ended up splitting time at center with Jim Schrader. He was the starter at the position in 1954, his senior year. The Baltimore Colts selected him in the second round of the 1955 NFL draft, and he had a thirteen-year career in Baltimore.

SZYMANSKI, FRANK
Center (1943–44), 6'0", 190 lbs.

It's safe to say that not many players in Notre Dame history had as unusual a career as Frank Szymanski. A former all-state tackle at Northwestern High School in Detroit, Michigan, Szymanski began his career in promising fashion, seeing plenty of field time as a second-string center on the national championship team that went 9–1 in 1943. After the season he entered the navy's V-12 program and was not expected to play for Notre Dame in 1944. But he returned to South Bend after a case of rheumatic fever granted him a medical discharge from Naval Pre-Flight School. He was back at Notre Dame in the fall and back on the football team in time to be part of a 59–10 loss to eventual national champion Army. Notre Dame won its final three games by a combined score of 70–7, and finished the year at 8–2.

In the spring of 1945, Szymanski was named Notre Dame's captain for the upcoming season, but that never came to pass—he had signed a professional contract with the Chicago Bears. Although he thought the contract would not come into effect until after his senior season was completed, it was enough to end his college career. The NFL later agreed with the player's interpretation, ruling that Szymanski was not a free agent because he had a year of eligibility past the 1945 season, so the contract was not binding. However, that summer the Big Ten issued a ruling stating that any player who "enters into an agreement or signs a contract" with a professional team is ineligible to play in college. It was within Szymanski's rights to appeal the rule, but he chose not to; he didn't want to "embarrass the university," he said, and resigned his captain's post and position on the team.

Szymanski was still a hot commodity in the NFL. His hometown Detroit Lions selected him in the first round of the 1945 draft, and he played for the Lions until the end of the 1947 season. The next year he played for the Philadelphia Eagles, and in 1949 for the Chicago Bears.

TATUM, KINNON
Linebacker (1993–96), 6'0", 226 lbs.

Before coming to Notre Dame, Tatum was an all-state performer at Douglas Byrd High School in Fayetteville, North Carolina, where he set a state high school record with 12 interceptions as a junior. He was also a three-year letter winner in track and captained both the track and football teams.

At Notre Dame, Tatum was a reserve linebacker during his first two seasons, climbing the depth chart to second string as a sophomore. He followed up his junior season, in which he made 77 tackles (50 solos and 27 assists) with 77 more tackles (45 solos and 32 assists) during his senior campaign. Tatum's senior total was good enough to lead the Fighting Irish, and he also shared the team lead in tackles, with 9, for a combined loss of 25 yards. He finished up his college career with 116 solo tackles and 72 assists for 188 total hits. The Carolina Panthers selected him in the third round of the 1997 NFL draft, and he was still with them through the 1999 season. Tatum joined the Tampa Bay Buccaneers in 2000.

TAYLOR, AARON
Guard/Tackle (1990–93), 6'4", 299 lbs.

Taylor won virtually every award a college lineman can win while protecting Fighting Irish quarterbacks from blind-side rushes. He was the complete package: size, speed, agility, and strength.

Before enrolling at Notre Dame, Taylor was a two-time all-state performer at DeLa Salle High School in Concord, California, and a first-team high school All-American in 1989. He began his college football career in 1990, but played only 7:56 in two games as a reserve guard. The following season, Taylor broke through. He started ten of the season's twelve games at left guard and played 239:13. As a junior in 1992, he started all twelve games at left guard, seeing 269:07 of action. He was named a consensus All-American and was a finalist for the Lombardi Award, an honor bestowed on the best lineman in college football.

All-American guard Aaron Taylor won the Lombardi Award as the nation's top lineman, and was voted the Nick Pietrosante Award by his teammates. He later won a Super Bowl ring with the Green Bay Packers.

During his senior season, Taylor built on his success with a Fighting Irish team that went 11–1 and ranked number two in the nation. He moved to left tackle and dominated play for 298:57. He was a unanimous first-team All-American, won the Lombardi Award as the nation's top lineman, and was voted the Nick Pietrosante Award, which is presented annually to the Notre Dame player who best exemplifies the courage, pride, and dedication of the late fullback. Taylor was also a finalist for the Outland Trophy, which goes to the best interior lineman in college football. And Taylor was no slouch in the classroom. He had a 3.229 grade point average in the spring semester of his junior year and graduated a semester early.

The Green Bay Packers selected Taylor as the sixteenth overall pick in the 1994 NFL draft. There he became a protector of quarterback Brett Favre and was a member of the Super Bowl championship team in 1997 and the runners-up in 1998. He began playing for the San Diego Chargers in 1998.

TAYLOR, BOBBY
Free safety/Cornerback (1992–94),
6'3", 201 lbs.

Taylor was one of the best cover guys ever to play in Notre Dame's defensive backfield. He was fast, which is understandable considering that his father Robert, in the 1972 Olympics in Munich, Germany, won a gold medal as a member of the 400-meter relay team and a silver medal in the 100-meter run.

As a schoolboy in Longview, Texas, Taylor was both a *USA Today* and *Parade* magazine Prep All-American. Notre Dame won a heated recruiting battle for Taylor, who scored 1,225 points and was the state 5-A Player of the Year in basketball, and also a high school track star. As a Notre Dame freshman he started in six games as a free safety, made 28 solo tackles, 9 assists, broke up 9 passes, and blocked a kick. He was also a contributor on special-teams coverage. In all, he played 175:13, the most of any Fighting Irish freshman.

In 1993, Taylor won the team's starting cornerback position and often neutralized the opponent's best receiver. He led the team in interceptions, with 4, which he returned for 100 yards. He made 45 solo tackles and assisted on 6 others, sacked a quarterback, recovered a fumble, scored a touchdown, broke up 9 passes, and blocked 2 kicks. In short, he kept busy during his 265:09, which also included a lot of special-teams work. In Notre Dame's 24–21 victory over Texas A&M in the Cotton Bowl, Taylor made 7 tackles, blocked a field goal, and recovered a fumble. He was named a first-team All-American and was also a finalist for the Thorpe Award, which is presented each year to the top defensive back in the country.

Taylor was the only starting defensive player to return to South Bend in 1994. Expectations were high, since several publications named him the top defensive back in the nation in their preseason issues. However, Taylor played hurt for half the season. He fractured his right hand in a 34–15 victory over Stanford (he blocked a field goal, broke up a touchdown pass, and made 6 tackles), but played with a cast and didn't miss any subsequent games. He played 281:57 minutes as one of Notre Dame's starting cornerbacks, had 29 solo tackles, 17 assists, and a sack. He also intercepted a pass, defended 3 passes, and recovered a fumble and returned it for a 57-yard score. Taylor, a consensus pick, was Notre Dame's only All-American from the 1994 season, and the Columbus Touchdown Club named him its Defensive Back of the Year.

There was no senior season for Taylor, who left Notre Dame after his junior year to go pro. The Philadelphia Eagles selected him in the second round (fiftieth overall) of the 1995 NFL draft. He made the NFL's All-Rookie team in 1995, and was still playing with the team in 2000.

TERRELL, PATRICK CHRISTOPHER
Defensive back/Split end (1986–89),
6'0", 195 lbs.

All it took was a switch from split end to free safety for Terrell to step up to the top level of college football. At Lakewood High School, in St. Petersburg, Florida, he was an All-American wide receiver, a position he played during his first two seasons at Notre Dame. But in 1988 defense called, and Terrell started six games at free safety. He made 38 tackles and had 2 interceptions to help Notre Dame win all twelve of its games and a national championship.

The next season, as a senior, Terrell started all thirteen games. He compiled 44 tackles and finished second on the team in interceptions, with 5. In Notre Dame's 21–6 Orange Bowl victory over the University of Colorado, Terrell had 9 tackles and recovered a fumble, and postseason honors included being named a first-team All-American. The Los Angeles Rams selected him in the second round of the 1990 NFL draft, and he played with the Rams through the 1993 season. From there he went to play for the New York Jets in 1994 and 1995, and for the Carolina Panthers in 1995 and 1996.

THAYER, TOM
Defensive tackle/Tackle/Guard/Center
(1979–82), 6'5", 268 lbs.

There seemingly wasn't a line position that Thayer, a big, strong lineman from Joliet, Illinois, couldn't play, and he was as equally adept at pass blocking as pulling for downfield blocking. He began his college career in 1979 as a backup defensive tackle, making 3 tackles for the season. As a sophomore, he moved to offense and right guard, where he started six games and led all guards in minutes played. In 1981, as a junior, he started at left tackle and led the entire offense in field time. In 1982, he was all over the line. Injuries to other players made it necessary for

him to start three games at strong guard, four at center, and four at quick guard.

The Chicago Bears selected Thayer in the fourth round of the 1983 NFL draft. He played with the team from 1985 to 1992, and on the Super Bowl XX championship squad. He spent the 1993 season with the Miami Dolphins before retiring from football.

THEISMANN, JOE
Quarterback (1968–70), 6'0", 170 lbs.

Theismann, of South River, New Jersey, got more than most athletes from his time at Notre Dame. He certainly excelled in both the classroom and on the playing field. He also got a name change, or at least a pronunciation change. His father's name was pronounced "Thees-man," and that's what Joe went by for most of his life.

Enter Notre Dame's sports information department, looking for an angle to promote Theismann as a Heisman Trophy candidate. "Thise-man," of course, rhymes with Heisman. "Thees-man" doesn't. The player called his father and asked how to pronounce the family name. The father asked why, and Joe told him. The reply was quick and confident: "Thise-man," said the father to his son. The slogan "Theismann . . . as in Heisman" was born, although he finished second in the voting. To this day, whether in the broadcast booth or on the speaking circuit, at home or in public, the name is Theismann—as in Heisman.

Theismann enrolled at Notre Dame in 1967. He played backup to All-American quarterback Terry Hanratty, who was hurt at the end of the season, clearing the way for Theismann to start three games. He displayed an outstanding arm, the ability to scramble and read defenses, a quick release, confidence, and the toughness of a man much bigger than 170 pounds. He completed 27 of 49 passes for 451 yards and 2 touchdowns, rushed 59 times for 259 yards, and caught a pass for 13 yards. He also pitched in on special teams, returning 14 punts for 99 yards.

In 1969, Hanratty was gone and Theismann became Notre Dame's full-time starter. He passed for 1,531 yards and 13 touchdowns, and rushed for 378 yards and 6 touchdowns. He also set a Cotton Bowl record for passing yardage (231) and total yardage (279) in Notre Dame's 21–17 loss to top-ranked Texas. Theismann led the Fighting Irish to an 8–2–1 record.

His 1970 season was virtually as good as it gets, and, at the time, the best on record for a Notre Dame quarterback. It stood as the standard for twenty-seven years, until Ron Powlus's 1997 season eclipsed it. Theismann passed for 2,529 yards while completing 58 percent of his attempts for 16 touchdowns. He also rushed for 406 yards and 6 touchdowns, caught a pass for 7 yards, and scored on a 2-point conversion. In one game, a 38–28 loss to USC, he was 33 for 58 (most completions and second most attempts in a game) for 526 yards (most passing yards in a game).

Theismann, an All-American, was second behind Stanford's Jim Plunkett in Heisman Trophy voting. He was also an Academic All-American. His total offense of 5,432 yards on 807 attempts (a 6.7-yard average) ranks fourth on the school's all-time list. He is the school's sixth-all-time leading passer.

By the time he graduated, Theismann had rewritten the school's record books. He ranks third in passing attempts for a season (268), eighth in passing attempts for a career (509 in only three seasons), third in completions for a season (155), third in career passing percentage (.569), second in passing yards in a season (2,529), and fifth in passing yards for a career (4,411). He is also first in passing yards per game in a season (242.29), fifth in passing yards per game in a career (152.1), fourth in passing yards per attempt in a career (8.67), third in touchdown passes for a season (16), fourth in touchdown passes for a career (31), and third in touchdown passes per game in a career (1.07).

The Miami Dolphins selected Theismann in the fourth round of the 1971 NFL draft. His size kept him from being taken ear-

lier. The Dolphins intended to use him as a defensive back, so he left the country and signed with the Toronto Argonauts of the Canadian Football League, where he passed for more than 6,000 yards and 40 touchdowns in three seasons. That was enough to rekindle the interest of NFL scouts, and Theismann became a member of the Washington Redskins in 1974.

Theismann took over the offense in 1978 and spent the following eight seasons as one of the top offensive threats in the league. He led the Redskins to back-to-back Super Bowls after the 1982 and 1983 seasons, winning one Super Bowl ring against the Dolphins, who had let him get away. In 1983, he was also named the NFL's Player of the Year.

His playing career ended on November 18, 1985, when he suffered one of the most gruesome injuries ever witnessed on ABC's *Monday Night Football*. New York Giants' linebacker Lawrence Taylor sacked Theismann, causing a compound fracture of his right leg. The grisly replay was shown more times than the Zapruder film of the John F. Kennedy assassination.

In twelve NFL seasons, Theismann passed for more than 25,000 yards and 160 touchdowns. After retiring from the NFL, he became a public speaker and a football color commentator as well as a studio analyst for ESPN.

CAREER STATS

PASSING

Year	Att.	Comp.	Pct.	Yards	TDs
1968	49	27	.551	451	2
1969	192	108	.562	1,531	13
1970	268	155	.578	2,529	16
Total	509	290	.569	4,411	31

RUSHING

Year	Att.	Yards	Avg.	TDs
1968	59	259	4.4	4
1969	116	378	3.3	6
1970	141	406	2.9	6
Total	316	1,043	3.3	16

THOMAS, BOB
Placekicker (1971–73), 5′10″, 178 lbs.

Thomas, from Rochester, New York, did as much as a placekicker can do to help his team win a national championship. In the 1973 Sugar Bowl, he helped preserve Notre Dame's undefeated record with a 19-yard field goal with 4:26 to play to lift the Fighting Irish to a 24–23 victory over the previously undefeated Crimson Tide of Alabama.

That kick capped an outstanding season for Thomas, who led the Fighting Irish with 70 points. He made 43 of 45 extra points and half of his 18 field goal attempts. He also continued a streak of 62 consecutive extra points, which began in 1972 and at the time was the second longest in NCAA history. For his career he made 98 of 101 extra points, third on the school's all-time percentage list. He also led the team in scoring during two of his three seasons.

Thomas first kicked for Notre Dame in 1971. He led the team with 36 points on 21 of 22 extra points and 5 of 9 field goals. In 1972, he was second on the team in scoring, with 55 points—34 of 34 extra points and 7 of 11 field goals. The Los Angeles Rams selected him in the fifteenth round of the 1974 NFL draft. He played with the Chicago Bears from 1975 through 1984, for the Detroit Lions in 1982, and for the San Diego Chargers in 1985. As a pro he made 303 of 330 extra points and 151 of 239 field goals.

TONEFF, BOB
Tackle (1949–51), 6′2″, 230 lbs.

Toneff played a considerable amount of time on both offense and defense as a three-year starter at Notre Dame. However, it was as an offensive lineman that he distinguished himself as a college football player.

Toneff came to South Bend from Barberton, Ohio, in 1948, and was the starting right defensive tackle on the 1949 national championship team that won all ten of its games. The following season he started on both sides of the line of scrimmage. In his senior season, Toneff played primarily offense and was recognized as one of the best linemen in the country, rating first-team All-American honors after the season. The San Francisco 49ers selected him in the second round of the 1952 NFL draft. He enjoyed a thirteen-year career with San Francisco (1952–58) and the Washington Redskins (1959–64).

TONELLI, MARIO
Fullback (1936–38), 5′11″, 188 lbs.

Tonelli, who was an all-state running back at DePaul Academy in Chicago, enrolled at Notre Dame in 1935. He was a reserve fullback on the varsity football team the following year and became a starter in 1937. That year, his junior season, Tonelli's playing time was limited due to several injuries. He did get healthy in time to score the winning touchdown, in a 20–13 victory over USC in the season finale. In 1938, Tonelli was Notre Dame's second-leading rusher, with 259 yards on 42 carries (a 6.2-yards-per-carry average).

After he graduated, Tonelli signed a professional contract with the Chicago Cardinals. He entered the armed forces in 1941, and in 1942 he was one of the American soldiers who fought at Bataan in the Philippines, where the troops ran out of supplies and capitulated because of encroaching starvation. He also took part in the Bataan Death March, in which U.S. and Filipino soldiers were marched two hundred miles in seven days to detention camps. On New Year's Eve 1942, Tonelli was reported missing in action. Three years later he was released from a Japanese prisoner of war camp, and during his captivity he had lost 60 pounds. He eventually regained his strength and played one more season in Chicago, wearing number 58—not only the number that he wore for the Fighting Irish and the Cardinals, but his number in the last of several POW camps.

TORAN, STACEY
Defensive back (1980–83), 6′4″, 206 lbs.

Toran, from Indianapolis, Indiana, started for four seasons (minus four games) in the Notre Dame defensive backfield and will be remembered as one of the best ever to play the position in South Bend.

Toran had tremendous size and speed, and he could lay a receiver out with a hit. He started at cornerback in 1980, beginning with the third game of his freshman year. He made 30 tackles, broke up 6 passes, and had an interception. The following year, he started every game and made 54 tackles, broke up 4 passes, and had 2 interceptions. As a junior in 1982, he led all Notre Dame defensive backs and was third on the team in tackles, with 77, including 7 for losses. He also broke up 6 passes and had 2 interceptions in 316 minutes played, and was named an honorable mention All-American. Toran was named Notre Dame's defensive captain in 1983, but that season his effectiveness was limited because of arm injuries. He missed two games, and his 23 tackles were the lowest total in his college career. He also broke up a pass. The Los Angeles Raiders selected Toran in the sixth round of the 1984 NFL draft, and he played for the franchise until 1988.

TOWNSEND, MIKE
Defensive back (1971–73), 6'3", 183 lbs.

Townsend, of Hamilton, Ohio, was an outstanding athlete with good speed, size, and leaping ability. Those characteristics also came in handy on the basketball court, as Townsend made the Notre Dame hoops team as a walk-on.

It was in football, though, that he was truly a star. In 1971, as a sophomore, he was only a backup safety and made just 5 tackles, but his junior year was nothing short of sensational. Townsend, the starter at left cornerback, set a Notre Dame record for interceptions in a season, with 10, which also led the nation. He also made 34 tackles and broke up 4 passes. As a senior, Townsend started at free safety and made 3 interceptions and 26 tackles and recovered 3 fumbles, as Notre Dame won all of its eleven games and the national title. Townsend earned consensus All-American honors.

All-American defensive back Mike Townsend holds the Notre Dame record for interceptions in a season with 10 picks.

The Minnesota Vikings selected Townsend in the fourth round of the 1974 NFL draft. He didn't play in the NFL, opting instead for the Florida Sharks of the World Football League.

CAREER STATS

Year	Int.	Yards	Avg.	TDs
1971	No interceptions			
1972	10	39	3.9	0
1973	3	47	15.7	0
Total	13	86	6.6	0

TRAFTON, GEORGE
Center (1919), 6'2", 190 lbs.

Trafton's two-timing ways cut short what could have been an outstanding college football career. But it was his same disregard for the rules that lengthened his professional career.

Trafton was the starting center on head coach Knute Rockne's 1919 team, which won all nine of its games. That wasn't enough action for Trafton, who, it was later discovered, was playing semipro football on the side. He was dismissed from the Notre Dame team.

Just like that, he went from amateur and semipro to full-fledged professional. In 1920 he signed with the Decatur Staleys, which evolved into the Chicago Staleys in 1921 and the Chicago Bears the following year. Trafton, meanwhile, evolved into one of the best linemen in the early days of professional ball. He played thirteen seasons as a pro, and considered playing dirty part of his job description. In his rookie season, Trafton put such a beating on Rock Island center Harry Gunderson that he left the game with a broken hand and requiring eleven stitches over his left eye and two stitches in his lip. In an unrelated event, another Rock Island player once suffered a broken leg compliments of Trafton, who ran him down out of bounds and tackled him into a fence. That day Trafton knew when it was time to go. Before he even changed out of his uniform, he caught a cab and left to avoid being assaulted by the angry mob of spectators. "You had to be tough to stay alive in those days," he would say many years after the fact. "And believe me, bub, I lived."

In his hometown of Chicago, Trafton was a member of head coach George Halas's teams which earned the moniker Monsters of the Midway. He was an All-Pro in 1923, 1924, and 1926, and retired in 1932 after playing in 201 games for a total of 158 hours. Thirty-two years later he was inducted into the Pro Football Hall of Fame.

Quarterback Frank Tripucka led the Fighting Irish to a 9–0–1 record in 1948.

TRIPUCKA, FRANK
Quarterback (1945–48), 6′2″, 172 lbs.

The Bloomfield, New Jersey, native sat behind John Lujack for three seasons before being able to prove his worth. Tripucka, whose son Kelly would be a star in the NBA four decades later, took over the Notre Dame offense as a senior in 1948 and was ready for action. He completed 53 of 91 passes for 660 yards and was selected to play in the College Football All-Star Game.

Tripucka's career began far more humbly. As a freshman, in 1945, he completed the only pass he attempted, for 21 yards. The next season he connected on 1 of 5 passes for 19 yards. In 1947, the year Lujack won the Heisman Trophy and Notre Dame the national championship, Tripucka completed 25 of 44 passes for 422 yards.

Despite Tripucka's lack of college experience, the Philadelphia Eagles selected him in the first round of the 1949 draft. He played for the Eagles and the Detroit Lions in 1949, the Chicago Cardinals from 1950 through 1952, the Dallas Texans in 1952, and the Denver Broncos from 1960 through 1963.

TWOMEY, TED
Tackle (1928–29), 6'1", 205 lbs.

As legend, or at least legendary quarterback Harry Stuhldreher, has it, Twomey, of Duluth, Minnesota, was so mean and so tough that head coach Knute Rockne wouldn't even let him play in intrasquad scrimmages. That ban, however, did not carry over to games.

Twomey was a two-time starter at tackle and, in 1929, his senior season, he was named a second-team All-American. That season, the Fighting Irish were 9–0 and won the national title. Twomey served as an assistant coach for schools such as Georgia, Kentucky, Texas, and Florida in the first twenty years after his graduation. In the late 1940s he entered the business world.

URBAN, GASPER GEORGE
Guard/Tackle (1943, 1946–47),
6′2″, 200 lbs.

Urban's career at Notre Dame was interrupted by World War II, but in three seasons over five years he was a member of teams that won twenty-six games, lost one, and tied one while capturing three national championships.

"Urb," from Lynn, Massachusetts, won his first letter as a second-string guard on Notre Dame's 1943 national championship team, which won nine of ten games. He missed the next two seasons while serving in the Marine Corps during World War II. Urban returned to South Bend in 1946 and helped Notre Dame (8–0–1) win another title. In 1947, he backed up All-American tackle George Connor. Notre Dame was 9–0 and again was crowned the top program in the land. Urban played one season of professional football as a member of the All-American Football Conference's Chicago Rockets in 1948.

VAIRO, DOM
End (1932–34), 6′2″, 196 lbs.

By his senior year at Notre Dame, Vairo, from Calumet, Michigan, had worked his way up to team captain. That was quite an accomplishment for a guy who quit the freshman team because of an unpaid bill. Vairo reported for freshman football practice one day to find his uniform missing. He denied responsibility and insisted that there had been an error in the equipment office. He was still charged for the uniform and had to quit the team because he could not afford to pay for it. In 1932, he was back on the team and earned a letter. The following year, he shared time at left end with Wayne Millner and was switched to right end and was named captain for his senior season. Vairo played one season of professional football, in 1935, for the Green Bay Packers.

VARRICHIONE, FRANK
Guard/Offensive tackle/Defensive tackle (1951–54), 6′0″, 210 lbs.

Varrichione was a four-year varsity player and an All-American at Notre Dame, but he is probably best remembered for faking an injury. With only 2 seconds to play in the first half against the University of Iowa in 1953, Varrichione groaned in apparent pain and clutched his lower back. Officials called an injury time-out, stopping the clock and giving the Fighting Irish an opportunity to score a touchdown. The game ended in a 7–7 tie. The strategy, which Iowa had used earlier in the season, was legal at the time.

Varrichione came to South Bend after spending his final year of high school at Aquinas Institute in Rochester, New York. In his sophomore season he won a starting spot at offensive guard, and as a junior and senior

he started both ways at tackle. When he was a senior, in 1954, Varrichione was a key contributor to head coach Terry Brennan's winning start at Notre Dame. The Fighting Irish went 9–1, and Varrichione made first-team All-American. The Pittsburgh Steelers selected him in the first round of the 1955 NFL draft. He played with the Steelers through the 1960 season and for the Los Angeles Rams from 1961 through 1965.

VAUGHAN, PETE
Fullback (1908–09), 6′0″, 195 lbs.

Vaughan, of Crawfordsville, Indiana, has claim to a couple of pieces of Notre Dame football lore. Not only is he credited by some for coming up with the nickname Fighting Irish, he was also the first player in school history to break a goalpost. Both historic events happened in the same game, an 11–3 victory at Michigan in 1909.

As legend has it, Vaughan was upset that his teammates were not playing tough enough against the Wolverines and accused them of not "fighting like Irishmen." At least eleven of the twenty-one players on the 1909 roster, with names such as Maloney, Lynch, Brennan, Kelly, Duffy, Dolan, and Ryan, were of Irish descent. In that game, Vaughan leveled a goalpost by running into it with either his head, his shoulder, both, or neither. (Seeing as how he couldn't remember what he hit it with, the smart money is on the head.)

In 1908, Vaughan started at fullback. He scored 2 touchdowns in a 39–0 victory over Hillsdale, and Notre Dame's only touchdown in a 12–6 loss to the University of Michigan (on a 50-yard run during which he shook off eight defenders). He also scored against Chicago Physicians & Surgeons and

Ohio Northern. In 1909, Vaughn again started at fullback. In a season-opening 58–0 victory over Olivet he ran for a career-high 3 touchdowns in a game, but he tied his mark the following week in a 60–11 romp over Rose Poly. The next week Vaughan was held to only 2 touchdowns in a 17–0 victory over Michigan State. He then scored a touchdown and took out a goalpost, and maybe coined the most famous nickname in all of college sports, in an 11–3 victory at Michigan in game five. At the time, it was the most important game in the history of the program.

VERGARA, GEORGE
Guard/End (1922–23), 6'1", 187 lbs.

Vergara began his college football career at Fordham University in the Bronx, where he grew up. He transferred to Notre Dame in 1922 and fit right in with the football program, starting at right end as Notre Dame won eight games, tied one, and lost another. He played guard in 1923, when Notre Dame was 9–1, and was all set to start on the 1924 team that would win all ten of its games and a national championship. However, Vergara had seen some action as a freshman on the Fordham varsity team and had used up his eligibility. He remained at Notre Dame in 1924 anyway, serving as the freshman football coach while finishing up his degree. He played for the Green Bay Packers in 1925 and eventually became a politician. Thirty-one years after retiring from football, he was named the mayor of New Rochelle, New York, in Westchester County.

WADSWORTH, MIKE
Defensive line/Center (1963–65);
Athletic director (1995–2000)

Wadsworth, from Toronto, Ontario, was named to head up the Fighting Irish athletic department on August 1, 1994, but he'd been there before. His first tour at Notre Dame began in 1962, as a freshman fresh from Toronto's DeLaSalle High School, where his football team had lost just three games in three seasons. Because of knee injuries, Wadsworth was a somewhat ordinary player for the Fighting Irish, though he earned a letter in 1964 as a defensive lineman. As in high school, he suffered only three defeats at Notre Dame—the Irish went 16–3–1 while he was on the varsity squad.

Wadsworth graduated in 1966 with a degree in political science. For the next five years he played in the Canadian Football League, earning Rookie of the Year honors in 1966. While playing in the CFL, he went to Osgoode Hall Law School in Toronto, and it was through his efforts that the CFL players negotiated their contract with the owners and improved their conditions. Wadsworth later became the first president of the CFL Players Association.

After his playing days, Wadsworth began practicing law. He was a litigator of high regard for a decade and argued several cases before Canada's Supreme Court. As if that wasn't enough to fill his time, he also wrote columns for the *Toronto Daily Star* and was a commentator on televised broadcasts for CFL games. He spent the next nine years in the business world, rising through the ranks to become senior vice president of U.S. operations for the Crown Life Insurance Company. In 1989, Wadsworth became the Canadian ambassador to Ireland and lived there until late 1994. At that point it was time to move back to the land of the Fighting Irish. Wadsworth brought financial, legal, and athletic expertise to the job of athletic director, as well as all the assets that continue the fine tradition of sports administration in South Bend.

WALLNER, FRED
Fullback/Guard (1948–50), 6'2", 212 lbs.

Wallner beat incredible odds to make it to Notre Dame, let alone earn three letters and start on a national championship team. He was critically injured in a car crash in 1946 when he was a high school senior in Greenfield, Massachusetts. Fortunately, he made a speedy recovery and was back in playing shape in time to serve as a reserve fullback at Notre Dame in 1948. The next year head coach Frank Leahy decided that Wallner was big enough to play offensive guard, where he was a line mate of All-Americans and team captains Leon Hart and Jim Martin. Wallner also started at linebacker, as did future Hall of Famer Jerry Groom. All of the talent added up to a 10–0 season and a national championship. Wallner was again a two-way starter in 1950, his senior season. The Chicago Cardinals selected him in the twentieth round of the draft. He played for the Cardinals in 1951, 1952, 1954, and 1955, and he played for Houston Oilers in 1960.

WALSH, ADAM
Center (1922–24), 6'0", 187 lbs.

Not only was Walsh the heart and soul of the Seven Mules—the brave bunch who paved the way for the famed Four

Horsemen—he came up with the name. They may have toiled in obscurity, but the name gave them cachet and recognition outside of the football program.

Walsh was born in Churchville, Iowa, and grew up in Hollywood, California. He lettered in football, baseball, and track at Hollywood High School and was captain of the 1919 undefeated gridiron team. His gift was the ability to snap the ball to each individual Horseman just the way he liked it. Walsh began his varsity career as the starting center on head coach Knute Rockne's team that went 8–1–1 in 1922. He held the same position in 1923 and was named captain of the 1924 team, comprised of the Horsemen and the Mules, which won all ten of its games.

Walsh was a fierce competitor whose toughness can't be questioned. In 1924, he played with two broken hands in a 13–7 victory over Army at the Polo Grounds in 1924. Despite the injuries he did not make one bad snap, and intercepted a pass late in the fourth quarter to preserve the victory. He was also part of an impenetrable goal-line stand in Notre Dame's 27–10 Rose Bowl victory over Stanford. He was named to several All-American teams.

Football was not enough for Walsh. He also participated in basketball and track and field, despite having to work thirty hours a week at the Northern Indiana Gas and Electric Company to subsidize his education. Walsh was on course to earn a mechanical engineering degree until a throat infection caused him to fall behind. He never earned his diploma; instead, he married and took a job as a coach to support his family. At the tender age of twenty-three, Walsh was named head football coach and athletic director at the University of Santa Clara. He guided the tiny school with just three hundred students to a 19–18–2 record while playing against bigger schools with established programs, such as Cal–Berkeley, Stanford, and USC.

Walsh's next stop was Yale, in 1929, where he served as line coach. In 1934, he moved to Harvard, becoming the first man to work on the football coaching staffs at both of the fierce rivals. By 1935 he was on the move again. This time it was to accept another head coaching position at Bowdoin College, which he turned into one of the best small-college football teams in the East. In 1937, Bowdoin allowed just 27 points. The following year his charges won the New England small-college championship. In eight seasons, Bowdoin won thirty-four games, lost sixteen, and tied two.

Bowdoin dropped football during World War II and Walsh took a leave of absence. Not one to take a break, he returned to South Bend to work as an assistant coach. The following year, 1945, he made it to the pros as the head coach of the NFL's Cleveland Rams. In his rookie campaign he was named Coach of the Year as the Rams went 13–2 and won the league championship.

Walsh, a loyal man, returned to Bowdoin in 1947 and remained at the school until 1958, when he entered the business world. He was inducted into the College Football Hall of Fame in 1968.

WALSH, BILL
Center (1945–48), 6'3", 205 lbs.

Walsh, from Shawnee Mission, Kansas, started at center during three of his four years at Notre Dame, including 1947, when Notre Dame was 9–0 and won the national title. He was a starter as a freshman, but backed up George Strohmeyer the following year, 1946, and was back on the first team for the perfect 1947 season. Not only did Walsh regain his starting position, he rarely left the field. He played 300 minutes, sharing iron man honors with Bill Fischer. Walsh finished his career exactly as he began it, as Notre Dame's starting center.

The Pittsburgh Steelers selected Walsh in the third round of the 1949 NFL draft. He played in Pittsburgh for five seasons and later, during his subsequent coaching career, returned to South Bend to work as an assistant.

WATTERS, RICKY
Running back/Flanker (1987–90),
6'2", 205 lbs.

Watters, one in a long line of explosive and versatile offensive weapons to play for head coach Lou Holtz, came to Notre Dame with great credentials. He was a three-sport standout and football All-American at McDevitt High School in Harrisburg, Pennsylvania.

Watters started his college career in 1987 as a tailback. As a freshman, he played behind Mark Green and appeared in all twelve games, finishing with 373 yards and 3 touchdowns on 69 carries. As a sophomore he moved to flanker and settled in nicely, leading the Fighting Irish with 15 receptions for 286 yards. He also replaced 1987 Heisman Trophy winner Tim Brown as the team's most feared special-teams player. Watters led Notre Dame in punt returns, with 19, for 253 yards and 2 touchdowns. With 3 career touchdowns on punt returns, he is tied for tops in Notre Dame history along with Brown, Nick Rassas, and Allen Rossum.

Green graduated in 1988, and Watters was back at tailback. He was the team's second-leading rusher, behind quarterback Tony Rice, with 791 yards and 10 touchdowns on 118 carries, for a healthy 6.7-yards-per-carry average. He also caught 13 passes for 196 yards and returned 15 punts for 201 yards, including one for a 97-yard touchdown against SMU. The run is still a school record. Watters, who was named an honorable mention All-American, was limited to just two carries in Notre Dame's 21–6 victory over the University of Colorado in the Orange Bowl because of a bruised knee.

Watters was named captain for his senior season and finished up his career in fine fashion. After a slow start, he wound up with 579 yards and 8 touchdowns on 108 carries, including a 174-yard effort in a 34–29 victory over the University of Tennessee in the third-to-last game of the season. During the season he also caught 7 passes for 58 yards

Running back Ricky Watters was a versatile player who was a special teams standout and played receiver as well as tailback. He his a five-time Pro Bowl selection as well as a Super Bowl ring recipient in the pros. (Bill Panzica)

and was named an honorable mention All-American for the second consecutive year.

Despite playing at flanker during his sophomore season, Watters finished his Notre Dame career with 1,814 yards rushing, which at the time was fourteenth best in school history but is now nineteenth. The San Francisco 49ers selected him in the second round of the 1991 NFL draft, and he was a key member of the 1994 team that won the Super Bowl. He was traded to the Philadelphia Eagles in 1995, and then signed as a free agent with the Seattle Seahawks in 1998. Watters, who made the Pro Bowl in five of his first six seasons in the league, gained 6,643 yards and scored 56 touchdowns through his first eight years in the pros. He also caught 301 passes for 2,768 yards. In four seasons with San Francisco he gained 2,840 yards, which is tenth on the franchise's all-time list. In three seasons in Philadelphia, Watters gained 3,794 yards, a total surpassed by only three other Eagles. He moved on to the Seattle Seahawks in 1998.

CAREER STATS

RUSHING

Year	Att.	Yards	Avg.	TDs
1987	69	373	5.4	3
1988	30	71	2.4	0
1989	118	791	6.7	10
1990	108	579	5.4	8
Total	325	1,814	5.6	21

RECEIVING

Year	Rec.	Yards	Avg.	TDs
1987	6	70	11.7	0
1988	15	286	19.1	2
1989	13	196	15.1	0
1990	7	58	8.3	0
Total	41	610	14.9	2

WAYMER, DAVE
Defensive back/Flanker (1976–79), 6′3″, 188 lbs.

Waymer was an exceptional wide receiver and defensive back at West Charlotte High School, in North Carolina. He excelled at both positions in college as well. As a freshman he split time between flanker and cornerback, but in 1977, as a sophomore, he started at flanker and made 10 receptions for 164 yards. One catch resulted in a 68-yard scoring play in a 69–14 victory over Georgia Tech. Later that season, in the Cotton Bowl, Waymer was good for 3 catches for 38 yards as Notre Dame defeated Texas, 38–10, and was subsequently named national champion. He was moved back to cornerback for his final two college seasons, and as a junior he made 51 tackles and had 3 interceptions. Waymer was a team tri-captain as a senior, when he made 41 tackles and had 4 interceptions.

The New Orleans Saints selected Waymer in the second round of the 1980 NFL draft, and he played the first ten years of his thirteen-year career in New Orleans.

In 1990 and 1991 he played with the San Francisco 49ers, and with the Los Angeles Raiders in 1992.

WENDELL, MARTY
Fullback/Center/Guard (1944, 1946–48), 5′11″, 198 lbs.

Wendell, a Chicago native, was one of the most versatile players in the history of Notre Dame football as well as a well-rounded individual. He was the second player in school history to letter at three different positions; he had his college career interrupted for military service, and was also the vice president of his senior class.

Wendell played fullback on the 1944 Notre Dame squad, gaining 82 yards and scoring a touchdown on 32 carries. The next season he went off to serve in the military but returned to South Bend in 1946 and was shifted to center by head coach Frank Leahy, who also returned from his military stint that year. Wendell finally settled in at right guard, a position he held as a starter during his junior and senior seasons. He was named a first-team All-American as a senior, a year in which the Fighting Irish won the national championship. He played one season of pro football in 1949 with the Chicago Hornets of the All-American Football Conference.

WESTON, JEFF
Defensive tackle (1974–78), 6′4″, 258 lbs.

If it hadn't been for a knee injury in the opening game of his junior season, Jeff Weston might have gone down as one of the best defensive linemen ever to suit up for the Fighting Irish. As it stands, he was a quick and mobile defender who bridged the gap between the Ara Parseghian and Dan Devine eras.

Weston, who played his prep ball at Cardinal Mooney High School in Rochester, New York, was a backup defensive tackle as a freshman in 1974. He showed his potential by making 31 tackles in just 91 minutes of action. Predictably, he earned a spot in the starting lineup as a sophomore and had what would turn out to be his best season: he made 101 tackles, which trailed only Steve Niehaus for the team lead. The highlight of his year, and what would be a season for many players, came in a 31–10 victory over Navy in Devine's first season as coach. He made 5 solo tackles and assisted on 17 others. He also caused a fumble, recovered another, and ran back an interception of a fake punt for a 53-yard touchdown.

Watson's career hit a major snag in 1976, when he injured his knee after playing just 8:17. He had only 3 tackles in the season-opening loss to the University of Pittsburgh, but he was back in the starting lineup in 1977, splitting time with Mike Calhoun at tackle for the national champs. He made 57 tackles and recovered a fumble, but needed a second knee surgery after the season. Weston recovered in time to take advantage of his extra season of eligibility, in 1978. He started at right tackle and made 75 tackles, broke up 3 passes, and recovered 2 fumbles. His career totals were 267 tackles (20 for a total of -141 yards), 4 fumbles recovered, 3 passes defended, and 1 interception. Weston went undrafted in 1979 but played four seasons for the New York Giants.

WETOSKA, BOB
End (1956–58), 6'3", 225 lbs.

Wetoska, of Minneapolis, Minnesota, played two seasons as a backup at Notre Dame before breaking into the starting lineup in 1958, when he caught 12 passes for 210 yards. In addition to being the third-best receiver on the team, Wetoska was also an Academic All-American. The Washington Redskins selected him in the fifth round of the 1959 NFL draft. He didn't play for the Redskins and he didn't play end as a professional. Instead, he spent his entire ten-year professional career with the Chicago Bears as a tackle.

WHITE, KEVIN
Athletic director (2000–present)

White may not have a Notre Dame pedigree, but University President, Rev. Edward A. Molloy, C.S.C., knew he was the right man to run the massive athletic department at Notre Dame, including the winningest Division I College Football Team of all time. White's success in athletics and academics (he holds a Ph.D. in education and has taught classes every year of his career), as well as his sharp business acumen wherever he has worked more than made up for the fact that he wasn't previously a member of the Fighting Irish family. Now he's the family patriarch, and in a re-structuring move in South Bend, will be the first athletic director to report directly to the University President. White, who was 49 when he received his new position on March 13, 2000, had previously been athletic director at Arizona State, Tulane University, the University of Maine, and Loras College in Dubuque, Iowa.

A well-respected administrator, White has served on several NCAA committees, including the NCAA Council, formerly the association's highest governing body, as well as the executive committee of the Division I-A Athletic Director's Association. At Arizona State, he was chairman of the Pac-10 Conference's television and bowl committees.

Most recently, as athletic director of Arizona State, White led the athletic program from 23rd to 10th in the Sears Directors Cup rankings of overall athletic success. In 1998–99, Arizona State placed three teams in the top five in the nation, along with four in the top ten and eight in the top twenty. Academically, 233 student-athletes at the institution scored a B-average or better. In the meantime, White was busy. He planned the addition of two women's sports, renegotiated the school's radio contracts, hired new staff (including five head coaches), and increased the budget by more than 50%—or nearly $10 million—to $26 million, while turning a $3 million deficit into a $1 million surplus.

White's reputation was as solid at Tulane and Maine. At Tulane, from 1991–96, White led the Green Wave to success in both the classroom and on the playing fields and courts. The men's basketball team, which had been scandalized by a point-shaving scandal before White arrived, made it to the postseason five times in as many years during his tenure. At Maine, the school had nearly across-the-board athletic success. At Loras he was vice president for student affairs and vice president for development in addition to athletic director.

White, from Amityville, New York, earned a Ph.D. from Southern Illinois in 1985 and completed postdoctoral work at Harvard University's Institute for Educational Management. He also holds a master's degree in athletics administration from Central Michigan and a bachelor's degree in business administration from St. Joseph's College in Rensselaer, Indiana, where he was a sprinter on the track and field team. His wife, Jane, earned a master's degree in physical education, where she was head track and field coach. The Whites have five children—Maureen, Michael, Daniel, Brian, and Mariah.

WHITTINGTON, MIKE
Linebacker (1977–79), 6′2″, 219 lbs.

Whittington, of Miami, Florida, got his chance to prove his worth to Notre Dame head football coach Dan Devine in 1978, when fellow linebacker Bobby Leopold went down with an injury with four games remaining in the season. Whittington played well, and when Leopold was back the following season, Devine put both players in the starting lineup. In his three varsity seasons, Whittington made 197 tackles, 108 of them as a senior. The only Fighting Irish player who made more tackles that season was Bob Crable, who set a school record with 187. Whittington was not drafted to play in the National Football League, but still spent four years, from 1980 through 1983, with the New York Giants.

WILLIAMS, BOB
Quarterback (1948–50), 6′1″, 185 lbs.

Patience paid off for both Bob Williams and the University of Notre Dame. Although he had an outstanding high school football career at Loyola High School in Towson,

Maryland, he was not high on the list of many major colleges. Williams was a prep All-American as a senior and had also made all-state in both baseball and football.

Notre Dame was lukewarm on Williams and did not even offer him a football scholarship until June of his senior year of high school, when another recruit chose another school. It didn't take too much salesmanship to convince Williams to come to South Bend: he had dreamed of playing for the Fighting Irish since he was eight years old, when he had visited his older brother, Harold, a Notre Dame student, and Harold introduced him to head football coach Elmer Layden. That was a defining moment in the young boy's life, and for the next decade he concentrated on becoming a Notre Dame football player. The accurate passer and kicker turned out to be more than a consolation prize, as Williams led Notre Dame to a national championship in his first season as a starter.

As a sophomore in 1948, Williams played backup to Frank Tripucka at quarterback. He ran the ball 6 times for 11 yards, completed 8 of 14 passes for 110 yards and 2 touchdowns, and punted twice for 80 yards. As a junior in 1949, Williams burst into the starting lineup and led Notre Dame to a 10–0 record and a national championship. He completed 83 of 147 passes and topped Angelo Bertelli's single-season marks for yardage, with 1,347, and touchdowns, with 16. He also ran the ball 34 times for 63 yards and a touchdown and punted 42 times for a 38.6 average.

In a 34–21 victory over Michigan State, Williams set a single-game record by completing 13 of 16 passes. But it was just another day at the stadium for Williams, whose passing efficiency rating of 161.4 is still the school's best mark. He was a consensus All-American and finished fifth in the voting for the Heisman Trophy, just four spots behind teammate Leon Hart, who won the award.

Williams repeated as an All-American in 1950, but Notre Dame was far from the powerhouse it had been in his junior year.

All-American quarterback
Bob Williams (holding for
end Vince Meschievitz)
led Notre Dame to a 10–0
season and a national
championship on his way
to the College Football
Hall of Fame.

The team was rebuilding and went 4–4–1; Williams completed 99 of 210 passes for 1,035 yards, 10 touchdowns, and 15 interceptions. He also rushed 40 times for 115 yards and 2 touchdowns and punted 42 times for a 39.2 average. Along with his first-team All-American status, Williams also finished sixth in the Heisman race. The Chicago Bears selected him in the first round of the 1951 NFL draft. He played for the Bears in 1951, 1952, and 1955. He was enshrined in the College Football Hall of Fame in 1988.

CAREER STATS

Year	Att.	Comp.	Pct.	Yards	TDs
1948	14	8	.571	110	2
1949	147	83	.565	1,374	16
1950	210	99	.471	1,035	10
Total	371	190	.512	2,519	28

WILLIAMS, BOB
Quarterback (1956–58), 6'2", 190 lbs.

For the second time in less than a decade, Notre Dame relied on Bob Williams to lead its offense. The other Bob Williams played in South Bend from 1948 to 1950.

After spending a year's apprenticeship under the stellar Paul Hornung—a year in which he connected on 16 of 31 passes for a touchdown and 4 interceptions, rushed for 46 yards and a touchdown on 22 carries, and returned 3 kickoffs for 45 yards—Williams, from Wilkes-Barre, Pennsylvania, was ready to start. In 1957 he took the snaps with the first team and rushed for 144 yards and 2 touchdowns on 62 carries. He also completed half of his passes (53 of 106) for 559 yards, 3 touchdowns, and 5 interceptions. Williams got back 3 of the interceptions on defense and also made 19 tackles and returned 6 kickoffs for 102 yards.

As a senior in 1958, Williams was the starter at quarterback, but split time with George Izo. He completed 26 of 65 passes for 344 yards, 4 touchdowns, and 9 interceptions. He also rushed for 140 yards and 4 touchdowns on 44 carries, and on defense broke up 3 passes and made 23 tackles. He finished his career with 1,935 yards in total offense.

In 1959, the Chicago Bears selected their second quarterback named Bob Williams out of Notre Dame in less than a decade. This Bob Williams, however, was not drafted until the twenty-eighth round and never played in the NFL.

WILLIAMS, BROCK
Cornerback (1997–98, 2000), 5'10", 190 lbs.

Williams has the quickness and strength to play man-to-man defense from his cornerback position, and couples those qualities with an energetic style and a fearless hitting style.

The graduate of Hammond High School in Louisiana was one of only six freshmen to letter in 1997, seeing action in seven games. Williams broke into the starting lineup at cornerback the fourth game of his sophomore season and made 35 tackles, 8 assists. He also blocked 2 extra points against LSU. Williams was suspended from the team for violations regarding curfew, alcohol use, and parking. But he was back and showed a tremendous growth in maturity to lead the 2000 Notre Dame defense in playing time as a senior. He had his best season ever with 39 tackles and 10 assists. Williams also had a sack, an interception, and broke up 8 passes.

The New England Patriots selected Williams with the eighty-sixth overall pick, in the third round, of the 2001 National Football League draft.

WILLIAMS, LARRY
Guard/Offensive tackle (1981–84), 6'6", 276 lbs.

Williams arrived at Notre Dame in the fall of 1981 weighing in at 225 pounds, and

he gained more than 50 pounds in his four years in college. The Santa Ana, California, native not only got bigger during his time in South Bend, he also got better—much better.

Williams earned a letter as a freshman reserve and won a starting tackle spot as a sophomore. He injured his ankle during his junior season and missed the final two games of the year, but still played well enough to make second-team All-American. As a senior, Williams was switched to guard, and he responded with his second consecutive All-American season.

The Cleveland Browns selected Williams in the tenth round of the 1985 NFL draft. He played for Cleveland from 1986 through 1988, the San Diego Chargers in 1989, the New Orleans Saints in 1990 and 1991, and the New England Patriots in 1992.

WISNE, JERRY
Offensive guard (1995–98), 6'7", 295 lbs.

Wisne came to Notre Dame as an All-American defensive lineman from Jenks High School in Tulsa, Oklahoma. The Irish coaching staff moved the mobile lineman to offensive guard, where he eventually flourished, exhibiting excellent pass protecting and trapping skills. After playing only 4 minutes and 8 seconds in one game as a freshman and 97:56 as a sophomore, Wisne started all thirteen games as a junior in 1997—including the 1998 Independence Bowl—totaling 330:54 minutes in the regular season. His senior year mirrored his junior season through the first nine games, all starts in which he logged 249:06. However, torn knee ligaments prematurely ended Wisne's season. The middle of three Notre Dame linemen to be selected in the 1999 National Football League draft, Wisne went to the Chicago Bears in the fifth round, six picks before teammate Mike Rosenthal. Line mate Luke Petitgout was a first-round selection.

WOLSKI, BILL
Halfback (1963–65), 5'11", 195 lbs.

Wolski, a rugged and durable running back from Muskegon, Michigan, helped Ara

Parseghian enjoy instant success at Notre Dame. Wolski began his career as a backup for head coach Joe Kuharich in 1963. He ran the ball 70 times for 320 yards and 2 touchdowns, caught 3 passes for 11 yards, led the team in kickoff returns, with 16 for 379 yards, and ran back 6 punts for 31 yards. The following season Parseghian entered the scene, and Wolski emerged as a starter at left halfback. He was the team's leading rusher with 657 yards and 9 touchdowns on 136 carries. He also led the team in points with 66, was third in receiving with 8 receptions for 130 yards, and ran back 2 kickoffs for 49 yards. He scored 3 touchdowns in a 28–6 victory over Stanford, including one on a 54-yard pass play from Heisman Trophy–winning quarterback John Huarte.

Wolski again started at left halfback in 1965 and continued his scoring ways. He set a modern record with 5 touchdowns in one game in a 69–13 drubbing of the University of Pittsburgh. For the year he led the Fighting Irish in points, with 52, which included 8 touchdowns and two 2-point conversions. He was part of a powerful backfield, playing alongside halfback Nick Eddy and fullback Larry Conjar. Wolski finished with 452 yards on 103 carries while scoring 8 touchdowns. He also caught an 8-yard pass, led the team in kickoff returns, with 6 for 131 yards, and even made 7 tackles. He finished his career with 2,168 yards of total offense.

The Atlanta Falcons selected Wolski in the fifth round of the 1966 NFL draft, but he played just one season for the franchise.

CAREER STATS

Year	Att.	Yards	Avg.	TDs
1963	70	320	4.6	2
1964	136	657	4.8	9
1965	103	452	4.4	8
Total	309	1,429	4.6	19

WOODEN, SHAWN
Cornerback (1991, 1993–95),
5′11″, 188 lbs.

Wooden was a fifth-year player in the Notre Dame secondary in 1995, and one of five team captains. A prep All-American from Willow Grove, Pennsylvania, he missed most of his first two college seasons with back problems and was granted a fifth year of eligibility to make up for missing the 1992 season. He was making strides and in good health for most of the 1993 season before injuring his knee in the season's penultimate game and requiring arthroscopic surgery.

In 1991, Wooden only made it into five games for a total of 3:01, and did not make any tackles. After missing the 1992 season, he was back on the team in 1993. He played in eight games for a total of 48:04 and made 16 tackles and had an interception. Wooden made his way into the starting lineup in 1994, and in eleven games (playing 261:50), he made 59 tackles and had an interception. As a fifth-year senior, Wooden started all eleven games again, playing 278:09, while making 63 tackles and 3 interceptions.

The Miami Dolphins selected Wooden in the sixth round of the 1996 NFL draft. He was second on the team in tackles in each of his first two professional seasons. He played in Miami through the 1999 season and, at press time, he was on the roster of the Chicago Bears.

WORDEN, NEIL
Fullback (1951–53), 5′11″, 185 lbs.

Worden had no problem living up to his nickname, "Bull." He was a rugged, nearly unstoppable running and scoring machine who packed a lot of power into a relatively small package. Worden, a Milwaukee native, was a starter for head coach Frank Leahy in his first season on the Notre Dame varsity, and he scored 4 touchdowns in his first game, a 30–9 victory over Purdue. That year he was the team's leading rusher and scorer (181 carries for 676 yards, 48 points).

As a junior in 1952, Worden was the team's second-leading rusher with 504 yards on 150 carries, and he again led the team in scoring, with 60 points. Notre Dame finished third in the final Associated Press poll, thanks in part to the dependable Worden. The following season he led the Notre Dame offense during a spectacular season. The Fighting Irish were 9–0–1 and ranked second in the final poll. Worden led the team in rushing with 859 yards on 145 carries (nearly 6 yards per run), and in scoring, with 66 points. His career total of 2,039 yards was, at the time, third in school history. As of 2000, he ranked tenth. The Philadelphia Eagles selected him in the first round of the 1954 NFL draft after his teammates, Johnny Lattner (Pittsburgh) and Art Hunter (Green Bay), had already been selected. Worden played two seasons in Philadelphia (1954 and 1957) before retiring from pro football.

CAREER STATS

Year	Att.	Yards	Avg.	TDs
1951	181	676	3.7	8
1952	150	504	3.4	10
1953	145	859	5.9	11
Total	476	2,039	4.3	29

WRIGHT, HARRY
Fullback/Quarterback/Guard (1940–42), 6'0", 190 lbs.

From fullback to quarterback to offensive guard, Wright, from Hempstead, New York, kept changing positions and getting better at Notre Dame. He joined the varsity football team in 1940 as a reserve fullback. The following season his versatility came in handy, as he was named the team's starting quarterback. In 1942, to make room for quarterback Angelo Bertelli, an emerging superstar, Wright was moved to, of all places, the offensive line. He made the transition smoothly and was named a second-team All-American.

WUJCIAK, AL
Guard (1973–75), 6'2", 228 lbs.

Wujciak, of Newark, New Jersey, did not earn a letter until his junior year at Notre Dame, but he turned out to be one of the team's best linemen during an outstand-

ing offensive season. He was the team's starting left guard as a junior and was third on the team in minutes played, with 335. He was a pulling guard and a good blocker who helped Notre Dame rush for 3,119 yards during the regular season. In 1975, Wujciak started again and was named the Offensive Most Valuable Player by the Monogram Club.

WYNN, RENALDO
Outside linebacker/Defensive end (1993–96), 6'3", 275 lbs.

Wynn steadily improved in each of his years at Notre Dame to the point that he was the school's best defensive player and deemed good enough to be selected twenty-first overall by the Jacksonville Jaguars in the 1997 NFL draft. He arrived at Notre Dame after an outstanding athletic career (on the football, basketball, and baseball teams) at De-LaSalle Institute in Chicago, the same school at which former Notre Dame star Norm Barry coached, and which Moose Krause, another legendary Fighting Irish figure, attended.

Wynn did not play as a freshman, but used the year of eligibility on the back end of his career as a fifth-year senior. He began his college career as an outside linebacker, but lasted at the position for only three games. Head coach Lou Holtz moved the giant run-stuffer to defensive end for virtually the rest of his college career. As a second-year freshman, Wynn started five games and appeared in eleven overall. He made 15 solo tackles and assisted on 4 others, and also made 1.5 tackles for losses and 3 sacks. In 1994, his sophomore year, he played in eleven games as a linebacker and defensive lineman and started nine, missing one game because of turf toe. He finished with 33 solo tackles, 14 assists, 4 tackles for losses, and a sack in 231:38, more field time than any other defensive lineman.

The Fighting Irish had a full-time player at left defensive end in 1995. Wynn started all twelve games and played a career-high 274:33, again more than any other

National Monogram Club MVP defensive end Renaldo Wynn is one of the better linemen to come out of Notre Dame in recent years and was chosen in the first round of the NFL draft by the Jacksonville Jaguars.

defensive lineman on the team. He also led the team in sacks, with 6.5, and was credited with 42 tackles, 15 assists, and 6 hits for losses.

The fifth-year senior was no secret entering his final college season. In 222:48, Wynn made 41 tackles and assisted on 20 others for a career-high total of 61 hits. He also made a career-high 9 sacks and was credited with 6 tackles for losses. Wynn ended his career with a string of twenty-four consecutive starts, and was selected to play in the Senior Bowl. He was voted by his Notre Dame teammates as the team's Most Valuable Player, an award that is presented by the local chapter of the National Monogram Club, and he was named Notre Dame Lineman of the Year by the Moose Krause Chapter of the National Football Foundation.

Wynn made use of his fifth year in school by taking graduate courses with the goal of becoming a counselor or educational administrator. After being selected in the first round by the Jacksonville Jaguars, any other career path would have to wait. He was named to several All-Rookie teams and appears to have a long career ahead of him in the NFL.

WYNNE, CHET
Fullback (1918–21), 6'0", 168 lbs.

Wynne wasn't even supposed to play football at Notre Dame. He came to South Bend from Norton, Kansas, with the intention of running track, but football coach Knute Rockne was also the track coach (and a chemistry professor). Despite the risk of ruining Wynne's track career, Rockne utilized him in football.

Wynne turned out to have power, speed, and the ability to play defense. He was a backup fullback in 1918, and again in 1919, as Notre Dame won all nine of its games. The following season, Wynne became a first-team backfield mate of the legendary George Gipp (as a matter of fact, it was Gipp who urged Rockne to use Wynne). After two and a half seasons riding the bench, Wynne became a factor in the Army game during his junior season. He had fumbled early in the game, but Gipp's confidence in his teammate rubbed off on Rockne. Wynne went on to score on a 20-yard sideline run in Notre Dame's 27–17 victory. He was a scrub no more, starting at fullback for much of the remainder of the season. Notre Dame was again undefeated.

The next year Wynne, who was also the captain of the track team, started every game. He also led Notre Dame in interceptions, with 4. On offense, Wynne scored 2 touchdowns over Kalamazoo (including an 80-yard touchdown return), 2 against DePauw, and 1 against Indiana. He scored on a 45-yard touchdown against Army and further built on his reputation back east with a touchdown versus Rutgers (against whom he also had a 51-yard reception and an interception). He also scored a touchdown against Marquette University and another against Michigan State. Notre Dame's lone loss of the season was to the University of Iowa, and the team finished the season 10–1. After his college career, Wynne played for the Rochester Jeffersons in 1922 before entering coaching. He was the head coach at Creighton University, Auburn University, and the University of Kentucky.

YARR, TOMMY
Center (1929–31), 5'11", 195 lbs.

Midway through his college football career, Tommy Yarr did not seem destined for stardom, but he came on strong in the second half and finished up with a career worthy of induction into the College Football Hall of Fame. He was a member of head coach Knute Rockne's final two teams, which did not lose a game and won back-to-back national titles.

In the first of those two seasons, Yarr, who was a star at Chimacum Prep in Dabob, Washington, played sparingly as the team's third-string center. The next year, 1929, Yarr impressed Rockne to the tune of being named a starter. He excelled on offense as well as defense and was a typical Rockne lineman—a tad small, with supreme quickness and great fundamentals. He was a tenacious defender as well. Yarr helped preserve the Fighting Irish's undefeated season, with 2 interceptions in the final minutes of a 20–14 victory over SMU. He also intercepted and broke up a pass against Drake University in a 28–7 victory.

Yarr was named team captain in 1931, head coach "Hunk" Anderson's first season and Yarr's last. He proved to be tough as well as talented, playing the season's final three games with a cast on his hand. After the season he was named a first-team All-American. Yarr stayed at Notre Dame, serving as an assistant football coach in 1932. He signed a professional contract with the Chicago Cardinals in 1933, his lone year of pro football. He returned to coaching, taking over the helm at Carroll College. Yarr was inducted into the College Football Hall of Fame in 1987.

YONAKOR, JOHN
End (1942–43), 6'4", 222 lbs.

Offensive ends and leading receivers aren't generally the biggest players on a football team, but John Yonakor bucked that conventional wisdom. The Dorchester, Massachusetts, native was the biggest starter on Notre Dame's 1943 national championship team. He caught 15 passes for 323 yards to lead the Fighting Irish. He also scored 4 touchdowns, including one on a 30-yard pass to help Notre Dame to a 26–0 victory over third-ranked Army. Yonakor was a consensus All-American and was invited to play in the College Football All-Star Game.

After Yonakor's outstanding senior season, the Philadelphia Eagles selected him in the first round of the 1945 NFL draft. From 1946 through 1949, he played both offensive and defensive end for the Cleveland Browns of the All-American Football Conference. He then played for the NFL's New York Yankees in 1950, the Canadian Football League's Montreal Alouettes in 1950, and the NFL Washington Redskins in 1952.

YOUNG, BRYANT
Defensive tackle (1990–93), 6'3", 277 lbs.

Young, from Chicago Heights, Illinois, was a dominant interior lineman for head coach Lou Holtz. He was big and strong, with exceptional moves, and was a nightmare matchup for virtually any offensive lineman in a one-on-one situation.

Young earned four letters and began his career rather humbly as a special-teams player. In 31:48, he made 4 solo tackles and assisted on 4 others. He was named Notre Dame's

All-American defensive tackle Bryant Young went on to a Pro Bowl career with the San Francisco 49ers, including a Super Bowl championship.

than any defensive lineman (258:09) and was named an honorable mention All-American. He started at defensive tackle and led the team in sacks (7.5 for -64 yards) and tackles for losses (5.5 for -10 yards), and finished with 37 solo tackles and 14 assists. He also recovered a fumble and broke up a pass. Young was named one of four team captains in 1993. He played 266:16 and finished third on the team in tackles, with 67 (44 solo hits, 23 assists). He also made 7 tackles for -23 yards and 6.5 sacks for -49 yards, recovered a fumble, and broke up a pass. He capped his career with 9 tackles and a sack in Notre Dame's 24–21 victory over Texas A&M in the Cotton Bowl. He was named a first-team All-American.

Young was the first of three Fighting Irish players to be selected in the first round of the 1994 NFL draft. The San Francisco 49ers took him as the seventh pick. Offensive guard Aaron Taylor was selected sixteenth by the Green Bay Packers, and free safety Jeff Burris went to the Buffalo Bills, who had the twenty-seventh pick. In 1995, Young was seventh in sacks in the NFL, with 11.5, was named to the All-Pro and Pro Bowl rosters, and was a member of San Francisco's Super Bowl XXIX championship team. In 1996, he was selected by his teammates as the recipient of the Len Eshmont Award, which is presented annually to the San Francisco player who best exemplifies courage and leadership. In 1997, Young was a Pro Bowl alternate despite having ankle and foot problems.

starting left tackle in 1991, his sophomore season, played there for one game, and was then moved to nose tackle. He broke a bone in his left ankle during the season's seventh game and lost some playing time. Still, he finished fourth on the team, with 32 solo tackles and 18 assists. Nine of Young's tackles were for a combined -27 yards, and he led the team in sacks, with 4. In 232:32, he also recovered 2 fumbles and batted down 2 passes.

Young was back and 100 percent healthy in 1992. He played more minutes

Z

ZAVAGNIN, MARK
Linebacker (1979–82), 6'2", 228 lbs.

Zavagnin was all-city, all-state, and a Catholic All-American at Chicago's St. Rita High School. He had three great years for Notre Dame. He became a starter at weakside linebacker as a sophomore and was second on the team in tackles for two consecutive seasons. The only player who made more hits than Zavagnin during his sophomore and junior years was All-American linebacker Bob Crable.

Crable had graduated by 1982, and Zavagnin replaced him at middle linebacker. Now it was his turn to lead the team in tackles (with 113). After the season, Zavagnin was named a second-team All-American. The Chicago Bears selected him in the ninth round of the 1983 NFL draft, but he did not play professionally.

ZEIGLER, CURTIS DUSTIN
Guard (1993–95), 6'6", 292 lbs.

Dusty Zeigler was a mainstay on the Notre Dame offensive line during his final two college seasons. He was an honorable mention high school All-American while playing at Effingham County High School in Springfield, Georgia. As a junior in South Bend, he started all eleven games for a grand total of 276:26 of playing time. Head coach Lou Holtz said of his near-300-pounder, "Zeigler is playing as well as any offensive lineman I've had since I've been at Notre Dame. If he's not an All-American, we don't have one."

Zeigler was named an All-American, but not until his senior season, when he served as one of five Fighting Irish captains and saw 299:58 of action. His final Notre Dame team steamrolled past several opponents, compiling some outstanding running games. Notre Dame finished the season with an average of 233.5 yards rushing per game, sixth-best in the country. The Buffalo Bills selected Zeigler in the sixth round of the 1996 NFL draft, and he was a full-time starter by the 1998 season. He moved east to the New York Giants in 2000, joining two other former Irish linemen, Luke Petitgout and Mike Rosenthal.

ZELLARS, RAY
Fullback (1991–94), 5'11", 221 lbs.

Ray Zellars did not see much action at Notre Dame until All-American Jerome Bettis left the school and opened up the fullback spot for him. Before coming to Notre Dame, Zellars attended Pittsburgh's Oliver High School, where he rushed for 1,237 yards and 11 touchdowns as a senior, leading his school to the City League championship. He was also captain of the track, wrestling, and baseball teams, and the student council president.

During his first two seasons in South Bend, Zellars carried the ball only 32 times. When Bettis went to play professionally in Pittsburgh, Zellars stepped forward and proved to be an all-around back. He could run, catch, and block, and he was powerful as well as quick.

Zellars's junior year was not only his breakthrough year in college, it was also his best season. He was the team's starting fullback, playing a career-high 215:58, and he gained 494 yards and scored 5 touchdowns on 99 carries. He also caught 14 passes for 109 yards and 3 scores. Zellars had a great game against the University of Pittsburgh, against whom he rushed 12 times for 67 yards and 2 touchdowns. He was named an honorable mention All-American.

Many major publications predicted big things for Zellars in his senior season. In its preseason issue, the *Sporting News* ranked him the third-best fullback in the nation. If Zellars had remained healthy, he may have lived up to the great expectations, but one week after setting a career mark with 156 yards on just 14 carries, he sprained his left ankle against Stanford. He subsequently missed most of a month, including games against Boston College, Brigham Young, and Navy. The next week he carried the ball just 5 times as a backup against Florida State.

As a senior, Zellars gained 466 yards on 79 carries, with 3 rushing touchdowns. He also caught 12 passes for 114 yards and 2 touchdowns. After his eligibility was up he played in the Senior Bowl, and proved to scouts that he was healthy. The New Orleans Saints selected him in the second round of the 1995 NFL draft. In 1996, Zellars was second on the team and twentieth in the NFC in rushing.

CAREER STATS

Year	Att.	Yards	Avg.	TDs
1991	6	51	8.5	0
1992	26	124	4.8	0
1993	99	494	5.0	5
1994	79	466	5.9	3
Total	210	1,135	5.4	8

ZETTEK, SCOTT
Defensive tackle (1976–80), 6'5", 245 lbs.

Zettek, from Elk Grove Village, Illinois, seemed to spend as much time in the training room as he did on the field, but luckily for him and the Fighting Irish, both pursuits turned out to be successful.

Zettek made 21 tackles as a freshman. Then, during the 1977 spring drills, he suffered the first of several knee injuries that would plague him during his college career. In the fall of 1977 he was back in the start-

ing lineup and made 51 tackles. More knee problems kept him inactive for most of the 1978 season, and he underwent surgery the following spring. During his fourth fall on campus, Zettek made 61 tackles in eight games. But he missed three games with—you guessed it—a sprained knee. Zettek took advantage of his fifth year of eligibility and remained healthy the entire season. He was third on the team in tackles, with 70, and was named a first-team All-American. The Chicago Bears selected him in the eighth round of the 1982 NFL draft. He did not play in the league.

ZILLY, JACK
End (1943, 1946), 6'2", 200 lbs.

Zilly, of Southington, Connecticut, was part of two national championship teams at Notre Dame that sandwiched a tour of duty in the Pacific during World War II.

Zilly played behind John Yonakor at end on the 1943 Fighting Irish team that won nine of ten games and the national title. Following the season, he was assigned to active duty in the navy. He was discharged in the spring of 1946 and was back in South Bend that fall in time to be part of another national championship team, as Notre Dame went 8–0–1.

San Francisco of the All-American Football Conference selected Zilly in the sixth round of the 1947 draft. He played for the Los Angeles Rams from 1947 through 1951, and for the Philadelphia Eagles in 1952. After retiring from playing football, he took a job in private business. In 1955, he entered coaching as an assistant with the Los Angeles Rams, and joined the staff of the Fighting Irish the following season.

ZONTINI, LOU
Halfback (1937–39), 5'9", 181 lbs.

Zontini, of Whitesville, West Virginia, must have been happy when he scored an 84-yard touchdown in a 19–0 victory over the University of Minnesota in 1938, but there was no way he could have known how much a part of Notre Dame history that romp would become. It was edited into the final print of the motion picture *Knute Rockne, All-American*. Zontini was, however, far more than a one-play wonder. He was a two-year starter at right halfback and in 1938 was second on the team in yards rushing, with 319, despite being one of the best blockers on the team.

Zontini played for the Chicago Cardinals in 1940 and 1941, and the Cleveland Rams in 1944. In 1946, after a hitch in the navy at the tail end of World War II, he played one year for the Buffalo Bills of the All-American Football Conference.

ZORICH, CHRISTOPHER ROBERT
Defensive tackle (1988–90), 6'1", 266 lbs.

Generally, players who switch positions from high school to college move to a "smaller" position. Chris Zorich was asked to do the opposite. He started for four years as a linebacker at Vocational High School in Chicago, where he was all-state and an honorable mention All-American as a senior. When he came to Notre Dame, he was asked to play nose tackle. It took him a season to get the hang of the new spot, but once he did, the results were phenomenal.

Zorich, an amazing combination of strength and speed (he could bench press more than 475 pounds and run a 4.68 40-yard dash), had three of the best years of any Notre Dame player. He seemed to change a two- or three-on-one situation to his advantage, and even ran down receivers and runners who had turned the corner.

After failing to play on the varsity level as a freshman, Zorich applied himself and worked hard to learn his new position in time for his sophomore season. He made the starting lineup of a Fighting Irish team that won all twelve of its games and the national championship. He finished the season with 70 tackles (third on the team), including 4 for -8 yards. He also made 3.5 sacks, recovered 3 fumbles, and broke up 3 passes in a season that earned him first-team All-American honors.

Zorich continued to improve. As a junior he made 92 tackles, 5 for -12 yards, and 3 sacks. He also caused a fumble, recovered 2, and broke up 2 passes. Zorich's efforts were rewarded with consensus first-team All-

Three-time All-American Chris Zorich was an outstanding nose tackle and the recipient of the Lombardi Award in 1990.

American status, and he was also a finalist for the Lombardi Award, presented annually to the nation's top lineman.

Despite missing two games with a partially dislocated kneecap in 1990, Zorich had another stellar campaign. He was a tri-captain and made 57 tackles (12 for -26 yards) and 4 sacks, and also caused 2 fumbles, recovered 1, and broke up a pass. He was a unanimous first-team All-American, won the Lombardi Award, and was a semifinalist for the Outland Trophy, which goes to the top interior lineman in the country. Zorich capped his all-star career with 10 tackles in the Orange Bowl. He was Notre Dame's Most Valuable Player in the 10–9 loss to Colorado.

The Chicago Bears selected their hometown hero in the second round of the 1991 NFL draft. He played for the Bears from 1991 through 1997, and the following season for the Washington Redskins before retiring from the game.

Zorich was, however, more than just a football player. He started the Chris Zorich Foundation, which lends financial support to many community outreach programs in the Chicago area. In 1995, because of Zorich's charitable work, *USA Weekend* named him one of its Most Caring Athletes. Each year he distributes Thanksgiving dinners in his old neighborhood on the South Side of Chicago.

NOTRE DAME
BY THE NUMBERS

THE NOTRE DAME DREAM TEAM

OFFENSE

Tackles:	George Connor, Bill Fischer
Guards:	Larry DiNardo, Jack Cannon
Center:	Tommy Yarr
Wide receivers:	Tom Gatewood, Tim Brown
Quarterback:	Paul Hornung
Tight end:	Dave Casper
Running backs:	George Gipp, Vagas Ferguson

DEFENSE

Ends:	Alan Page, Ross Browner
Nose tackle:	Chris Zorich
Linebackers:	Jerry Groom, Bob Golic, Bob Crable, Michael Stonebreaker
Cornerbacks:	Bobby Taylor, Mike Townsend
Strong safety:	Luther Bradley
Free safety:	Jeff Burris

SPECIAL TEAMS

Placekicker:	John Carney
Punter:	Craig Hentrich
Kick returner:	Raghib Ismail
Punt returner:	Allen Rossum
Coach:	Knute Rockne
Assistants:	Ara Parseghian, Elmer Layden, Frank Leahy, Terry Brennan, Lou Holtz
Mascot:	Daniel "Rudy" Ruettiger
Cheerleader:	Regis Philbin

ALL-TIME RESULTS

1887
Coach: None
Record: 0–1–0
Captain: Henry Luhn

11/23	L	Michigan	0–8	H

1888
Coach: None
Record: 1–2–0
Captain: Edward Prudhomme

4/20	L	Michigan	6–26	H
4/21	L	Michigan	4–10	H
12/6	W	Harvard Prep	20–0	H
		Total Points	30–36	

1889
Coach: None
Record: 17–0–0
Captain: Edward Prudhomme

11/14	W	Northwestern	9–0	A

1890–1891
No team

1892
Coach: None
Record: 1–0–1
Captain: Pat Coady

10/19	W	South Bend H.S.	56–0	H
11/24	T	Hillsdale	10–10	H
		Total Points	66–10	

1893
Coach: None
Record: 4–1–0
Captain: Frank Keough

10/25	W	Kalamazoo	34–0	H
11/11	W	Albion	8–6	H
11/23	W	DeLaSalle	28–0	H
11/30	W	Hillsdale	22–10	H

1/1	L	Chicago	0–8	A
		Total Points	92–24	

1894
Coach: James L. Morison
Record: 3–1–1
Captain: Frank Keough

10/13	W	Hillsdale	14–0	H
10/20	T	Albion	6–6	H
11/15	W	Wabash	30–0	H
11/22	W	Rush Medical	18–6	H
11/29	L	Albion	12–19	H
		Total Points	80–31	

1895
Coach: H. G. Hadden
Record: 3–1–0
Captain: Dan Casey

10/19	W	Northwestern Law School	20–0	H
11/7	W	Illinois Cycling Club	18–2	H
11/22	L	Indianapolis Artillery	0–18	H
11/28	W	Chicago Physicians & Surgeons	32–0	H
		Total Points	70–20	

1896
Coach: Frank E. Hering
Record: 4–3–0
Captain: Frank E. Hering

10/8	L	Chicago Physicians & Surgeons	0–4	H
10/14	L	Chicago	0–18	H
10/27	W	South Bend A.C.	46–0	H
10/31	W	Albion	24–0	H
11/14	L	Purdue	22–28	H
11/20	W	Highland Views	82–0	H
11/26	W	Beloit	8–0	H
		Total Points	182–50	

1897

Coach: Frank E. Hering
Record: 4–1–1
Captain: Jack Mullen

10/13	T	Rush Medical	0–0	H
10/23	W	DePauw	4–0	H
10/28	W	Chicago Dental Surgeons	62–0	H
11/6	L	Chicago	5–34	A
11/13	W	St. Viator	60–0	H
11/25	W	Mich State	34–6	H
		Total Points	165–40	

1898

Coach: Frank E. Hering
Record: 4–2–0
Captain: Jack Mullen

10/8	W	Illinois	5–0	A
10/15	W	Michigan State	53–0	H
10/23	L	Michigan	0–23	A
10/29	W	DePauw	32–0	H
11/11	L	Indiana	5–11	H
11/19	W	Albion	60–0	A
		Total Points	155–34	

1899

Coach: James McWeeney
Record: 6–3–1
Captain: Jack Mullen

9/27	W	Englewood High School	29–5	H
9/30	W	Michigan State	40–0	H
10/4	L	Chicago	6–23	A
10/14	W	Lake Forest	38–0	H
10/18	L	Michigan	0–12	A
10/23	W	Indiana	17–0	H
10/27	W	Northwestern	12–0	H
11/4	W	Rush Medical	17–0	H
11/18	T	Purdue	10–10	A
11/30	L	Chicago Physicians & Surgeons	0–5	H
		Total Points	169–55	

1900

Coach: Pat O'Dea
Record: 6–3–1
Captain: John Farley

9/29	W	Goshen	55–0	H
10/6	W	Englewood High School	68–0	H
10/13	W	South Bend Howard Park	64–0	H
10/20	W	Cincinnati	58–0	H
10/25	L	Indiana	0–6	A
11/3	T	Beloit	6–6	H
11/10	L	Wisconsin	0–54	A
11/17	L	Michigan	0–7	A
11/24	W	Rush Medical	5–0	H
11/29	W	Chicago Physicians & Surgeons	5–0	H
		Total Points	261–73	

1901

Coach: Pat O'Dea
Record: 8–1–1
Captain: Al Fortin

9/28	T	South Bend A.C.	0–0	H
10/5	W	Ohio Medical	6–0	A
10/12	L	Northwestern	0–2	A
10/19	W	Chicago Medical	32–0	H
10/26	W	Beloit	5–0	A
11/2	W	Lake Forest	16–0	H
11/9	W	Purdue	12–6	H
11/16	W	Indiana	18–5	H
11/23	W	Chicago Physicians & Surgeons	34–0	H
11/28	W	South Bend A.C.	22–6	H
		Total Points	145–19	

1902

Coach: James F. Faragher
Record: 6–2–1
Captain: Louis "Red" Salmon

9/27	W	Michigan State	33–0	H
10/11	W	Lake Forest	28–0	H
10/18	L	Michigan (at Toledo)	0–23	N
10/25	W	Indiana	11–5	A
11/1	W	Ohio Medical	6–5	A
11/8	L	Knox	5–12	A
11/15	W	American Medical	92–0	H
11/22	W	DePauw	22–0	H
11/27	T	Purdue	6–6	A
		Total Points	203–51	

1903

Coach: James F. Faragher
Record: 8–0–1
Captain: Louis "Red" Salmon

10/3	W	Michigan State	12–0	H
10/10	W	Lake Forest	28–10	H
10/17	W	DePauw	56–0	H
10/24	W	American Medical	52–0	H
10/29	W	Chicago Physicians & Surgeons	46–0	H
11/7	W	Missouri Osteopaths	28–0	H

11/14	T	Northwestern	0–0	A
11/21	W	Ohio Medical	35–0	A
11/26	W	Wabash	35–0	A
		Total Points	292–10	

1904
Coach: Louis "Red" Salmon
Record: 5–3–0
Captain: Frank Shaughnessy

10/1	W	Wabash	12–4	H
10/8	W	American Medical	44–0	H
10/15	L	Wisconsin (at Milwaukee)	0–58	N
10/22	W	Ohio Medical	17–5	A
10/27	W	Toledo Athletic Association	6–0	H
11/5	L	Kansas	5–24	A
11/19	W	DePauw	10–0	H
11/24	L	Purdue	0–36	A
		Total Points	94–127	

1905
Coach: Henry J. McGlew
Record: 5–4–0
Captain: Pat Beacom

9/30	W	North Division H.S.	44–0	H
10/7	W	Michigan State	28–0	H
10/14	L	Wisconsin (at Milwaukee)	0–21	N
10/21	L	Wabash	0–5	H
10/28	W	American Medical	142–0*	H
11/4	W	DePauw	71–0	H
11/11	L	Indiana	5–22	A
11/18	W	Bennett Medical	22–0	H
11/24	L	Purdue	0–32	A
		Total Points	312–80	

* After a 25-minute first half, with Notre Dame leading 121–0, the second half was shortened to only 8 minutes to permit the "Doctors" time to eat before catching a train to Chicago. Notre Dame scored 27 touchdowns, but missed 20 extra points.

1906
Coach: Thomas A. Barry
Record: 6–1–0
Captain: Bob Bracken

10/6	W	Franklin	26–0	H
10/13	W	Hillsdale	17–0	H
10/20	W	Chicago Physicians & Surgeons	28–0	H
10/27	W	Michigan State	5–0	H
11/3	W	Purdue	2–0	A
11/10	L	Indiana	0–12	N
11/24	W	Beloit	29–0	H
		Total Points	107–12	

1907
Coach: Thomas A. Barry
Record: 6–0–1
Captain: Dom Callicrate

10/12	W	Chicago Physicians & Surgeons	32–0	H
10/19	W	Franklin	23–0	H
10/26	W	Olivet	22–4	H
11/2	T	Indiana	0–0	H
11/9	W	Knox	22–4	H
11/23	W	Purdue	17–0	H
11/28	W	St. Vincent's	21–12	A
		Total Points	137–20	

1908
Coach: Victor M. Place
Record: 8–1–0
Captain: Harry Miller

10/3	W	Hillsdale	39–0	H
10/10	W	Franklin	64–0	H
10/17	L	Michigan	6–12	A
10/24	W	Chicago Physicians & Surgeons	88–0	H
10/29	W	Ohio Northern	58–4	H
11/7	W	Indiana	11–0	N
11/13	W	Wabash	8–4	A
11/18	W	St. Viator	46–0	H
11/26	W	Marquette	6–0	A
		Total Points	326–20	

1909
Coach: Frank C. Longman
Record: 7–0–1
Captain: Howard Edwards
"The Notre Dame Victory March" was introduced this season.

10/9	W	Olivet	58–0	H
10/16	W	Rose Poly	60–11	H
10/23	W	Michigan State	17–0	H
10/30	W	Pittsburgh	6–0	A
11/6	W	Michigan	11–3	A
11/13	W	Miami (of Ohio)	46–0	H
11/20	W	Wabash	38–0	H
11/25	T	Marquette	0–0	A
		Total Points	236–14	

1910

Coach: Frank C. Longman
Record: 4–1–1
Captain: Ralph Dimmick

10/8	W	Olivet	48–0	H
10/22	W	Butchel (Akron)	51–0	H
11/5	L	Michigan State	0–17	A
11/12	W	Rose Poly	41–3	A
11/19	W	Ohio Northern	47–0*	H
11/24	T	Marquette	5–5	A
		Total Points	192–25	

*Notre Dame's one-hundredth victory

1911

Coach: John L. Marks
Record: 6–0–2
Captain: Luke Kelly

10/7	W	Ohio Northern	32–6	H
10/14	W	St. Viator	43–0	H
10/21	W	Butler	27–0	H
10/28	W	Loyola (of Chicago)	80–0	H
11/4	T	Pittsburgh	0–0	A
11/11	W	St. Bonaventure	34–0	H
11/20	W	Wabash	6–3	A
11/30	T	Marquette	0–0	A
		Total Points	222–9	

1912

Coach: John L. Marks
Record: 7–0–0
Captain: Charles "Gus" Dorais

10/5	W	St. Viator	116–7	H
10/12	W	Adrian	74–7	H
10/19	W	Morris Harvey	39–0	H
10/26	W	Wabash	41–6	H
11/2	W	Pittsburgh	3–0	A
11/9	W	St. Louis	47–7	A
11/28	W	Marquette	69–0	N
		Total Points	389–27	

THE JESSE HARPER YEARS
Five seasons: 34–5–1 (.863)

1913

Coach: Jesse Harper
Record: 7–0–0
Captain: Knute Rockne

10/4	W	Ohio Northern	87–0	H
10/18	W	South Dakota	20–7	H
10/25	W	Alma	62–0	H
11/1	W	Army	35–13	A
11/7	W	Penn State	14–7	A

11/22	W	Christian Brothers	20–7	A
11/27	W	Texas	30–7	A
		Total Points	268–41	

1914

Coach: Jesse Harper
Record: 6–2–0
Captain: Keith Jones

10/3	W	Alma	56–0	H
10/10	W	Rose Poly	103–0	H
10/17	L	Yale	0–28	A
10/24	W	South Dakota	33–0	N
10/31	W	Haskell	20–7	H
11/7	L	Army	7–20	A
11/14	W	Carlisle	48–6	N
11/26	W	Syracuse	20–0	A
		Total Points	287–61	

1915

Coach: Jesse Harper
Record: 7–1–0
Captain: Freeman Fitzgerald

10/2	W	Alma	32–0	H
10/9	W	Haskell	34–0	H
10/23	L	Nebraska	19–20	A
10/30	W	South Dakota	6–0	H
11/6	W	Army	7–0	A
11/13	W	Creighton	41–0	A
11/25	W	Texas	36–7	A
11/27	W	Rice	55–2	A
		Total Points	230–29	

1916

Coach: Jesse Harper
Record: 8–1–0
Captain: Stan Cofall

9/30	W	Case Tech	48–0	H
10/7	W	Western Reserve	48–0	A
10/14	W	Haskell	26–0	H
10/28	W	Wabash	60–0	H
11/4	L	Army	10–30	A
11/11	W	South Dakota	21–0	N
11/18	W	Michigan State	14–0	A
11/25	W	Alma	46–0	H
11/30	W	Nebraska	20–0	A
		Total Points	293–30	

1917

Coach: Jesse Harper
Record: 6–1–1
Captain: Jim Phelan

10/6	W	Kalamazoo	55–0	H
10/13	T	Wisconsin	0–0	A

10/20	L	Nebraska	0–7	A
10/27	W	South Dakota	40–0	H
11/3	W	Army	7–2	A
11/10	W	Morningside	13–0	A
11/17	W	Michigan State	23–0	H
11/24	W	Washington and Jefferson	3–0	A
		Total Points	141–9	

THE KNUTE ROCKNE YEARS
Thirteen seasons: 105–12–5 (.881)

1918
Coach: Knute Rockne
Record: 3–1–2
Captain: Leonard Bahan

9/28	W	Case Tech	26–6	A
11/2	W	Wabash	67–7	A
11/9	T	Great Lakes	7–7	H
11/16	L	Michigan State	7–13	A
11/23	W	Purdue	26–6	A
11/28	T	Nebraska	0–0	A
		Total Points	133–39	

1919
Coach: Knute Rockne
Record: 9–0–0
Captain: Leonard Bahan

10/4	W	Kalamazoo	14–0	H
10/11	W	Mount Union	60–7	H
10/18	W	Nebraska	14–9	A
10/25	W	Western Michigan	53–0	H
11/1	W	Indiana	16–3	N
11/8	W	Army	12–9	A
11/15	W	Michigan State	13–0	H
11/22	W	Purdue	33–13	A
11/27	W	Morningside	14–6	A
		Total Points	229–47	

1920
Coach: Knute Rockne
Record: 9–0–0
Captain: Frank Coughlin

10/2	W	Kalamazoo	39–0	H
10/9	W	Western Michigan	42–0	H
10/16	W	Nebraska	16–7	A
10/23	W	Valparaiso	28–3	H
10/30	W	Army	27–17	A
11/6	W	Purdue	28–0	H
11/13	W	Indiana (at Indianapolis)	13–10	N
11/20	W	Northwestern	33–7*	A

11/25	W	Michigan State	25–0	A
		Total Points	251–44	

*George Gipp's last game. He contracted a strep throat and died from complications of the disease on December 14 at the age of twenty-five.

1921
Coach: Knute Rockne
Record: 10–1–0
Captain: Eddie Anderson

9/24	W	Kalamazoo	56–0	H
10/1	W	DePauw	57–10	H
10/8	L	Iowa	7–10	A
10/15	W	Purdue	33–0	A
10/22	W	Nebraska	7–0	H
10/29	W	Indiana (at Indianapolis)	28–7	N
11/5	W	Army	28–0	A
11/8	W	Rutgers (Polo Grounds)	48–0	N
11/12	W	Haskell	42–7	H
11/19	W	Marquette	21–7	A
11/24	W	Michigan State	48–0	H
		Total Points	375–41	

1922
Coach: Knute Rockne
Captain: Glen Carberry
Record: 8–1–1

9/20	W	Kalamazoo	46–0	H
10/7	W	St. Louis	26–0	H
10/14	W	Purdue	20–0	A
10/21	W	DePauw	34–7	H
10/28	W	Georgia Tech	13–3	A
11/4	W	Indiana	27–0	H
11/11	T	Army	0–0	A
11/18	W	Butler	31–3	A
11/25	W	Carnegie Tech	19–0	A
11/30	L	Nebraska	6–14	A
		Total Points	222–27	

1923
Coach: Knute Rockne
Record: 9–1–0
Captain: Harvey Brown

9/29	W	Kalamazoo	74–0	H
10/6	W	Lombard	14–0	H
10/13	W	Army (at Brooklyn)	13–0	N
10/20	W	Princeton	25–2	A
10/27	W	Georgia Tech	35–7	H
11/3	W	Purdue	34–7	H
11/10	L	Nebraska	7–14	A
11/17	W	Butler	34–7	H

11/24	W	Carnegie Tech	26–0	A
11/29	W	St. Louis	13–0	A
		Total Points	275–37	

1924
Coach: Knute Rockne
Record: 10–0–0
Captain: Adam Walsh

10/4	W	Lombard	40–0	H
10/11	W	Wabash	34–0	H
10/18	W	Army (at Polo Grounds)	13–7	N
10/25	W	Princeton	12–0	A
11/1	W	Georgia Tech	34–3*	H
11/8	W	Wisconsin	38–3	A
11/15	W	Nebraska	34–6	H
11/22	W	Northwestern	13–6	N
11/29	W	Carnegie Tech	40–19	A
		Total Points	258–44	

*Notre Dame's two-hundredth victory
ROSE BOWL

1/1	W	Stanford (Pasadena)	27–10	N

1925
Coach: Knute Rockne
Record: 7–2–1
Captain: Clem Crowe

9/26	W	Baylor	41–0	H
10/3	W	Lombard	69–0	H
10/10	W	Beloit	19–3	H
10/17	L	Army (at Yankee Stadium)	0–27	N
10/24	W	Minnesota	19–7	A
10/31	W	Georgia Tech	13–0	A
11/7	T	Penn State	0–0	A
11/14	W	Carnegie Tech	26–0	H
11/21	W	Northwestern	13–10	H
11/26	L	Nebraska	0–17	A
		Total Points	200–64	

1926
Coach: Knute Rockne
Record: 9–1–0
Co-Captains: Gene Edwards, Tom Hearden

10/2	W	Beloit	77–0	H
10/9	W	Minnesota	20–7	A
10/16	W	Penn State	28–0	H
10/23	W	Northwestern	6–0	A
10/30	W	Georgia Tech	12–0	H
11/6	W	Indiana	26–0	H
11/13	W	Army (at Yankee Stadium)	7–0	N
11/20	W	Drake	21–0	H

11/27	L	Carnegie Tech	0–19	A
12/4	W	USC	13–12	A
		Total Points	210–38	

1927
Coach: Knute Rockne
Record: 7–1–1
Captain: John Smith

10/1	W	Coe College	28–7	H
10/8	W	Detroit	20–0	A
10/15	W	Navy (at Baltimore)	19–6	N
10/22	W	Indiana	19–6	A
10/29	W	Georgia Tech	26–7	H
11/5	T	Minnesota	7–7	H
11/12	L	Army (at Yankee Stadium)	0–18	N
11/19	W	Drake	32–0	A
11/26	W	USC (at Soldier Field)	7–6	N
		Total Points	158–57	

1928
Coach: Knute Rockne
Record: 5–4–0
Captain: Fred Miller

9/29	W	Loyola (of New Orleans)	12–6	H
10/6	L	Wisconsin	6–22	A
10/13	W	Navy (at Soldier Field)	7–0	N
10/20	L	Georgia Tech	0–13	A
10/27	W	Drake	32–6	H
11/3	W	Penn State (at Philadelphia)	9–0	N
11/10	W	Army (at Yankee Stadium)	12–6	N
11/17	L	Carnegie Tech	7–27*	H
12/1	L	USC	14–27	A
		Total Points	99–107	

*First defeat at home since 1905

1929
Coach: Knute Rockne
Record: 9–0–0
Captain: John Law

10/5	W	Indiana	14–0	A
10/12	W	Navy (at Baltimore)	14–7	N
10/19	W	Wisconsin (at Soldier Field)	19–0	N
10/26	W	Carnegie Tech	7–0	A
11/2	W	Georgia Tech	26–6	A
11/9	W	Drake (at Soldier Field)	19–7	N

11/16	W	USC (at Soldier Field)	13–12	N
11/23	W	Northwestern	26–6	A
11/30	W	Army (at Yankee Stadium)	7–0	N
		Total Points	145–38	

No home games; Notre Dame Stadium was under construction

1930
Coach: Knute Rockne
Record: 10–0–0
Captain: Tom Conley

10/4	W	SMU	20–14	H
10/11	W	Navy*	26–2	H
10/18	W	Carnegie Tech	21–6	H
10/25	W	Pittsburgh	35–19	A
11/1	W	Indiana	27–0	H
11/8	W	Pennsylvania	60–20	A
11/15	W	Drake	28–7	H
11/22	W	Northwestern	14–0	A
11/29	W	Army (at Soldier Field)	7–6	N
12/6	W	USC	27–0	A
		Total Points	265–74	

*Dedication of Notre Dame Stadium

THE HEARLEY "HUNK" ANDERSON YEARS
Three seasons: 16–9–2 (.630)

1931
Coach: "Hunk" Anderson
Record: 6–2–1
Captain: Tommy Yarr

10/3	W	Indiana	25–0	A
10/10	T	Northwestern (at Soldier Field)	0–0	N
10/17	W	Drake	63–0	H
10/24	W	Pittsburgh	25–12	H
10/31	W	Carnegie Tech	19–0	A
11/7	W	Pennsylvania	49–0	H
11/14	W	Navy (at Baltimore)	20–0	N
11/21	L	USC	14–16	H
11/28	L	Army (at Yankee Stadium)	0–12	N
		Total Points	215–40	

1932
Coach: "Hunk" Anderson
Record: 7–2–0
Captain: Paul Host

10/8	W	Haskell	73–0	H
10/15	W	Drake	62–0	H

10/22	W	Carnegie Tech	42–0	H
10/29	L	Pittsburgh	0–12	A
11/5	W	Kansas	24–6	A
11/12	W	Northwestern	21–0	H
11/19	W	Navy (at Cleveland)	12–0	N
11/26	W	Army (at Yankee Stadium)	21–0	N
12/10	L	USC	0–13	A
		Total Points	255–31	

1933
Coach: "Hunk" Anderson
Record: 3–5–1
Captains: Hugh Devore/Tom Gorman

10/7	T	Kansas	0–0	H
10/14	W	Indiana	12–2	A
10/21	L	Carnegie Tech	0–7	A
10/28	L	Pittsburgh	0–14	H
11/4	L	Navy (at Baltimore)	0–7	N
11/11	L	Purdue	0–19	H
11/18	W	Northwestern	7–0	A
11/25	L	USC	0–19	H
12/2	W	Army (at Yankee Stadium)	13–12	N
		Total Points	32–80	

THE ELMER LAYDEN YEARS
Seven seasons: 47–13–3 (.770)

1934
Coach: Elmer Layden
Record: 6–3–0
Captain: Dom Vairo

10/6	L	Texas	6–7	H
10/13	W	Purdue	18–7	H
10/20	W	Carnegie Tech	13–0	H
10/27	W	Wisconsin	19–0	H
11/3	L	Pittsburgh	0–19	A
11/10	L	Navy (at Cleveland)	6–10	N
11/17	W	Northwestern	20–7	A
11/24	W	Army (at Yankee Stadium)	12–6	N
12/8	W	USC	14–0	A
		Total Points	108–56	

1935
Coach: Elmer Layden
Record: 7–1–1
Captain: Joe Sullivan*

9/28	W	Kansas	28–7	H
10/5	W	Carnegie Tech	14–3	A
10/12	W	Wisconsin	27–0	A
10/19	W	Pittsburgh	9–6	H

10/26	W	Navy (at Baltimore)	14–0	N
11/2	W	Ohio State	18–13	A
11/9	L	Northwestern	7–14	H
11/16	T	Army (at Yankee Stadium)	6–6	N
11/23	W	USC	20–13	H
		Total Points	143–62	

*Died from complications of pneumonia, March 1935

1936
Coach: Elmer Layden
Record: 6–2–1
Captain: Bill Smith, then John Lautar*

10/3	W	Carnegie Tech	21–7	H
10/10	W	Washington (of St. Louis)	14–6	H
10/17	W	Wisconsin	27–0	H
10/24	L	Pittsburgh	0–26	A
10/31	W	Ohio State	7–2	H
11/7	L	Navy (at Baltimore)	0–3	N
11/14	W	Army (at Yankee Stadium)	20–6	N
11/21	W	Northwestern	26–6	H
12/5	T	USC	13–13	A
		Total Points	128–69	

*Captain-elect Smith resigned his captaincy because of illness and Lautar was elected acting captain.

1937
Coach: Elmer Layden
Record: 6–2–1
Captain: Joe Zwers

10/2	W	Drake	21–0	H
10/9	T	Illinois	0–0	A
10/16	L	Carnegie Tech	7–9	A
10/23	W	Navy	9–7	H
10/30	W	Minnesota	7–6	A
11/6	L	Pittsburgh	6–21	H
11/13	W	Army (at Yankee Stadium)	7–0	N
11/20	W	Northwestern	7–0	A
11/27	W	USC	13–6	H
		Total Points	77–49	

1938
Coach: Elmer Layden
Record: 8–1–0
Captain: Jim McGoldrick

10/1	W	Kansas	52–0	H
10/8	W	Georgia Tech	14–6	A
10/15	W	Illinois	14–6	H

10/22	W	Carnegie Tech	7–0	H
10/29	W	Army (at Yankee Stadium)	19–7	N
11/5	W	Navy (at Baltimore)	15–0	N
11/12	W	Minnesota	19–0*	H
11/19	W	Northwestern	9–7	A
12/3	L	USC	0–13	A
		Total Points	149–39	

*Notre Dame's three-hundredth victory

1939
Coach: Elmer Layden
Record: 7–2–0
Captain: Johnny Kelly

9/30	W	Purdue	3–0	H
10/7	W	Georgia Tech	17–14	H
10/14	W	SMU	20–19	H
10/21	W	Navy (at Cleveland)	14–7	N
10/28	W	Carnegie Tech	7–6	A
11/4	W	Army (at Yankee Stadium)	14–0	N
11/11	L	Iowa	6–7	A
11/18	W	Northwestern	7–0	H
11/25	L	USC	12–20	H
		Total Points	100–73	

1940
Coach: Elmer Layden
Record: 7–2–0
Captain: Milt Piepul

10/5	W	College of the Pacific	25–7	H
10/12	W	Georgia Tech	26–20	H
10/19	W	Carnegie Tech	61–0	H
10/26	W	Illinois	26–0	A
11/2	W	Army (at Yankee Stadium)	7–0	N
11/9	W	Navy (at Baltimore)	13–7	N
11/16	L	Iowa	0–7	H
11/23	L	Northwestern	0–20	A
12/7	W	USC	10–6	A
		Total Points	168–67	

THE FRANK LEAHY YEARS
Eleven seasons: 87–11–9 (.855)

1941
Coach: Frank Leahy
Record: 8–0–1
Captain: Paul Lillis

9/27	W	Arizona	38–7	H
10/4	W	Indiana	19–6	H

10/11	W	Georgia Tech	20–0	A
10/18	W	Carnegie Tech	16–0	A
10/25	W	Illinois	49–14	H
11/1	T	Army (at Yankee Stadium)	0–0	N
11/8	W	Navy (at Baltimore)	20–13	N
11/15	W	Northwestern	7–6	A
11/22	W	USC	20–18	H
		Total Points	189–64	

1942
Coach: Frank Leahy
Record: 7–2–2
Captain: George Murphy

9/26	T	Wisconsin	7–7	A
10/3	L	Georgia Tech	6–13	H
10/10	W	Stanford	27–0	H
10/17	W	Iowa Pre-Flight	28–0	H
10/24	W	Illinois	21–14	A
10/31	W	Navy (at Cleveland)	9–0	N
11/7	W	Army (at Yankee Stadium)	13–0	N
11/14	L	Michigan	20–32	H
11/21	W	Northwestern	27–20	H
11/28	W	USC	13–0	A
12/5	T	Great Lakes (at Soldier Field)	13–13	N
		Total Points	184–99	

1943
Coach: Frank Leahy
Captain: Pat Filley
Record: 9–1–0

9/25	W	Pittsburgh	41–0	A
10/2	W	Georgia Tech	55–13	H
10/9	W	Michigan	35–12	A
10/16	W	Wisconsin	50–0	A
10/23	W	Illinois	47–0	H
10/30	W	Navy (at Cleveland)	33–6	N
11/6	W	Army (at Yankee Stadium)	26–0	N
11/13	W	Northwestern	25–6	A
11/20	W	Iowa Pre-Flight	14–13	H
11/27	L	Great Lakes	14–19	A
		Total Points	340–69	

1944
Coach: Ed McKeever
Record: 8–2–0
Captain: Pat Filley

9/30	W	Pittsburgh	58–0	A
10/7	W	Tulane	26–0	H

10/14	W	Dartmouth (at Fenway Park, Boston)	64–0	N
10/21	W	Wisconsin	28–13	H
10/28	W	Illinois	13–7	A
11/4	L	Navy (at Baltimore)	13–32	N
11/11	L	Army (at Yankee Stadium)	0–59	N
11/18	W	Northwestern	21–0	H
11/25	W	Georgia Tech	21–0	A
12/2	W	Great Lakes	28–7	H
		Total Points	272–118	

1945
Coach: Hugh Devore
Record: 7–2–1
Captain: Frank Dancewicz

9/29	W	Illinois	7–0	H
10/6	W	Georgia Tech	40–7	A
10/13	W	Dartmouth	34–0	H
10/20	W	Pittsburgh	39–9	A
10/27	W	Iowa	56–0	H
11/3	T	Navy (at Cleveland)	6–6	N
11/10	L	Army (at Yankee Stadium)	0–48	N
11/17	W	Northwestern	34–7	A
11/24	W	Tulane	32–6	A
12/1	L	Great Lakes	7–39	A
		Total Points	255–122	

1946
Coach: Frank Leahy
Record: 8–0–1

9/28	W	Illinois	26–6	A
10/5	W	Pittsburgh	33–0	H
10/12	W	Purdue	49–6	H
10/26	W	Iowa	41–6	A
11/2	W	Navy (at Baltimore)	28–0	N
11/9	T	Army (at Yankee Stadium)	0–0	N
11/16	W	Northwestern	27–0	H
11/23	W	Tulane	41–0	A
11/30	W	USC	26–6	H
		Total Points	271–24	

1947
Coach: Frank Leahy
Record: 9–0–0
Captain: George Connor

10/4	W	Pittsburgh	40–6	A
10/11	W	Purdue	22–7	A
10/18	W	Nebraska	31–0	H

10/25	W	Iowa	21–0	H
11/1	W	Navy (at Cleveland)	27–0	N
11/8	W	Army	27–7	H
11/15	W	Northwestern	26–19	A
11/22	W	Tulane	59–6	H
12/6	W	USC	38–7	A
		Total Points	291–52	

1948
Coach: Frank Leahy
Record: 9–0–1
Captain: Bill Fischer

9/25	W	Purdue	28–27	H
10/2	W	Pittsburgh	40–0	A
10/9	W	Michigan State	26–7	H
10/16	W	Nebraska	44–13	A
10/23	W	Iowa	27–12	A
10/30	W	Navy (at Baltimore)	41–7	N
11/6	W	Indiana	42–6	A
11/13	W	Northwestern	12–7	H
11/27	W	Washington	46–0	H
12/4	T	USC	14–14	A
		Total Points	320–93	

1949
Coach: Frank Leahy
Record: 10–0–0
Captains: Leon Hart, Jim Martin

9/24	W	Indiana	49–6	H
10/1	W	Washington	27–7	A
10/8	W	Purdue	35–12	A
10/15	W	Tulane	46–7	H
10/29	W	Navy (at Baltimore)	40–0	N
11/5	W	Michigan State	34–21	A
11/12	W	North Carolina (at Yankee Stadium)	42–6	N
11/19	W	Iowa	28–7	H
11/26	W	USC	32–0	H
12/3	W	SMU	27–20	A
		Total Points	360–86	

1950
Coach: Frank Leahy
Record: 4–4–1
Captain: Jerry Groom

9/30	W	North Carolina	14–7	H
10/7	L	Purdue	14–28	H
10/14	W	Tulane	13–9	A
10/21	L	Indiana	7–20	A
10/28	L	Michigan State	33–36	H
11/4	W	Navy (at Cleveland)	19–10	N
11/11	W	Pittsburgh	18–7	H
11/18	T	Iowa	14–14	A
12/2	L	USC	7–9	A
		Total Points	139–140	

1951
Coach: Frank Leahy
Record: 7–2–1
Captain: Jim Mutscheller

9/29	W	Indiana	48–6	H
10/5	W	Detroit	40–6	N
10/13	L	SMU	20–27	H
10/20	W	Pittsburgh	33–0	A
10/27	W	Purdue	30–9	H
11/3	W	Navy (at Baltimore)	19–0	N
11/10	L	Michigan State	0–35	A
11/17	W	North Carolina	12–7*	A
11/24	T	Iowa	20–20	H
12/1	W	USC	19–12	A
		Total Points	241–122	

*Notre Dame's four-hundredth victory

1952
Coach: Frank Leahy
Record: 7–2–1
Captain: Jack Alessandrini

9/27	T	Pennsylvania	7–7	A
10/4	W	Texas	14–3	A
10/11	L	Pittsburgh	19–22	H
10/18	W	Purdue	26–14	A
10/25	W	North Carolina	34–14	H
11/1	W	Navy (at Cleveland)	17–6	N
11/8	W	Oklahoma	27–21	H
11/15	L	Michigan State	3–21	A
11/22	W	Iowa	27–0	A
11/29	W	USC	9–0	H
		Total Points	183–108	

1953
Coach: Frank Leahy
Record: 9–0–1
Captain: Don Penza

9/26	W	Oklahoma	28–21	A
10/3	W	Purdue	37–7	A
10/17	W	Pittsburgh	23–14	H
10/24	W	Georgia Tech	27–14	H
10/31	W	Navy	38–7	H
11/7	W	Pennsylvania	28–20	A
11/14	W	North Carolina	34–14	A
11/21	T	Iowa	14–14	H
11/28	W	USC	48–14	A
12/5	W	SMU	40–14	H
		Total Points	317–139	

THE TERRY BRENNAN YEARS
Five seasons: 32–18–0 (.640)

1954
Coach: Terry Brennan
Record: 9–1–0
Captains: Paul Matz, Dan Shannon

9/25	W	Texas	21–0	H
10/2	L	Purdue	14–27	H
10/9	W	Pittsburgh	33–0	A
10/16	W	Michigan State	20–19	H
10/30	W	Navy (at Baltimore)	6–0	N
11/6	W	Pennsylvania	42–7	A
11/13	W	North Carolina	42–13	H
11/20	W	Iowa	34–18	A
11/27	W	USC	23–17	H
12/4	W	SMU	26–14	A
		Total Points	261–115	

1955
Coach: Terry Brennan
Record: 8–2–0
Captain: Ray Lemek

9/24	W	SMU	17–0	H
10/1	W	Indiana	19–0	H
10/7	W	Miami	14–0	A
10/15	L	Michigan State	7–21	A
10/22	W	Purdue	22–7	A
10/29	W	Navy	21–7	H
11/5	W	Pennsylvania	46–14	A
11/12	W	North Carolina	27–7	A
11/19	W	Iowa	17–14	H
11/26	L	USC	20–42	A
		Total Points	210–112	

1956
Coach: Terry Brennan
Record: 2–8–0
Captain: Jim Morse

9/22	L	SMU	13–19	A
10/6	W	Indiana	20–6	H
10/13	L	Purdue	14–28	H
10/20	L	Michigan State	14–47	H
10/27	L	Oklahoma	0–40	H
11/3	L	Navy (at Baltimore)	7–33	N
11/10	L	Pittsburgh	13–26	A
11/17	W	North Carolina	21–14	H
11/24	L	Iowa	8–48	A
12/1	L	USC	20–28	A
		Total Points	130–289	

1957
Coach: Terry Brennan
Record: 7–3–0
Captains: Dick Prendergast, Ed Sullivan

9/28	W	Purdue	12–0	A
10/5	W	Indiana	26–0	H
10/12	W	Army (at Philadelphia)	23–21	N
10/26	W	Pittsburgh	13–7	H
11/2	L	Navy	6–20	H
11/9	L	Michigan State	6–34	A
11/16	W	Oklahoma	7–0	A
11/23	L	Iowa	13–21	H
11/30	W	USC	40–12	H
12/7	W	SMU	54–21	A
		Total Points	200–136	

1958
Coach: Terry Brennan
Record: 6–4–0
Captains: Al Ecuyer, Chuck Puntillo

9/27	W	Indiana	18–0	H
10/4	W	SMU	14–6	A
10/11	L	Army	2–14	H
10/18	W	Duke	9–7	H
10/25	L	Purdue	22–29	H
11/1	W	Navy (at Baltimore)	40–20	N
11/8	L	Pittsburgh	26–29	A
11/15	W	North Carolina	34–24	H
11/22	L	Iowa	21–31	A
11/29	W	USC	20–13	A
		Total Points	206–173	

THE JOE KUHARICH YEARS
Four seasons: 17–23–0 (.425)

1959
Coach: Joe Kuharich
Record: 5–5–0
Captain: Ken Adamson

9/26	W	North Carolina	28–8	H
10/3	L	Purdue	7–28	A
10/10	W	California	28–6	A
10/17	L	Michigan State	0–19	A
10/24	L	Northwestern	24–30	H
10/31	W	Navy	25–22	H
11/7	L	Georgia Tech	10–14	H
11/14	L	Pittsburgh	13–28	A
11/21	W	Iowa	20–19	A
11/28	W	USC	16–6	H
		Total Points	171–180	

1960
Coach: Joe Kuharich
Record: 2–8–0
Captain: Myron Pottios

9/24	W	Cal–Berkley	21–7	H
10/1	L	Purdue	19–51	H
10/8	L	North Carolina	7–12	A

10/15	L	Michigan State	0–21	H
10/22	L	Northwestern	6–7	A
10/29	L	Navy	7–14	N
		(at Philadelphia)		
11/5	L	Pittsburgh	13–20	H
11/12	L	Miami (of Florida)	21–28	A
11/19	L	Iowa	20–28	H
11/26	W	USC	17–0	A
		Total Points	111–188	

1961
Coach: Joe Kuharich
Record: 5–5–0
Captains: N. Roy, Nick Buoniconti

9/30	W	Oklahoma	19–6	H
10/7	W	Purdue	22–20	A
10/14	W	USC	30–0	H
10/21	L	Michigan State	7–17	A
10/28	L	Northwestern	10–12	H
11/4	L	Navy	10–13	H
11/11	W	Pittsburgh	26–20	A
11/18	W	Syracuse	17–15	H
11/25	L	Iowa	21–42	A
12/2	L	Duke	13–37	A
		Total Points	175–182	

1962
Coach: Joe Kuharich
Record: 5–5–0
Captain: Mike Lind

9/29	W	Oklahoma	13–7	A
10/6	L	Purdue	6–24	H
10/13	L	Wisconsin	8–17	A
10/20	L	Michigan State	7–31	H
10/27	L	Northwestern	6–35	A
11/3	W	Navy (at Phila)	20–12	N
11/10	W	Pittsburgh	43–22	H
11/17	W	North Carolina	21–7	H
11/24	W	Iowa	35–12	H
12/1	L	USC	0–25	A
		Total Points	159–192	

1963
Coach: Hugh Devore
Record: 2–7–0
Captain: Bob Lehmann

9/28	L	Wisconsin	9–14	H
10/5	L	Purdue	6–7	A
10/12	W	USC	17–14	H
10/19	W	UCLA	27–12	H
10/26	L	Stanford	14–24	A
11/2	L	Navy	14–35	H
11/9	L	Pittsburgh	7–27	H
11/16	L	Michigan State	7–12	A
11/23		Iowa*		A

11/28	L	Syracuse	7–14	N
		(at Yankee Stadium)		
		Total Points	108–159	

*Game cancelled because of the death of President John F. Kennedy

THE ARA PARSEGHIAN YEARS
Eleven seasons: 95–17–4 (.836)

1964
Coach: Ara Parseghian
Record: 9–1–0
Captain: Jim Carroll

9/26	W	Wisconsin	31–7	A
10/3	W	Purdue	34–15	H
10/10	W	Air Force	34–7	A
10/17	W	UCLA	24–0	H
10/24	W	Stanford	28–6	H
10/31	W	Navy (at	40–0	N
		Philadelphia)		
11/7	W	Pittsburgh	17–15	A
11/14	W	Michigan State	34–7	H
11/21	W	Iowa	28–0	H
11/28	L	USC	17–20	A
		Total Points	287–77	

1965
Coach: Ara Parseghian
Record: 7–2–1
Captain: Phil Sheridan

9/18	W	Cal–Berkeley	48–6	A
9/25	L	Purdue	21–25	A
10/2	W	Northwestern	38–7	H
10/9	W	Army (at Shea	17–0	N
		Stadium)		
10/23	W	USC	28–7	H
10/30	W	Navy	29–3	H
11/6	W	Pittsburgh	69–13	A
11/13	W	North Carolina	17–0	H
11/20	L	Michigan State	3–12	H
11/27	T	Miami (of Florida)	0–0	A
		Total Points	270–73	

1966
Coach: Ara Parseghian
Record: 9–0–1
Captain: Jim Lynch

9/24	W	Purdue	26–14	H
10/1	W	Northwestern	35–7	A
10/8	W	Army	35–0	H
10/15	W	North Carolina	32–0	H
10/22	W	Oklahoma	38–0	A

10/29	W	Navy	31–7	N
		(at Philadelphia)		
11/5	W	Pittsburgh	40–0	H
11/12	W	Duke	64–0	H
11/19	T	Michigan State	10–10	A
11/26	W	USC	51–0	A
		Total Points	362–38	

1967
Coach: Ara Parseghian
Record: 8–2–0
Captain: Bob (Rocky) Bleier

9/23	W	Cal–Berkeley	41–8	H
9/30	L	Purdue	21–28	A
10/7	W	Iowa	56–6	H
10/14	L	USC	7–24	H
10/21	W	Illinois	47–7	A
10/28	W	Michigan State	24–12	H
11/4	W	Navy	43–14	H
11/11	W	Pittsburgh	38–0	A
11/18	W	Georgia Tech	36–3*	A
11/24	W	Miami (of Florida)	24–22	A
		Total Points	337–124	

*Notre Dame's five-hundredth victory

1968
Coach: Ara Parseghian
Record: 7–2–1
Captains: George Kunz, Bob Olson

9/21	W	Oklahoma	45–21	H
9/28	L	Purdue	22–37	H
10/5	W	Iowa	51–28	A
10/12	W	Northwestern	27–7	H
10/19	W	Illinois	58–8	H
10/26	L	Michigan State	17–21	A
11/2	W	Navy (at	45–14	N
		Philadelphia)		
11/9	W	Pittsburgh	56–7	
11/16	W	Georgia Tech	34–6	H
11/30	T	USC	21–21	A
		Total Points	376–170	

1969
Coach: Ara Parseghian
Record: 8–2–1
Captains: Bob Olson, Mike Oriard

9/20	W	Northwestern	35–10	H
9/27	L	Purdue	14–28	A
10/4	W	Michigan State	42–28	H
10/11	W	Army (at Yankee	45–0	N
		Stadium)		
10/18	T	USC	14–14	H
10/25	W	Tulane	37–0	A
11/1	W	Navy	47–0	H
11/8	W	Pittsburgh	49–7	A

11/15	W	Georgia Tech	38–20	A
11/22	W	Air Force	13–6	H
		Total Points	334–113	

COTTON BOWL

1/1	L	Texas (at Dallas)	17–21	N

1970
Coach: Ara Parseghian
Record: 10–1–0
Captains: Larry DiNardo, Tim Kelly

9/19	W	Northwestern	35–14	A
9/26	W	Purdue	48–0	H
10/3	W	Michigan State	29–0	A
10/10	W	Army	51–10	H
10/17	W	Missouri	24–7	A
10/31	W	Navy (at	56–7	N
		Philadelphia)		
11/7	W	Pittsburgh	46–14	H
11/14	W	Georgia Tech	10–7	H
11/21	W	Louisiana State	3–0	H
11/28	L	USC	28–38	A
		Total Points	330–97	

COTTON BOWL

1/1	W	Texas (at Dallas)	24–11	N

1971
Coach: Ara Parseghian
Record: 8–2–0
Captains: Walt Patulski, Tom Gatewood

9/18	W	Northwestern	50–7	H
9/25	W	Purdue	8–7	A
10/2	W	Michigan State	14–2	H
10/9	W	Miami (of Florida)	17–0	A
10/16	W	North Carolina	16–0	H
10/23	L	USC	14–28	H
10/30	W	Navy	21–0	H
11/6	W	Pittsburgh	56–7	A
11/13	W	Tulane	21–7	H
11/20	L	Louisiana State	8–28	A
		Total Points	225–86	

1972
Coach: Ara Parseghian
Record: 8–3–0
Captains: John Dampeer, Greg Marx

9/23	W	Northwestern	37–0	A
9/30	W	Purdue	35–14	H
10/7	W	Michigan State	16–0	A
10/14	W	Pittsburgh	42–16	H
10/21	L	Missouri	26–30	H
10/28	W	Texas Christian	21–0	H
11/4	W	Navy (at	42–23	N
		Philadelphia)		
11/11	W	Air Force	21–7	A
11/18	W	Miami (of Florida)	20–17	H

12/2	L	USC	23–45	A
		Total Points	283–152	

ORANGE BOWL

1/1	L	Nebraska	6–40	N
		(at Miami)		

1973
Coach: Ara Parseghian
Record: 11–0–0
Captains: Dave Casper, Frank Pomarico,
Mike Townsend

9/22	W	Northwestern	44–0	H
9/29	W	Purdue	20–7	A
10/6	W	Michigan State	14–10	H
10/13	W	Rice	28–0	A
10/20	W	Army	62–3	A
10/27	W	USC	23–14	H
11/3	W	Navy	44–7	H
11/10	W	Pittsburgh	31–10	A
11/22	W	Air Force	48–15	H
12/1	W	Miami (of Florida)	44–0	A
		Total Points	358–66	

SUGAR BOWL

12/31	W	Alabama	24–23	N
		(at New Orleans)		

1974
Coach: Ara Parseghian
Record: 10–2–0
Captains: Tom Clements, Greg Collins

9/9	W	Georgia Tech	31–7	A
9/21	W	Northwestern	49–3	A
9/28	L	Purdue	20–31	H
10/5	W	Michigan State	19–14	A
10/12	W	Rice	10–3	H
10/19	W	Army	48–0	H
10/26	W	Miami (of Florida)	38–7	H
11/2	W	Navy (at Philadelphia)	14–6	N
11/16	W	Pittsburgh	14–10	H
11/23	W	Air Force	38–0	H
11/30	L	USC	24–55	A
		Total Points	305–136	

ORANGE BOWL

1/1	W	Alabama (at Miami)	13–11	N

THE DAN DEVINE YEARS
Six seasons: 53–16–1 (.764)

1975
Coach: Dan Devine
Record: 8–3–0
Captains: Ed Bauer, Jim Stock

9/15	W	Boston College	17–3	N
9/20	W	Purdue	17–0	A
9/27	W	Northwestern	31–7	H
10/4	L	Michigan State	3–10	H
10/11	W	North Carolina	21–14	A
10/18	W	Air Force	31–30	A
10/25	L	USC	17–24	H
11/1	W	Navy	31–10	H
11/8	W	Georgia Tech	24–3	H
11/15	L	Pittsburgh	20–34	A
11/22	W	Miami (at Florida)	32–9	A
		Total Points	244–144	

1976
Coach: Dan Devine
Record: 9–3–0
Captains: Mark McLane, Willie Fry

9/11	L	Pittsburgh	10–31	H
9/18	W	Purdue	23–0	H
9/25	W	Northwestern	48–0	A
10/2	W	Michigan State	24–6	A
10/16	W	Oregon	41–0	H
10/23	W	South Carolina	13–6	A
10/30	W	Navy (at Cleveland)	27–21	N
11/6	L	Georgia Tech	14–23	A
11/13	W	Alabama	21–18	H
11/20	W	Miami (of Florida)	40–27	H
11/27	L	USC	13–17	A
		Total Points	274–149	

GATOR BOWL

12/27	W	Penn State (at Jacksonville)	20–9	N

1977
Coach: Dan Devine
Record: 11–1–0
Captains: Ross Browner, Terry Eurick, Willie Fry

9/10	W	Pittsburgh	19–9	A
9/17	L	Mississippi (at Jacksonville)	13–20	N
9/24	W	Purdue	31–24	A
10/1	W	Michigan State	16–6	H
10/15	W	Army (at Giants Stadium)	24–0	N
10/22	W	USC	49–19	H
10/29	W	Navy	43–10	H
11/5	W	Georgia Tech	69–14	H
11/12	W	Clemson	21–17	A
11/19	W	Air Force	49–0	H
12/3	W	Miami (of Florida)	48–10	A
		Total Points	382–129	

COTTON BOWL

1/2	W	Texas (at Dallas)	38–10	N

1978
Coach: Dan Devine
Record: 9–3–0
Captains: Bob Golic, Jerome Heavens,
Joe Montana

9/9	L	Missouri	0–3	H
9/23	L	Michigan	14–28	H
9/30	W	Purdue	10–6	H
10/7	W	Michigan State	29–25	A
10/14	W	Pittsburgh	26–17	H
10/21	W	Air Force	38–15	A
10/28	W	Miami (of Florida)	20–0	H
11/4	W	Navy (at Cleveland)	27–7	N
11/11	W	Tennessee	31–14	H
11/18	W	Georgia Tech	38–21	A
11/25	L	USC	25–27	A
		Total Points	258–163	

COTTON BOWL

1/1	W	Houston (at Dallas)	35–34*	N

*Notre Dame's six-hundredth victory

1979
Coach: Dan Devine
Record: 7–4–0
Captains: Vagas Ferguson, Tim Foley,
Dave Waymer

9/15	W	Michigan	12–10	A
9/22	L	Purdue	22–28	A
9/29	W	Michigan State	27–3	H
10/6	W	Georgia Tech	21–13	H
10/13	W	Air Force	38–13	A
10/20	L	USC	23–42	H
10/27	W	South Carolina	18–17	H
11/3	W	Navy	14–0	H
11/10	L	Tennessee	18–40	A
11/17	L	Clemson	10–16	H
11/24	W	Miami (of Florida)*	40–15	N
		Total Points	243–197	

*National Olympic Stadium, Tokyo, Japan

1980
Coach: Dan Devine
Record: 9–2–1
Captains: Bob Crable, Tom Gibbons, John
Scully

9/6	W	Purdue	31–10	H
9/20	W	Michigan	29–27	H
10/4	W	Michigan State	26–21	A
10/11	W	Miami	32–14	H
10/18	W	Army	30–3	H
10/25	W	Arizona	20–3	A
11/1	W	Navy (at Giants Stadium)	33–0	N

11/8	T	Georgia Tech	3–3	A
11/15	W	Alabama*	7–0	A
11/22	W	Air Force	24–10	H
12/6	L	USC	3–20	A
		Total Points	238–111	

*Legion Field, Birmingham, Alabama
SUGAR BOWL

1/1	L	Georgia (at New Orleans)	10–17	N

THE GERRY FAUST YEARS
Five seasons: 30–26–1 (.535)

1981
Coach: Gerry Faust
Record: 5–6–0
Captains: Bob Crable and Phil Carter

9/12	W	Louisiana State	27–9	H
9/19	L	Michigan	7–25	A
9/26	L	Purdue	14–15	A
10/3	W	Michigan State	20–7	H
10/10	L	Florida State	13–19	H
10/24	L	USC	7–14	H
10/31	W	Navy	38–0	H
11/7	W	Georgia Tech	35–3	H
11/14	W	Air Force	35–7	A
11/21	L	Penn State	21–24	A
11/27	L	Miami	15–37	A
		Total Points	232–160	

1982
Coach: Gerry Faust
Record: 6–4–1
Captains: Phil Carter, Dave Duerson,
Mark Zavagnin

9/18	W	Michigan	23–17	H
9/25	W	Purdue	28–14	H
10/2	W	Michigan St.	11–3	A
10/9	W	Miami	16–14	H
10/16	L	Arizona	13–16	H
10/23	T	Oregon	13–13	A
10/30	W	Navy (at Giants Stadium)	27–10	N
11/6	W	Pittsburgh	31–16	A
11/13	L	Penn State	14–24	H
11/20	L	Air Force	17–30	A
11/27	L	USC	13–17	A
		Total Points	206–174	

1983
Coach: Gerry Faust
Record: 7–5–0
Captains: Blair Kiel, Stacey Toran

9/10	W	Purdue	52–6	A
9/17	L	Michigan State	23–28	H
9/24	L	Miami	0–20	A
10/1	W	Colorado	27–3	A
10/8	W	South Carolina	30–6	A
10/15	W	Army (at Giants Stadium)	42–0	N
10/22	W	USC	27–6	H
10/29	W	Navy	28–12	H
11/5	L	Pittsburgh	16–21	H
11/12	L	Penn State	30–34	A
11/19	L	Air Force	22–23	H
		Total Points	297–159	

LIBERTY BOWL

12/29	W	Boston College (at Memphis)	19–18	N

1984

Coach: Gerry Faust
Record: 7–5–0
Captains: Mike Golic, Joe Johnson, Larry Williams

9/8	L	Purdue (Hoosier Dome)	21–23	N
9/15	W	Michigan State	24–20	A
9/22	W	Colorado	55–14	H
9/29	W	Missouri	16–14	A
10/6	L	Miami	13–31	H
10/13	L	Air Force	7–21	H
10/20	L	South Carolina	32–36	H
10/27	W	Louisiana State	30–22	A
11/3	W	Navy (at Giants Stadium)	18–17	N
11/17	W	Penn State	44–7	H
11/24	W	USC	19–7	A
		Total Points	279–212	

ALOHA BOWL

12/29	L	SMU (at Honolulu)	20–27	N

1985

Coach: Gerry Faust
Record: 5–6–0
Captains: Anthony Furjanic, Mike Larkin, Allen Pinkett, Tim Scannell

9/14	L	Michigan	12–20	A
9/21	W	Michigan State	27–10	H
9/28	L	Purdue	17–35	A
10/5	L	Air Force	15–21	A
10/19	W	Army	24–10	H
10/26	W	USC	37–3	H
11/2	W	Navy	41–17	H
11/9	W	Mississippi	37–14	H
11/16	L	Penn State	6–36	A

11/23	L	Louisiana State	7–10	H
11/30	L	Miami	7–58	A
		Total Points	230–234	

THE LOU HOLTZ YEARS

Eight seasons: 77–19–1 (.799)

1986

Coach: Lou Holtz
Record: 5–6–0
Captain: Mike Kovaleski

9/13	L	Michigan	23–24	H
9/20	L	Michigan State	15–20	A
9/27	W	Purdue	41–9	H
10/4	L	Alabama	10–28	A*
10/11	L	Pittsburgh	9–10	H
10/18	W	Air Force	31–3	H
11/1	W	Navy (at Baltimore)	33–14	N
11/8	W	SMU	61–29	H
11/15	L	Penn State	19–24	H
11/22	L	Louisiana State	19–21	A
11/29	W	USC	38–37	A
		Total Points	299–219	

*at Legion Field, Birmingham, Alabama

1987

Coach: Lou Holtz
Record: 8–4–0
Captains: Chuck Lanza, Byron Spruell

9/12	W	Michigan	26–7	A
9/19	W	Michigan State	31–8	H
9/26	W	Purdue	44–20	A
10/10	L	Pittsburgh	22–30	A
10/17	W	Air Force	35–14	A
10/24	W	USC	26–15	H
10/31	W	Navy	56–13	H
11/7	W	Boston College	32–25	H
11/14	W	Alabama	37–6	H
11/21	L	Penn State	20–21	A
11/28	L	Miami	0–24	A
		Total Points	329–183	

COTTON BOWL

1/1	L	Texas A&M (at Dallas)	10–35	N

1988

Coach: Lou Holtz
Record: 12–0–0
Captains: Ned Bolcar, Mark Green, Andy Heck

9/10	W	Michigan	19–17	H
9/17	W	Michigan State	20–3	A

9/24	W	Purdue	52–7	H
10/1	W	Stanford	42–14	H
10/8	W	Pittsburgh	30–20	A
10/15	W	Miami	31–30	H
10/22	W	Air Force	41–13	H
10/29	W	Navy (at Baltimore)	22–7	N
11/5	W	Rice	54–11	H
11/19	W	Penn State	21–3	H
11/26	W	USC	27–10	A
		Total Points	359–135	

FIESTA BOWL

1/2	W	West Virginia (at Tempe, Ariz.)	34–21	N

1989

Coach: Lou Holtz
Record: 12–1–0
Captains: Ned Bolcar, Anthony Johnson, Tony Rice

8/31	W	Virginia (at Giants Stadium)	36–13	N
9/16	W	Michigan	24–19	A
9/23	W	Michigan State	21–3	H
9/30	W	Purdue	40–7	A
10/7	W	Stanford	27–17	A
10/14	W	Air Force	41–27	A
10/21	W	USC	28–24	H
10/28	W	Pittsburgh	45–7	H
11/4	W	Navy	41–0	H
11/11	W	SMU	59–6	H
11/18	W	Penn State	34–23	A
11/25	L	Miami	10–27	A
		Total Points	406–173	

ORANGE BOWL

1/1	W	Colorado (at Miami)	21–6	N

1990

Coach: Lou Holtz
Record: 9–3–0
Captains: Mike Heldt, Todd Lyght, Ricky Watters, Chris Zorich

9/15	W	Michigan	28–24	H
9/22	W	Michigan State	20–19	A
9/29	W	Purdue	37–11	H
10/6	L	Stanford	31–36	H
10/13	W	Air Force	57–27	H
10/20	W	Miami	29–20	H
10/27	W	Pittsburgh	31–22	A
11/3	W	Navy (at Giants Stadium)	52–31	N
11/10	W	Tennessee	34–29	A

11/17	L	Penn State	21–24	H
11/24	W	USC	10–6	A
		Total Points	350–249	

ORANGE BOWL

1/1	L	Colorado (at Miami)	9–10	N

1991

Coach: Lou Holtz
Record: 10–3–0
Captain: Rodney Culver

9/7	W	Indiana	49–27	H
9/14	L	Michigan	14–24	A
9/21	W	Michigan State	49–10	H
9/28	W	Purdue	45–20	A
10/5	W	Stanford	42–26	A
10/12	W	Pittsburgh	42–7	H
10/19	W	Air Force	28–15	A
10/26	W	USC	24–20	H
11/2	W	Navy	38–0*	H
11/9	L	Tennessee	34–35**	H
11/16	L	Penn State	13–35	A
11/30	W	Hawaii	48–42	A
		Total Points	426–261	

* Three-hundredth game played in Notre Dame Stadium
** Notre Dame's seven-hundredth victory

SUGAR BOWL

1/1	W	Florida (at New Orleans)	39–28	N

1992

Coach: Lou Holtz
Record: 10–1–1
Captains: Demetrius DuBose, Rick Mirer

9/5	W	Northwestern (at Soldier Field)	42–7	N
9/12	T	Michigan	17–17	H
9/19	W	Michigan State	52–31	A
9/26	W	Purdue	48–0	H
10/3	L	Stanford	16–33	H
10/10	W	Pittsburgh	52–21	A
10/24	W	Brigham Young	42–16	H
10/31	W	Navy (at Giants Stadium)	38–7	N
11/7	W	Boston College	54–7	H
11/14	W	Penn State	17–16	H
11/28	W	USC	31–23	A
		Total Points	409–178	

COTTON BOWL

1/1	W	Texas A&M (at Dallas)	28–3	N

1993
Coach: Lou Holtz
Record: 11–1–0
Captains: Jeff Burris, Tom Ruddy, Aaron Taylor,
Bryant Young

9/4	W	Northwestern	27–12	H
9/11	W	Michigan	27–23	A
9/18	W	Michigan State	36–14	H
9/25	W	Purdue	17–0	A
10/2	W	Stanford	48–20	A
10/9	W	Pittsburgh	44–0	H
10/16	W	Brigham Young	45–20	A
10/23	W	USC	31–13	H
10/30	W	Navy (at Veterans Stadium)	58–27	N
11/13	W	Florida State	31–24	H
11/20	L	Boston College	39–41	H
		Total Points	403–194	

COTTON BOWL

1/1	W	Texas A&M (at Dallas)	24–21	N

1994
Coach: Lou Holtz
Record: 6–5–1
Captains: Lee Becton, Justin Goheen, Brian
Hamilton, Ryan Leahy

9/3	W	Northwestern (at Soldier Field)	42–15	N
9/10	L	Michigan	24–26	H
9/17	W	Michigan State	21–20	A
9/24	W	Purdue	39–21	H
10/1	W	Stanford	34–15	H
10/8	L	Boston College	11–30	A
10/15	L	Brigham Young	14–21	H
10/29	W	Navy	58–21	H
11/12	L	Florida State (at Citrus Bowl)	16–23	N
11/19	W	Air Force	42–30	H
11/26	T	USC	17–17	A
		Total Points	318–239	

FIESTA BOWL

1/2	L	Colorado (at Tempe, Ariz.)	24–41	N

1995
Coach: Lou Holtz
Record: 9–3–0
Captains: Paul Grasmanis, Ryan Leahy,
Derrick Mayes, S. Wooden, D. Zeigler

9/2	L	Northwestern	15–17	H
9/9	W	Purdue	35–28	A
9/16	W	Vanderbilt	41–0	H

9/23	W	Texas	55–27	H
9/30	L	Ohio State	26–45	A
10/7	W	Washington	29–21	A
10/14	W	Army (at Giants Stadium)	28–27	N
10/21	W	USC	38–10	H
10/28	W	Boston College	20–10	W
11/4	W	Navy	35–17	W
11/18	W	Air Force	44–14	W
		Total Points	366–216	

ORANGE BOWL

1/1	L	Florida State (at Miami)	26–31	N

1996
Coach: Lou Holtz
Record: 8–3–0
Captains: Lyron Cobbins, Marc Edwards,
Ron Powlus

9/5	W	Vanderbilt	14–7	A
9/14	W	Purdue	35–0	H
9/21	W	Texas	27–24	A
9/28	L	Ohio State	16–29	H
10/12	W	Washington	54–20	H
10/19	L	Air Force	17–20*	H
11/2	W	Navy	54–27	N
11/9	W	Boston College	48–21	A
11/16	W	Pittsburgh	60–6	H
11/23	W	Rutgers	62–0	H
11/30	L	USC	20–27**	A
		Total Points	407–181	

*one overtime
**Notre Dame's thousandth game

THE BOB DAVIE YEARS
Two seasons: 16–9 (.640)

1997
Coach: Bob Davie
Record: 7–6–0
Captains: Melvin Dansby, Ron Powlus,
Allen Rossum

9/6	W	Georgia Tech	17–13	H
9/13	L	Purdue	17–28	A
9/20	L	Michigan State	7–23	H
9/27	L	Michigan	14–21	A
10/4	L	Stanford	15–33	A
10/11	W	Pittsburgh	45–21	A
10/18	L	USC	17–20	H
10/25	W	Boston College	52–20	H
11/1	W	Navy	21–17	H
11/15	W	Louisiana State	24–6	A

11/22	W	West Virginia	21–14	H
11/29	W	Hawaii	23–22	A
		Total Points	273–238	

INDEPENDENCE BOWL

12/28	L	Louisiana State (at Shreveport, La.)	9–27	N

1998

Coach: Bob Davie
Record: 9–3
Captains: Bobbie Howard, Kory Minor, Mike Rosenthal
Rededication of Notre Dame Stadium

9/5	W	Michigan	36–20	H
9/12	L	Michigan State	23–45	A
9/26	W	Purdue	31–30	H
10/3	W	Stanford	35–17	H
10/10	W	Arizona State	28–9	A
10/24	W	Army	20–17	H
10/31	W	Baylor	27–3	H
11/7	W	Boston College	31–26	A
11/14	W	Navy (at Jack Kent Cooke Stadium)	30–0	A
11/21	W	Louisiana State	39–36	H
11/28	L	USC	0–10	A
		Total Points	300–213	

GATOR BOWL

1/1	L	Georgia Tech (at Jacksonville)	28–35	N

1999

Coach: Bob Davie
Record: 5–7
Captain: Jarious Jackson

8/28	W	Kansas*	48–13	H
9/4	L	Michigan	22–26	A#
9/11	L	Purdue	23–28	A
9/18	L	Michigan State	13–23	H
10/2	W	Oklahoma	34–30	H
10/9	W	Arizona State	48–17	H
10/16	W	USC	25–24	H
10/30	W	Navy	28–24	H
11/6	L	Tennessee	14–38	A
11/13	L	Pittsburgh	27–37	A
11/20	L	Boston College	29–31	H
11/27	L	Stanford	37–40	A
		Total Points	348–331	

*State of Indiana Eddie Robinson Classic
#Largest regular-season attendance in NCAA history at time of game

2000

Coach: Bob Davie
Record: 9–3
Captains: Anthony Denman, Jabari Holloway, Grant Irons, Dan O'Leary

9/2	W	Texas A&M	24–10	H
9/9	L	Nebraska	24–27	H
9/16	W	Purdue	23–21	H
9/23	L	Michigan State	21–27	A
10/7	W	Stanford	20–14	H
10/14	W	Navy (at Orlando, FL)	45–14	N
10/21	W	West Virginia	42–28	A
10/28	W	Air Force	34–31	H
11/11	W	Boston College	28–16	H
11/18	W	Rutgers	45–17	A
11/25	W	USC	38–21	A
		Total Points	344–226	

FIESTA BOWL

1/1	L	Oregon State (at Tempe, AZ)	9–41	N

NOTRE DAME'S CONSENSUS NATIONAL CHAMPIONSHIPS

Year	Record	Coach	Year	Record	Coach
1924	10–0	Knute Rockne	1949	10–0	Frank Leahy
1929	9–0	Knute Rockne	1966	9–0–1	Ara Parseghian
1930	10–0	Knute Rockne	1973	11–0	Ara Parseghian
1943	9–1	Frank Leahy	1977	11–1	Dan Devine
1946	8–0–1	Frank Leahy	1988	12–0	Lou Holtz
1947	9–0	Frank Leahy			

NOTRE DAME'S BOWL APPEARANCES

Bowl	Date	Opponent	Score	Bowl	Date	Opponent	Score
Rose	1/1/25	Stanford	27-10 (W)	Cotton	1/1/88	Texas A&M	35-10 (L)
Cotton	1/1/70	Texas	21-17 (L)	Fiesta	1/2/89	West Virginia	34-21 (W)
Cotton	1/1/71	Texas	24-11 (W)	Orange	1/1/90	Colorado	21-6 (W)
Orange	1/1/73	Nebraska	40-6 (L)	Orange	1/1/91	Colorado	10-9 (L)
Sugar	12/31/73	Alabama	24-23 (W)	Sugar	1/1/92	Florida	39-28 (W)
Orange	1/1/75	Alabama	13-11 (W)	Cotton	1/1/93	Texas A&M	28-3 (W)
Gator	12/27/76	Penn State	20-9 (W)	Cotton	1/1/94	Texas A&M	24-21 (W)
Cotton	1/2/78	Texas	38-10 (W)	Fiesta	1/2/95	Colorado	41-24 (L)
Cotton	1/1/79	Houston	35-34 (W)	Orange	1/1/96	Florida State	31-26 (L)
Sugar	1/1/81	Georgia	17-10 (L)	Independence	12/28/97	LSU	27-9 (L)
Liberty	12/29/83	Boston College	19-18 (W)	Gator	1/1/99	Georgia Tech	31-28 (L)
Aloha	12/29/84	SMU	27-20 (L)	Fiesta	1/1/01	Oregon Tech	41-9 (L)

Notre Dame's College Football Hall of Fame Inductees

Year	Player	Position	Year	Player	Position
1951	George Gipp	HB	1978	Frank Hoffman	G
	Elmer Layden	FB	1979	John Lattner	HB
1954	Frank Carideo	QB	1982	Bert Metzger	G
1958	Harry Stuhldreher	QB	1983	Bill Fischer	G
1960	Johnny Lujack	QB		Bill Shakespeare	HB
1963	George Connor	OT	1984	Emil Sitko	HB
1965	Jack Cannon	G	1985	Paul Hornung	QB
1966	Edgar Miller	OT		Fred Miller	T
1968	Adam Walsh	C	1987	Tommy Yarr	C
1970	Don Miller	HB	1988	Bob Williams	QB
1971	Louis Salmon	FB	1990	Wayne Miller	E
1972	Angelo Bertelli	QB	1992	Jim Lynch	LB
	Ray Eichenlaub	FB	1993	Alan Page	DE
1973	Leon Hart	TE	1994	Jerry Groom	C/LB
1974	Marchmont Schwartz	HB	1995	Jim Martin	E/T
1974	Heartley Anderson	G	1997	Ken MacAfee	TE
1975	John Smith	G	1999	Ross Brenner	DE
1976	Creighton Miller	HB	2000	Bob Dove	E
1977	Ziggy Czarobski	OT			

Notre Dame's Pro Football Hall of Fame Inductees

Player	Team(s)	Position	Player	Team(s)	Position
Curly Lambeau	Green Bay	FB/Coach	George Connor	Chicago	C
George Trafton	Chicago	C	Paul Hornung	Green Bay	HB
Wayne Millner	Boston/ Washington	E	Alan Page	Minnesota/ Chicago	DE

Notre Dame's Head Coaches

Year(s)	Coach	W	L	T	Pct.	Year(s)	Coach	W	L	T	Pct.
1887–89, 92–93	No head coaches	7	4	1	.625	1918–30	Knute Rockne	105	12	5	.881
						1931–33	Hunk Anderson	16	9	2	.630
1894	J. L. Morison	3	1	1	.700	1934–40	Elmer Layden	47	13	3	.770
1895	H. G. Hadden	3	1	0	.750	1941–43, 46–53	Frank Leahy	87	11	9	.855
1896–98	Frank E. Hering	12	6	1	.658						
1899	James McWeeney	6	3	1	.650	1944	Ed McKeever	8	2	0	.800
1900–01	Patrick O'Dea	14	4	2	.750	1945–63	Hugh Devore	9	9	1	.500
1902–03	James Faragher	14	2	2	.833	1954–58	Terry Brennan	32	18	0	.640
1904	Louis Salmon	5	3	0	.625	1959–62	Joe Kuharich	17	23	0	.425
1905	Henry J. McGlew	5	4	0	.556	1964–74	Ara Parseghian	95	17	4	.836
1906–07	Thomas Barry	12	1	1	.893	1975–80	Dan Devine	53	16	1	.764
1908	Victor M. Place	8	1	0	.889	1981–85	Gerry Faust	30	26	1	.535
1909–10	Frank C. Longman	11	1	2	.857	1986–96	Lou Holtz	100	30	2	.765
1911–12	John L. Marks	13	0	2	.933	1997–present	Bob Davie	16	9	0	.640
1913–17	Jesse C. Harper	34	5	1	.863						

Coach of the Year Award Winners

The American Football Coaches Association (AFCA), in conjunction with Kodak, has honored a Coach of the Year since 1935, and the Football Writers Association of America (FWAA) has done the same since 1957. Since these awards have been presented, three Notre Dame coaches have been the recipients:

1941   (AFCA) Frank Leahy
1964   (AFCA) Ara Parseghian (a tie with Frank Broyles of Arkansas)
1964   (FWAA) Ara Parseghian
1988   (FWAA) Lou Holtz

In 1988, Holtz also was named Coach of the Year by the *Sporting News*, United Press International, CBS Sports, and *Football News*. He was one of four finalists for the FWAA award, named for former University of Alabama coach Paul "Bear" Bryant, in three straight seasons (1987–89).

Holtz was one of three finalists for the 1993 *Football News* Coach of the Year award.

Notre Dame's NCAA Records

INDIVIDUAL RECORDS, ANNUAL CHAMPIONS

Rushing—Creighton Miller, 1943, 151 carries for 911 yards

Punt Returns—Nick Rassas, 1965, 24 for 459 yards; Allen Rossum, 1996, 15 for 344 yards

Interceptions—Tony Carey, 8 for 121 yards; Mike Townsend, 1972, 10 for 39 yards

Kick Scoring—Menil Mavraides, 1953, 27 points

Kickoff Returns—Raghib Ismail, 1988, 36.1-yard average (12 returns for 433 yards)

Highest Percentage of Field Goals Made of 40 Yards or More—John Carney, 1984, .909 (10 of 11)

Highest Percentage of Field Goals Made of 40 to 49 Yards—John Carney, 1984, 1.000 (10 of 10)

OTHER RECORDS

Most Consecutive Career Field Goals Made of 40 to 49 Yards—John Carney, 1984–85, 12

Most Touchdowns Scored on Punt Returns in a Single Game—Tim Brown, 1987 vs. Michigan State, 2; Allen Rossum, 1996 vs. Pittsburgh, 2 (held by many others)

Most Touchdowns Scored on Kickoff Returns in a Single Game—Raghib Ismail, 1988 vs. Rice, 2; 1989 vs. Michigan, 2 (held by six others, though Ismail is the only player in history to score twice in two games)

Most returns for touchdowns—Allen Rossum (9): kickoff returns, 3 (99 yards, Sept. 14, 1996, vs. Purdue; 93 yards, Oct. 11, 1997 vs. Pittsburgh; 80 yards, Oct. 25, 1997, vs. Boston College); punt returns, 3 (57 yards, Oct. 19, 1996, vs. Air Force; 55 yards, Nov. 16, 1996, vs. Pittsburgh; 83 yards, Nov. 17, 1996, vs. Pittsburgh); interception returns, 3 (29 yards, Sept. 23, 1995, vs. Texas; 76 yards, Oct. 7, 1995, vs. Washington; 37 yards, Nov. 29, 1997, vs. Hawaii).

TEAM RECORDS, ANNUAL CHAMPIONS

Total Offense—1943, 418.0 yards per game; 1946, 441.3 yards per game; 1949, 434.8 yards per game.

Rushing Offense—1943, 313.7 yards per game; 1946, 340.1 yards per game.

Scoring Offense—1966, 36.2 points per game.

Punt Returns—1958, 17.6 yards per return.

Kickoff Returns—1957, 27.6 yards per return; 1966, 29.6 yards per return.

Total Defense—1946, 141.7 yards per game; 1974, 195.2 yards per game.

Rushing Defense—1974, 102.8 yards per game.

Scoring Defense—1946, 2.7 points per game.

Total Offense in a Season, Most Plays per Game—92.4, 1970 (924 in 10 games).

Pass Defense, Lowest Completion Percentage Allowed in a Season (minimum of 200 attempts)—.333, 1967 (102 of 306).

Pass Defense, Fewest Yards Allowed per Attempt in a Season (minimum of 300 attempts)—3.78, 1967 (306 for 1,158 yards).

Pass Defense, Fewest Yards Allowed per Completion in a Season (minimum of 150 completions)—9.5, 1993 (263 for 2,502 yards).

Pass Defense, Lowest Completion Percentage Allowed in a Season (minimum 200 attempts)—.333, 1967 (102 of 306).

Punt Return Defense, Fewest Returns Allowed in a Season—5 (for 52 yards), 1968 (tied with Nebraska in 1995).

Touchdowns Scored on Kickoff Returns in a Single Game—2, vs. Rice, 1988, 2, vs. Michigan 1989 (held by many teams).

Touchdowns Scored on Punt Returns in a Single Game—3, vs. Pittsburgh, 1996 (held by many teams).

Defensive Extra Point Attempts Against in a Single Game—2, vs. Rice 1988 (2 returns, 1 scored).

Notre Dame's All-Time Leaders (Through 2000)

(* indicates a Notre Dame record)

RUSHING, CAREER (Based on Net Yards)

Year	Carries	Yards	Avg.	TDs	Year	Carries	Yards	Avg.	TDs
1. Autry Denson					7. Randy Kinder				
1995	137	695	5.1	8	1993	89	537	6.0	2
1996	202	1,179	5.8	8	1994	119	702	5.9	4
1997	264	1,268	5.1	12	1995	143	809	5.7	9
1998	251	1,274	5.1	15	1996	53	247	4.7	3
Total	854	4,318*	5.1	43	Total	404	2,295	5.7	18
2. Allen Pinkett					8. Tony Brooks				
1982	107	532	5.0	5	1987	54	262	4.9	1
1983	252	1,394	5.5	16	1988	117	667	5.7	2
1984	275	1,105	4.0	17	1990	105	451	4.3	4
1985	255	1,100	4.3	11	1991	147	894	6.1	5
Total	889*	4,131	4.6	49*	Total	423	2,274	5.4	12
3. Vagas Ferguson					9. Emil Sitko				
1976	81	350	4.3	2	1946	54	346	6.4	3
1977	80	493	6.2	6	1947	60	426	7.1	4
1978	211	1,192	5.6	7	1948	129	742	5.8	9
1979	301	1,437	4.8	17	1949	120	712	5.9	9
Total	673	3,472	5.2	32	Total	362	2,226	6.1	25
4. Jerome Heavens					10. Neil Worden				
1975	129	756	5.9	5	1951	181	676	3.7	8
1976	54	204	3.8	0	1952	150	504	3.4	10
1977	229	994	4.3	6	1953	145	859	5.9	11
1978	178	728	4.1	4	Total	476	2,039	4.3	29
Total	590	2,682	4.5	15	11. Lee Becton				
5. Phil Carter					1991	15	62	4.1	0
1979	27	145	5.4	0	1992	68	373	5.5	3
1980	186	822	4.4	6	1993	164	1,044	6.4	6
1981	165	727	4.4	6	1994	100	550	5.5	3
1982	179	715	4.0	2	Total	347	2,029	5.8	12
Total	557	2,409	4.3	4	12. Mark Green				
6. George Gipp					1985	5	64	12.8	0
1917	63	244	3.9	0	1986	96	406	4.2	2
1918	98	541	5.5	6	1987	146	861	5.9	6
1919	106	729	6.9	7	1988	135	646	4.8	7
1920	102	827	8.1	8	Total	382	1,977	5.2	15
Total	369	2,341	6.3	21					

Year	Carries	Yards	Avg.	TDs
13. Marchy Schwartz				
1929	65	326	5.0	3
1930	124	927	7.5	9
1931	146	692	4.7	5
Total	335	1,945	5.8	17
14. Don Miller				
1922	87	472	5.4	3
1923	89	698	7.5	9
1924	107	763	7.1	5
Total	283	1933	6.8*	17
15. Tony Rice				
1987	89	337	3.8	7
1988	121	700	5.8	9
1989	174	884	5.1	7
Total	384	1,921	4.9	23
16. Jerome Bettis				
1990	15	115	7.7	1
1991	168	972	5.8	16
1992	154	825	5.4	10
Total	337	1,912	5.7	27
17. Jim Crowley				
1922	75	566	7.5	5
1923	88	536	6.1	4
1924	131	739	5.6	6
Total	294	1,841	6.3	15
18. Christie Flanagan				
1925	99	556	5.6	7
1926	68	535	7.9	4
1927	118	731	6.2	4
Total	285	1,822	6.4	15
19. Ricky Watters				
1987	69	373	5.4	3
1988	30	71	2.4	0
1989	118	791	6.7	10
1990	108	579	5.4	8
Total	325	1,814	5.6	21
20. Al Hunter				
1973	32	150	4.7	3
1975	117	558	4.8	8
1976	233	1,058	4.5	12
Total	382	1,766	4.6	23

RUSHING, SEASON

Year	Carries	Yards	Avg.	TDs
1. Vagas Ferguson				
1979	301*	1,437*	4.8	17*
2. Allen Pinkett				
1983	252	1,394	5.5	16
3. Reggie Brooks				
1992	167	1,343	8.0	13
4. Autry Denson				
1998	251	1,274	5.1	15
5. Vagas Ferguson				
1978	211	1,192	5.6	7
6. Autry Denson				
1996	202	1,179	5.8	8
7. Allen Pinkett				
1984	275	1,105	4.0	17*
8. Allen Pinkett				
1985	255	1,100	4.3	11
9. Al Hunter				
1976	233	1,058	4.5	12
10. Lee Becton				
1993	164	1,044	6.4	6
11. Jerome Heavens				
1977	229	994	4.3	6
12. Jerome Bettis				
1991	168	972	5.8	16
13. Marchy Schwartz				
1930	124	927	7.5	9
14. Creighton Miller				
1943	151	911	6.0	10
15. Jim Stone				
1980	192	908	4.7	7
16. Tony Brooks				
1991	147	894	6.1	5
17. Tony Rice				
1989	174	884	5.1	7
18. Mark Green				
1987	146	861	5.9	6
19. Neil Worden				
1953	145	859	5.9	11
20. Wayne Bullock				
1974	203	855	4.2	12
21. George Gipp				
1920	102	827	8.1*	8

RUSHING, GAME

Carries	Yards	Avg.	TDs
1. Vagas Ferguson (vs. Georgia Tech., 1978)			
30	255*	8.5	1
2. Phil Carter (vs. Michigan State, 1980)			
40*	254	6.4	1
3. Reggie Brooks (vs. USC, 1992)			
19	227	11.9	3
4. Jim Stone (vs. Miami, 1980)			
38	224	5.9	1
5. Vagas Ferguson (vs. Navy, 1978)			
18	219	12.2	1
6. Allen Pinkett (vs. Penn State, 1983)			
36	217	6.0	4
7. Jim Stone (vs. Navy, 1980)			
33	211	6.4	2

RUSHING, GAME (cont'd)

Carries	Yards	Avg.	TDs
8. Reggie Brooks (vs. Purdue, 1992)			
15	205	13.6	3
9. Jerome Heavens (vs. Army, 1977)			
34	200	5.9	1
10. Allen Pinkett (vs. Air Force, 1983)			
27	197	7.3	1
11. Autry Denson (vs. Baylor, 1998)			
24	189	7.9	1
Allen Pinkett (vs. Penn State, l984)			
34	189	5.6	4
12. Emil Sitko (vs. Michigan State, 1948)			
24	186	7.8	1
13. Marchy Schwartz (vs. Carnegie Tech., 1931)			
18	185	10.3	1
Vagas Ferguson (vs. USC, 1979)			
25	185	7.4	2
14. George Gipp (vs. Kalamazoo, 1920)			
16	183	11.4	1
15. Phil Carter (vs. Air Force, 1980)			
29	181	6.2	1
Al Hunter (vs. South Carolina, 1976)			
32	181	5.7	0
16. Jim Morse (vs. USC, 1954)			
19	179	9.4	1
17. Jerome Bettis (vs. Stanford, 1991)			
24	179	7.5	3

PASSING, CAREER (Based on Completions)

	Att.	Comp.	Int.	Pct.	Yards	TDs
1. Ron Powlus						
1994	222	119	9	.536	1,729	19
1995	217	124	7	.571	1,853	12
1996	232	133	4	.573	1,942	12
1997	298	182	7	.611	2,078	9
Total	969*	558*	27	.575	7,602*	52*
2. Steve Beuerlein						
1983	145	75	6	.517	1,061	4
1984	232	140	18	.603	1,920	7
1985	214	107	13	.500	1,335	3
1986	259	151	7	.583	2,211	13
Total	850	473	44*	.556	6,527	27
3. Rick Mirer						
1989	30	15	1	.500	180	0
1990	200	110	6	.550	1,824	8
1991	234	132	10	.564	2,117	18
1992	234	120	6	.513	1,876	15
Total	698	377	23	.540	5,997	41
4. Jarious Jackson						
1996	15	10	0	.667	181	3
1997	17	8	1	.471	146	1
1998	188	104	6	.553	1,740	13

	Att.	Comp.	Int.	Pct.	Yards	TDs
1999	316	184	14	.582	2,753	17
Total	536	306	21	.571	4,820	34
5. Terry Hanratty						
1966	147	78	10	.531	1,247	8
1967	206	110	15	.534	1,439	9
1968	197	116	9	.588	1,466	10
Total	550	304	34	.533	4,152	27
6. Blair Kiel						
1980	124	48	5	.387	531	0
1981	151	67	10	.444	936	7
1982	219	118	10	.539	1,273	3
1983	115	64	7	.557	910	7
Total	609	297	32	.488	3,650	17
7. Joe Theismann						
1968	49	27	5	.551	451	2
1969	192	108	16	.562	1,531	13
1970	268	155	14	.578	2,529	16
Total	509	290	35	.569	4,411	31
8. Joe Montana						
1975	66	28	8	.424	507	4
1977	189	99	8	.524	1,604	11
1978	260	141	9	.542	2,010	10
Total	515	268	25	.520	4,121	25
9. Tom Clements						
1972	162	83	12	.512	1,163	8
1973	113	60	6	.531	882	8
1974	215	122	11	.567	1,549	8
Total	490	265	29	.541	3,594	24
10. Ralph Guglielmi						
1951	53	27	4	.509	438	0
1952	142	61	9	.429	683	4
1953	113	52	5	.460	792	8
1954	127	68	7	.535	1,160	6
Total	435	208	24	.478	3,117	18

PASSING, SEASON

	Att.	Comp.	Int.	Pct.	Yards	TDs
1. Jarious Jackson						
(1997)	316*	184*	14	.592	2,753*	17
2. Ron Powlus						
(1997)	298	182	7	.611	2,078	9
3. Joe Theismann						
(1970)	268	155	14	.578	2,429	16
4. Steve Beuerlein						
(1986)	259	151	7	.583	2,211	13
5. Joe Montana						
(1978)	260	141	9	.542	2,010	10
6. Steve Beuerlein						
(1984)	232	140	18	.603*	1,920	7
7. Ron Powlus						
(1996)	232	133	4	.573	1,942	12

	Att.	Comp.	Int.	Pct.	Yards	TDs
8. Rick Mirer						
(1991)	234	132	10	.564	2,117	18
9. Ron Powlus						
(1995)	217	124	7	.571	1,853	12
10. Tom Clements						
(1974)	215	122	11	.567	1,549	8

PASS RECEIVING, CAREER
(Based on Receptions)

	Rec.	Yards	Avg.	TDs
1. Tom Gatewood				
1969	47	743	15.8	8
1970	77	1,123	14.6	7
1971	33	417	12.6	4
Total	157*	2,283	14.5	19
2. Jim Seymour				
1966	48	862	17.9	8
1967	37	515	13.9	4
1968	53	736	13.9	4
Total	138	2,113	15.3	16
3. Tim Brown				
1984	28	340	12.1	1
1985	25	397	15.9	3
1986	45	910	20.2	5
1987	39	846	21.7	3
Total	137	2,493	18.2	12
4. Derrick Mayes				
1992	10	272	27.2	3
1993	24	512	21.3	2
1994	47	847	18.0	11
1995	48	881	18.4	6
Total	129	2,512*	19.4	22*
5. Ken MacAfee				
1974	14	146	10.4	1
1975	26	333	12.8	5
1976	34	483	14.2	3
1977	54	797	14.8	6
Total	128	1,759	13.7	15
6. Tony Hunter				
1979	27	690	25.5	2
1980	23	303	13.2	1
1981	28	397	14.2	2
1982	42	507	12.1	0
Total	120	1,897	15.8	5
7. Malcolm Johnson				
1995	0	0	0	0
1996	25	449	18.0	2
1997	42	596	14.2	2
1998	43	692	16.1	6
Total	110	1,737	15.7	10

PASS RECEIVING, SEASON

	Rec.	Yards	Avg.	TDs
1. Tom Gatewood				
(1970)	77*	1,123*	14.6	7
2. Jack Snow				
(1964)	60	1,114	18.6	9
3. Ken MacAfee				
(1977)	54	797	14.8	6
4. Jim Seymour				
(1968)	53	736	13.9	4
5. Jim Seymour				
(1966)	48	862	17.9	8
Derrick Mayes				
(1995)	48	881	18.4	6
6. Derrick Mayes				
(1994)	47	847	18.0	11*
Tom Gatewood				
(1969)	47	743	15.8	8
7. Tim Brown				
(1986)	45	910	20.2	5
Bobby Brown				
(1997)	45	543	12.1	6

TOTAL OFFENSE, CAREER
(Based on Total Offensive Yards)

	Plays	Yards	Avg.
1. Ron Powlus			
1994	300	1,681	5.6
1995	275	1,819	6.6
1996	285	1,950	6.8
1997	344	2,029	6.0
Total	1204*	7,479*	6.2
2. Rick Mirer			
1989	42	212	5.0
1990	298	2,022	6.8
1991	309	2,423	7.8
1992	302	2,034	6.7
Total	951	6,691*	7.0
3. Steve Beuerlein			
1983	168	1,052	6.3
1984	290	1,845	6.4
1985	257	1,316	5.1
1986	312	2,246	7.2
Total	1027*	6,459	6.3
4. Jarious Jackson			
1996	26	197	7.6
1997	25	182	7.3
1998	280	2,101	7.5
1999	456	3,217	7.1
Total	787	5,697	7.2
5. Joe Theismann			
1968	118	710	6.0
1969	308	1,909	6.2

TOTAL OFFENSE, CAREER *(cont'd)*
(Based on Total Offensive Yards)

	Plays	Yards	Avg.
1970	391	2,813	7.2
Total	807	5,432	6.7
6. Tony Rice			
1987	171	1,000	5.8
1988	259	1,876	7.2
1989	311	2,006	6.5
Total	741	4,882	6.6
7. Terry Hanratty			
1966	197	1,371	7.0
1967	281	1,622	5.8
1968	253	1,745	6.9
Total	731	4,738	6.5

TOTAL OFFENSE, SEASON

	Plays	Yards	Avg.
1. Jarious Jackson (1999)	456*	3,297	7.1
2. Joe Theismann (1970)	391*	2,813*	7.2
3. Rick Mirer (1991)	309	2,423	7.8
4. Steve Beuerlein (1986)	312	2,246	7.2
5. Joe Montana (1978)	332	2,114	6.4
6. Jarious Jackson (1998)	280	2,101	7.5
7. John Huarte (1964)	242	2,069	8.5
6. Rick Mirer (1992)	302	2,034	6.7
7. Ron Powlus (1997)	344	2,029	5.9
8. Rick Mirer (1990)	298	2,022	6.8

PUNT RETURNS, CAREER
(Based on Average per Return)

	No.	Yards	Avg.	TDs
1. Allen Rossum				
1994	0	0	0.0	0
1995	0	0	0.0	0
1996	15	344	22.9	3
1997	12	83	6.9	0
Total	27	427	15.8*	3*
2. Nick Rassas				
1963	0	0	0.0	0
1964	15	153	10.2	0
1965	24	459	19.1	3
Total	39	612	15.7	3*
3. Raghib Ismail				
1988	5	72	14.4	0

	No.	Yards	Avg.	TDs
1989	7	113	16.1	1
1990	13	151	11.6	0
Total	25	336	13.4	1
4. Ricky Watters				
1988	19	253	13.3	2
1989	15	201	13.4	1
Total	34	454	13.35	3*
5. Tim Brown				
1986	2	753	7.5	0
1987	34	401	11.8	3
Total	36	476	13.2	3*
6. Bill Gay				
1947	1	20	20.0	0
1948	12	210	17.5	0
1949	19	254	13.4	0
1950	14	96	6.9	0
Total	46	580	12.6	0
7. Andy Puplis				
1935	2	68	34.0	0
1936	24	178	7.4	0
1937	21	281	13.4	0
Total	47	527	11.2	0

PUNT RETURNS, SEASON
(Minimum of 1.5 per Game)

	No.	Yards	Avg.	TDs
1. Allen Rossum (1996)	15	344**	20.2*	3*
2. Nick Rassas (1965)	244	59*	19.1*	3*
3. Andy Puplis (1937)	21	281	13.38	0
4. Bill Gay (1949)	19	254	13.37	0
5. Frank Dancewicz (1945)	18	240	13.33	0
6. Ricky Watters (1988)	19	253	13.31	2
7. Steve Juzwik (1941)	22	280	12.7	0
8. Jeff Burris (1991)	18	227	12.6	0
9. Frank Carideo (1929)	33	405	12.3	1
10. Tim Brown (1987)	34	401	11.8	3

**In 1996, Rossum had only 15 punt returns, which does not meet the 1.5 per game requirement. However, he still holds the record based on his return yards (344) divided by the minimum return amount of 17. Rossum actually averaged 22.9 yards per return in 1996.

KICKOFF RETURNS, CAREER
(Based on Average per Return)

	No.	Yards	Avg.	TDs
1. Paul Castner				
1920	2	55	27.5	0
1921	8	222	27.8	0
1922	11	490	44.5	2
Total	21	767	36.5*	2
2. Allen Rossum				
1995	3	84	31.3	0
1996	6	227	37.8	1
1997	20	570	28.5	2
Total	29	881	30.4	3
3. Nick Eddy				
1964	7	148	21.2	0
1965	3	63	21.0	0
1966	4	193	48.3	2
Total	14	404	28.9	2
4. Paul Hornung				
1954	1	58	58.0	0
1955	6	109	18.3	0
1956	16	496	31.0	1
Total	23	663	28.82	1
5. Clint Johnson				
1991	9	217	24.1	1
1992	8	152	19.0	0
1993	10	409	40.9	1
Total	27	778	28.81	2
6. Raghib Ismail				
1988	12	433	36.1	2
1989	20	502	25.1	2
1990	14	336	24.0	1
Total	46	1,271	27.6	5*

KICKOFF RETURNS, SEASON
(Minimum of 0.5 per Game)

	No.	Yards	Avg.	TDs
1. Paul Castner				
(1922)	114	90	44.5*	2*
2. John Lattner				
(1953)	8	331	41.4	2*
3. Clint Johnson				
(1993)	10	409	40.9	1
4. Allen Rossum				
(1996)	6	227	37.8	1
5. Raghib Ismail				
(1988)	12	433	36.1	2*
6. Paul Hornung				
(1956)	16	496	31.0	1
7. Christie Flanagan				
(1926)	6	183	30.5	1
8. Hiawatha Francisco				
(1984)	6	178	29.7	0

	No.	Yards	Avg.	TDs
9. Mike Miller				
(1992)	9	261	29.0	0
10. Chet Wynne				
(1921)	9	258	28.7	1
11. Greg Bell				
(1981)	13	371	28.5	1

PUNTING, CAREER
(Based on Average per Punt)

	No.	Yards	Avg.
1. Craig Hentrich			
1989	26	1,159	44.6
1990	34	1,526	44.9
1991	23	986	42.9
1992	35	1,534	43.8
Total	118	5,204	44.1*
2. Vince Phelan			
1987	50	2,044	40.9
3. Hunter Smith			
1995	38	1,382	36.4
1996	44	1,906	43.3
1997	35	1,462	41.8
Total	117	4,750	40.6
4. Bill Shakespeare			
1933	5	266	53.2
1934	41	1,638	40.0
1935	45	1,801	40.0
Total	91	3,705	40.71
5. Blair Kiel			
1980	66	2,649	40.1
1981	73	2,914	39.9
1982	77	3,267	42.4
1983	43	1,704	39.6
Total	259*	10,534*	40.67
6. Joe Restic			
1975	40	1,739	43.5
1976	63	2,627	41.7
1977	45	1,713	38.1
1978	61	2,330	38.2
Total	209	8,409	40.2
7. Brian Doherty			
1971	58	2,259	38.9
1972	43	1,650	38.4
1973	39	1,664	42.7
Total	140	5,573	39.8

PUNTING, SEASON

	No.	Yards	Avg.
1. Craig Hentrich			
(1990)	34	1,526	44.9*
2. Craig Hentrich			
(1989)	26	1,159	44.6
3. Craig Hentrich			
(1992)	35	1,534	43.8

PUNTING, SEASON *(cont'd)*

	No.	Yards	Avg.
4. Joe Restic			
(1975)	40	1,739	43.5
5. Hunter Smith			
(1996)	44	1,906	43.3
6. Craig Hentrich			
(1991)	23	986	42.9
7. Brian Doherty			
(1973)	39	1,664	42.7
8. Blair Kiel			
(1982)	77*	3,267*	42.4
9. Hunter Smith			
(1997)	35	2132	42.6
10. Joe Restic			
(1976)	63	2627	41.7

INTERCEPTIONS, CAREERS

	No.	Yards	Avg.	TDs
1. Luther Bradley				
1973	6	37	6.2	0
1975	4	135	33.8	1
1976	2	0	0.0	0
1977	5	46	9.2	0
Total	17*	218	12.8	1
2. Tom MacDonald				
1961	1	23	23.0	0
1962	9	81	9.0	0
1963	5	63	12.6	1
Total	15	167	11.1	1
3. Ralph Stepaniak				
1969	4	84	21.0	0
1970	6	55	9.2	0
1971	3	40	13.3	1
Total	13	179	13.8	1
Joe Restic				
1975	0	0	0.0	0
1976	4	92	23.0	0
1977	6	25	4.2	0
1978	3	59	19.7	1
Total	13	176	13.5	1
Clarence Ellis				
1969	3	98	32.6	1
1970	7	25	3.6	0
1971	3	34	11.3	0
Total	13	157	12.1	1
John Lattner				
1951	5	66	13.2	1
1952	4	58	14.5	0
1953	4	4	1.0	0
Total	13	128	9.8	1

	No.	Yards	Avg.	TDs
Mike Townsend				
1971	0	0	0.0	0
1972	10	39	3.9	0
1973	3	47	15.7	0
Total	13	86	6.6	0

INTERCEPTIONS, SEASON

	No.	Yards	Avg.	TDs
1. Mike Townsend				
(1972)	10*	39	3.9	0
2. Tom MacDonald				
(1962)	9	81	9.0	0
3. Tony Carey				
(1964)	8	121	15.1	0
Todd Lyght				
(1989)	8	42	5.3	0
Angelo Bertelli				
(1942)	8	41	5.1	0
4. Tom Schoen				
(1966)	7	118	16.0	2
Dave Duerson				
(1982)	7	104	14.9	0
5. Nick Rassas				
(1965)	6	197*	32.8	1
Luther Bradley				
(1973)	6	37	6.2	0
Joe Restic				
(1977)	6	25	4.2	0

SCORING, CAREER
(† indicates 2-point conversion)

	TDs	PATs	FGs	Pts.
1. Allen Pinkett				
1982	6	0	0	36
1983	18	1	0	110
1984	18	0	0	108
1985	11	0	0	66
Total	53*	1†	0	320*
2. Craig Hentrich				
1989	0	44	8	68
1990	0	41	16	89
1991	0	48	5	63
1992	0	44	10	74
Total	0	177*	39	294
3. Autry Denson				
1995	8	0	0	48
1996	10	0	0	60
1997	13	0	0	78
1998	15	0	0	90
Total	46	0	0	276

	TDs	PATs	FGs	Pts.
4. Louis "Red" Salmon				
1900	3	0	0	15
1901	7	13	1	53
1902	11	17	1	77
1903	15	30	0	105
Total	36	60	2	250
5. Dave Reeve				
1974	0	38	7	59
1975	0	24	11	57
1976	0	29	9	56
1977	0	39	12	75
Total	0	130	39	247
6. Stan Cofall				
1914	9	25	1	82
1915	9	17	0	71
1916	12	12	0	84
Total	30	60	2	246
7. John Carney				
1984	0	25	17	76
1985	0	21	13	60
1986	0	24	21	87
Total	0	70	51*	223

SCORING, SEASON

(† indicates 2-point conversion)

	No.	Yards	Avg.	TDs
1. Jerome Bettis				
(1991)	20*	00		120*
2. Allen Pinkett				
(1983)	18	1†	0	110
3. Allen Pinkett				
(1984)	18		0	108
4. Louis "Red" Salmon				
(1903)	15	30	0	105
5. Vagas Ferguson				
(1979)	17		0	102
6. Autry Denson				
(1988)	15		0	90
7. Craig Hentrich				
(1990)	0	41	16	89
8. Kevin Pendergast				
(1993)	0	45	14	87
John Carney				
(1986)	0	24	21*	87
10. Reggie Brooks				
(1992)	14	1†	0	86

FIELD GOALS, CAREER

	No.	Att.	Long	Under 40	Over 40
1. John Carney					
1984	17	19	48	7–8	10–11
1985	13	22	48	8–11	5–11
1986	21	28	49	16–18	5–10
Total	51*	69*	49	31–37	20–32
2. Craig Hentrich					
1989	8	15	32	8–11	0–4
1990	16	20	44	13–13	3–7
1991	5	8	35	5–7	0–1
1992	10	13	42	9–11	1–2
Total	39	56	44	35–42	4–14
3. Dave Reeve					
1974	7	10	45	6–	1–
1975	11	16	48	8–	3–
1976	9	18	53	5–	4–
1977	13	20	51	8–11	4–9
Total	39	64	53*	27–41	12–23
4. Mike Johnston					
1982	19	22	48	10–11	9–11
1983	12	21	49	10–14	2–7
Total	31	43	49	20–25	11–18
5. Harry Oliver					
1980	18	23	51	12–15	6–8
1981	6	13	43	5–8	1–5
Total	24	36	51	17–23	7–13
6. Chuck Male					
1978	9	12	47	6–7	3–5
1979	13	20	49	5–7	8–13
Total	22	32	49	11–14	11–18
7. Jim Sanson					
1996	6	9	39	6–8	0–1
1997	5	10	45	4–7	1–3
1998	11	15	48	10–11	1–4
Total	22	34	48	20–26	2–8

FIELD GOALS, SEASON

	No.	Att.	Long	Under 40	Over 40
1. John Carney					
(1986)	21*	28*	49	16–18	5–10
2. Mike Johnston					
(1982)	19	22	48	10–11	9–11
3. Harry Oliver					
(1980)	18	23	51	12–15	6–8

FIELD GOALS, SEASON *(cont'd)*

	No.	Att.	Long	Under 40	Over 40
4. John Carney					
(1984)	17	19	48	7–8	10–11
5. Craig Hentrich					
(1990)	16	20	44	13–13	3–7
6. Kevin Pendergast					
(1993)	14	19	47	11–14	3–5
Ted Gradel					
(1987)	14	18	49	11–13	3–5
7. John Carney					
(1985)	13	22	48	8–11	5–11
Chuck Male					
(1979)	13	20	49	5–7	8–13
Dave Reeve					
(1977)	13	20	51	8–11	4–9

NOTRE DAME'S YEARLY LEADERS

(* indicates a Notre Dame record)

RUSHING

		Carries	Yards			Carries	Yards
1918	George Gipp	98	541	1956	Paul Hornung	94	420
1919	George Gipp	106	729	1957	Nick Pietrosante	90	449
1920	George Gipp	102	827	1958	Nick Pietrosante	117	549
1921	John Mohardt	136	781	1959	Gerry Gray	50	256
1922	Jim Crowley	75	566	1960	Angelo Dabiero	80	325
1923	Don Miller	89	698	1961	Angelo Dabiero	92	637
1924	Don Miller	107	763	1962	Don Hogan	90	454
1925	Christie Flanagan	99	556	1963	Joe Kantor	88	330
1926	Christie Flanagan	68	535	1964	Bill Wolski	136	657
1927	Christie Flanagan	118	731	1965	Nick Eddy	115	582
1928	Jack Chevigny	120	539	1966	Nick Eddy	78	553
1929	Joe Savoldi	112	597	1967	Jeff Zimmerman	133	591
1930	Marchy Schwartz	124	927	1968	Bob Gladieux	152	713
1931	Marchy Schwartz	146	692	1969	Denny Allan	148	612
1932	George Melinkovich	88	503	1970	Ed Gulyas	118	534
1933	Nick Lukats	107	339	1971	Bob Minnix	78	337
1934	George Melinkovich	73	324	1972	Eric Penick	124	726
1935	Bill Shakespeare	104	374	1973	Wayne Bullock	162	752
1936	Bob Wilke	132	434	1974	Wayne Bullock	203	855
1937	Bunny McCormick	91	347	1975	Jerome Heavens	129	756
1938	Bob Saggau	60	353	1976	Al Hunter	233	1,058
1939	Milt Piepul	82	414	1977	Jerome Heavens	229	994
1940	Steve Juzwik	71	407	1978	Vagas Ferguson	211	1,192
1941	Fred Evans	141	490	1979	Vagas Ferguson	301*	1,437*
1942	Corwin Clatt	138	698	1980	Jim Stone	192	908
1943	Creighton Miller	151	911	1981	Phil Carter	165	727
1944	Bob Kelly	136	681	1982	Phil Carter	179	715
1945	Elmer Angsman	87	616	1983	Allen Pinkett	252	1394
1946	Emil Sitko	53	346	1984	Allen Pinkett	275	1,105
1947	Emil Sitko	60	426	1985	Allen Pinkett	255	1,100
1948	Emil Sitko	129	742	1986	Mark Green	96	406
1949	Emil Sitko	120	712	1987	Mark Green	146	861
1950	Jack Landry	109	491	1988	Tony Rice	121	700
1951	Neil Worden	181	676	1989	Tony Rice	174	884
1952	John Lattner	148	732	1990	Rodney Culver	150	710
1953	Neil Worden	145	859	1991	Jerome Bettis	168	972
1954	Don Schaefer	141	766	1992	Reggie Brooks	167	1343
1955	Don Schaefer	145	638	1993	Lee Becton	164	1,044

RUSHING (cont'd)

		Carries	Yards
1994	Randy Kinder	119	702
1995	Randy Kinder	143	809
1996	Autry Denson	202	1,179
1997	Autry Denson	264	1,268
1998	Autry Denson	232	1,215
1999	Tony Fisher	156	811
2000	Julius Jones	162	657

PASSING

		Att.	Comp.	Yards	TDs
1918	George Gipp	45	19	293	1
1919	George Gipp	72	41	727	3
1920	George Gipp	62	30	709	3
1921	John Mohardt	98	53	995	9
1922	Jim Crowley	21	10	154	1
1923	Jim Crowley	36	13	154	1
1924	Harry Stuhldreher	33	25	471	4
1925	Harry O'Boyle	21	7	107	0
1926	Christ Flanagan	29	12	207	0
1927	John Niemiec	33	14	187	0
1928	John Niemiec	108	37	456	3
1929	Jack Elder	25	8	187	1
1930	Marchy Schwartz	56	17	319	3
1931	Marchy Schwartz	51	9	174	3
1932	Nick Lukats	28	13	252	2
1933	Nick Lukats	67	21	329	0
1934	Bill Shakespeare	29	9	230	2
1935	Bill Shakespeare	66	19	267	3
1936	Bob Wilke	52	19	365	2
1937	Jack McCarthy	53	16	225	3
1938	Bob Saggau	28	8	179	3
1939	Harry Stevenson	50	14	236	1
1940	Bob Saggau	60	21	483	4
1941	Angelo Bertelli	123	70	1,027	8
1942	Angelo Bertelli	159	72	1,039	10
1943	Johnny Lujack	71	34	525	4
1944	Frank Dancewicz	163	68	989	9
1945	Frank Dancewicz	90	30	489	5
1946	Johnny Lujack	100	49	778	6
1947	Johnny Lujack	109	61	777	9
1948	Frank Tripucka	91	53	660	11
1949	Bob Williams	147	83	1,374	16
1950	Bob Williams	210	99	1,035	10
1951	John Mazur	110	48	645	5
1952	Ralph Guglielmi	143	62	725	4
1953	Ralph Guglielmi	113	52	792	8
1954	Ralph Guglielmi	127	68	1,162	6
1955	Paul Hornung	103	46	743	9
1956	Paul Hornung	111	59	917	3
1957	Bob Williams	106	53	565	3
1958	George Izo	118	68	1,067	9
1959	George Izo	95	44	661	6
1960	George Haffner	108	30	548	3
1961	Frank Budka	95	40	636	3
1962	Daryle Lamonica	128	64	821	6
1963	Frank Budka	40	21	239	4
1964	John Huarte	205	114	2,062	16
1965	Bill Zloch	88	36	558	3
1966	Terry Hanratty	147	78	1,247	8
1967	Terry Hanratty	206	110	1,439	9
1968	Terry Hanratty	197	116	1,466	10
1969	Joe Theismann	192	108	1,531	13
1970	Joe Theismann	268	155	2,429*	16
1971	Cliff Brown	111	56	669	4
1972	Tom Clements	162	83	1,163	8
1973	Tom Clements	113	60	882	8
1974	Tom Clements	215	122	1,549	8
1975	Rick Slager	139	66	686	2
1976	Rick Slager	172	86	1,281	11
1977	Joe Montana	189	99	1,604	11
1978	Joe Montana	260	141	2,010	10
1979	Rusty Lisch	208	108	1,781	4
1980	Blair Kiel	124	48	531	0
1981	Blair Kiel	151	67	936	7
1982	Blair Kiel	219	118	1,273	3
1983	Steve Beuerlein	145	75	1,061	4
1984	Steve Beuerlein	232	140	1,920	7
1985	Steve Beuerlein	214	107	1,335	3
1986	Steve Beuerlein	259	151	2,211	13
1987	Tony Rice	82	35	663	1
1988	Tony Rice	138	70	1,176	8
1989	Tony Rice	137	68	1,122	2
1990	Rick Mirer	200	110	1,824	8
1991	Rick Mirer	234	132	2,117	18
1992	Rick Mirer	234	120	1,876	15
1993	Kevin McDougal	159	98	1,541	7
1994	Ron Powlus	222	119	1,729	19*
1995	Ron Powlus	217	124	1,853	12
1996	Ron Powlus	232	133	1,942	12
1997	Ron Powlus	298*	182*	2,078	9
1998	Jarious Jackson	188	104	1,740	13
1999	Jarious Jackson	316	184	2,753*	17
2000	Matt LoVecchio	125	73	980	11

RECEIVING

		Rec.	Yards	TDs
1918	Bernie Kirk	7	102	1
1919	Bernie Kirk	21	372	2
1920	Eddie Anderson	17	293	3
1921	Eddie Anderson	26	394	2
1922	Don Miller	6	144	1
1923	Don Miller	9	149	1
1924	Don Miller	16	297	2
1925	Gene Edwards	4	28	0
1926	Ike Voedisch	6	95	0

Year	Player	Rec.	Yards	TDs
1927	John Colrick	11	126	1
1928	John Colrick	18	199	2
1929	John Colrick	4	90	0
1930	Ed Kosky	4	76	1
1931	Paul Host	6	48	2
1932	George Melinkovich	7	106	1
1933	Steve Banas	6	59	0
1934	Dom Vairo	4	135	2
1935	Wally Fromhart	11	174	1
1936	Joe O'Neill	8	140	1
1937	Andy Puplis	5	86	1
1938	Earl Brown	6	192	4
1939	Bud Kerr	6	129	0
1940	Bob Hargrave	9	98	1
1941	Steve Juzwik	18	307	2
1942	Bob Livingstone	17	272	3
1943	John Yonakor	15	323	4
1944	Bob Kelly	18	283	5
1945	Bob Skoglund	9	100	1
1946	Terry Brennan	10	154	2
1947	Terry Brennan	16	181	4
1948	Leon Hart	16	231	4
1949	Leon Hart	19	257	5
1950	Jim Mutscheller	35	426	7
1951	Jim Mutscheller	20	305	2
1952	Joe Heap	29	437	2
1953	Joe Heap	22	335	5
1954	Joe Heap	18	369	0
1955	Jim Morse	17	424	3
1956	Jim Morse	20	442	1
1957	Dick Lynch	13	128	0
1958	Monty Stickles	20	328	7
1959	Bob Scarpitto	15	297	4
1960	Les Traver	14	225	0
1961	Les Traver	17	349	2
1962	Jim Kelly	41	523	4
1963	Jim Kelly	18	264	2
1964	Jack Snow	60	1,114	9
1965	Nick Eddy	13	233	2
1966	Jim Seymour	48	862	8
1967	Jim Seymour	37	515	4
1968	Jim Seymour	53	736	4
1969	Tom Gatewood	47	743	8
1970	Tom Gatewood	77*	1,123*	7
1971	Tom Gatewood	33	417	4
1972	Willie Townsend	25	369	4
1973	Pete Demmerle	26	404	5
1974	Pete Demmerle	43	667	6
1975	Ken MacAfee	26	333	5
1976	Ken MacAfee	34	483	3
1977	Ken MacAfee	54	797	6
1978	Kris Haines	32	699	5
1979	Dean Masztak	28	428	2
1980	Tony Hunter	23	303	1
1981	Tony Hunter	28	387	2
1982	Tony Hunter	42	507	0
1983	Allen Pinkett	28	288	2
1984	Mark Bavaro	32	395	1
1985	Tim Brown	25	397	3
1986	Tim Brown	45	910	5
1987	Tim Brown	39	846	3
1988	Ricky Watters	15	286	2
1989	Raghib Ismail	27	535	0
1990	Raghib Ismail	32	699	2
1991	Tony Smith	42	789	4
1992	Lake Dawson	25	462	1
1993	Lake Dawson	25	395	2
1994	Derrick Mayes	47	847	11*
1995	Derrick Mayes	48	881	6
1996	Pete Chryplewicz	27	331	4
1997	Bobby Brown	45	543	6
1998	Malcolm Johnson	43	692	6
1999	Bobby Brown	36	608	5
2000	David Givens	25	310	2

SCORING

(† indicates one 2-point conversion;
†† indicates two 2-point conversions)

Year	Player	TDs	Xps	FGs	Pts.
1918	George Gipp	6	7	0	43
1919	George Gipp	7	4	1	49
1920	George Gipp	8	16	0	64
1921	John Mohardt	12	0	0	72
1922	Paul Castner	8	10	2	64
1923	Don Miller	10	0	0	60
	Red Maher	10	0	0	60
1924	Jim Crowley	9	17	0	71
1925	Christie Flanagan	7	3	0	45
1926	Bucky Dahman	6	5	0	41
1927	John Niemiec	4	7	0	31
1928	Jack Chevigny	3	0	0	18
1929	Jack Elder	7	0	0	42
1930	Marchy Schwartz	9	0	0	54
1931	Marchy Schwartz	5	0	0	30
1932	George Melinkovich	8	0	0	48
1933	Nick Lukats	2	0	0	12
1934	George Melinkovich	6	0	0	36
1935	Bill Shakespeare	4	0	0	24
1936	Bob Wilke	6	0	0	36
1937	Andy Puplis	3	6	0	24
1938	Benny Sheridan	4	0	0	24
	Earl Brown	4	0	0	24
1939	Milt Piepul	6	0	0	36
1940	Steve Juzwik	7	1	0	43
1941	Fred Evans	11	1	0	67

SCORING (cont'd)

		TDs	Xps	FGs	Pts.
1942	Corwin Clatt	5	0	4	30
	Creighton Miller	5	0	0	30
1943	Creighton Miller	13	0	0	78
1944	Bob Kelly	13	6	0	84
1945	Elmer Angsman	7	0	0	42
1946	Terry Brennan	6	0	0	36
	Jim Mello	6	0	0	36
1947	Terry Brennan	11	0	0	66
1948	Emil Sitko	9	0	0	54
1949	Emil Sitko	9	0	0	54
	Billy Barrett	9	0	0	54
1950	Jim Mutscheller	7	0	0	42
1951	Neil Worden	8	0	0	48
1952	Neil Worden	10	0	0	60
1953	Neil Worden	11	0	0	66
1954	Joe Heap	8	0	0	48
1955	Paul Hornung	6	5	2	47
1956	Paul Hornung	7	14	0	56
1957	Monty Stickles	3	11	1	32
1958	Monty Stickles	7	15	1	60
1959	Bob Scarpitto	8	0	0	48
1960	Bob Scarpitto	5	0	0	30
1961	Joe Perkowski	0	16	5	31
1962	Joe Farrell	4	0	0	24
	Jim Kelly	4	0	0	24
	Daryle Lamonica	4	0	0	24
1963	Frank Budka	4	0	0	24
1964	Bill Wolski	11	0	0	66
1965	Bill Wolski	8	4	0	52
1966	Nick Eddy	10	0	0	60
1967	Joe Azzaro	0	37	8	61
1968	Bob Gladieux	14	0	0	84
1969	Scott Hempel	0	41	5	56
1970	Scott Hempel	0	36	4	48
1971	Robert Thomas	0	21	5	36
1972	Andy Huff	10	0	0	60
1973	Bob Thomas	0	43	9	70
1974	Wayne Bullock	12	0	0	72
1975	Dave Reeve	0	24	11	57
1976	Al Hunter	13	0	0	78
1977	Dave Reeve	0	39	12	75
1978	Vagas Ferguson	8	0	0	48
1979	Vagas Ferguson	17	0	0	102
1980	Harry Oliver	0	19	18	73
1981	Harry Oliver	0	28	6	46
1982	Mike Johnston	0	19	19	76
1983	Allen Pinkett	18	1†	0	110
1984	Allen Pinkett	18	0	0	108
1985	Allen Pinkett	11	0	0	66
1986	John Carney	0	24	21*	87
1987	Ted Gradel	0	33	14	75

		TDs	Xps	FGs	Pts.
1988	Reggie Ho	0	32	9	59
1989	Anthony Johnson	13	0	0	78
1990	Craig Hentrich	0	41	16	89
1991	Jerome Bettis	20*	0	0	120*
1992	Reggie Brooks	14	1†	0	86
1993	Kevin Pendergast	0	45	14	87
1994	Derrick Mayes	11	1†	0	68
1995	Marc Edwards	12	2††	0	76
1996	Autry Denson	11	0	0	66
1997	Autry Denson	13	0	0	78
1998	Autry Denson	15	0	0	90
1999	Tony Fisher	7	11	0	44
2000	Nick Setta	1	44	8	74

TACKLES

1956	Ed Sullivan	79
1957	Jim Schaaf, Al Ecuyer	88
1958	Al Ecuyer	78
1959	Bob Scholtz, Ken Adamson	84
1960	Myron Pottios	74
1961	Nick Buoniconti	74
1962	Ed Hoerster	73
1963	Bill Pfeiffer	101
1964	Jim Carroll	140
1965	Jim Lynch	108
1966	Jim Lynch	106
1967	Bob Olson	98
1968	Bob Olson	129
1969	Bob Olson	142
1970	Jim Wright	110
1971	Mike Kadish	97
1972	Jim O'Malley	122
1973	Greg Collins	133
1974	Greg Collins	144
1975	Steve Niehaus	113
1976	Steve Heimkreiter	118
1977	Bob Golic	146
1978	Steve Heimkreiter	160
1979	Bob Crable	187*
1980	Bob Crable	154
1981	Bob Crable	167
1982	Mark Zavagnin	113
1983	Tony Furjanic	142
1984	Mike Kovaleski	108
1985	Tony Furjanic	147
1986	Mike Kovaleski	88
1987	Ned Bolcar	106
1988	Wes Pritchett	112
1989	Ned Bolcar	109
1990	Michael Stonebreaker	95
1991	Demetrius DuBose	127
1992	Demetrius DuBose	87

1993	Justin Goheen	92
1994	Brian Magee	81
1995	Lyron Cobbins	105
1996	Kinnon Tatum	77
1997	Jimmy Friday	109
1998	Bobbie Howard	108
1999	Al Jani Sanders	91
2000	Anthony Denman	84

PUNT RETURN AVERAGE
(Minimum of 5 returns through 1969; minimum of 1.0 returns per game from 1970)

		No.	Yards	Avg.
1919	Joe Brandy	26	186	7.2
1920	Joe Brandy	27	249	9.2
1921	None			
1922	Frank Thomas	21	196	9.3
1923	Harry Stuhldreher	32	308	9.6
1924	Harry Stuhldreher	22	194	8.8
1925	Charlie Riley	7	38	5.4
1926	Vince McNally	8	153	19.1
1927	Charles McKinney	5	36	7.2
1928	Frank Carideo	22	239	10.9
1929	Frank Carideo	33	405	12.3
1930	Frank Carideo	37	303	8.2
1931	Emmett Murphy	10	105	10.5
1932	Chuck Jaskwhich	23	254	11.0
1933	Andy Pilney	9	124	13.8
1934	Wally Fromhart	33	288	8.7
1935	Andy Pilney	13	148	11.4
1936	Bob Wilke	5	73	14.6
1937	Andy Puplis	21	281	13.4
1938	Benny Sheridan	11	194	17.6
1939	Benny Sheridan	8	107	13.4
1940	Bob Hargrave	24	176	7.3
1941	Steve Juzwik	22	280	12.7
1942	Pete Ashbaugh	13	196	15.1
1943	Creighton Miller	7	151	21.6
1944	Bob Kelly	12	129	10.8
1945	Frank Dancewicz	18	240	13.3
1946	Bob Livingstone	7	103	14.7
1947	Coy McGee	6	162	27.0
1948	Lancaster Smith	5	157	31.4
1949	Bill Gay	19	254	13.4
1950	Bill Gay	14	96	6.9
1951	Billy Barrett	5	107	21.4
1952	John Lattner	7	113	16.1
1953	Joe Heap	8	143	17.9
1954	Dean Studer	5	62	12.4
1955	Dean Studer	6	92	15.3
1956	Aubrey Lewis	5	46	9.2
1957	None			

		No.	Yards	Avg.
1958	Pat Doyle	7	64	9.1
1959	Bob Scarpitto	7	118	16.9
1960	Angelo Dabiero	8	102	12.8
1961	Angelo Dabiero	11	97	8.8
1962	Frank Minik	6	41	6.8
1963	Bill Wolski	6	31	5.2
1964	Nick Rassas	15	153	10.2
1965	Nick Rassas	24	459*	19.1*
1966	Tom Schoen	29	253	8.7
1967	Tom Schoen	42*	447	10.6
1968	Bob Gladieux	6	91	15.2
1969	Brian Lewallen	7	75	10.7
1970	Mike Crotty	19	100	5.3
1971	Mike Crotty	33	297	9.0
1972	Ken Schlezes	10	138	13.8
1973	Bob Zanot	19	141	7.4
1974	Ted Burgmeier	6	46	7.7
1975	Ted Burgmeier	9	52	5.8
1976	Steve Schmitz	18	168	9.3
1977	Steve Schmitz	14	127	9.1
1978	Dave Waymer	25	175	7.0
1979	Dave Duerson	12	209	17.4
1980	Dave Duerson	25	194	7.8
1981	Dave Duerson	32	221	6.9
1982	Dave Duerson	34	245	7.2
1983	Joe Howard	28	202	7.2
1984	Troy Wilson	11	84	7.6
1985	Troy Wilson	17	144	8.5
1986	Troy Wilson	26	222	8.5
1987	Tim Brown	34	401	11.8
1988	Ricky Watters	19	253	13.3
1989	Ricky Watters	15	201	13.4
1990	Raghib Ismail	13	151	11.6
1991	Jeff Burris	18	227	12.6
1992	Michael Miller	25	172	6.9
1993	Michael Miller	26	213	8.2
1994	None			
1995	None			
1996	Allen Rossum	15	344	22.9
1997	Allen Rossum	12	83	6.9
1998	Joey Getherall	15	143	9.5
1999	Julius Jones	15	195	13.0
2000	Joey Getherall	24	392	16.3

KICKOFF RETURN AVERAGE
(Minimum of 4 returns through 1969; minimum of 0.5 returns per game from 1970)

		No.	Yards	Avg.
1919	George Gipp	8	166	20.8
1920	George Gipp	11	208	18.9
1921	Chet Wynne	9	258	28.7

KICKOFF RETURN AVERAGE (cont'd)

		No.	Yards	Avg.
1922	Paul Castner	11	490	44.5*
1923	Willie Maher	4	184	46.0
1924	Elmer Layden	5	111	22.2
1925	Rex Enright	4	86	21.5
1926	Christie Flanagan	6	183	30.5
1927	Jack Chevigny	4	91	22.8
1928	Jack Chevigny	5	115	23.0
1929	Joe Savoldi	4	81	20.3
1930	Joe Savoldi	4	186	46.5
1931	None			
1932	George Melinkovich	4	164	41.0
1933	Ray Brancheau	7	109	15.6
1934	Bill Shakespeare	4	60	15.0
1935	Bill Shakespeare	5	123	24.6
1936	Andy Puplis	5	136	27.2
1937	None			
1938	None			
1939	Harry Stevenson	5	85	17.0
1940	Milt Piepul	4	122	30.5
1941	Fred Evans	9	206	22.9
1942	Bob Livingstone	8	184	23.0
1943	Creighton Miller	4	53	13.3
1944	Bob Kelly	8	213	26.6
1945	Phil Colella	5	105	21.0
1946	None			
1947	None			
1948	Larry Coutre	4	70	17.5
1949	Emil Sitko	4	89	22.3
1950	Jack Landry	11	195	17.7
1951	Billy Barrett	4	86	21.5
1952	Joe Heap	6	145	24.2
1953	John Lattner	8	331	41.4
1954	Jim Morse	5	166	33.2
1955	Dean Studer	5	115	23.0
1956	Paul Hornung	16	496	31.0
1957	Dick Lynch	5	159	31.8
1958	Jim Crotty	12	297	24.8
1959	Bob Scarpitto	12	247	20.6
1960	George Sefcik	7	167	23.9
1961	Angelo Dabiero	8	193	24.1
1962	Ron Bliey	13	309	23.8
1963	Ron Bliey	5	131	26.2
1964	Nick Rassas	4	103	25.8
1965	Bill Wolski	6	131	21.8
1966	Nick Eddy	4	193	48.3
1967	Dave Haley	5	119	23.8
1968	Coley O'Brien	4	156	39.0
1969	Mike Crotty	4	111	27.8
1970	Darryll Dewan	4	91	22.8
1971	Gary Diminick	7	199	28.4
1972	Gary Diminick	15	331	22.1

		No.	Yards	Avg.
1973	Gary Diminick	8	181	22.6
1974	Al Samuel	8	150	18.8
1975	Dan Knott	10	284	28.4
1976	Al Hunter	12	241	20.1
1977	Terry Eurick	9	211	23.4
1978	Jim Stone	13	242	18.6
1979	Jim Stone	19	493	25.9
1980	Jim Stone	17	344	20.2
1981	Greg Bell	13	371	28.5
1982	Allen Pinkett	14	354	25.3
1983	Alonzo Jefferson	10	174	17.4
1984	Hiawatha Francisco	6	178	29.7
1985	Tim Brown	14	338	24.1
1986	Tim Brown	25	698*	27.9
1987	Tim Brown	23	456	19.8
1988	Raghib Ismail	12	433	36.1
1989	Raghib Ismail	20	502	25.1
1990	Raghib Ismail	14	336	24.0
1991	Clint Johnson	9	217	24.1
1992	Michael Miller	9	261	29.0
1993	Clint Johnson	10	409	40.9
1994	Emmett Mosley	13	320	24.6
1995	Emmett Mosley	15	419	27.9
1996	Allen Rossum	6	227	37.8
1997	Allen Rossum	20	570	28.5
1998	Darcy Levy	7	163	23.3
1999	Julius Jones	26*	603	23.2
2000	Julius Jones	15	427	28.5

INTERCEPTIONS
(Minimum of 3)

		No.	Yards
1919	George Gipp	3	32
1920	None		
1921	Harry Mehre	4	97
	Chet Wynne	4	43
1922	None		
1923	Jim Crowley	4	31
1924	None		
1925	None		
1926	Vince McNally	3	0
1927	None		
1928	None		
1929	Frank Carideo	5	151
1930	Carl Cronin	3	26
	Marty Brill	3	8
	Tom Conley	3	4
1931	Nordy Hoffmann	3	32
1932	Mike Koken	4	18
1933	Nick Lukats	3	22
	Ray Brancheau	3	10

		No.	Yards				No.	Yards
1934	None				1980	None		
1935	None				1981	Mark Zavagnin	3	27
1936	Bob Wilke	3	33		1982	Dave Duerson	7	104
1937	Ed Simonich	3	10		1983	Rick Naylor	3	24
1938	None				1984	Pat Ballage	3	41
1939	None				1985	Steve Lawrence	3	57
1940	Steve Bagarus	4	26		1986	Steve Lawrence	3	28
1941	Bernie Crimmins	4	12		1987	Corny Southall	3	80
1942	Angelo Bertelli	8	41			Marv Spence	3	18
1943	Creighton Miller	6	78		1988	George Streeter	3	39
1944	Joe Gasparella	4	28			Jeff Alm	3	8
1945	Frank Dancewicz	3	31		1989	Todd Lyght	8	42
1946	Terry Brennan	3	18		1990	None		
1947	Johnny Lujack	3	44		1991	Tom Carter	5	79
1948	Bill Gay	6	83		1992	Jeff Burris	5	6
1949	Bill Gay	4	80			Tom Carter	5	0
1950	Dave Flood	4	28		1993	Bobby Taylor	4	100
1951	John Lattner	5	66		1994	None		
1952	John Lattner	4	58		1995	Lyron Cobbins	5	86
	Jack Whelan	4	35		1996	Benny Guilbeaux	4	42
1953	Ralph Guglielmi	5	50		1997	Benny Guilbeaux	4	76
1954	Ralph Guglielmi	5	50		1998	A'Jani Sanders	3	29
1955	Paul Hornung	5	59		1999	Deveron Harper	4	27
1956	Aubrey Lewis	3	39		2000	Ron Israel	3	41
1957	Bob Williams	3	28					
1958	George Izo	4	11		**PLAYING TIME**			
1959	Don White	3	39					
	George Sefcik	3	35					**Minutes**
1960	None				1947	William Fischer, Bill Walsh		300
1961	Angelo Dabiero	5	78		1948	Leon Hart		398
1962	Tom MacDonald	9	81		1949	Jim Martin		405
1963	Tom MacDonald	5	63		1950	Jerry Groom		465
1964	Tony Carey	8	121		1951	John Lattner		401
1965	Nick Rassas	6	197*		1952	John Lattner		422
1966	Tom Schoen	7	112		1953	Art Hunter		423
1967	Tom Schoen	4	108		1954	Paul Matz		438
	John Pergine	4	19		1955	Jim Mense		531:30*
1968	Chuck Zloch	5	31		1956	Paul Hornung		396
1969	Ralph Stepaniak	4	84		1957	Jim Schaaf		432
1970	Clarence Ellis	7	25		1958	Monty Stickles		350
1971	Ken Schlezes	4	63		1959	Bob Scholtz		423:22
1972	Mike Townsend	10*	39		1960	Les Traver		464:33
1973	Luther Bradley	6	37		1961	Angelo Dabiero		464:34
1974	None				1962	Ed Hoerster		413:40
1975	Luther Bradley	4	135		1963	Bob Lehmann		361
	Tom Lopienski	4	79		1964	Jack Snow		313:39
1976	Joe Restic	4	92		1965	Dick Arrington		338:27
1977	Joe Restic	6	25		1966	John Pergine		261:55
1978	Joe Restic	3	59		1967	Tom McKinley		277:47
	Tom Gibbons	3	48		1968	Bob Gladieux		289:55
	Dave Waymer	3	10		1969	Larry DiNardo		283:41
1979	Dave Waymer	4	77		1970	John Dampeer		300:19
					1971	Frank Pomarico		316:35

PLAYING TIME *(cont'd)*

		Minutes				Minutes
1972	Drew Mahalic	287:31	1986	Shawn Heffern		302:02
1973	Steve Sylvester	288:38	1987	Byron Spruell		282:22
1974	Gerry DiNardo	307:05	1988	Andy Heck, Mike Heldt		256:16
1975	Ernie Hughes	322:28	1989	Dean Brown		295:53
1976	Ernie Hughes	318:00	1990	Rick Mirer		301:24
1977	Ken MacAfee	296:23	1991	Tom Carter		334:28
1978	Dave Waymer	331:41	1992	Jeff Burris		289:40
1979	Bob Crable	319:23	1993	Tim Ruddy		298:57
1980	Phil Pozderac	315:40	1994	Bobby Taylor		281:57
1981	Bob Crable	308:20	1995	Ryan Leahy		316:10
1982	Dave Duerson	290:05	1996	Chris Clevenger		302:40
1983	Tony Furjanic	318:22	1997	Mike Doughty		337:33
1984	Tim Scannell	269:47	1998	John Merandi		308:14
1985	Tony Furjanic	327:11	1999	John Merandi		340:53
			2000	Jeff Faine		450:25

Longest Plays

RUSHING

Player	(Opponent, Year)	Yards	Player	(Opponent, Year)	Yards
Bob Livingstone	(USC, 1947)	92	Paul McDonald	(St. Vincent's, 1907)	85
Larry Coutre	(Navy, 1949)	91	Lou Zontini	(Minnesota, 1938)	84
Joe Heap	(SMU, 1954)	89	Emil Sitko	(Illinois, 1946)	*83
Eric Penick	(USC, 1973)	85	Corwin Clatt	(Great Lakes, 1942)	81
Bob Kelly	(Pittsburgh, 1944)	85	Robert Farmer	(Boston College, 1996)	81
Jack McCarthy	(Drake, 1937)	85	Larry Coutre	(Tulane, 1949)	81
Ulric Ruel	(Ohio Northern, 1908)	85			

*Did not score

PASSING

Pass–Receiver	(Opponent, Year)	Yards
Blair Kiel–Joe Howard	(Georgia Tech, 1981)	96
John Huarte–Nick Eddy	(Pittsburgh, 1964)	91
Steve Beuerlein–Tim Brown	(SMU, 1986)	84
Terry Hanratty–Jim Seymour	(Purdue, 1966)	84
Rick Mirer–Tony Smith	(Air Force, 1991)	83
Paul Failla–Derrick Mayes	(Stanford, 1993)	80
Joe Montana–Ted Burgmeier	(North Carolina, 1975)	80
Joe Theismann–Mike Creaney	(Pittsburgh, 1970)	78
Paul Hornung–Jim Morse	(USC, 1955)	78
Steve Beuerlein–Tim Brown	(Navy, 1986)	77
Rusty Lisch–Tony Hunter	(Air Force, 1979)	75
Bob Williams–Gary Myers	(Navy, 1958)	75
Harry Stuhldreher–Jim Crowley	(Nebraska, 1924)	75
Steve Beuerlein–Reggie Ward	(Missouri, 1984)	74
John Huarte–Nick Eddy	(Navy, 1964)	74
George Izo–Aubrey Lewis	(Pittsburgh, 1957)	74
George Izo–Red Mack	(Pittsburgh, 1958)	72*

*Did not score

INTERCEPTIONS

Player	(Opponent, Year)	Yards	Player	(Opponent, Year)	Yards
Jack Elder	(Army, 1929)	100	Wally Fromhart	(USC, 1935)	82*
Luther Bradley	(Purdue, 1975)	99	Art Parisien	(Minnesota, 1925)	82*
Nick Rassas	(Northwestern, 1965)	92	Tom Carter	(Tennessee, 1991)	79
Jack Elder	(Drake, 1927)	90	Allen Rossum	(Washington, 1995)	76
Dave Duerson	(Miami, 1981)	88	Lou Loncaric	(North Carolina, 1955)	75
Steve Juzwik	(Army, 1940)	85	Fred Carideo	(Purdue, 1934)	72
Mike Swistowicz	(North Carolina, 1949)	84			

*Did not score

KICKOFF RETURNS

Player	(Opponent, Year)	Yards
Alfred Bergman	(Loyola of Chicago, 1911)	105*
Clint Johnson	(Stanford, 1993)	100
Joe Savoldi	(SMU, 1930)	100
Allen Rossum	(Purdue, 1996)	99
Greg Bell	(Miami, 1981)	98
George Melinkovich	(Northwestern, 1932)	98
Terry Brennan	(Army, 1947)	97
Arthur Bergman	(Nebraska, 1919)	97
Tim Brown	(Louisiana State, 1986)	96
Nick Eddy	(Purdue, 1966)	96
Tim Brown	(Air Force, 1986)	95
Paul Castner	(Kalamazoo, 1922)	95
Don Miller	(St. Louis, 1922)	95
Bill Cerney	(DePauw, 1922)	95
Dom Callicrate	(Olivet, 1907)	95
Paul Hornung	(USC, 1956)	95

* The playing field was 110 yards long in 1911. Bergman received the kickoff on his own goal line and was downed on Loyola's 5-yard line.

PUNTS

Player	(Opponent, Year)	Yards
Bill Shakespeare	(Pittsburgh, 1935)	86
Elmer Layden	(Stanford, 1924)	80*
Craig Hentrich	(Colorado, 1990)	77
Hunter Smith	(Arizona State, 1998)	79
Bill Shakespeare	(Navy, 1935)	75

*Rose Bowl

FIELD GOALS

Player	(Opponent, Year)	Yards
Dave Reeve	(Pittsburgh, 1976)	53
John Carney	(SMU, 1984)*	51

Player	(Opponent, Year)	Yards
Harry Oliver	(Michigan, 1980)	51
Dave Reeve	(Michigan State, 1977)	51
Harry Oliver	(Navy, 1980)	50
Harry Oliver	(Georgia, 1980)**	50
Ted Gradel	(Alabama, 1987)	49
John Carney	(Purdue, 1986)	49
Mike Johnston	(South Carolina, 1983)	49
Harry Oliver	(Army, 1980)	49
Chuck Male	(Michigan State, 1979)	49
Joe Perkowski	(USC, 1961)	49

* Aloha Bowl
** Sugar Bowl

PUNT RETURNS

Player	(Opponent, Year)	Yards
Ricky Watters	(SMU, 1989)	97
Chet Grant	(Case Tech, 1916)	95
M. Harry "Red" Miller	(Olivet, 1909)	95
Joe Heap	(USC, 1953)	94
Joe Heap	(Pittsburgh, 1952)	92
John Lattner	(Iowa, 1952)	86
Lancaster Smith	(Pittsburgh, 1948)	85
Bob Scarpitto	(USC, 1958)	82
Ricky Watters	(Michigan, 1988)	81
Tom Schoen	(Pittsburgh, 1967)	78
Frank Carideo	(Georgia Tech, 1929)	75
Billy Barrett	(Navy, 1951)	74
Tim Brown	(Air Force, 1987)	74
Tim Simon	(Army, 1973)	73

* Did not score

FUMBLE RETURN

Player	(Opponent, Year)	Yards
Frank Shaughnessy	(Kansas, 1904)	107

Notre Dame's Record Versus Opponents

Opponent	First Game	Last Game	W	L	T	N.D.	Opp.
Adrian	1912	1912	1	0	0	74	7
Air Force	1964	2000	20	5	0	800	399
Akron	1910	1910	1	0	0	51	0
Alabama	1973	1987	5	1	0	112	86
Albion	1893	1898	3	1	1	110	31
Alma	1913	1916	4	0	0	196	0
American Medical College	1901	1905	5	0	0	362	0
Arizona	1941	1982	2	1	0	71	26
Arizona State	1998	1999	2	0	0	76	26
Army	1913	1998	36	8	4	828	423
Baylor	1925	1998	2	0	0	68	3
Beloit	1896	1926	5	0	1	144	9
Bennett Medical College	1905	1905	1	0	0	22	0
Boston College	1975	2000	9	3	0	300	248
Brigham Young	1992	1994	2	1	0	101	57
Butler	1911	1923	3	0	0	92	10
Cal–Berkeley	1959	1967	4	0	0	138	27
Carlisle	1914	1914	1	0	0	48	6
Carnegie Tech	1922	1941	15	4	0	353	103
Case Tech	1916	1918	2	0	0	74	6
Chicago	1894	1899	0	4	0	11	83
Chicago Dental	1897	1897	1	0	0	62	0
Chicago Phys & Surgeons	1895	1908	7	2	0	265	9
Christian Brothers	1913	1913	1	0	0	20	7
Cincinnati	1900	1900	1	0	0	58	0
Clemson	1977	1979	1	1	0	31	33
Coe	1927	1927	1	0	0	28	7
Colorado	1983	1994	3	2	0	136	74
Creighton	1915	1915	1	0	0	41	0
Dartmouth	1944	1945	2	0	0	98	0
DeLaSalle	1893	1893	1	0	0	28	0
DePauw	1897	1922	8	0	0	286	17
Detroit	1927	1951	2	0	0	60	6
Drake	1926	1937	8	0	0	278	20
Duke	1958	1966	2	1	0	86	44
Englewood High School	1899	1900	2	0	0	97	5
Florida	1991	1991	1	0	0	39	28
Florida State	1981	1995	1	3	0	86	97
Franklin	1906	1908	3	0	0	113	0

Opponent	First Game	Last Game	W	L	T	N.D.	Opp.
Georgia	1980	1980	0	1	0	10	17
Georgia Tech	1922	1998	26	5	1	800	304
Goshen	1900	1900	1	0	0	55	0
Great Lakes	1918	1945	1	2	2	69	85
Harvard Prep	1888	1888	1	0	0	20	0
Haskell	1914	1932	5	0	0	195	14
Hawaii	1991	1998	2	0	0	71	64
Highland Views	1896	1896	1	0	0	82	0
Hillsdale	1892	1908	4	0	1	102	20
Houston	1978	1978	1	0	0	35	34
Illinois	1898	1968	11	0	1	313	62
Illinois Cycling Club	1895	1895	1	0	0	18	2
Indiana	1898	1991	23	5	1	571	166
Indianapolis Artillery	1895	1895	0	1	0	0	18
Iowa	1921	1968	13	8	3	565	364
Iowa Pre-Flight	1942	1943	2	0	0	42	13
Kalamazoo	1893	1923	7	0	0	318	0
Kansas	1904	1999	4	1	1	157	50
Knox	1902	1907	1	1	0	27	16
Lake Forest	1899	1903	4	0	0	110	0
Lombard	1923	1925	3	0	0	123	0
Louisiana State	1970	1998	5	5	0	205	195
Loyola (Chicago)	1911	1911	1	0	0	80	0
Loyola (New Orleans)	1928	1928	1	0	0	12	6
Marquette	1908	1921	3	0	3	101	12
Miami (Florida)	1955	1990	15	7	1	511	410
Miami (Ohio)	1909	1909	1	0	0	46	0
Michigan	1887	1999	11	17	1	453	533
Michigan State	1897	2000	41	22	1	1,297	888
Minnesota	1925	1938	4	0	1	72	27
Mississippi	1977	1985	1	1	0	50	34
Missouri	1970	1984	2	2	0	66	54
Missouri Osteopaths	1903	1903	1	0	0	28	0
Morningside	1917	1919	2	0	0	27	6
Morris Harvey	1912	1912	1	0	0	39	0
Mount Union	1919	1919	1	0	0	60	7
Navy	1927	2000	64	9	1	1,980	723
Nebraska	1915	2000	7	7	1	228	174
North Carolina	1949	1975	15	1	0	402	147
North Division High School	1905	1905	1	0	0	44	0
Northwestern	1889	1995	37	8	2	1,010	347
Northwestern Law	1895	1895	1	0	0	20	0
Ohio Medical University	1901	1904	4	0	0	64	10
Ohio Northern	1908	1913	4	0	0	224	10
Ohio State	1935	1996	2	2	0	67	89
Oklahoma	1952	1968	8	1	0	211	146
Olivet	1907	1910	3	0	0	128	4
Oregon	1976	1982	1	0	1	54	13
Oregon St.	2001	2001	0	1	1	9	41
Pacific	1940	1940	1	0	0	25	7
Penn State	1913	1992	8	8	1	331	287
Pennsylvania	1930	1955	5	0	1	232	68
Pittsburgh	1909	1999	40	17	1	1,602	774

Opponent	First Game	Last Game	W	L	T	N.D.	Opp.
Princeton	1923	1924	2	0	0	37	2
Purdue	1896	2000	47	23	2	1,711	1,098
Rice	1915	1988	4	0	0	147	16
Rose Poly	1909	1914	3	0	0	204	14
Rush Medical	1894	1900	3	0	1	40	6
Rutgers	1921	2000	3	0	0	155	17
St. Bonaventure	1911	1911	1	0	0	34	0
St. Louis	1912	1923	3	0	0	86	7
St. Viator	1897	1912	4	0	0	265	7
St. Vincent's	1907	1907	1	0	0	21	12
South Bend Athletic Club	1901	1901	1	0	1	22	6
South Bend Commercial Athletic Club	1896	1896	1	0	0	46	0
South Bend High School	1892	1892	1	0	0	56	0
South Bend Howard Park	1900	1900	1	0	0	64	0
South Carolina	1976	1984	3	1	0	93	65
South Dakota	1913	1917	5	0	0	120	7
SMU	1930	1989	10	3	0	391	216
Stanford	1924	2000	10	5	0	443	305
Syracuse	1914	1963	2	1	0	44	29
Tennessee	1978	1999	2	3	0	131	156
Texas	1913	1996	8	2	0	268	117
Texas A&M	1987	2000	3	1	0	86	69
Texas Christian	1972	1972	1	0	0	21	0
Toledo Athletic Assoc.	1904	1904	1	0	0	6	0
Tulane	1944	1971	8	0	0	275	35
UCLA	1963	1964	2	0	0	51	12
USC	1926	1998	41	26	5	1,452	1,152
Valparaiso	1920	1920	1	0	0	28	3
Vanderbilt	1995	1996	2	0	0	55	6
Virginia	1989	1989	1	0	0	36	13
Wabash	1894	1924	10	1	0	331	29
Washington	1948	1996	4	0	0	156	48
Washington (St. Louis)	1936	1936	1	0	0	14	6
Washington and Jefferson	1917	1917	1	0	0	3	0
West Virginia	1988	2000	3	0	0	97	63
Western Michigan	1919	1920	2	0	0	95	0
Western Reserve	1916	1916	1	0	0	48	0
Wisconsin	1900	1964	8	6	2	269	216
Yale	1914	1914	0	1	0	0	28
Totals			776	241	26	26,642	11,828

Professional Players from Notre Dame

Notre Dame has had 387 players who have gone on to appear on an active roster in either the National Football League (1920 to present), the fourth American Football League (1960 to 1969), or the All-American Football Conference (1946 to 1949).

Adams, John "Tree", T, Washington, 1945–49

Adamson, Ken, G, Denver, 1960–62

Alm, Jeff, DT, Houston, 1990–93

Anderson, Eddie, E, Rochester, 1922; Chicago Cardinals, 1922–25; Chicago Bears, 1923

Anderson, Heartley "Hunk", G, Chicago Bears, 1922–25

Angsman, Elmer, HB, Chicago Cardinals, 1946–52

Bagarus, Steve, HB, Washington, 1945–46; 1948; Los Angeles Rams, 1947

Banas, Steve, QB, Detroit, 1935; Philadelphia, 1935

Banks, Robert, DE, Houston, 1988, 1991; Cleveland, 1989–90

Barry, Norm, QB, Chicago Cardinals, 1921; Green Bay, 1921

Baujan, Harry, E, Cleveland, 1920–21

Bavaro, Mark, TE, New York Giants, 1985–90; Cleveland, 1992; Philadelphia, 1993–94

Beams, Byron, T, Pittsburgh, 1959–60; Houston, 1961

Becker, Doug, LB, Chicago Bears, 1978; Buffalo, 1978

Beinor, Ed, T, Chicago Cardinals, 1940–41; Washington, 1941–42

Belden, Bob, QB, Dallas, 1969–70

Bell, Greg, RB, Buffalo, 1984–87; Los Angeles Rams, 1988–89; Los Angeles Raiders, 1990–91

Bercich, Pete, LB, Minnesota, 1994–

Berezney, Pete, T, Los Angeles Dons (AAFC), 1947; Baltimore (AAFC), 1948

Berry, Bert, LB, Indianapolis, 1997–99

Bertelli, Angelo, QB, Los Angeles Dons (AAFC), 1946; Chicago Rockets, 1947–48

Bettis, Jerome, FB, Los Angeles Rams, 1993–95; Pittsburgh, 1996–

Beuerlein, Steve, QB, Los Angeles Raiders, 1987–90; Dallas, 1991–92; Arizona, 1993–94; Jacksonville, 1995; Carolina, 1996–

Bleier, Robert "Rocky", RB, Pittsburgh, 1968, 1971–80

Bolcar, Ned, LB, Seattle, 1990; Miami, 1991–92

Bradley, Luther, CB, Detroit, 1978–81

Brennan, Mike, T, Cincinnati, 1990; Phoenix, 1991; Buffalo, 1991–92

Brooks, Reggie, TB, Washington, 1993–95

Brooks, Tony, FB, Philadelphia, 1992–93

Brown, Chris, DB, Pittsburgh, 1984–85

Brown, Dean, T, San Diego, 1990

Brown, Derek, TE, New York Giants, 1992–94; Jacksonville, 1995–97; Oakland, 1998–

Brown, Tim, WR, Oakland/Los Angeles Raiders, 1988–present

Browner, Jim, S, Cincinnati, 1979–80

Browner, Ross, DE, Cincinnati, 1979–86; Green Bay, 1987

Bryant, Junior, DE, San Francisco, 1993–

Budka, Frank, DB, Los Angeles Rams, 1964

Buoniconti, Nick, LB, Boston, 1962–68; Miami, 1969–74, 1976

Burgmeier, Ted, S, Kansas City, 1978

Burnell, Max, HB, Chicago Bears, 1944

Burris, Jeff, Buffalo, 1994–97; Indianapolis, 1998–

Calhoun, Mike, DT, San Francisco, 1980; Tampa Bay, 1980

Carberry, Glen, E, Buffalo, 1923–24; Cleveland, 1925

Carney, John, K, Tampa Bay, 1989; San Diego, 1990–

Carollo, Joe, T, Los Angeles Rams, 1962–68, 1971; Philadelphia, 1969; Cleveland, 1972–73

Carroll, Jim, LB, New York Giants, 1965–66; Washington, 1966–68; New York Jets, 1969

Carter, Tom, DB, Washington, 1993–96; Chicago Bears, 1996–

Casper, Dave, TE, Oakland, 1974–80; Houston, 1980–83; Minnesota, 1983; Los Angeles Raiders, 1984

Chryplewicz, Pete, TE, Detroit Lions 1997–

Cifelli, Gus, T, Detroit, 1950–52; Green Bay, 1953; Philadelphia, 1954; Pittsburgh, 1954

Clark, Willie, CB, San Diego, 1994–97

Clasby, Bob, DT, St. Louis/Phoenix, 1986–90

Clatt, Corwin, FB, Chicago Cardinals, 1948–49

Clements, Tom, QB, Kansas City, 1980

Cobbins, Lyron, LB, Arizona 1997

Cofall, Stanley, HB, Cleveland, 1920; New York Giants, 1921

Coleman, Herb, C. Chicago Rockets (AAFC), 1946–48; Baltimore (AAFC), 1948

Collins, Greg, LB, San Francisco, 1975; Seattle, 1976; Buffalo, 1977

Commisa, Vince, G, Boston, 1944

Conjar, Larry, RB, Cleveland, 1967; Philadelphia, 1968; Baltimore, 1969–70

Connor, George, T/DT/LB, Chicago Bears, 1948–55

Cook, Ed, T, Chicago Cardinals, 1958–59; St. Louis, 1960–65; Atlanta, 1966–67

Corgan, Mike, FB, Detroit, 1943

Costa, Paul, TE/T, Buffalo, 1965–72

Cotton, Forest "Fod", T, Rock Island, 1923–25

Coughlin, Danny, HB, Minnesota, 1923

Coughlin, Frank, T, Detroit, 1921; Green Bay, 1921; Rock Island, 1921

Coutre, Larry, HB, Green Bay, 1950, 1953; Baltimore, 1953

Covington, John, DB, Indianapolis, 1994–95

Cowhig, Gerry, FB, Los Angeles Rams, 1947–49; Chicago Cardinals, 1950; Philadelphia, 1951

Crable, Bob, LB, New York Jets, 1982–85

Crimmins, Bernie, G, Green Bay, 1945

Crotty, Jim, DB, Washington, 1960–61; Buffalo, 1961–62

Crowley, Jim, HB, Green Bay, 1925; Providence, 1925

Culver, Al, T, Chicago Bears, 1932; Green Bay, 1932

Culver, Rodney, FB, Indianapolis, 1992–93; San Diego 1994–95

Czarobski, Ziggy, G, Chicago Rockets (AAFC), 1948; Chicago Hornets (AAFC), 1949

Dahl, Bob, T, Cleveland, 1992–95; Washington, 1996–97

Dalvin, Mike, OT, Washington 1995

Dancewicz, Frank, QB, Boston 1946–48

Davis, Arch, HB, Columbus, 1925–26

Davis, Travis, S, New Orleans 1995; Jacksonville 1995–98; Pittsburgh 1999–

Dawson, Lake, WR, Kansas City, 1994–97; Indianapolis, 1999

DeGree, Cy, G, Detroit, 1921

Denson, Autry, RB, Miami, 1999–

DiBernardo, Rick, LB, St. Louis, 1986

Dorsey, Eric, DT, New York Giants, 1986–92

Dove, Bob, E/DE, Chicago Rockets (AAFC), 1946–47; Chicago Cardinals, 1948–53; Detroit, 1953–42

DuBose, Demetrius, LB, Tampa Bay, 1993–96; New York Jets, 1997

Duerson, Dave, S, Chicago Bears, 1983–89, New York Giants, 1990; Arizona, 1991–93

Duggan, Ed, HB, Rock Island, 1921

Duranko, Pete, DE–LB, Denver, 1967–70, 1972–74

Ebli, Ray, E, Chicago Cardinals, 1942; Buffalo (AAFC), 1946; Chicago Rockets (AAFC), 1947

Eddy, Nick, RB, Detroit, 1968–72

Edwards, Gene, G, Canton, 1920–21; Toledo, 1922; Cleveland, 1923–35

Edwards, Marc, RB, San Francisco 1997–98; Cleveland 1999–

Eichenlaub, Ray, FB, Columbus, 1925; Cleveland, 1925

Eilers, Pat, S, Minnesota, 1990–91; Phoenix, 1992; Washington, 1993–94; Chicago, 1995

Ellis, Clarence, CB, Atlanta, 1972–74

Enright, Rex, FB, Green Bay, 1926–27

Evans, Fred, HB, Cleveland (AAFC), 1946; Buffalo (AAFC), 1947; Chicago Rockets (AAFC), 1947–48; Chicago Bears, 1948

Fanning, Mike, DE–DT, Los Angeles Rams, 1975–82; Detroit, 1983; Seattle, 1984

Feeney, Al, C, Canton, 1920–21

Ferguson, Vagas, RB, New England, 1980–82; Houston, 1983; Cleveland, 1983

Figaro, Cedric, LB, San Diego, 1988–90; Cleveland, 1991–92

Fischer, Bill, "Moose", T, Chicago Cardinals, 1949–53

Fitzgerald, Freeman, C, Rock Island, 1920–21

Flanigan, Jim, DT, Chicago Bears, 1994–

Foley, Tim, T, Baltimore, 1981

Furjanic, Anthony, LB, Buffalo, 1986–88; Miami, 1988

Gann, Mike, DE, Atlanta, 1985–93
Garvey, Hec, T, Chicago Bears, 1922–25,
    Hartford, 1926; Brooklyn, 1926, 1930; New
    York Giants, 1927–28; Providence, 1929;
    Staten Island, 1931
Gasparella, Joe, QB/LB, Pittsburgh, 1948,
    1950–51; Chicago Cardinals, 1951
Gatewood, Tom, WR, New York Giants,
    1972–73
Gaul, Frank, T, New York Bulldogs, 1949
Gay, Bill, DB, Chicago Cardinals, 1951–52
Gibson, Oliver, NG, Pittsburgh 1995–98;
    Cincinnati 1999–
Gladieux, Bob, RB, Buffalo, 1979; Boston, 1969;
    New England, 1970–72
Goeddeke, George, C/G, Denver, 1967–72
Golic, Bob, LB/NT, New England, 1979–82;
    Cleveland, 1982–88; Los Angeles Raiders,
    1989–92
Golic, Mike, DT, Houston, 1985–87;
    Philadelphia, 1988–92; Miami, 1993
Gompers, Bill, HB, Buffalo (AAFC), 1948
Grasmanis, Paul, DL, Chicago 1996–98; St.
    Louis 1999; Denver 1999–
Green, Mark, HB, Chicago Bears, 1989–92
Greeney, Norm, G, Green Bay, 1933; Pittsburgh,
    1934–35
Groom, Jerry, C, Chicago Cardinals, 1951–55
Grunhard, Tim, C, Kansas City, 1990–
Guglielmi, Ralph, QB, Washington, 1955,
    1958–60; St. Louis, 1961; New York Giants,
    1962–63; Philadelphia, 1963
Haines, Kris, WR, Washington, 1979; Chicago
    Bears, 1979–81
Halperin, Robert, QB, Brooklyn, 1932
Hanratty, Terry, QB, Pittsburgh, 1969–75;
    Tampa Bay, 1976
Hardy, Kevin, DE/DT, San Francisco, 1968;
    Green Bay, 1970; San Diego, 1971–72
Hart, Leon, E/FB, Detroit, 1950–57
Hayes, Dave, E, Green Bay, 1921–22
Hayes, Jerry, E, Rock Island, 1921
Heap, Joe, HB, New York Giants, 1955
Hearden, Tom "Red", HB, Green Bay, 1927–28;
    Chicago Bears, 1928
Heck, Andy, T, Seattle, 1989–93; Chicago,
    1994–present
Heenan, Pat, SE/DB, Washington, 1960
Heimkreiter, Steve, LB, Baltimore, 1980
Heldt, Mike, C, Indianapolis, 1992–93
Helwig, John, G, Chicago Bears, 1953–56
Hentrich, Craig, P, Green Bay, 1994–97;
    Tennessee Oilers/Titans, 1998–
Higgins, Luke, G, Baltimore (AAFC), 1947

Holohan, Pete, TE, San Diego, 1981–87; Los
    Angeles Rams, 1988–90; Kansas City, 1991;
    Cleveland, 1992
Hornung, Paul, HB/K, Green Bay, 1957–62,
    1964–66
Howard, Joe, SE, Buffalo, 1986–88; Washington,
    1989–91
Huarte, John, QB, Boston, 1966–67;
    Philadelphia, 1968; Kansas City, 1970–71;
    Chicago Bears, 1972
Huffman, Dave, C/G/T, Minnesota, 1979–83,
    1985–90
Huffman, Tim, G/T, Green Bay, 1981–85
Hughes, Ernie, G, San Francisco, 1978, 1980;
    New York Giants, 1981–83
Hunter, Al, RB, Seattle, 1977–80
Hunter, Art, C, Green Bay, 1954; Cleveland,
    1956–59; Los Angeles Rams, 1960–64;
    Pittsburgh, 1965
Hunter, Tony, TE, Buffalo, 1983–84; Los
    Angeles Rams, 1985–87
Ismail, Raghib, WR, Oakland/Los Angeles
    Raiders, 1993–96; Carolina, 1996–98; Dallas,
    1999
Izo, George, QB, St. Louis, 1960; Washington,
    1961–64; Detroit, 1965; Pittsburgh, 1966
Johnson, Anthony, FB, Indianapolis, 1990–93;
    New York Jets, 1994; Chicago Bears, 1995–
Jones, Andre, LB, Detroit, 1992
Jones, Jerry, G, Decatur, 1920; Rock Island,
    1922; Cleveland, 1924
Jurkovic, Mirko, G, Chicago Bears, 1992
Juzwik, Steve, HB, Washington, 1942; Buffalo
    (AAFC), 1946–47; Chicago Rockets
    (AAFC), 1948
Kadish, Mike, DT, Buffalo, 1973–81
Kantor, Joe, RB, Washington, 1966
Kasper, Tom, HB, Rochester, 1923
Keefe, Emmett, G, Chicago Tigers, 1920; Green
    Bay, 1921; Rock Island, 1921–22; Milwaukee,
    1922
Kell, Paul, T, Green Bay, 1939–40
Kelley, Mike, T/G, Houston, 1985–87;
    Philadelphia, 1988
Kelly, Bob, HB, Los Angeles Dons (AAFC),
    1947–48; Baltimore (AAFC), 1949
Kelly, Jim, TE, Pittsburgh, 1963; Philadelphia,
    1965, 1967
Kerr, Bill, E, Los Angeles Dons (AAFC), 1946
Kiel, Blair, QB, Tampa Bay, 1984; Indianapolis,
    1986–87; Green Bay, 1988–91
Kiley, Roger, E, Chicago Cardinals, 1923
Kinder, Randy, RB, Philadelphia 1997–99
Knafelc, Greg, QB, New Orleans, 1983

Knapp, Lindsay, G, Kansas City, 1993–95
Koken, Mike, HB, Chicago Cardinals, 1933
Kosikowski, Frank, E, Cleveland (AAFC), 1948; Buffalo (AAFC), 1948
Kovatch, John, E, Washington, 1942, 1946; Green Bay, 1947
Kowalkowski, Scott, LB, Philadelphia, 1991–93; Detroit, 1994–
Koziak, Mike, G, Duluth, 1924–25
Krimm, John, S, New Orleans, 1982–83
Kuchta, Frank, C, Washington, 1958–59; Denver, 1960
Kuechenberg, Bob, G/T, Miami, 1970–83
Kuharich, Joe, G, Chicago Cardinals, 1940–41, 1945
Kulbitski, Vic, FB, Buffalo (AAFC), 1946–48
Kunz, George, T, Atlanta, 1969–74, Baltimore, 1975–77, 1980
Kurth, Joe, T, Green Bay, 1933–34
Lambeau, Earl "Curly", HB, Green Bay, 1921–29
Lamonica, Daryle, QB, Buffalo, 1963–66; Oakland, 1967–74
Lansing, Vince, T/G, Evansville, 1921
Lanza, Chuck, C, Pittsburgh, 1988–90
Larson, Fred, C, Chicago Bears, 1922; Milwaukee, 1923–24; Green Bay, 1925; Chicago Cardinals, 1929
Lattner, Johnny, HB, Pittsburgh, 1954
Law, John, T, Newark, 1930
Lawrence, Don, T, Washington, 1959–61
Leahy, Bernie, HB, Chicago Bears, 1932
Lemek, Ray, G, Washington, 1957–61; Pittsburgh, 1962–65
Leonard, Bill, DE, Baltimore (AAFC) 1949
Leonard, Jim, FB/QB, Philadelphia, 1934–37
Leopold, Bobby, LB, San Francisco, 1980–83
Lind, Mike, FB, San Francisco 1963–67
Lisch, Rusty, QB/S, St. Louis, 1980–83; Chicago Bears, 1984
Livingston, Bob, HB, Chicago Rockets (AAFC), 1948; Chicago Hornets (AAFC), 1949; Buffalo (AAFC), 1949; Baltimore, 1950
Longo, Tom, DB, New York Giants, 1969; St. Louis, 1971
Lujack, Johnny, QB/DB, Chicago Bears, 1948–51
Lyght, Todd, CB, Los Angeles Rams, 1991–
Lynch, Dick, DB, Washington, 1958; New York Giants, 1959–66
Lynch, Jim, LB, Kansas City, 1967–77
MacAfee, Ken, TE, San Francisco, 1978–79
Mack, Bill, FL, Pittsburgh, 1961–63, 1965; Philadelphia, 1964; Atlanta, 1966; Green Bay, 1966

Maddock, Bob, G, Chicago Cardinals, 1942, 1946
Maggioli, Achille "Chick", HB, Buffalo (AAFC), 1948; Detroit, 1949; Baltimore, 1950
Mahalic, Drew, LB, San Diego, 1975; Philadelphia, 1976–78
Malone, Grover, HB, Chicago Tigers, 1920; Green Bay, 1921; Akron, 1923
Marelli, Ray, G, Chicago Cardinals, 1928
Martin, Dave, LB, Kansas City, 1968; Chicago Bears, 1969
Martin, Jim, LB/K, Cleveland, 1950; Detroit, 1951–61; Baltimore, 1963; Washington, 1964
Martz, Bob, T, Tampa, 1991
Marx, Greg, DE, Atlanta, 1973
Mastrangelo, Johnny, G, Pittsburgh, 1947–48; New York Yankees (AAFC), 1949; New York Giants, 1950
Mavraides, Menil "Minnie", G, Philadelphia, 1954, 1957
Mayer, Frank, G, Green Bay, 1927
Mayes, Derrick, WR, Green Bay 1996–98; Seattle 1999–
Mayl, Gene, E, Dayton, 1925–26
McBride, Oscar, TE, Arizona 1995
McCoy, Mike, DT, Green Bay, 1970–76; Oakland, 1977–78; New York Giants, 1979–80; Detroit, 1980
McDonald, Devon, LB, Indianapolis, 1993–96
McGill, Karmeeleyah, LB, Cincinnati, 1993
McGill, Mike, LB, Minnesota, 1968–70; St. Louis, 1971–72
McGuire, Gene, C, New Orleans, 1992–93; Green Bay, 1995
McInerny, Arnie, C–FB, Chicago Cardinals, 1920–27
McMullan, John, G, New York Titans, 1960–61
McNulty, Paul, E, Chicago Cardinals, 1924–25
Meagher, Jack, E, Chicago Tigers, 1920
Mehre, Henry, C, Minneapolis, 1923–24
Mello, Jim, FB, Boston, 1947; Los Angeles Rams, 1948; Chicago Rockets (AAFC), 1948; Detroit, 1949
Mergenthal, Art, G, Cleveland, 1945; Los Angeles Rams, 1946
Meyer, John, LB, Houston, 1966
Mieszkowski, Ed, T, Brooklyn (AAFC), 1946–47
Miller, Don, HB, Providence, 1925
Millner, Wayne, E, Boston, 1936; Washington, 1937–41, 1945
Mirer, Rick, QB, Seattle, 1993–96; Chicago Bears, 1997–98; Green Bay, 1999

Mohardt, Johnny, HB, Chicago Cardinals, 1922–23; Racine, 1924; Chicago Bears, 1925

Montana, Joe, QB, San Francisco, 1979–92, Kansas City, 1993–94

Moriarty, Larry, RB, Houston, 1983–86; Kansas City, 1986–91

Moynihan, Tim, C, Chicago Cardinals, 1932–33

Mundee, Fred, C, Chicago Bears, 1943–45

Mutscheller, Jim, E–TE, Baltimore, 1954–61

Nemeth, Steve, HB–QB, Cleveland, 1945, Chicago Rockets (AAFC), 1946; Baltimore (AAFC), 1947

Niehaus, Steve, DT, Seattle, 1976–78; Minnesota, 1979

Norman, Todd, T, Seattle 1995

O'Boyle, Harry, HB, Green Bay, 1928–29, 1932; Philadelphia, 1933

O'Connor, Bill "Zeke", E, Buffalo (AAFC), 1948; Cleveland (AAFC), 1949; New York Yankees, 1951

O'Malley, Jim, LB, Denver, 1973–75

O'Neil, Bob, G, Pittsburgh, 1956–57; New York Titans, 1961

Oriard, Mike, C, Kansas City, 1970–73

Ostrowski, Chet, DE, Washington, 1954–59

Page, Alan, DT, Minnesota, 1967–78; Chicago Bears, 1978–81

Palumbo, Sam, LB, Cleveland, 1955–56; Green Bay, 1957; Buffalo, 1960

Panelli, John "Pep", FB/LB, Detroit, 1949–50; Chicago Cardinals, 1951–53

Pasquesi, Toni, DT, Chicago Cardinals, 1955–57

Patulski, Walt, DE, Buffalo, 1972–75; St. Louis, 1977

Pearson, Dud, QB, Racine, 1922

Pergine, John, LB, Los Angeles Rams, 1969–72; Washington, 1973–75

Peterson, Anthony, LB, San Francisco, 1994–96; Chicago Bears, 1997; San Francisco, 1998–

Petitbon, John, HB, Dallas, 1952; Cleveland, 1955–56; Green Bay, 1957

Petitgout, Luke, OL, N.Y. Giants 1999–

Phelan, Bob, HB, Toledo, 1922; Rock Island, 1923–24

Piepul, Milt, FB, Detroit, 1941

Pietrosante, Nick, FB, Detroit, 1959–65; Cleveland, 1966–67

Pilska, Joe, HB, Hammond, 1920–21

Pinkett, Allen, RB, Houston, 1986–91

Pivarnik, Joe, G, Philadelphia, 1936

Pivec, Dave, TE, Los Angeles Rams, 1966–68; Denver, 1969

Pottios, Myron, LB, Pittsburgh, 1961, 1963–65; Los Angeles Rams, 1966–70; Washington, 1971–74

Powers, John, SE, Pittsburgh, 1962–66

Pozderac, Phil, T, Dallas, 1982–87

Pritchett, Wes, LB, Buffalo, 1989–90, Atlanta, 1991

Puplis, Andy, HB, Chicago Cardinals, 1943

Quinn, Steve, C, Houston, 1966

Rassas, Nick, DB, Atlanta, 1966–68

Ratigan, Brian, LB, Indianapolis, 1994–95

Ratkowski, Ray, HB, Boston, 1961

Ratterman, George, QB, Buffalo (AAFC), 1947–49, New York Yankees, 1950–51, Cleveland, 1952–56

Regner, Tom, G/T, Houston, 1967–72

Rehder, Tom, T, New England, 1988–89, New York Giants, 1990, Minnesota, 1992

Reilly, Jim, G, Buffalo, 1970–71

Riffle, Charley, G, Cleveland, 1944; New York Yankees (AAFC), 1946–48

Rogers, John, C, Cincinnati, 1933–34

Rosenthal, Mike, OL, N.Y. Giants 1999–

Rossum, Allen, CB, Philadelphia 1998–

Ruddy, Tim, C, Miami, 1994–

Rudnick, Tim, S, Baltimore, 1974

Ruetz, Joe, G, Chicago Rockets (AAFC), 1946, 1948

Rutkowski, Ed, HB/FL/QB, Buffalo, 1963–66

Ryan, Jim, HB, Rock Island, 1924; Chicago Cardinals, 1924

Ryan, Tim, G, Tampa, 1991–93

Rydzewski, Frank, T, Cleveland, 1920; Chicago Tigers, 1920; Hammond, 1920, 1922–26; Chicago Cardinals, 1921; Chicago Bears, 1923; Milwaukee, 1925

Rykovich, Julie, HB-DB, Buffalo (AAFC) 1947–48; Chicago Rockets (AAFC) 1948; Chicago Bears 1949–51

Rymkus, Lou, T, Washington, 1943; Cleveland, 1946–51

Savoldi, Joe, FB, Chicago Bears, 1930

Scarpitto, Bob, FL/P, San Diego, 1961; Denver, 1962–67; Boston, 1968

Schaefer, Don, FB, Philadelphia, 1956

Scharer, Eddie, QB, Detroit, 1926, 1928; Pottsville, 1927

Schoen, Tom, S, Cleveland, 1970

Scholtz, Bob, C, Detroit, 1960–64; New York Giants, 1965–66

Schrader, Jim, C, Washington, 1954, 1956–61; Philadelphia, 1962–64

Scibelli, Joe, G, Los Angeles Rams, 1961–75

Scott, Vince, G, Buffalo (AAFC), 1947–48

Scully, John, G/C, Atlanta, 1981–90

Seiler, Paul, T/C, New York Jets, 1967, 1969; Oakland, 1971–73

Seyfrit, Mike "Si", E, Toledo, 1923; Hammond, 1924

Seymour, Jim, WR, Chicago Bears, 1970–72

Shellog, Alec, T, Brooklyn, 1939; Chicago Bears, 1939

Signaigo, Joe, OG-DG, New York (AAFC) 1948–49; New York Yankees 1950

Simmons, Floyd, HB, Chicago Rockets (AAFC), 1948

Sitko, Emil "Red", HB, San Francisco, 1950; Chicago Cardinals, 1951–52

Skoglund, Bob, E, Green Bay, 1947

Slackford, Fred, FB, Dayton, 1920; Canton, 1921

Smagala, Stan, CB, Dallas, 1990; Pittsburgh, 1992–93

Smith, Chris, FB, Kansas City, 1986–87

Smith, Dick "Red", QB, Green Bay, 1927, 1929; New York Yankees, 1928; Newark, 1930; New York Giants, 1931

Smith, Hunter, P, Indianapolis, 1999–

Smith, Irv, TE, New Orleans, 1993–97; San Francisco, 1998; Cleveland, 1999–

Smith, Rod, DB, New England, 1992–94; Carolina, 1995; Minnesota, 1996

Smith, Tony, SE, Kansas City, 1992

Snow, Jack, SE, Los Angeles Rams, 1965–75

Snowden, Jim, T/DE, Washington, 1965–71

Spaniel, Frank, HB, Baltimore, 1950; Washington, 1950

Stams, Frank, DE, Los Angeles Rams, 1989–91; Cleveland, 1992–94; Carolina, 1995

Statuto, Art C, Buffalo (AAFC) 1948–49; Los Angeles Rams 1950

Steinkemper, Bill, T, Chicago Bears, 1943

Stenger, Brian, LB, Pittsburgh, 1969–72; New England, 1973

Stevenson, Mark, G, Columbus, 1922

Stewart, Ralph, C-LB, New York (AAFC) 1947–48; Baltimore (AAFC) 1948

Stickles, Monty, TE, San Francisco, 1960–67; New Orleans, 1968

Stonebreaker, Michael, LB, Chicago, 1991; Atlanta, 1993–94

Streeter, George, S, Chicago Bears, 1989; Los Angeles Raiders, 1990

Strohmeyer, George, C, Brooklyn (AAFC), 1948; Chicago Hornets (AAFC), 1949

Stuhldreher, Harry, QB, Brooklyn, 1926

Sullivan, George, E, Boston, 1948

Swatland, Dick, G, Houston, 1968

Swistowicz, Mike, FB, New York Yankees, 1950; Chicago Cardinals, 1950

Sylvester, Steve, G/T/C, Oakland, 1975–81; Los Angeles Raiders, 1982–83

Szymanski, Dick, C/LB, Baltimore, 1955, 1957–68

Szymanski, Frank, C/LB, Detroit, 1945–47

Tatum, Kinnon, LB, Carolina 1997–99; Tampa Bay 2000–

Taylor, Aaron, G, Green Bay 1994–97; San Diego 1998–99

Taylor, Bobby, CB, Philadelphia Eagles, 1995–

Terlep, George, QB, Buffalo (AAFC), 1946–48; Cleveland (AAFC), 1948

Terrell, Pat, S, Los Angeles Rams, 1990–93; New York Jets, 1994–

Thayer, Tom, G–C, Chicago Bears, 1985–92, Miami, 1993

Theismann, Joe, QB/KR, Washington, 1974–85

Thomas, Bob, K, Chicago Bears, 1975–84; Detroit, 1982; San Diego, 1985

Tobin, George, G, New York Giants, 1947

Toneff, Bob, DT, San Francisco, 1952, 1954–58; Washington, 1959–64

Tonelli, Mario, HB, Chicago Cardinals, 1940, 1945

Toran, Stacey, S, Los Angeles Raiders, 1984–88

Trafton, George, C, Decatur, 1920; Chicago Staleys, 1921; Chicago Bears, 1922–32

Tripucka, Frank, QB, Philadelphia, 1949; Detroit, 1949; Chicago Cardinals, 1950–52; Dallas, 1952; Denver, 1960–63

Urban, Gasper, G, Chicago Rockets (AAFC), 1948

Vairo, Dom, E, Green Bay, 1935

Varrichione, Frank, T, Pittsburgh, 1955–60; Los Angeles Rams, 1961–65

Vasys, Arunas, LB, Philadelphia, 1966–68

Vergara, George, E, Green Bay, 1925

Wallace, John, E, Chicago Bears, 1928; Dayton, 1929

Wallner, Fred, G, Chicago Cardinals, 1951–52, 1954–55; Houston, 1960

Walsh, Bill, C, Pittsburgh, 1949–54

Ward, Gillie, T, Dayton, 1923

Watters, Ricky, RB, San Francisco, 1991–94; Philadelphia, 1995–97; Seattle, 1998–

Waymer, Dave, CB, New Orleans, 1980–89; San Francisco, 1990–91, Los Angeles Raiders, 1992

Wendell, Marty, G, Chicago Hornets (AAFC), 1949

Weston, Jeff, DT, New York Giants, 1979–82

Wetoska, Bob, T, Chicago Bears, 1960–69

Whipple, Ray, E, Detroit, 1920
White, Jim, T, New York Giants, 1946–50
Whittington, Mike, LB, New York Giants, 1980–83
Wightkin, Bill, T/DE, Chicago Bears, 1950–57
Williams, Bob, QB, Chicago Bears, 1951–52, 1955
Williams, George, DT, Cleveland, 1992
Williams, Joel, TE, Miami, 1987
Williams, Larry, G, Cleveland, 1986–88, San Diego, 1989; New Orleans, 1990–91; New England, 1992
Wisne, Jerry, OL, Chicago 1999–
Wolski, Bill, HB, Atlanta, 1966
Wooden, Shawn, S, Miami 1996–99; Chicago 2000–
Worden, Neil "Bull", FB, Philadelphia, 1954, 1957
Wunsch, Harry, G, Green Bay, 1934

Wynn, Renaldo, DT, Jacksonville, 1997–
Wynne, Chet, FB, Rochester, 1922
Wynne, Elmer, FB, Chicago Bears, 1928; Dayton, 1929
Yarr, Tom, C, Chicago Cardinals, 1933
Yonaker, John, E/DE, Cleveland (AAFC), 1946–49; New York Yankees, 1950; Washington, 1952
Young, Bryant, DT, San Francisco, 1994–
Zalejski, Ernie, HB, Baltimore, 1950
Zeigler, Dusty, G, Buffalo 1996–99; N.Y. Giants 2000–
Zellars, Ray, FB, New Orleans 1995–98
Zilly, Jack, E, Los Angeles Rams, 1947–51; Philadelphia, 1952
Zoia, Clyde, G, Chicago Cardinals, 1920–23
Zontini, Lou, HB, Chicago Cardinals, 1940–41; Cleveland, 1944; Buffalo (AAFC), 1946
Zorich, Chris, DT, Chicago Bears, 1991–97

IRISH NFL DRAFT PICKS

Since the National Football League began drafting players in 1936, starting with the initial draft on February 8, 1936, at the Ritz-Carlton Hotel in Philadelphia, 410 Notre Dame football players have been chosen by NFL teams.

Notre Dame has had 55 first-round draft picks, beginning with Bill Shakespeare by Pittsburgh in 1936. Overall, the Irish have had five players (more than any other school) chosen as the first pick in the entire draft: quarterback Angelo Bertelli by Boston in 1944; quarterback Frank Dancewicz by Boston in 1946; end Leon Hart by Detroit in 1950; quarterback Paul Hornung by Green Bay in 1957; and defensive tackle Walt Patulski by Buffalo in 1972. Here's a listing of first-round selections by current NFL teams:

1936	Bill Shakespeare, B, Pittsburgh	1969	George Kunz, T, Atlanta
1944	Angelo Bertelli, QB, Boston		Jim Seymour, E, Los Angeles Rams
1945	Frank Szymanski, C, Detroit	1970	Mike McCoy, Green Bay
	John Yonakor, E, Philadelphia	1972	Clarence Ellis, DB, Atlanta
1946	Frank Dancewicz, QB, Boston		Walt Patulski, DE, Buffalo
	Johnny Lujack, QB, Chicago		Mike Kadish, DT, Miami
	Emil Sitko, RB, Los Angeles Rams	1975	Mike Fanning, DT, Los Angeles Rams
	George Connor, T, New York Giants	1976	Steve Niehaus, DT, Seattle
1949	Frank Tripucka, QB, Philadelphia	1978	Ross Browner, DE, Cincinnati
	Bill Fischer, G, Chicago Cardinals		Luther Bradley, DB, Detroit
1950	Leon Hart, E, Detroit		Ken MacAfee, TE, San Francisco
1951	Bob Williams, QB, Chicago	1980	Vagas Ferguson, RB, New England
	Jerry Groom, C, Chicago Cardinals	1982	Bob Crable, LB, New York Jets
1954	Art Hunter, TH, Green Bay	1983	Tony Hunter, TE, Buffalo
	John Lattner, HB, Pittsburgh	1984	Greg Bell, RB, Buffalo
	Neil Worden, FB, Philadelphia	1986	Eric Dorsey, DT, New York Giants
1955	Joe Heap, HB, New York Giants	1988	Tim Brown, WR, Los Angeles
	Ralph Guglielmi, QB, Washington		Raiders
	Frank Varrichione, T, Pittsburgh	1989	Andy Heck, T, Seattle
1957	Paul Hornung, B, Green Bay	1991	Todd Lyght, CB, Los Angeles Rams
1959	Nick Pietrosante, FB, Detroit	1992	Derek Brown, TE, New York Giants
1960	George Izo, QB, New York Jets,	1993	Rick Mirer, QB, Seattle
	Chicago Cardinals		Jerome Bettis, FB, Los Angeles Rams
	Monty Stickles, E, San Diego,		Tom Carter, CB, Washington
	San Francisco		Irv Smith, TE, New Orleans
1965	Jack Snow, WR, Minnesota	1994	Bryant Young, DT, San Francisco
1967	Tom Regner, G, Houston		Aaron Taylor, G, Green Bay
	Alan Page, DT, Minnesota		Jeff Burris, S, Buffalo
	Tom Seiler, G, New York Jets	1997	Renaldo Wynn, DE, Jacksonville
1968	Kevin Hardy, DE, New Orleans	1999	Luke Petitgout, G, New York Giants

Here's a complete listing of all Notre Dame draft picks, including three years of All-America Football Conference picks from 1947 to 1949:

1936
1.   Bill Shakespeare, QB, Pittsburgh
3.   Andy Pilney, HB, Detroit
7.   Marty Peters, E, Pittsburgh
7.   Wally Fromhart, B, Green Bay
8.   Wayne Millner, E, Boston

1938
8.   Pat McCarty, C, Pittsburgh
10. Joe Kuharich, G, Pittsburgh

1939
4.   Ed Beinor, T, Brooklyn
6.   Paul Kell, T, Green Bay
9.   Earl Brown, E, Chicago Cardinals
17. Ed Simonich, B, Chicago Bears
17. Ed Longhi, C, Pittsburgh
19. Mario Tonelli, FB, New York Giants
19. Bill Hofer, B, Green Bay

1940
12. Bud Kerr, E, Green Bay
20. Steve Sitko, B, Washington

1941
11. Milt Piepul, FB, Detroit
15. Bob Saggau, B, Green Bay
18. Bob Osterman, C, Chicago Bears

1942
11. John Kovatch, E, Washington
19. Steve Juzwik, B, Washington

1943
2.   Fred "Dippy" Evans, RB, Chicago Bears
3.   Bob Dove, E, Washington
4.   Wally Ziemba, C, Washington
5.   Lou Rymkus, T, Washington
11. Tom Brock, C, Green Bay
11. Henry Wright, G, Washington
26. Bob Neff, T, Philadelphia
28. Dick Creevy B, Chicago Bears

1944
1.   Angelo Bertelli, QB, Boston
2.   Creighton Miller, HB, Brooklyn
9.   Matthew Bolger, E, Detroit
10. Pat Filley, G, Cleveland
15. Bob McBride, G, Cleveland

17. John Creevey, B, Cleveland
25. John McGinnis, E, Chicago Cardinals
27. Russ Ashbaugh, B, Pittsburgh
27.   Bill Earley, B, Chicago Cardinals
30. Stan Kudlacz, C, Cleveland

1945
1.   Frank Szymanski, C, Detroit
1.   John Yonakor, E, Philadelphia
2.   John "Tree" Adams, T, Washington
6.   Corwin "Cornie" Clatt, FB, Chicago Cardinals
6.   Jerry Cowhig, RB, Cleveland
6.   Jim Mello, FB, Boston
7.   Ziggy Czarobski, T, Chicago Cardinals
12. Herb Coleman, C, Boston
14. John Creevey, B, Chicago Bears
15. George Connor, T, Pittsburgh
20. Bob Livingston, HB, Chicago Bears
23. Luke Higgins, T, Cleveland
28. Paul Limont, E, Detroit

1946
1.   Frank Dancewicz, QB, Boston
1.   George Connor, T, New York Giants
1.   Johnny Lujack, QB, Chicago Bears
1.   Emil Sitko, RB, Los Angeles Rams
3.   Elmer Angsman, RB, Chicago Cardinals
5.   Pete Berenzy, T, Detroit
7.   Ed Mieszkowski, T, Boston
7.   Bob Skoglund, E, Washington
8.   Joe Signaigo, G, Los Angeles Rams
11. George Strohmeyer, C, Los Angeles Rams
12. Bob Palladino, B, Los Angeles Rams
15. Fred Rovai, G, Chicago Cardinals
15. Gasper Urban, G, Los Angeles Rams
17. Jerry Ford, E, Los Angeles Rams
20. Bill Heywood, B, Chicago Cardinals
20. Frank Ruggerio, B, Boston

NFL
1947
2.   John Mastrangelo, G, Pittsburgh
6.   George Sullivan, T, Boston
8.   Bob Kelly, HB, Green Bay
11. Bob Skoglund, E, Green Bay
13. John Fallon, T, New York Giants
24. Ralph Stewart, C, New York Giants
25. Bob Palladino, B, Green Bay

AAFC
1947
1.   George Sullivan, T, Chicago Rockets (4)

2. Gerry Cowhig, RB, Cleveland (16)
5. John Mastrangelo, G, Buffalo (34)
6. John Zilly, E, San Francisco (46)
8. Matt Bolger, E, Chicago Rockets (60)
8. George Strohmeyer, C, New York Yankees (63)
14. Bob Livingstone, HB, Chicago Rockets (108)
14. Joe Signaigo, B, Cleveland (112)
16. John Kosikowski, E, Buffalo (122)
16. Johnny Lujack, QB, Chicago Rockets

NFL
1948
4. Joe Gasperallo, QB, Pittsburgh
6. Marty Wendell, G, Philadelphia
14. George Ratterman, QB, Boston
15. John Fallon, G, Chicago Bears
16. Bill O'Connor, G, Los Angeles Rams
22. Floyd Simmons, RB, Pittsburgh
25. Coy McGee, B, Detroit
27. John Panelli, FB, Green Bay
29. Art Statuto, C, Philadelphia
30. Bill Fischer, G, Chicago Cardinals

AAFC
1948
3. Bill Gompers, HB, Buffalo (16)
4. Bill O'Connor, E, Buffalo (24)
5. John Walsh, C, Chicago Rockets (25)
6. Marty Wendell, G, Buffalo (33)
18. Doug Waybright, E, Buffalo (119)
19. Pete Ashbaugh, B, Cleveland (129)
26. John Panelli, FB, New York Yankees (184)

NFL
1949
1. Bill Fischer, G, Chicago Cardinals
1. Frank Tripucka, QB, Philadelphia
2. John Panelli, FB, Detroit
3. Bill Walsh, C, Pittsburgh
5. Terry Brennan, HB, Philadelphia
8. Bill Wightkin, E, Chicago Bears
20. Frank Gaul, T, Boston
24. Don McAuliffe, B, New York Giants

AAFC
1949
2. John Panelli, FB, New York Yankees (13)
5. Frank Gaul, G, Buffalo (35)

1950
1. Leon Hart, E, Detroit

2. Jim Martin, E, Cleveland
4. Larry Coutre, HB, Green Bay
5. Mike Swistowicz, HB, New York Bulldogs
5. Frank Spaniel, HB, Washington
5. Ernie Zalejski, HB, Chicago Bears
7. Billy Gay, B, Chicago Cardinals
10. Walt Grothaus, C, Chicago Cardinals
11. John Helwig, G, Chicago Bears
18. Ray Espanan, E, Chicago Cardinals
19. Gus Cifelli, T, Detroit
19. Frank Gaul, T, Pittsburgh
30. Ed Hudak, T, Pittsburgh

1951
1. Jerry Groom, C, Chicago Cardinals
1. Bob Williams, QB, Chicago Bears
12. Jack Landry, B, Chicago Cardinals
20. Fred Wallner, G, Chicago Cardinals
29. Bob Livingston, HB, Chicago Cardinals

1952
2. Bob Toneff, T, San Francisco
7. John Petitbon, HB, Texas
10. Chet Ostrowski, E, Washington
12. Jim Mutscheller, E, Texas
13. Dave Flood, B, Pittsburgh
16. Paul Burns, G, New York Giants
28. Billy Barrett, B, Green Bay

1953
8. Don Beck, B, New York Giants
15. Bob O'Neil, E, Pittsburgh
29. Jack Alessandrini, G, Baltimore
30. Bill Gaudreau, B, Chicago Cardinals

1954
1. Johnny Lattner, HB, Pittsburgh
1. Art Hunter, T, Green Bay
1. Neil Worden, FB, Philadelphia
2. Jim Schrader, C, Washington
4. Minnie Mavraides, G, Philadelphia
4. Frank Paterra, B, Chicago Bears
6. Tom McHugh, B, Chicago Cardinals
10. Joe Katchik, E, Los Angeles Rams
15. Sam Palumbo, G, San Francisco
18. Don Penza, E, Pittsburgh
28. Joe Bush, G, Pittsburgh

1955
1. Ralph Guglielmi, QB, Washington
1. Frank Varrichione, T, Pittsburgh
1. Joe Heap, B, New York Giants
2. Dick Szymanski, C, Baltimore

1955 (cont'd)
3. Tony Pasquesi, T, Chicago Cardinals
4. Paul Reynolds, B, Cleveland
4. Sam Palumbo, C, Cleveland
6. Dan Shannon, E, Chicago Bears
24. Bob Ready, T, Washington

1956
3. Don Schaefer, B, Philadelphia
9. Wayne Edmonds, G, Pittsburgh
13. Jim Mense, C, Green Bay
14. John McMullan, G, New York Giants
15. Dick Fitzgerald, B, Chicago Bears
19. Ray Lemek, G, Washington
21. Gene Kapish, E, Cleveland
21. Gene Martell, T, Pittsburgh
22. George Nicula, T, Washington
29. Pat Bisceglia, G, Washington

1957
1. Paul Hornung, QB, Green Bay
12. Ed Sullivan, C, Green Bay
13. Jim Morse, B, Green Bay
20. Byron Beams, T, Los Angeles Rams

1958
6. Dick Lynch, HB, Washington
9. Frank Kuchta, C, Washington
10. Aubrey Lewis, B, Chicago Bears

1959
1. Nick Pietrosante, FB, Detroit
5. Frank Geremia, T, San Francisco
5. Bob Wetoska, T, Washington
7. Don Lawrence, T, Washington
10. Ron Toth, T, Washington
10. Bronko Nagurski,* T, San Francisco
18. Al Ecuyer, G, New York Giants
27. Norm Odyniec, FB, Washington
28. Bob Williams, QB, Chicago Bears
29. Dick Loncaric, T, Pittsburgh
30. Angelo Mosca, T, Philadelphia
* Not to be confused with University of
Minnesota and Chicago Bears fullback Bronko
Nagurski who played from the 1920s to the
1940s.

1960
1. George Izo, QB, Chicago Cardinals/New
   York Titans
1. Monty Stickles, E, San Francisco/Los
   Angeles Chargers
3. Bob Scholtz, C, Detroit/Los Angeles
   Chargers

12. Jim Crotty, HB, Washington/Dallas
17. Mike Graney, E, Philadelphia/Buffalo

1961
2. Myron Pottios, LB, Pittsburgh/Oakland
9. Bob Scarpitto, HB, Los Angeles Chargers
10. Bill Mack, HB, Pittsburgh/Buffalo
10. Joe Scibelli, HB, Los Angeles Rams/New
    York Titans
20. Ray Ratkowski, HB, Green Bay/Boston

1962
2. Bob Bill, T, New York Giants/San Diego
2. Joe Carollo, T, Los Angeles Rams/Dallas
   Texans
5. Mike Lind, HB, San Francisco/San Diego
9. John Powers, E, Pittsburgh
13. Nick Buoniconti, G, Boston
13. Joe Perkowski, B, Chicago Bears

1963
9. Ed Burke, T, Houston
10. Ed Hoerster, LB, Chicago Bears/Buffalo
12. Daryle Lamonica, QB, Green Bay/Buffalo
16. John Slafkosky, T, St. Louis

1964
2. Jim Kelly, E, Pittsburgh/Boston
4. Frank Budka, HB, Chicago Bears
4. Paul Costa, HB, Green Bay/Kansas City
5. Jim Snowden, FB, Washington/Kansas
   City
7. John Simon, E, Kansas City
8. George Bednar, G, St. Louis/Oakland
10. Clay Stephens, E, Kansas City
13. Tom MacDonald, DB, Washington
17. Dave Humenik, T, New York
    Giants/Boston
17. Bob Lehmann, G–LB, New York Jets

1965
1. Jack Snow, E, Minnesota/San Diego
6. Tony Carey, HB, Chicago Bears/San Diego
6. John Huarte, QB, Philadelphia/New York
   Jets
8. John Meyer, LB, St. Louis/ Buffalo
12. Jim Carroll, LB, New York Giants
14. Tom Longo, DB, Philadelphia/Oakland
14. Dave Pivec, E, Chicago Bears
18. Dick Arrington, G, Cleveland/Boston

1966
2. Nick Eddy, HB, Detroit/Denver
2. Nick Rassas, DB, Atlanta/San Diego

3. Phil Sheridan, E, Atlanta/New York Jets
4. Pete Duranko, DE/LB, Cleveland/Denver
5. Bill Wolski, HB, Atlanta/New York Jets
8. Tom Talaga, E, Cleveland/Denver
16. Arunas Vasys, LB, Philadelphia

1967
1. Paul Seiler, G, New York Jets (12)
1. Alan Page, DE, Minnesota (15)
1. Tom Regner, G, Houston (23)
2. Larry Conjar, FB, Cleveland (46)
2. Jim Lynch, LB, Kansas City (47)
3. George Goeddeke, C, Denver (59)
4. Tom Rhoads, DE, Buffalo (70)
16. Allen Sack, LB, Los Angeles Rams (408)
16. Paul Hornung, HB, New Orleans, (Expansion)
16. Bob Scholtz, T, New Orleans, (Expansion)

1968
1. Kevin Hardy, DE, New Orleans (7)
3. Mike McGill, LB, Minnesota (76)
5. Jim Smithberger, DB, Boston (116)
6. Dave Martin, DB, Philadelphia (157)
8. Dick Swatland, G/T, New Orleans (195)
8. Tom Schoen, DB, Cleveland (212)
11. John Pergine, LB, Los Angeles Rams (297)
16. "Rocky" Bleier, RB, Pittsburgh (417)

1969
1. George Kunz, T, Atlanta (2)
1. Jim Seymour, SE, Los Angeles Rams (10)
2. Terry Hanratty, QB, Pittsburgh (30)
4. Bob Kuechenberg, G, Philadelphia (80)
5. Jim Winegardner, TE, Chicago Bears (119)
6. Ed Tuck, G, Miami (141)
8. Bob Gladieux, RB, Boston (186)
11. Eric Norri, DT, Washington (269)
12. Bob Belden, QB, Dallas (308)
12. John Lavin, LB, Kansas City (309)
13. Tom Quinn, DB, Chicago Bears (325)

1970
1. Mike McCoy, DT, Green Bay (2)
3. Jim Reilly, G, Buffalo (57)
5. Bob Olson, LB, Boston (107)
5. Mike Oriard, C, Kansas City (130)
7. Terry Brennan, T, Philadelphia (158)

1971
4. Joe Theismann, QB, Miami (99)
5. Tim Kelly, LB, Boston (106)
7. Larry DiNardo, G, New Orleans (158)
15. Jim Wright, LB, New York Giants (382)

1972
1. Walt Patulski, DE, Buffalo (1)
1. Clarence Ellis, DB, Atlanta (15)
1. Mike Kadish, DT, Miami (25)
3. Fred Swendsen, DE, Buffalo (53)
4. Eric Patton, LB, Green Bay (86)
5. Tom Gatewood, WR, New York Giants (107)
7. Ralph Stepaniak, DB, Buffalo (157)
7. Mike Zikas, DT, New York Giants (177)

1973
2. Greg Marx, DT, Atlanta (39)
6. Mike Creaney, C, Chicago Bears (138)
9. John Dampeer, G, Cincinnati (224)
12. Jim O'Malley, LB, Denver (296)
13. John Cieszkowski, RB, Chicago Bears (320)
15. Ken Schlezes, DB, Philadelphia (367)

1974
2. Dave Casper, TE, Oakland (45)
4. Mike Townsend, DB, Minnesota (86)
9. Brian Doherty, P, Buffalo (226)
11. Tim Rudnick, DB, Baltimore (285)
14. Frank Pomarico, G, Kansas (353)
15. Bob Thomas, K, LosAngeles Rams (388)
17. Cliff Brown, RB, Philadelphia (427)
17. Willie Townsend, WR, Los Angeles Rams (440)

1975
1. Mike Fanning, DT, Los Angeles Rams (9)
2. Greg Collins LB, San Francisco (35)
3. Drew Mahalic, LB, Denver (69)
5. Kevin Nosbusch, DT, San Diego (111)
5. Wayne Bullock, RB, San Francisco (114)
10. Steve Sylvester, T, Oakland (259)
13. Pete Demmerle, WR, San Diego (320)
13. Eric Penick, RB, Denver (329)
14. Reggie Barnett, DB, San Diego (345)
16. Tom Fine, TE, Buffalo (406)

1976
1. Steve Niehaus, DT, Seattle (2)
7. Ed Bauer, G, New Orleans (201)

1978
1. Ken MacAfee, TE, San Francisco (7)
1. Ross Browner, DT, Cincinnati (8)
1. Luther Bradley, DB, Detroit (11)
2. Willie Fry, DE, Pittsburgh (49)
3. Ernie Hughes, G, San Francisco (79)
4. Al Hunter, RB, Seattle (1977 supplemental draft)

1978 *(cont'd)*

5.   Ted Burgmeier, DB, Miami (111)
9.   Steve McDaniels, T, San Francisco (249)
10. Doug Becker, LB, Pittsburgh (258)

1979

2.   Dave Huffman, C, Minnesota (43)
2.   Bob Golic, LB, New England (52)
3.   Joe Montana, QB, San Francisco (82)
8.   Steve Heimkreiter, LB, Baltimore (197)
9.   Jerome Heavens, RB, Chicago Bears (230)
9.   Kris Haines, WR, Washington (233)
9.   Jeff Weston, DT, Miami (244)
10. Joe Restic, DB, Chicago Bears (257)
10. Mike Calhoun, DT, Dallas (274)
12. Jim Browner, DB, Cincinnati (304)

1980

1.   Vagas Ferguson, RB, New England (25)
2.   Dave Waymer, DB, New Orleans (41)
2.   Tim Foley, T, Baltimore (51)
4.   Rusty Lisch, QB, St. Louis (89)
8.   Bobby Leopold, LB, San Francisco (210)
10. Rob Martinovich, T, Kansas City (51)

1981

4.   John Scully, C, Atlanta (109)
7.   Pete Holohan, TE, San Diego (189)
8.   Scott Zettek, DT, Chicago Bears (205)
9.   Jim Stone, RB, Seattle (223)
9.   Tim Huffman, T, Green Bay (227)
12. John Hankerd, LB, Denver (317)

1982

1.   Bob Crable, LB, New York Jets (23)
3.   John Krimm, DB, New Orleans (76)
5.   Phil Pozderac, T, Dallas (137)

1983

1.   Tony Hunter, TE, Buffalo (12)
3.   Dave Duerson, DB, Chicago Bears (64)
4.   Tom Thayer, C, Chicago Bears (91)
5.   Larry Moriarty, RB, Houston (114)
9.   Mark Zavagnin, LB, Chicago Bears (235)
9.   Bob Clasby, T, Seattle (236)

1984

1.   Greg Bell, RB, Buffalo (26)
6.   Chris Brown, DB, Pittsburgh (164)
6.   Stacey Toran, DB, Los Angeles Raiders (168)
9.   Neil Maune, G, Dallas (249)
11. Blair Kiel, QB, Tampa Bay (281)

1985

2.   Mike Gann, DE, Atlanta (45)
3.   Mike Kelley, C, Houston (82)
4.   Mark Bavaro, TE, New York Giants (100)
10. Mike Golic, DT, Houston (255)
10. Larry Williams, G, Cleveland (259)

1986

1.   Eric Dorsey, DE, New York Giants (19)
3.   Allen Pinkett, RB, Houston (61)
8.   Antony Furjanic, LB, Buffalo (202)
8.   Mike Perrino, T, San Diego (209)

1987

2.   Wally Kleine, T, Washington (48)
4.   Steve Beuerlein, QB, Los Angeles Raiders (110)
7.   Robert Banks, DT, Houston(176)
8.   Joel Williams, TE, Miami (210)

1988

1.   Tim Brown, WR, Los Angeles Raiders (6)
3.   Tom Rehder, T, New England (69)
3.   Chuck Lanza, C, Pittsburgh (70)
6.   Cedric Figaro, LB, San Diego (152)
9.   Brandy Wells, DB, Cincinnati (226)

1989

1.   Andy Heck, T, Seattle (15)
2.   Frank Stams, DE, Los Angeles Rams (44)
5.   Mark Green, RB, Chicago Bears (130)
6.   Wes Pritchett, LB, Miami (147)
11. George Streeter, S, Chicago Bears (304)

1990

2.   Anthony Johnson, FB, Indianapolis (36)
2.   Tim Grunhard, G, Kansas City (40)
2.   Jeff Alm, DT, Houston (41)
2.   Pat Terrell, S, Los Angeles Rams (49)
4.   Mike Brennan, T, Cincinnati (92)
5.   Stan Smagala, CB, Los Angeles Raiders (122)
6.   Ned Bolcar, LB, Seattle (146)
10. D'Juan Francisco, S, Washington (262)
12. Dean Brown, T, Indianapolis (316)

1991

1.   Todd Lyght, CB, Los Angeles Rams (5)
2.   Ricky Watters, RB, San Francisco (45)
2.   Chris Zorich, NT, Chicago Bears (49)
3.   Bob Dahl, DT, Cincinnati (72)

4. Raghib Ismail, FL, Los Angeles Raiders (100)
5. Tim Ryan, G, Tampa Bay (136)
7. Andre Jones, LB, Pittsburgh (185)
8. Scott Kowalkowski, LB, Philadelphia (216)
9. Michael Stonebreaker, LB, Chicago (245)
10. Mike Heldt, C, San Diego (257)

1992

1. Derek Brown, TE, New York Giants (14)
2. Rod Smith, DB, New England (35)
4. Rodney Culver, FB, Indianapolis (85)
4. Tony Brooks, FB, Philadelphia (92)
4. Gene McGuire, C, New Orleans (95)
6. Tony Smith, SE, Kansas City (159)
6. George Williams, DT, Cleveland (163)
9. Mirko Jurkovic, G, Chicago Bears (246)

1993

1. Rick Mirer, QB, Seattle (2)
1. Jerome Bettis, FB, Los Angeles Rams (10)
1. Tom Carter, CB, Washington (17)
1. Irv Smith, TE, New Orleans (20)
2. Demetrius DuBose, LB, Tampa Bay (34)
2. Reggie Brooks, TB, Washington (45)
4. Devon McDonald, LB, Indianapolis (107)
5. Lindsay Knapp, G, Kansas City (130)
8. Craig Hentrich, K–P, New York Jets (200)

1994

1. Bryant Young, DT, San Francisco (7)
1. Aaron Taylor, G, Green Bay (16)
1. Jeff Burris, S, Buffalo (27)
2. Tim Ruddy, C, Miami (65)
3. Jim Flanigan, DT, Chicago (74)
3. Willie Clark, CB, San Diego (82)
3. Lake Dawson, SE, Kansas City (92)
5. John Covington, S, Indianapolis (133)
5. Anthony Peterson, LB, San Francisco (153)
7. Pete Bercich, LB, Minnesota (211)

1995

2. Ray Zellars, FB, New Orleans (44)
2. Bobby Taylor, CB, Philadelphia (50)
4. Oliver Gibson, NG, Pittsburgh (120)
5. Michael Miller, FL, Cleveland (147)
7. Travis Davis, S, New Orleans (242)

1996

2. Derrick Mayes, SE, Green Bay (56)
4. Paul Grasmanis, NG, Chicago Bears (116)
6. Shawn Wooden, CB, Miami (189)
   Dusty Zeigler, G, Buffalo (202)

1997

1. Renaldo Wynn, DL, Jacksonville (21)
2. Marc Edwards, RB, San Francisco (55)
3. Bert Berry, LB, Indianapolis (86)
3. Kinnon Tarum, LB, Carolina (87)
5. Pete Chryplewicz, TE, Detroit (135)

1998

3. Allen Rossum, DB, Philadelphia (85)

1999

1. Luke Petigout, OL, New York Giants (19)
5. Jerry Wisne, OL, Chicago Bears (143)
5. Mike Rosenthal, OL, New York Giants (149)
5. Malcolm Johnson, WR, Pittsburgh (166)
7. Hunter Smith, P, Indianapolis (5th) (210)
7. Autry Denson, RB, Tampa Bayy (233)
7. Kory Minor, LB, San Francisco (234)

2000

7. Jarious Jackson, QB, Denver Broncos (214)

2001

3. Mike Gandy, OG, Chicago (68)
3. Brock Williams, CB, New England (86)
4. Jabari Holloway, TE, New England (119)
6. Tony Driver, S, Buffalo (178)
6. Dan O'Leary, TE, Buffalo (195)
7. Anthony Denman, LB, Jacksonville (213)

1998 Final Depth Chart

OFFENSE

Quick Tackle
Luke Petitgout***
MATT BRENNAN

Quick Guard
Jerry Wisne***
KURT VOLLERS
John Wagner*

Center
JOHN MERANDI**
ROB MOWL

Strong Guard
Tim Ridder***
MIKE GANDY*
JIM JONES
BRENDAN O'CONNOR

Strong Tackle
Mike Rosenthal****
JOHN TEASDALE*

Split End
Malcolm Johnson****
RAKI NELSON***
DAVID GIVENS*
JAY JOHNSON**
JONATHAN HERBERT*

Quarterback
JARIOUS JACKSON***
ARNAZ BATTLE*
ERICK CHAPPELL

Tight End
JABARI HOLLOWAY**
DAN O'LEARY**
JOHN OWENS

Fullback
Jamie Spencer***
JOEY GOODSPEED***
JASON MURRAY*
MIKE McNAIR

Tailback
Autry Denson****
TONY FISHER*
DARCEY LEVY*
Jay Vickers

Flanker
BOBBY BROWN***
JOEY GETHERALL**
JAVIN HUNTER

Kicker
JIM SANSON***

Punter
Hunter Smith****

DEFENSE

Outside Linebacker
Kory Minor****
ANTHONY DENMAN**
ROCKY BOIMAN*
ANTHONY BRANNAN

Left End
ANTHONY WEAVER*
JASON CHING*

Nose Guard
LANCE LEGREE**
ANTWON JONES***
ANDY WISNE

Right End
BRAD WILLIAMS***
B.J. SCOTT*

Outside Linebacker
LAMONT BRYANT***
GRANT IRONS**
JOE FERRER**

Inside Linebacker
Bobbie Howard****
TYREO HARRISON
Hugh Holmes*

Inside Linebacker
Jimmy Friday***
Joe Thomas**
RONNIE NICKS**

Left Cornerback
DEVERON HARPER***
CLIFFORD JEFFERSON
Tim Lynch*

Free Safety
A'JANI SANDERS***
DEKE COOPER***
RON ISRAEL*
TERRANCE HOWARD

Strong Safety
Benny Guilbeaux***
TONY DRIVER**
LEE LAFAYETTE**
Kevin Rice*

Right Cornerback
BROCK WILLIAMS**
Ty Goode***
JUSTIN SMITH

Includes every player who played at least one second in one game in 1998. Returnees in all caps. Italics indicate walk-on members of squad. Asterisks indicate number of letters won.

292

1999 Final Depth Chart

OFFENSE

Quick Tackle
JORDAN BLACK*
KURT VOLLERS*
CASEY ROBIN*

Quick Guard
JIM JONES*
RYAN SCAROLA*
*Brendan O'Connor**

Center
John Merandi***
B.J. SCOTT*

Strong Guard
MIKE GANDY**
Matt Brennan*
Rob Mowl*

Strong Tackle
JOHN TEASDALE**
SEAN MAHAN*

Split End
Bobby Brown*****
JAVIN HUNTER*
JAY JOHNSON***
*Johnathan Hebert***

Quarterback
Jarious Jackson****
ARNAZ BATTLE**

Tight End
JABARI HOLLOWAY***
DAN O'LEARY***
JOHN OWENS*
GERALD MORGAN

Fullback
Joey Goodspeed****
TOM LOPIENSKI*
MIKE MCNAIR
JEREMY JUAREZ

Tailback
TONY FISHER**
JULIUS JONES*
TERRANCE HOWARD*
TONY DRIVER**
TIM McNEIL

Flanker
JOEY GETHERAL***
DAVID GIVENS**
*Raki Nelson****

Kicker
Jim Sanson****
DAVID MILLER

Holder
*James Caputo**

Punter
JOEY HILDBOLD*

DEFENSE

Left End
GRANT IRONS***
Jason Ching**

Left Tackle
ANTHONY WEAVER**
Antwon Jones****
Noah Van Hook-Drucker*
ANDREW DEMPSEY

Right Tackle
Brad Williams****
LANCE LEGREE***
ANDY WISNE*

Right End
Lamont Bryant****
RYAN ROBERTS*

Outside Linebacker
ROCKY BOIMAN**
Joe Ferrer***
JUSTIN THOMAS

Inside Linebacker
ANTHONY DENMAN***
CARLOS PIERRE-ANTOINE*
ANTHONY BRANNAN*

Inside Linebacker
Ronnie Nicks***
TYREO HARRISON*

Left Cornerback
CLIFFORD JEFFERSON*
Lee Lafayette**
JASON BECKSTROM*

Free Safety
A'Jani Sanders****
RON ISRAEL**
DONALD DYKES*
CHRIS YURA*

Strong Safety
Deke Cooper****
JUSTIN SMITH*
GEROME SAPP*
*Mike Grady**

Right Cornerback
Deveron Harper****
SHANE WALTON*

Includes every player who played at least one second in one game in 1999. Returnees in all caps. Italics indicate walk-on members of squad. Asterisks indicate number of letters won.

2000 Final Depth Chart

OFFENSE

Left Tackle
JORDAN BLACK**
BRENNAN CURTIN*
CASEY ROBIN**

Left Guard
Jim Jones**
SEAN MAHAN**
RYAN GILLIS

Center
JEFF FAINE*
J.W. JORDAN*
JOHN CROWTHER*

Right Guard
Mike Gandy****
RYAN SCAROLA**
SEAN MILLIGAN

Right Tackle
KURT VOLLERS**
JOHN TEASDALE***

Split End
JAVIN HUNTER**
Jay Johnson****

Quarterback
MATT LoVECCHIO*
ARNAZ BATTLE***

Tight End
Jabari Holloway****
Dan O'Leary****
JOHN OWENS***
GARY GODSEY*
Joe Recendez*
GERALD MORGAN

Fullback
TOM LOPIENSKI**
JASON MURRAY**
MIKE McNAIR

Tailback
JULIUS JONES**
TONY FISHER***
TERRANCE HOWARD**
CHRIS YURA**
TIM O'NEILL

Flanker
JOEY GETHERALL****
DAVID GIVENS***
OMAR JENKINS

Kicker
NICK SETTA*
Matt McNew (KOs)

Holder
ADAM TIBBLE*

Punter
JOEY HILDBOLD**

DEFENSE

Left End
ANTHONY WEAVER***
DARRELL CAMPBELL*
JIM MOLINARO

Defensive Tackle
B.J. Scott**
ANDY WISNE**

Nose Guard
Lance Legree****
CEDRIC HILLIARD

Right End
RYAN ROBERTS**
JOHN OWENS***

Outside Linebacker
ROCKY BOIMAN***
Anthony Brannan**
CHAD DeBOLT*

Inside Linebacker
Anthony Denman****
COURTNEY WATSON*
PATRICK RYAN*
MIKE GOOLSBY*
BRIAN DIERCKMAN*
Mike Zelenka*

Inside Linebacker
TYREO HARRISON**
CARLOS PIERRE-ANTOINE*

Left Cornerback
Brock Williams***
JASON BECKSTROM**
DWAYNE FRANCIS

Free Safety
Tony Driver****
DONALD DYKES**
JUSTIN SMITH*

Strong Safety
RON ISRAEL***
GLENN EARL*
GEROME SAPP**
MATT SARB*

Right Cornerback
SHANE WALTON**
CLIFFORD JEFFERSON**
VONTEZ DUFF*

Includes every player who played one second or more in 2000. Returnees in all caps. Italics indicate walk-on members of squad. Asterisks indicate number of letters won.

MONOGRAM MEN LOST AND RETURNING

OFFENSE		**DEFENSE**	
First Team Lost	4	First Team Lost	6
Second Team Lost	1	Second Team Lost	4
total Lost (includes Kickers)	10	Total Lost	12
First Team Returning	7	First Team Returning	5
Second Team Returning	10	Second Team Returning	7
Total Returning	24	Total Returning	18

Total Lost *19 — Total Returning *49

2001 Final Depth Chart

(as of September 2001)

OFFENSE

Pos	#	Name	Ht	Wt	Yr
SE	21	JAVIN HUNTER	6-0	191	Sr.
	18	Ronnie Rodamer	6-4	210	So.
LT	78	JORDAN BLACK	6-6	318	Sr.
	63	Brennan Curtin	6-8	305	Jr.
LG	79	SEAN MAHAN	6-3	292	Sr.
	67	Ryan Gillis	6-3	296	Jr.
C	52	JEFF FAINE	6-3	296	Jr.
	72	Ryan Scarola	6-5	308	Sr.
RG	65	SEAN MILLIGAN	6-4	295	Jr.
	76	John Teasdale	6-5	305	Sr.
RT	75	KURT VOLLERS	6-7	312	Sr.
	70	Jim Molinaro	6-6	295	Jr.
TE	84	JOHN OWENS	6-3	270	Sr.
	14	Gary Godsey	6-7	270	Jr.
FL	6	DAVID GIVENS	6-3	212	Sr.
	3	Arnaz Battle	6-1	210	Sr.
QB	10	MATT LOVECCHIO	6-4	205	So.
	7	Carlyle Holiday	6-3	218	So.
	or 1	Jared Clark	6-4	230	So.
FB	36	TOM LOPIENSKI	6-1	249	Sr.
	or 40	Jason Murray	6-1	260	Sr.
	or 47	Mick McNair	6-0	237	Sr.
TB	12	TONY FISHER	6-2	226	Sr.
	or 22	Julius Jones	5-10	220	Jr.
	or 32	Terrance Howard	6-1	195	Sr.

DEFENSE

Pos	#	Name	Ht	Wt	Yr
LE	98	ANTHONY WEAVER	6-3	286	Sr.
	92	Kyle Budinscak	6-4	265	So.
DT	60	DARRELL CAMPBELL	6-4	296	Jr.
	77	Greg Pauly	6-6	280	So.
NG	94	ANDY WISNE	6-3	285	Sr.
	50	Cedric Hilliard	6-2	290	Jr.
RE	44	GRANT IRONS	6-5	275	Sr.
	95	Ryan Roberts	6-2	262	Sr.
ILB	51	TYREO HARRISON	6-2	242	Sr.
	2	Carlos Pierre-Antoine	6-3	241	Sr.
ILB	33	COURTNEY WATSON	6-1	232	Jr.
	41	Mike Goolsby	6-3	240	So.
	or 57	Justin Thomas	6-1	245	Jr.
OLB	30	ROCKY BOIMAN	6-4	240	Sr.
	81	Jerome Collins	6-4	242	So.
LCB	42	SHANE WALTON	5-11	186	Sr.
	37	Preston Jackson	5-9	176	So.
	or 9	Jackson Beckstrom	5-10	190	So.
FS	28	DONALD DYKES	5-11	195	Sr.
	19	Glenn Earl	6-1	210	Jr.
SS	5	RON ISRAEL	6-0	212	Sr.
	20	Gerome Sapp	6-0	214	Jr.
RCB	15	CLIFFORD JEFFERSON	5-9	176	Sr.
	34	Vontez Duff	5-11	192	So.

SPECIALISTS

Pos	#	Name	Ht	Wt	Yr
KO	13	NICK SETTA	5-11	175	Jr.
PK	13	NICK SETTA	5-11	175	Jr.
	35	David Miller	5-11	208	Sr.
P	17	JOEY HILDBOLD	5-10	188	Jr.
	13	Nick Setta	5-11	175	Jr.
HLD	80	ADAM TIBBLE	5-11	286	Sr.
SNP	56	JOHN CROWTHER	6-2	240	Sr.
	91	JEFF THOMPSON	6-4	267	Fr.
PR	22	JULIUS JONES	5-10	220	Jr.
	34	VONTEZ DUFF	5-11	192	So.
KR	22	JULIUS JONES	5-10	206	So.
	34	VONTEZ DUFF	5-11	192	So.
	6	DAVID GIVENS	6-3	214	Jr.

NOTRE DAME'S ALL-AMERICANS

*Indicates Consensus All-American

1903
Louis "Red" Salmon, FB

1909
Harry Miller, HB

1913
Gus Dorais, QB
Ray Eichenlaub, FB
Knute Rockne, E

1916
Charlie Bachman, G
Stan Cofall, HB

1917
Frank Rydzewski, C

1920
George Gipp, HB
Roger Kiley, E

1921
Eddie Anderson, E
Heartley "Hunk" Anderson, G
Paul Castner, HB
Roger Kiley, E
Johnny Mohardt, HB
Buck Shaw, T

1922
Paul Castner, FB
Ed DeGree, G

1923
Harvey Brown, G
Elmer Layden, FB
Don Miller, HB

1924
Jim Crowley, HB
Elmer Layden, FB
Harry Stuhldreher, QB
Adam Walsh, C

1926
Art Boeringer, C
Christie Flanagan, HB

1927
Christie Flanagan, HB
John Polisky, T
John Smith, G

1928
Fred Miller, T

1929
Jack Cannon, G
Frank Carideo, QB*
Ted Twomey, T

1930
Marty Brill, HB
Frank Carideo, QB*
Tom Conley, E
Al Culver
Bert Metzger, G
Joe Savoldi, FB
Marchy Schwartz, HB

1931
Nordy Hoffmann, G
Joe Kurth, T
Marchy Schwartz, HB*
Tommy Yarr, C

1932
Ed Kosky, E
Joe Kurth, T*
Ed Krause, T
George Melinkovich, FB

1934
Jack Robinson, C

1935
Wayne Millner, E
Andy Pilney, HB
Bill Shakespeare, HB

1936
John Lautar, G

1937
Ed Beinor, T
Chuck Sweeney, E

1938
Ed Beinor, T*
Earl Brown, E
Jim McGoldrick, G

1939
Budd Kerr, E
Milt Piepul, FB

1940
Milt Piepul, FB

1941
Bernie Crimmins, G
Bob Dove, E

1942
Angelo Bertelli, QB
Bob Dove, E
Harry Wright, G

1943
Angelo Bertelli, QB
Herb Coleman, C
Pat Filley, G
Creighton Miller, HB
Jim White, T
John Yonakor, E

1944
Bob Kelly, HB
Pat Killey, G

1945
Frank Dancewicz, QB
John Mastrangelo, G

1946
George Connor, T
Johnny Lujack, QB*
John Mastrangelo, G
George Strohmeyer, C

1947
George Connor, T
Ziggy Czarobski, T
Leon, Hart E
Johnny Lujack, QB*

1948
Bill Fischer, G
Leon Hart, E
Emil Sitko, FB
Marty Wendell, G

1949
Leon Hart, E*
Jim Martin, T
Emil Sitko, FB*
Bob Williams, QB

1950
Jerry Groom, C
Bob Williams, QB

1951
Jim Mutscheller, E
Bob Toneff, T

1952
John Lattner, HB*
Bob O'Neill, DE

1953
Art Hunter, T
John Lattner, HB*
Don Penza, E

1954
Ralph Guglielmi, QB*
Dan Shannon, E
Frank Varrichione, T

1955
Pat Bisceglia, G
Paul Hornung, HB
Don Schaefer, FB

1956
Paul Hornung, QB

1957
Al Ecuyer, G
Nick Pietrosante, FB

1958
Al Ecuyer, G
Nick Pietrosante, FB
Monty Stickles, E

1959
Monty Stickles, E

1960
Myron Pottios, G

1961
Nick Buoniconti, G

1962
Jim Kelly, E
Daryle Lamonica, QB

1963
Jim Kelly, E
Bob Leumann, G

1964
Tony Carey, DB
Jim Carroll, LB
Kevin Hardy, DT

John Huarte, QB
Jack Snow, E

1965
Dick Arrington, G
Jim Lynch, LB
Nick Rassas, DB
Tom Regner, G

1966
Larry Conjar, FB
Pete Duranko, DT
Nick Eddy, HB*
Terry Hanratty, QB
Kevin Hardy, DT
Jim Lynch, LB*
Alan Page, DE
Tom Regner, G
Tom Schoen, DB
Jim Seymour, E

1967
Kevin Hardy, DE
Mike McGill, LB
John Pergine, LB
Tom Schoen, DB
Jim Seymour, E
Jim Smithberger, DB
Dick Swatland, G

1968
Terry Hanratty, QB
George Kunz, T
Jim Seymour, E

1969
Larry DiNardo, G
Mike McCoy, DT*
Bob Olson, LB
Mike Oriard, C
Jim Reilly, T

1970
Larry DiNardo, G
Clarence Ellis, DB
Tom Gatewood, E
Joe Theismann, QB

1971
Clarence Ellis, DB
Tom Gatewood, E

1971 (cont'd)
Mike Kadish, DT
Walt Patulski, DE*

1972
John Dampeer, T
Greg Marx, DT*

1973
Dave Casper, TE
Mike Townsend, DB

1974
Greg Collins, LB
Tom Clements, QB
Pete Demmerle, E
Gerry DiNardo, G
Mike Fanning, DT
Steve Niehaus, DT
Steve Sylvester, T

1975
Luther Bradley, DB
Ken MacAfee, TE
Steve Niehaus, T*

1976
Luther Bradley, DB
Ross Browner, DE*
Willie Fry, DE
Ken MacAfee, TE

1977
Luther Bradley, DB
Ross Browner, DE*
Ted Burgmeier, DB
Willie Fry, DE
Bob Golic, MG
Ernie Hughes, G
Ken MacAfee, TE*

1978
Bob Golic, LB*
Dave Huffman, C

1979
Bob Crable, LB
Vagas Ferguson, HB
Tim Foley, T

1980
Bob Crable, LB
Harry Oliver, K

John Scully, C*
Scott Zettek, DE

1981
Bob Crable, LB
Dave Duerson, CB
John Krimm, CB

1982
Dave Duerson, S
Tony Hunter, TE
Mike Johnston, K
Mark Zavagnin, LB

1983
Allen Pinkett, TB
Larry Williams, T

1984
Mark Bavaro, TE
Mike Gann, DT
Mike Kelley, C
Larry Williams, G

1985
Allen Pinkett, TB
Tim Scannell, G

1986
Tim Brown, FL
Cedric Figaro, LB
Wally Kleine, DT

1987
Ned Bolcar, LB
Tim Brown, FL*
Cedric Figaro, LB
Chuck Lanza, C

1988
Andy Heck, T
Wes Pritchett, LB
Frank Stams, DE
Michael Stonebreaker, LB
Chris Zorich, DT

1989
Jeff Alm, DT
Ned Bolcar, LB
Tim Grunhard, G

Raghib Ismail, FL
Todd Lyght, CB*
Tony Rice, QB
Chris Zorich, DT

1990
Mike Heldt, C
Raghib Ismail, FL*
Todd Lyght, CB
Michael Stonebreaker, LB*
Chris Zorich, DT*

1991
Jerome Bettis, FB
Derek Brown, TE
Demetrius DuBose, LB
Mirko Jurkovic, G

1992
Reggie Brooks, TB
Tom Carter, CB
Rick Mirer, QB
Irv Smith, TE
Aaron Taylor, G

1993
Jeff Burris, CB
Tim Ruddy, C
Aaron Taylor, T*
Bobby Taylor, S
Bryant Young, DT

1994
Bobby Taylor, CB

1995
Ryan Leahy, G
Derrick Mayes, SE
Dusty Zeigler, G

1996
Jeremy Akers, G

1998
Autry Denson, HB
Mike Rosenthal, T

2000
Anthony Denman, LB

Notre Dame's Heisman Trophy Winners

Angelo Bertelli, QB 1943
Johnny Lujack, QB 1947
Leon Hart, E 1949
John Lattner, HB 1953
Paul Hornung, QB 1956
John Huarte, QB 1964
Tim Brown, F 1987

Notre Dame's Lombardi Award Winners

1971   Walt Patulski, DE
1977   Ross Browner, DE
1990   Chris Zorich, DT
1993   Aaron Taylor, T

Notre Dame's Outland Trophy Winners

1946   George Connor, T
1948   Bill Fischer, 1948
1976   Ross Browner, DE
Aaron Taylor was one of three finalists for the award in 1993.

Notre Dame's Walter Camp Trophy Winners

1977   Ken MacAfee, TE
1987   Tim Brown, FL
1990   Raghib Ismail, FL

Notre Dame's Maxwell Award Winners

1949   Leon Hart, TE
1952   John Lattner, HB
1953   John Lattner, HB
1966   Jim Lynch, LB
1977   Ross Browner, DE

NICK PIETROSANTE AWARD WINNERS

The Nick Pietrosante Award is presented each year to the Notre Dame player who best exemplifies the courage, loyalty, teamwork, dedication, and pride of the late Fighting Irish All-American fullback. The award is determined by a vote of the players. Pietrosante died of cancer on February 6, 1988.

1988	Andy Heck, T	1995	Richard Rolle, WR
1989	Anthony Johnson, FB	1996	Kevin Carretta, TE
1990	Chris Zorich, NG	1997	Melvin Dansby, DE
1991	Ryan Mihalko, FB	1998	Bobby Howard, LB
1992	Demetrius DuBose, LB	1999	Lamont Bryant, DE
1993	Aaron Taylor, OT	2000	Joey Getherall, Flanker
1994	Oliver Gibson, NG; Justin Goheen, LB		

MOOSE KRAUSE LINEMAN OF THE YEAR AWARD WINNERS

First awarded in 1986, the Lineman of the Year Award is presented by the Moose Krause Chapter of the National Football Foundation and Hall of Fame to Notre Dame's most exceptional lineman.

1986	Robert Banks, DE	1994	Oliver Gibson, NG
1987	Chuck Lanza, C	1995	Ryan Leahy, G
1988	Frank Stams, DE	1996	Renaldo Wynn, DE
1989	Jeff Alm, DT	1997	Melvin Dansby, DE
1990	Chris Zorich, NT	1998	Mike Rosenthal, T
1991	Mirko Jurkovic, T	1999	Brad Williams, DT
1992	Lindsay Knapp, T	2000	Lance Legree, DT
1993	Aaron Taylor, T		

HESBURGH/JOYCE SCHOLARSHIP WINNERS

The Hesburgh/Joyce Hall of Fame Scholarship, presented by the National Football Foundation, was a postgraduate study grant previously given to a walk-on who contributed significantly to the success of the football program.

1988	Reggie Ho, K; Brad Alge, E	1991	Jeff Baker, WR
1989	Doug DiOrio, S; Chris Shey, LB	1992	Matt Johnson, QB
1990	Jerry Bodine, CB	1993	Jason Beckwith, G

JOHNNY UNITAS GOLDEN ARM AWARD WINNERS

The Kentucky chapter of the National Football Foundation and Hall of Fame annually honors the nation's top quarterback. Rick Mirer was selected as one of the six finalists for the award in 1992.

1989   Tony Rice

Notre Dame National Monogram Club Most Valuable Player Award Winners

The Notre Dame National Monogram Club MVP award is given annually, based on voting by team members.

1967	Terry Hanratty (offense), Tom Schoen (defense)		1980	Bob Crable
1968	Terry Hanratty (offense), Bob Kuechenberg (defense)		1981	Bob Crable
			1982	Dave Duerson
			1983	Allen Pinkett
1969	Bob Olson		1984	Allen Pinkett
1970	Joe Theismann (offense), Tim Kelly (defense)		1985	Allen Pinkett
			1986	Tim Brown
1971	Dan Novakov (offense), Walt Patulski (defense)		1987	Tim Brown
			1988	Tony Rice
1972	Andy Huff (offense), Jim O'Malley (defense)		1989	Tony Rice
			1990	Raghib Ismail
1973	Dave Casper (offense), Greg Collins (defense)		1991	Jerome Bettis, Rick Mirer
1974	Wayne Bullock (offense), Greg Collins (defense)		1992	Reggie Brooks
			1993	Jeff Burris
1975	Al Wujiack (offense), Steve Niehaus (defense)		1994	Derrick Mayes
			1995	Derrick Mayes
1976	Al Hunter (offense), Ross Browner (defense)		1996	Autry Denson
			1997	Autry Denson
1977	Ken MacAfee		1998	Autry Denson
1978	Joe Montana (offense), Bob Golic (defense)		1999	Jarious Jackson
			2000	Anthony Denman
1979	Vagas Ferguson			

CoSIDA/GTE Academic All-Americans

Each year, CoSIDA (College Sports Information Directors of America) and GTE honor an Academic All-America football team made up of top scholar athletes from universities around the country. A 3.2 minimum cumulative grade point average is required for nomination. A total of twenty-nine Notre Dame football players have been first-team selections. Two-time selections include Tom Gatewood, Greg Marx, Joe Restic, and Tim Ruddy. Joe Heap was a three-time honoree. Two others have received second-team recognition. Ruddy was named team member of the year in 1993.

First Team
1952	Joe Heap, HB
1953	Joe Heap, HB
1954	Joe Heap, HB
1955	Don Schaefer, FB
1958	Bob Wetoska, E
1963	Bob Lehmann, G
1966	Tom Regner, G
1966	Jim Lynch, LB
1967	Jim Smithberger, DB
1968	George Kunz, T
1969	Jim Reilly, T
1970	Joe Theismann, QB; Larry DiNardo, G; Tom Gatewood, SE
1971	Tom Gatewood, SE
1971	Greg Marx, DT
1972	Greg Marx, DT; Mike Creaney, TE

1973	Dave Casper, TE; Bob Thomas, K; Gary Potempa, LB
1974	Pete Demmerle, SE; Reggie Barnett, CB
1977	Ken MacAfee, TE; Dave Vinson, G; Joe Restic, S
1978	Joe Restic, S
1980	Bob Burger, G; Tom Gibbons, S
1981	John Krimm, CB
1985	Greg Dingens, DT
1987	Vince Phelan, P; Ted Gradel, K
1992	Tim Ruddy, C
1993	Tim Ruddy, C

Second Team
1988	Reggie Ho, K
1994	Mark Zataveski, C

GTE Academic All-America Hall of Fame

The GTE Academic All-America Hall of Fame recognizes former Academic All-Americans who graduated ten or more years ago and have community service accomplishments. To be nominated, a candidate must have been an Academic All-American with a cumulative grade point average of at least 3.0 on a 4.0 scale. The inductees are selected by a committee made up of officers of CoSIDA (College Sports Information Directors of America), GTE, and the media. The first class of inductees was in 1988. Notre Dame's members:

1990	Joe Theismann, QB
1996	Bob Thomas, K
1993	Dave Casper, TE

NCAA SCHOLARSHIP WINNERS

The National Collegiate Athletic Association each year honors student athletes from universities around the nation by presenting them with $5,000 postgraduate scholarships. The program began in 1964.

1967	Fred Schnurr, T		1975	Pete Demmerle, SE
1968	Jim Smithberger, DB		1975	Reggie Barnett, CB
1969	George Kunz, T		1979	Joe Restic, S
1970	Mike Oriard, C		1980	Tom Gibbons, S
1971	Larry DiNardo, G		1981	John Krimm, CB
1972	Tom Gatewood, SE		1985	Greg Dingens, DT
1973	Greg Marx, DT		1988	Reggie Ho, K
1974	Dave Casper, TE		1993	Tim Ruddy, C

Scholarship honorees must have a 3.0 grade point average on a 4.0 scale and have performed with distinction in their individual sports, epitomizing the term *scholar athlete*.

NATIONAL FOOTBALL FOUNDATION AND HALL OF FAME SCHOLARS

The National Football Foundation and Hall of Fame each year honors scholar athletes from universities around the nation by presenting them with $3,000 scholarships for postgraduate study. The program began in 1959.
Notre Dame's recipients:

1966	Jim Lynch, LB		1974	Pete Demmerle, SE
1968	George Kunz, LB		1977	Dave Vinson, G
1969	Mike Oriard, C		1978	Joe Restic, F
1970	Larry DiNardo, G		1980	Bob Burger, G
1971	Tom Gatewood, SE		1983	Mike Favorite, SE
1972	Greg Marx, DT		1985	Greg Dingens, DT
1973	Dave Casper, TE		1993	Tim Ruddy, C

Scholar-athlete honorees must be seniors and graduate school candidates chosen for their football ability and performance, academic application and performance, and outstanding leadership and citizenship.